Cambridge Primary Path

Foundation Level

Teacher's Edition

Lily Pane

CAMBRIDGE UNIVERSITY PRESS

LEVEL F: Scope and Sequence

1 Big Question: Who am I?

Reading	Vocabulary	Grammar
Nonfiction *We Are All Different!* **Reading Strategy** Similarities and Differences **Fiction** *Grandma Turtle* **Reading Strategy** Real or Fantasy?	**Key Words 1:** favorite, color, hair, girl, brown, boy **Key Words 2:** short, long, tall, curly, straight, blond **Key Words 3:** class, different **Key Words 4:** old, slow, fast, tired, young, happy	**Verb *to be*: Affirmative and Negative** I am six years old. I'm not tall. He is short. She isn't short. **Verb *to be*: Affirmative and Negative** You are young. You aren't old. They are happy. They aren't slow.

2 Big Question: What is school?

Reading	Vocabulary	Grammar
Nonfiction *Welcome to My School* **Reading Strategy** Classifying **Fiction** *I Can't Find My Things!* **Reading Strategy** Understanding a Character's Feelings	**Key Words 1:** desk, teacher, classroom, gym, bathroom, playground **Key Words 2:** library, schoolbag, pencil case, notebook, colored pencil, eraser **Key Words 3:** classmates, apple **Key Words 4:** story, sad, mad, hungry, lunchbox, surprised	***a / an*** a pencil an eraser **Possessive Adjectives** This is your desk. It is his first day at school. I can't find my book. Gemma shares her pencils with Max.

3 Big Question: What is a toy?

Reading	Vocabulary	Grammar
Nonfiction *Top Five Toys* **Reading Strategy** Classifying Words **Fiction** *Don't Touch!* **Reading Strategy** Ordering Story Events	**Key Words 1:** toy, box, house, paper, airplane, tablet **Key Words 2:** robot, fun, dollhouse, tent, train, jump rope **Key Words 3:** jump, children **Key Words 4:** monkey bars, bike, car, action figure, dinosaur, spaceship	**Commands** Listen! March! Stop! Stand! Sit! Jump! **Negative Commands** Don't touch my cars! Don't run!

4 Big Question: What makes a home?

Reading	Vocabulary	Grammar
Nonfiction *All Kinds of Homes* **Reading Strategy** Comparing **Fiction** *Snail Finds His Home* **Reading Strategy** Plot and Setting	**Key Words 1:** home, family, dining room, living room, bedroom, kitchen **Key Words 2:** apartment, room, water, garden, stove, bed **Key Words 3:** roof, stairs **Key Words 4:** snail, ladybug, forest, spider, butterfly, mouse	**Prepositions** It's in the kitchen. It's on the roof. It's under the tree house. **Verb *to be*: *Yes/No* Questions (Singular)** Is Mouse under a tree? No, he isn't. He's in a hole. Is Spider under the leaf? Yes, he is.

5 Big Question: Where do wild animals belong?

Reading	Vocabulary	Grammar
Nonfiction *Top Five Wild Animals* **Reading Strategy** Visualizing **Fiction** *The Rabbit on the Moon* **Reading Strategy** Predicting from Pictures	**Key Words 1:** zebra, land, elephant, octopus, ocean, dolphin **Key Words 2:** teeth, tail, beak, jungle, claw, fur **Key Words 3:** feathers, insects **Key Words 4:** rabbit, moon, snake, tongue, sun, stars	**Verb *to be*: *Wh–* Questions** What color are they? They are black and white. What are they? They're baby pandas. **Verb *to be*: *Yes/No* Questions (Plural)** Are Ketzi and the little rabbit near the stars? Yes, they are. / No, they aren't.

Oracy Skill	Phonics	Ready to Write	Listening	The Big Challenge	Speaking Mission
Ground Rules Listen to others. Take turns. Respect others. Share your ideas. Raise your hand to speak. **Cue Card:** **1** This is …	**The Alphabet**	**Learn to Write** Capital and Lowercase Letters	**Dialogue** Talking About Your Favorite Thing	**How can we talk about ourselves?**	**Saying Who You Are When You Are Lost**

Oracy Skill	Phonics	Ready to Write	Listening	The Big Challenge	Speaking Mission
Agreeing and Disagreeing **Cue Cards:** **2** Yes. **3** No.	**Initial Sounds** *c, p, t, n, b, h*	**Learn to Write** Alphabetical Order	**Song** Describing Your School	**How can we make a classroom map?**	**Borrowing Something at School**

Oracy Skill	Phonics	Ready to Write	Listening	The Big Challenge	Oracy Task
Active Listening **Cue Card:** **4** Please repeat that.	**Ending Sounds:** *-at, -en*	**Learn to Write** Complete Sentences	**Dialogue** Playing a Game	**How can we make a toy?**	**Collaboration** Agreeing on Buying a Toy

Oracy Skill	Phonics	Ready to Write	Listening	The Big Challenge	Speaking Mission
Taking Turns **Cue Cards:** **5** It's my turn. **6** It's your turn.	**Ending Sounds:** *-ut, -ig*	**Learn to Write** Nouns	**Poem** What Home Means to You	**How can I describe my home?**	**Describing an Object You Lost**

Oracy Skill	Phonics	Ready to Write	Listening	The Big Challenge	Speaking Mission
Participating Actively **Cue Card:** **7** Let's …	**Initial Sounds:** *q, s, f, j, g, r*	**Learn to Write** Identify Questions and Exclamations	**Guessing Game** Identifying Wild Animals	**How can we describe a wild animal?**	**Playing a Board Game**

LEVEL F: Scope and Sequence

6 Big Question: What can people do?

Reading	Vocabulary	Grammar
Nonfiction *Kids with Amazing Abilities* **Reading Strategy** Predicting from Titles **Fiction** *Hip-hop Hanna* **Reading Strategy** Cause and Effect	**Key Words 1:** ability, paint, run, skate, play basketball, talk **Key Words 2:** see, ride, climb, say, spell, swim **Key Words 3:** blind, backwards **Key Words 4:** music, love, dancer, practice, read, puppy	***I can / I can't*** I can ride a horse. I can't walk. ***Yes/No* Questions with *can* and *can't*** Can Hanna dance well? Yes, she can. No, she can't.

7 Big Question: Is all food healthy?

Reading	Vocabulary	Grammar
Nonfiction *Snacks from Around the World!* **Reading Strategy** Similarities and Differences **Fiction** *No Broccoli, Please!* **Reading Strategy** Main Idea	**Key Words 1:** fruit, banana, grapes, vegetable, spinach, sugar **Key Words 2:** juice, water, oil, yogurt, tomato, rice **Key Words 3:** fried, freezer **Key Words 4:** broccoli, fish, French fries, chocolate, soup, muffin	***like / don't like*** I like peanut butter sandwiches. I don't like cheese sandwiches. ***Yes/No* Questions with *like*** Do you like broccoli now? Yes, I do. No, I don't.

8 Big Question: Are routines important?

Reading	Vocabulary	Grammar
Nonfiction *Henry's Healthy Habits* **Reading Strategy** Summarizing **Fiction** *Andy Ant* **Reading Strategy** Making Judgments	**Key Words 1:** brush my teeth, eat breakfast, go to school, walk, ride my bike, take the bus **Key Words 2:** sleep, do exercise, have fun, take a bath, change clothes, wash my hands **Key Words 3:** before, after **Key Words 4:** wake up, collect, march, find, carry, clean	**Present Simple: Affirmative** I wash my hands. I sleep 10 hours each night. **Present Simple: Negative** I don't sleep on Saturdays! We don't work on Saturdays.

9 Big Question: Why do we wear different clothes?

Reading	Vocabulary	Grammar
Nonfiction *Traditional Clothes from Around the World* **Reading Strategy** Cause and Effect **Fiction** *The Emperor's New Clothes* **Reading Strategy** Beginning, Middle, and End	**Key Words 1:** clothes, cold, jacket, hot, T-shirt, shoes **Key Words 2:** wear, hat, skirt, pants, gloves, dress **Key Words 3:** wool, cool **Key Words 4:** emperor, thief, palace, expensive, smart, fool	**Present Continuous: Affirmative and Negative** I'm wearing gloves and big boots. I'm not wearing a hat. She's wearing a long skirt. He's not wearing a jacket. **Present Continuous: *Yes/No* Questions** Are you wearing magic clothes? Yes, I am. Are you wearing your new clothes? No, I'm not.

Oracy Skill	Phonics	Ready to Write	Listening	The Big Challenge	Oracy Task
Asking for Agreement **Cue Cards:** **2** Yes. **3** No. **8** Do you agree?	**Initial Sounds:** *h, t, p, m, b, d*	**Learn to Write** Verbs	**Dialogue** Asking for Help	**What different things can we do?**	**Discussion** Agreeing on a Game to Play

Oracy Skill	Phonics	Ready to Write	Listening	The Big Challenge	Speaking Mission
Giving and Responding to Positive Feedback **Cue Cards:** **9** Good job! **10** Thank you.	**Ending Sounds:** *x, m, b*	**Learn to Write** Adjectives	**Song** Healthy Food vs. Junk Food	**How can we make a healthy dessert?**	**Buying Groceries**

Oracy Skill	Phonics	Ready to Write	Listening	The Big Challenge	Speaking Mission
Speaking Up **Cue Cards:** **4** Please repeat that. **11** I don't understand.	**Ending Sounds** *-sk, -st, -nt*	**Learn to Write** Statements	**Presentation** Talking About Morning and Bedtime Routines	**How can we describe our routines?**	**Assigning Tasks to Follow a Class Routine**

Oracy Skill	Phonics	Ready to Write	Listening	The Big Challenge	Oracy Task
Standing Up Straight and Keeping Still **Cue Cards:** **1** This is… **12** These are …	**Initial Sounds:** *gr- pl-*	**Learn to Write** Questions	**Presentation** Describing What You Wear	**How do we dress for special occasions?**	**Presentation** Giving a Final Presentation

Cambridge Primary Path

For a Future Full of Opportunities

Better Learning within Cambridge Primary Path

***Cambridge Primary Path* is a 7-level English language and literacy course that will help young learners become articulate speakers and writers of English, empowering them to make the most of life's opportunities.**

Through three essential pillars, the course offers an effective approach to learning:

- Its comprehensive, **literacy-based approach** provides students with essential language support integral to literacy training that will ensure they become fully literate in English.
- Its groundbreaking **Oracy Framework** helps students become confident communicators, able to articulate their learning in multiple contexts.
- Its **creativity principles** encourage students to become better thinkers and problem solvers … and to have fun at the same time!

These three pillars are presented in a child-friendly design that emulates children's magazines and storybooks and are complemented by animated and real-world videos to ensure that *Cambridge Primary Path* offers a rich learning environment for both students and teachers.

Literacy-based Approach

Development of advanced reading skills using authentic-like fiction and non-fiction texts.

Students learn to read and then read to learn.

Oracy

Our research-based, systematic approach to strengthening communication skills.

Students become confident speakers, able to successfully articulate their ideas.

Creativity

Creative Journal and activities designed to build students' creativity.

Students become better thinkers and problem-solvers while enjoying themselves!

Course Components

- Student's Book with Creative Journal
- Activity Book with Practice Extra
- Grammar and Writing Workbook
- Teacher's Edition
- Flashcards (through Level 4)
- Class Audio
- Test Generator with Assessment Pack
- Presentation Plus (a digital resource with real-world videos and oracy animations)
- Teacher's Resource Bank (including Study Guides)
- Online Training: Teaching with *Cambridge Primary Path*

cambridge.org/primarypath/teachertraining

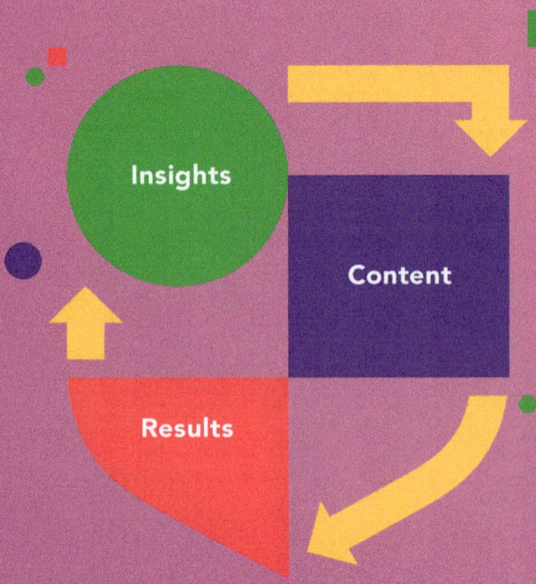

Better Learning within Cambridge Primary Path

Better Learning is our approach, connecting teachers and learners from around the world with the latest research and materials to build brighter futures together. It's a continuous cycle where our insights shape content that drives results.

Here's how our approach has shaped the three pillars of *Cambridge Primary Path*.

1 What is a literacy-based approach?

Insights
Skills in phonemic awareness, phonics, fluency, vocabulary, and comprehension are essential to literacy development. (National Reading Panel)

Content
Cambridge Primary Path creates a literacy-rich environment for students.

Results
Students become confident and articulate readers, writers, speakers, and listeners.

Literacy develops in the first language when children acquire oral language (listening and speaking) and then learn to read and write. But in a second language, children require much more support to acquire literacy.

The course's **literacy-based approach** provides this essential language support alongside the different aspects of literacy training. First, students *learn to read* in English, mastering phonics, spelling, and expanding their vocabulary. Then, as they learn to dig deeper and think more critically about texts, students begin to *read to learn*, or access information about the world in the second language.

How do we approach literacy in Cambridge Primary Path?

1 Inquiry-based Learning

Learning is not just about learning facts, or lists, or grammatical structures! Students' natural curiosity can be channeled so they identify, investigate, and find things out for themselves. This is known as inquiry-based learning. When students are encouraged to formulate their own questions about a topic, they will engage with the ideas and become more effective learners and problem-solvers.

The unit title works as **The Big Question** to get students thinking about the topic, thereby activating their prior knowledge. The **unit-opener video** challenges students to think about the topic from different angles and start to formulate their own questions. The Big Question is then strategically interwoven throughout each unit:

- Each unit is based around two major reading texts, nonfiction and fiction, in a variety of genres. The language of the unit emerges from those texts, and Big Question links encourage students to think critically about the content they are learning, discuss it, and relate it back to the Big Question.
- The **Listening** page provides additional real-world content to deepen students' exploration and curiosity surrounding the Big Question.
- Each unit culminates in a **Big Challenge** project and presentation that is linked to the Big Question and brings together the language and knowledge students acquired in the unit.

2 Reading Strategies

The course equips students with a variety of reading and comprehension strategies so they become better, more confident readers.

Each unit presents a fiction and nonfiction text that focus on a different reading strategy, from comparing and contrasting to identifying the author's purpose and predicting. These strategies give students a variety of techniques to dig deeper into the text's meaning. These strategies are reinforced in additional texts in the Activity Book.

3 Rich Vocabulary

Vocabulary is crucial for reading comprehension and for academic success. Students need to understand a majority of words in a text in order to fully understand it, and they also need a specialized vocabulary to learn content area material.

Students acquire a rich vocabulary in *Cambridge Primary Path*, from content-specific academic vocabulary in the reading texts and unit opener videos to everyday conversational language in the Speaking Missions.

4 Phonics, Spelling, and Word Patterns

Phonics instruction helps young readers understand the relationship between graphemes (letters and letter combinations) and phonemes (individual speech sounds). Initially this guides students to decode and read words accurately. As they progress, students become better spellers as they acquire English spelling patterns through guided word study.

5 Grammar in Context

Students need explicit grammar support to tackle higher-level, richer input in a second language. Students learn best when language is contextualized, so we challenge them to look at the context to infer grammatical rules.

- From Level 3 onward, students apply an inductive grammar approach, using context to infer rules for each grammar area.
- Students get two pages of grammar practice per unit in the Activity Book.
- An additional eight pages of grammar practice in the Grammar and Writing Workbook reinforces grammar points.

6 Structured Process Writing

How do you improve your writing? You read more! In *Cambridge Primary Path*, students read and analyze different text types as part of a structured writing program that enables them to produce more effective writing of their own.

- Students study various different model text types and genres.
- In the Activity Book, students progress through a **4-step process writing section** in which they plan, write, and edit their own text.
- **Improve Your Writing** (called *Ready to Write* in Foundation Level and *Learn to Write* in Levels 1–2) complements the process writing by focusing on elements of written language, such as correct capitalization or sequencing adverbs.
- Students produce a variety of written outputs as part of the **Big Challenge** project.

7 Dialogic Reading

Dialogic reading strategies create memorable, interactive reading classes and readers who think critically and engage in dialogues about what they are reading. Dialogic reading prompts are questions that initially come from you, the teacher. But, as students become more accustomed to the techniques, they start to ask their own questions and develop their own critical thinking when they read independently.

In the Teacher's Edition, you will find all the questions and prompts you need to guide students.

2 What is oracy?

Insights
Oracy skills are an essential component of exceptional communication.

Content
A structured oracy syllabus enables students to develop strong oracy skills.

Results
Students become highly effective, confident communicators.

Can you think of someone who is an excellent communicator? Not just a fine public speaker, but someone who is good at persuading others, at listening attentively, and at facilitating group decisions? That person has strong oracy skills.

Oracy is the **skill of communicating confidently** in a variety of situations, from giving presentations in front of an audience to successfully participating in group discussions and collaborative activities. It's also the skill of listening actively, reading group dynamics, and facilitating shared decision-making.

Oracy training includes **physical skills**, like projecting your voice and conveying confidence through your posture; **social-emotional skills**, like helping a group come to a collective decision; and **cognitive skills**, like structuring your ideas into a coherent argument. Acquiring oracy skills at a young age gives students confidence, develops their self-esteem, and sets them up for future success.

How do we approach oracy in Cambridge Primary Path?

1 A Comprehensive Oracy Skills Framework

Cambridge Primary Path's oracy syllabus is based on an oracy skills framework developed with leading oracy experts in the Department of Education at Cambridge University. The framework breaks students' skills down into physical, cognitive, and social-emotional skills. These skills are then mapped, with can-do statements, by level: Foundation (by end of Foundation Level); Apprentice (by end of Level 2); Developing (by end of Level 4); Confident (by end of Level 6).

2 Embedded Oracy Practice

Each unit includes an oracy page, on which the oracy characters—Oracy Morris and his friends—present the target oracy skill via an **animated oracy video**.

- a Students practice the oracy skill through a task and observe each other.
- b **Cue Cards** provide the functional language students need to complete the task.
- c Students reflect on their skills in **Check Your Oracy!**
- d **Oracy Reminders** are strategically interspersed throughout the units to remind students to use the oracy skills they have already learned.
- e An **Oracy Extension activity** on either the Listening or the Big Challenge page reinforces the target oracy skill in every unit.

3 Repetition and Extension

Students encounter each oracy skill multiple times across the levels to extend and build on their knowledge. Here's an example: Cognitive Descriptor #4 in the Oracy Framework is about learning to organize your talk. Notice how students progress through different elements of structuring a talk, circling back, and building on previous elements.

- **Apprentice:** I can use sequencers to mark the beginning, middle, and end.
- **Developing:** I can use sequencers and structure my talk into a beginning, middle, and end.
- **Confident:** I can organize the content and structure of my talk to convey clear meaning.

4 Oracy Performance Tasks

Oracy Performance Tasks (after every third unit) enable students to demonstrate the skills they've learned. Students self-assess after each Performance Task to reflect on their achievements and their learning needs.

Oracy FAQs

Are all speaking activities oracy?
Yes and no! All speaking activities provide opportunities for oracy. But for the purpose of introducing oracy, *Cambridge Primary Path* separates oracy skills work from the more traditional ELT speaking work reflected in the Speaking Missions (focus on everyday functional language and vocabulary) and in the Time to Talk! activities (focus on fluency).

The oracy language looks sparse. Shouldn't we be giving students more functional language?
No. The oracy language featured on the Cue Cards is intentionally simple so that students focus on the oracy skills rather than get distracted by too many variations in language. There are many ways to agree with someone, but "I agree" works well in all situations; if students know to say that, they can concentrate on the target oracy skill.

Oracy Framework

	Foundation (by end of Foundation)	Apprentice (by end of Level 2)	Developing (by end of Level 4)	Confident (by end of Level 6)
Physical	1 I can speak up so that others can hear me. 2 I can pronounce simple words and phrases clearly. 3 I can stand up straight and remain still when speaking in front of others.	1 I can project my voice so everyone can hear it. 2 I can pronounce my words clearly, and I aim to speak at a speed that my audience can understand. 3 I can stand up straight and remain still when speaking in front of others.	1 I know how to project my voice, adapting it to the situation. 2 I can speak clearly and talk at a speed that my audience can understand. 3 I can use appropriate gestures and body movements when speaking in front of others.	1 I can project my voice confidently and adapt it to the situation. 2 I can speak clearly and confidently and adapt the speed of delivery. 3 I can confidently use appropriate gestures and body movements when making a presentation.
Cognitive	1 I can agree and disagree with others using simple words. 2 I can show/express that I don't understand. 3 I can ask basic questions. 4 I can recognize the beginning, middle, and end of a story or presentation.	1 I can express my own opinion and agree or disagree with different opinions. 2 I can ask questions when things are not clear. 3 I can answer the question "Why?" for straightforward cause and effect scenarios. 4 I can use sequencers to mark the beginning, middle, and end.	1 I can express my opinion with supporting reasons and give reasons for agreeing or disagreeing with different opinions. 2 I can ask different types of questions to get further information, clarity, and repetition. 3 I can use evidence to support an argument. 4 I can use sequencers and structure my talk into a beginning, middle, and end.	1 I can confidently express my opinion with supporting reasons and give reasons for agreeing or disagreeing with different opinions. 2 I can ask a wide range of questions in different situations, including probing questions. 3 I can confidently use evidence to support an argument. 4 I can organize the content and structure of my talk to convey clear meaning.
Social/Emotional	1 I can speak in front of others. 2 I can take turns and listen to others. 3 I can understand and follow ground rules. 4 I can participate actively in pair work and whole-class activities. 5 I can listen patiently to others. 6 I can give and respond to positive feedback.	1 I can speak in front of an audience. 2 I can take turns and listen to others in a discussion. 3 I can suggest basic ground rules. 4 I can participate in a discussion. 5 I can listen patiently to others. 6 I can recognize the importance of being positive and can make positive comments on my classmates' ideas.	1 I can speak in front of an audience and interact with the audience. 2 I can recognize and respect the feelings and views of others in a discussion. 3 I can put ground rules into use. 4 I can participate in a discussion and elicit contributions from others. 5 I can listen actively and respond when appropriate. 6 I can regularly make positive comments on my classmates' ideas.	1 I can speak confidently and engage my audience in different ways. 2 I can respect and respond appropriately to the feelings and views of others in a discussion. 3 I can explain ground rules to others and remind them if necessary. 4 I can participate in a range of discussions and elicit contributions from others. 5 I can listen actively to what others are saying and can respond confidently. 6 I can confidently make positive comments on my classmates' ideas.

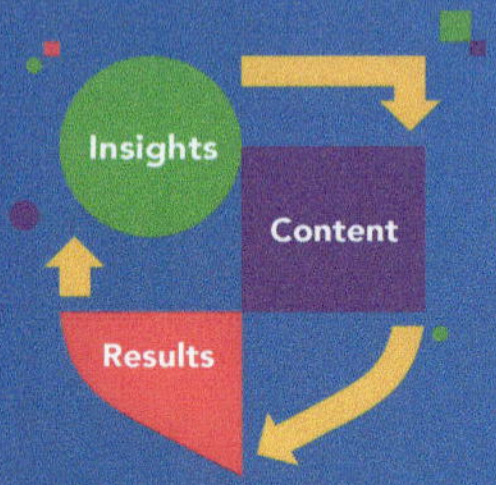

3 What is creativity?

Insights
Creative work and play motivate children while encouraging multiple perspectives.

Content
Topic-linked Creative Journal and Build Creativity! activities encourage students to get creative.

Results
Students become better critical thinkers and problem-solvers.

7 Reasons Building Creativity is Good for Kids

1 Creativity promotes critical thinking, problem-solving, and innovation.

2 Creativity lets kids express themselves.

3 Creativity encourages kids to take risks and learn from their mistakes.

4 Creativity lets kids relax and learn in a different way.

5 Creativity helps kids to focus better.

6 Creativity allows kids to have fun and enjoy tasks!

7 Creativity motivates kids to keep learning throughout their lives.

Learning is all about experimenting: about trying new things and exploring different perspectives. Adopting a playful and creative mindset develops learning strategies that foster not only language learning, but learning in general, so students become more effective critical thinkers and innovators.

Creative thinkers are **better critical thinkers and problem solvers**. Creativity activities promote the fun in learning and thinking about the world. They help students relax and approach learning in new ways. Students focus, learn why some things didn't work, and consider how multiple or new approaches might. Creativity encourages us to express our individuality and originality and to bring new approaches to the problems we confront inside and outside the classroom.

How do we approach creativity in Cambridge Primary Path?

Cambridge Primary Path is full of activities that promote creativity, all developed around the following principles:

1 **Flow:** Concentrating so hard on a task that you become totally immersed and lose track of time.

2 **Focus:** Doing just one thing, without distraction.

3 **Try, Try, and Try Again:** Finding new ways to solve problems and realizing that your mistakes and failures are part of the creative process.

4 **A Different Point of View:** Making the effort to see things in a different way or try new approaches.

5 **Take a Break:** Leaving a task, especially when stuck, and coming back later to consider new possibilities.

6 **Why, Why, Oh Why? (or Questions, Questions, Questions):** Being inquisitive opens your mind up to new possibilities, while justifying answers supports the retention of knowledge and encourages you to consider multiple perspectives.

7 **Start All Over Again:** Starting all over again when you get stuck often leads you to understand why something didn't work.

Build Creativity! activities in the Teacher's Edition break the routine and offer opportunities for developing students' creativity. But you don't have to wait for those activities; creative activities can be employed whenever you see fit!

The Creative Journal is a component that gets students to think creatively in class or at home.

- The first two pages of the journal are linked to unit language and topics and encourage students to manipulate them in non-conventional ways.
- A short reading text or new input linked to unit topics on the third page highlights real-world situations from an unusual perspective.
- On the fourth page, students can be especially playful with the content and really get their imaginations working!
- Creative Blasts following every three units offer additional bursts of thinking outside the box.

There is no right or wrong way to use the Creative Journal, but these recommendations will maximize its benefits:

- Do some pages in class first. Once students understand the approach, they can better enjoy using the journal on their own.
- Allow students to personalize the Creative Journal and truly own it. Each page has instructions and examples, but these are not rules. If students want to adapt the activities, all the better—they're being creative!
- If a student is unclear how to do an activity, encourage them to tell you what they think they should do or what they could do rather than explaining it to them. Some students may find this a little frustrating at first, but they will soon understand how to approach the tasks creatively.
- It's important that the Creative Journal be something students want to do. If it feels like a chore, let them take a break and do something different.
- Some activities can be done quickly; others slowly. In all cases, the process is what's important. Encourage students to repeat the process or say how they might change the task.
- Praise the process, not the result. Students will respond better when encouraged to keep working on a problem and given new challenges over finding the right answer.
- The activities can be done individually or in pairs/groups and shared in class. But creativity can be very personal, so keep in mind that some students may not be comfortable sharing.

FAQs on Creativity in the Classroom

I don't feel very creative! How can I help my learners be creative?
We are all creative, but we might not have much practice! Creativity isn't about being an artist; it's about seeing the world and its challenges in new ways. It's about believing that all problems have solutions, but the real challenge is discovering them. The best thing teachers can do is ask more questions and give encouragement: *Why? How? Why don't you try again?*

What if my students don't know what to do?
Encourage them to do the activity however they think they should, or ask guiding questions to help students think for themselves. Remind them that this is an opportunity for them to make up the rules they want.

How long should students spend on each task?
Try to avoid setting time limits. One of the objectives is for students to enter a state of flow by focusing on a task. Some students will finish quickly; others may become absorbed and take more time. The emphasis should be on the process, not on finishing in a given amount of time. Students can always return to any of the activities they want!

How can I persuade parents about the importance of creativity?
Parents want their children to be happy and ready for the future. Encouraging students' creativity skills meets those objectives by shaping students into critical thinkers and problem-solvers. Students will do a lot of coloring and drawing, but they will also train themselves to focus, challenge their brains, consider different perspectives, and solve puzzles—all while having fun!

Cambridge Primary Path Unit Walkthrough

Unit Opener

Every unit starts off with a **Big Question** that sets the context for the unit, fosters high-level thinking skills, and promotes a deeper exploration of the theme.

A **photo collage with exploration questions** activates prior knowledge and gets students thinking about the topic. The items pictured will be revisited in the unit.

Each unit includes a **unit-opener video** that introduces the topic and prompts students to start considering different angles of it.

The video also presents **Key Words 1**. These words are clearly marked and can be presented through full-color **Flashcards** (Foundation–Level 4).

Activity Book

Graphic organizers allow students to systematize the information from the video as well as provide a means for more profound understanding of the topic. Students also practice Key Words 1.

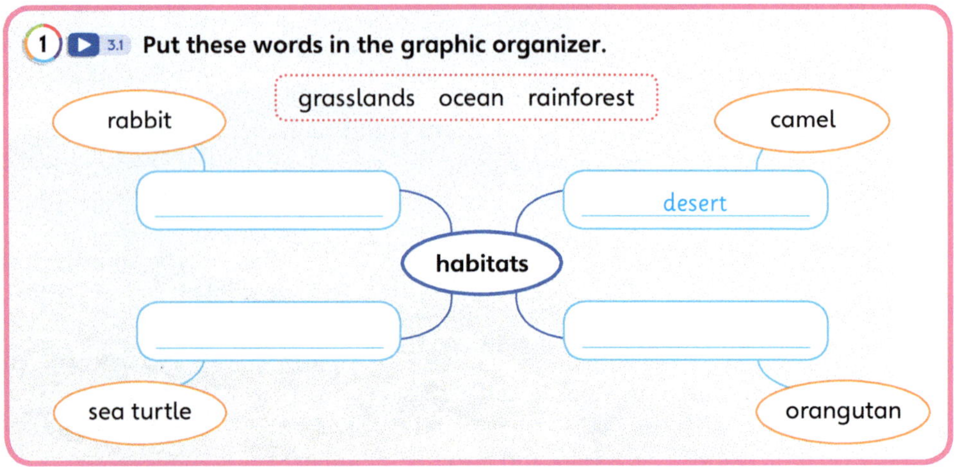

Nonfiction Reading

Ready to Read: Nonfiction introduces students to a **reading strategy** before they read the nonfiction text. Each text focuses on a different strategy, from comparing and contrasting to identifying the author's purpose and predicting, providing students with a variety of techniques to become better readers.

Nonfiction texts inspired by children's magazines provide meaningful content and language input on a wide range of topics. Students learn about the world and acquire language with appropriate scaffolding and support.

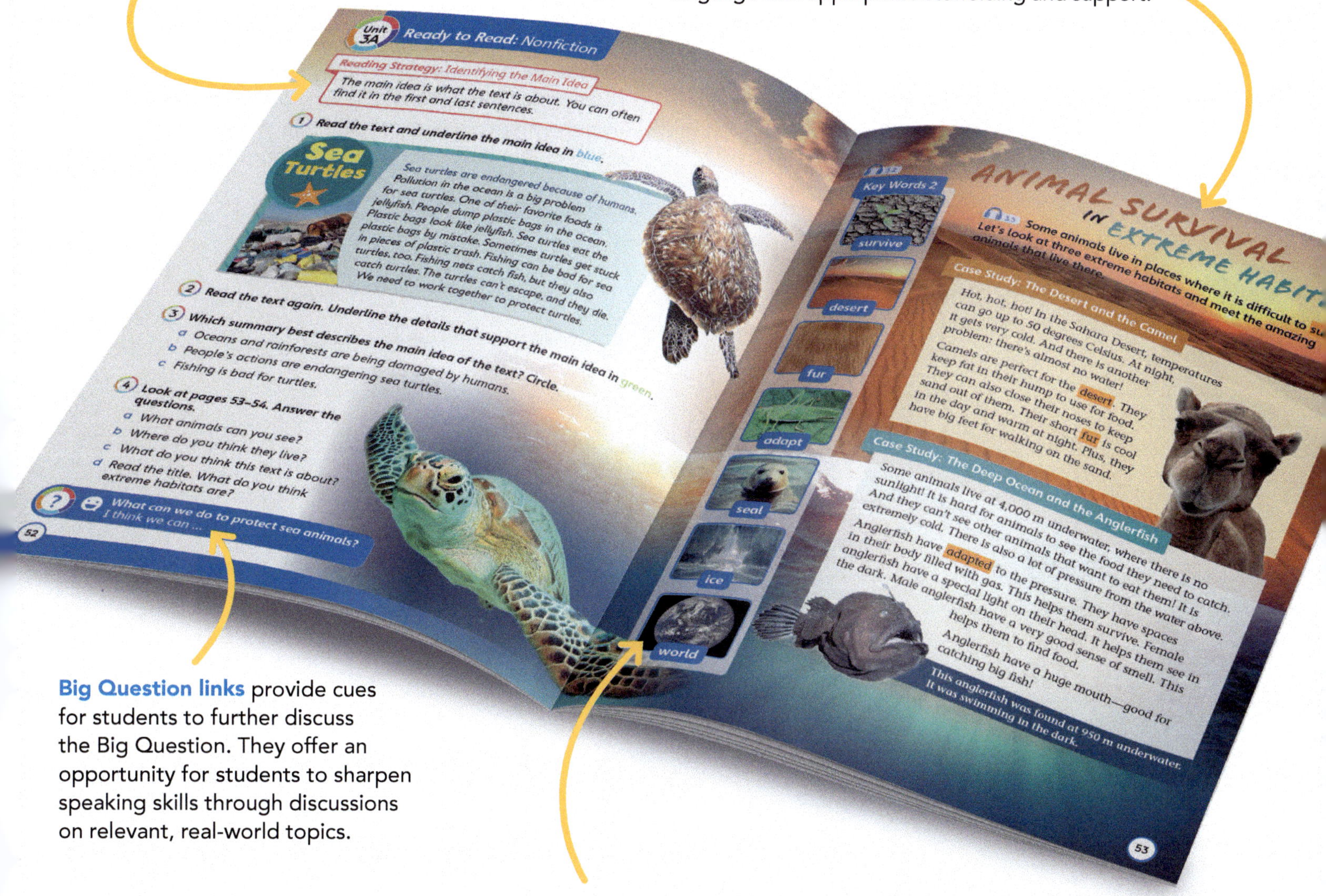

Big Question links provide cues for students to further discuss the Big Question. They offer an opportunity for students to sharpen speaking skills through discussions on relevant, real-world topics.

Key Words 2 help students comprehend the nonfiction text. These are clearly presented with photos and accompanying flashcards (Foundation–Level 4) and are highlighted in the body of the text.

Activity Book

Students practice Key Words 2 and reading strategies in another nonfiction text linked thematically to the unit topic.

Nonfiction Reading

Dialogic reading strategies create memorable, participative reading classes and young readers who think critically and talk about the texts. Dialogic reading prompts come from you initially, but, as students become more accustomed to the technique, they start to ask their own questions when they read independently. In the Teacher's Edition, you'll find all the questions and prompts you need to help students fully engage with the texts.

Teacher's Edition

Which habitat is this section about?
How is the Arctic extreme?
What do polar bears eat?
Why are polar bears' feet special?
What is the polar bear's fur like?
How does their fur help polar bears?
How does hiding help them?
How are polar bears like camels and anglerfish?
How are polar bears' feet like camels' feet?
What does "adapt" mean?
How have the three animals adapted to where they live?

Think boxes promote critical thinking skills and creativity.

On the **Explore the Text** page, students will practice the reading comprehension strategy they learned as well as implement a variety of other strategies to organize information and comprehend the text deeply.

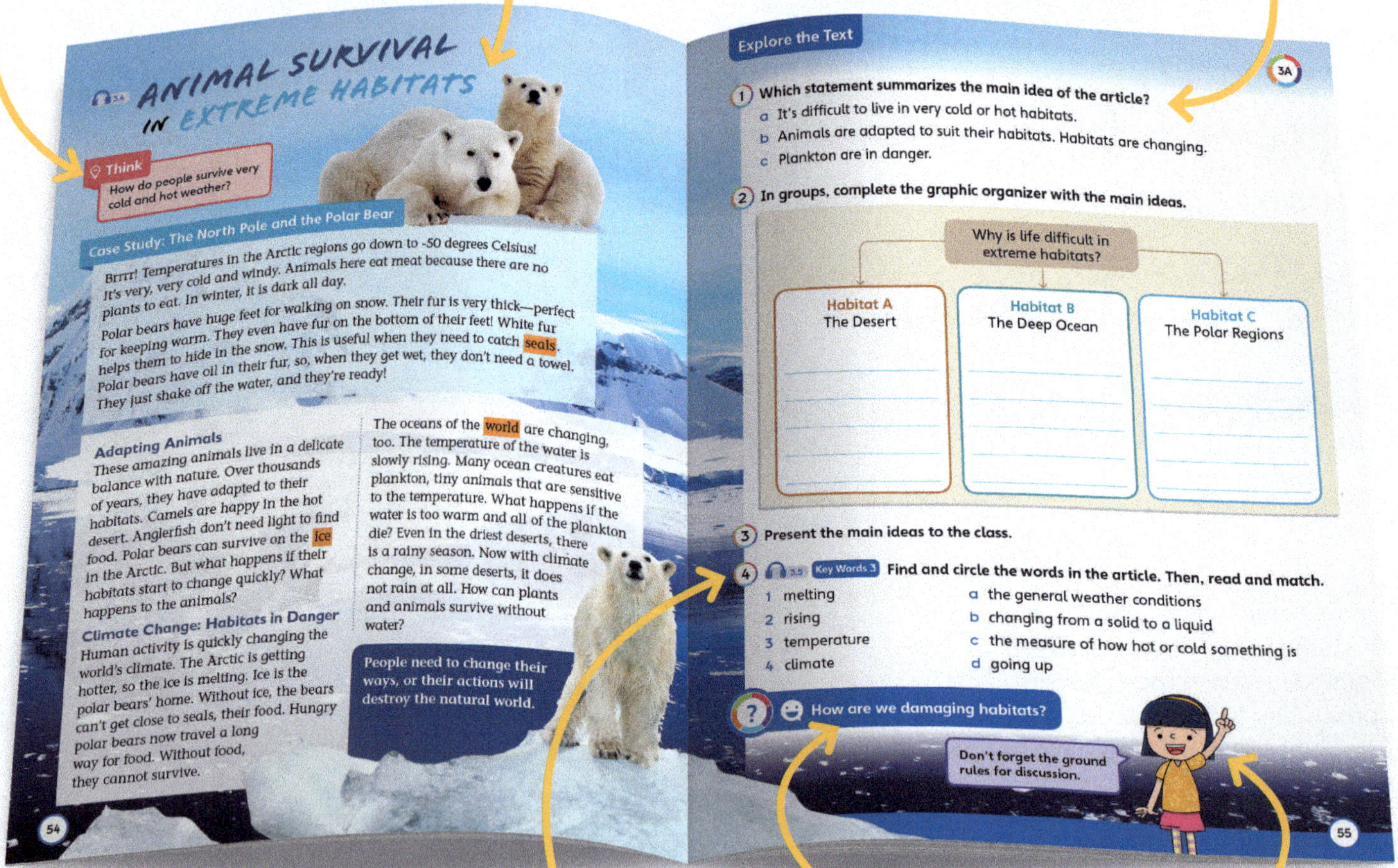

Key Words 3 (Words in Context) appear in the nonfiction text. Students learn techniques to deduce their meaning from context.

A Big Question link connects the nonfiction text to the Big Question.

Oracy Reminders encourage students to utilize their oracy skills when they discuss the Big Question link.

Activity Book

Students practice reading comprehension using the Activity Book nonfiction text.

Grammar and Phonics

The **Grammar in Context** page provides clear and systematic presentation and practice of key grammar structures. Students first reflect on the structure based on examples—at least one of which comes from the reading text—and then they explore the grammar rule. Finally, students practice using the structure through a song or chant or a speaking activity.

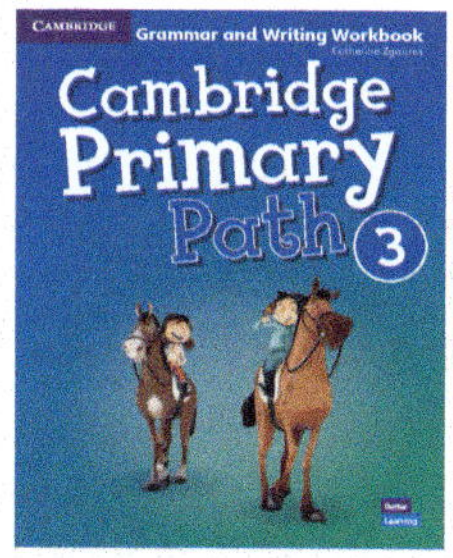

The **Grammar and Writing Workbook** offers two additional pages of grammar practice for each grammar point!

Activity Book

Students have two full pages of additional grammar practice per grammar point.

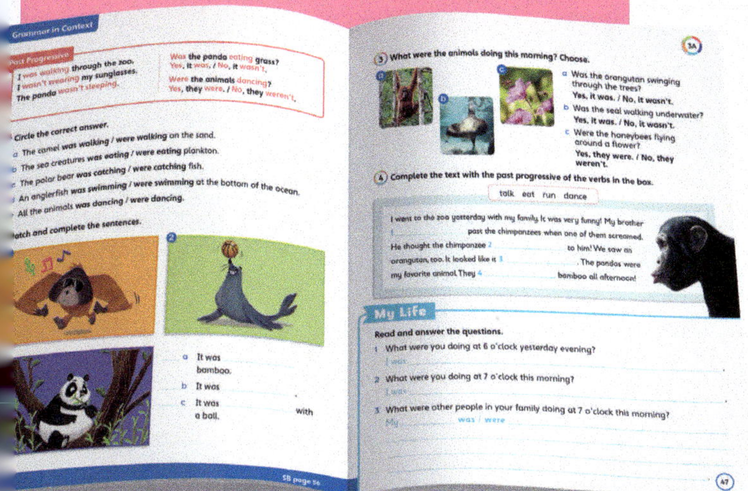

The **Phonics and Spelling** pages help young readers understand the relationship between graphemes (letters and letter combinations) and phonemes (individual speech sounds). Initially this helps children decode and read words accurately (Foundation–Level 3), and, as they progress, they become better spellers as they practice and acquire English spelling patterns through guided word study (Levels 4–6).

Activity Book

Students have additional practice with the target sounds, spelling, and word patterns.

Oracy

Oracy is the skill of communicating confidently and effectively in diverse situations, from presentations to participating in group discussions. At the core, oracy is about strengthening communication skills, but it goes well beyond the words we use. It includes physical skills, like projecting your voice and conveying confidence through your posture; social-emotional skills, like understanding group dynamics and helping a group come to a collective decision; and cognitive skills, like structuring your ideas into a coherent argument.

Each unit focuses on a different oracy skill. The oracy skills are revisited as students advance through the levels, allowing them to consolidate their skills and build confidence.

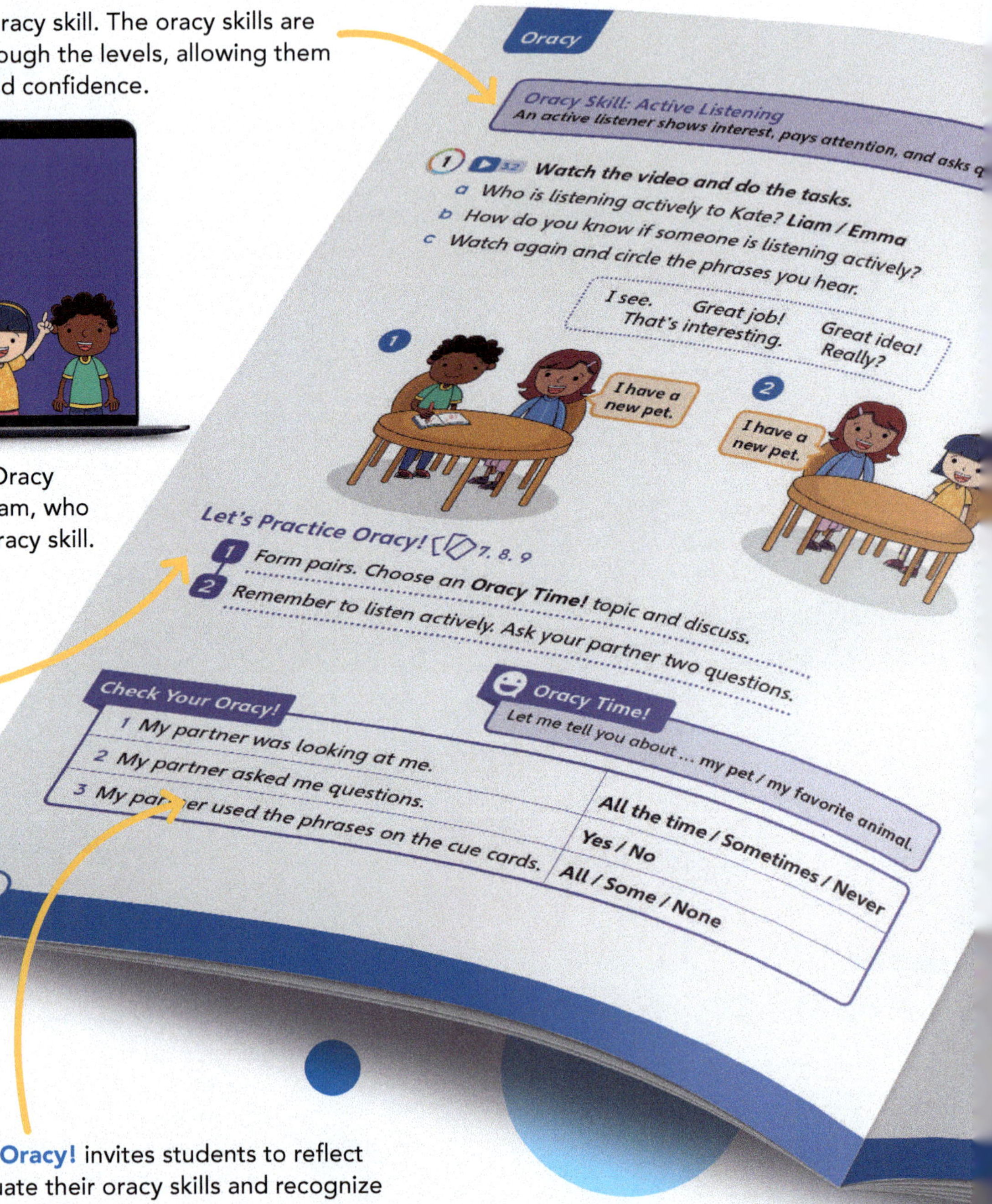

Animated **oracy videos** feature Oracy Morris, Kate, Jack, Emma, and Liam, who present and demonstrate each oracy skill.

In **Let's Practice Oracy!**, students practice oracy skills and observe each other. Cue Cards with key phrases—the same functional language that they saw in the animation—provide additional language support.

Check Your Oracy! invites students to reflect on and evaluate their oracy skills and recognize their own progress in oracy as they advance through the course.

Activity Book

Students review oracy skills and participate in self- and peer-assessment activities.

Writing

The **Writing** page is part of a structured process-writing program that enables students to produce more effective writing on their own. Each page begins with a model text that familiarizes students with a particular genre, such as a letter/email, brochure, or news report. Students analyze the genre to discover its key features and then practice writing their own texts.

The **Grammar and Writing Workbook** offers an additional three pages of writing practice.

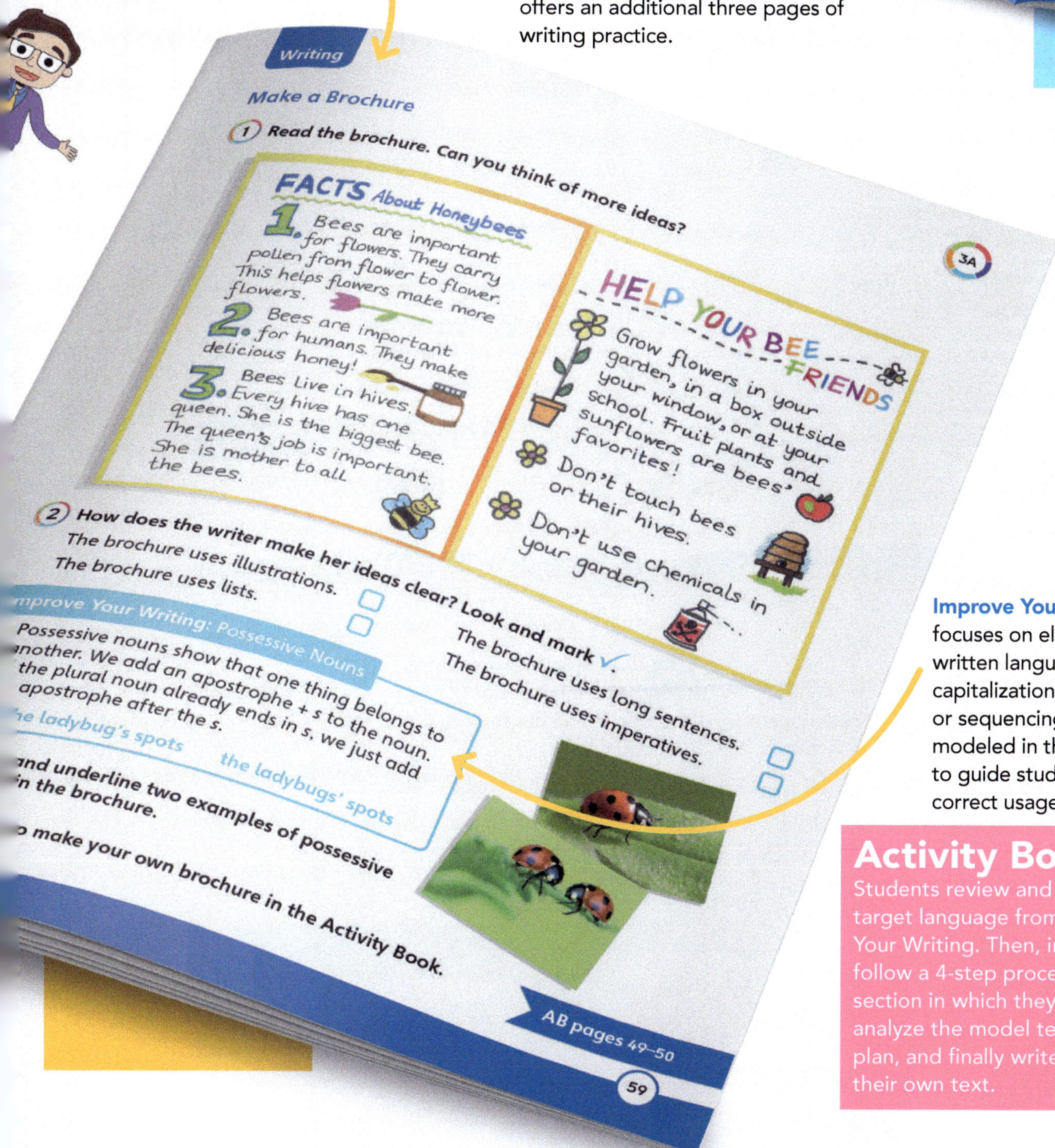

Improve Your Writing focuses on elements of written language such as capitalization, conjunctions, or sequencing adjectives modeled in the writing text to guide students in the correct usage.

Activity Book

Students review and practice the target language from Improve Your Writing. Then, in class, they follow a 4-step process-writing section in which they read and analyze the model text, make a plan, and finally write and edit their own text.

Fiction Reading

Ready to Read: Fiction starts with **Key Words 4**. These words are presented through images (Foundation–Level 4) and then practiced in a meaningful activity before students encounter them in a fiction text.

Students are again presented with a **reading strategy**—this time linked to a piece of fiction—and are given an opportunity to practice it before they apply it to the text.

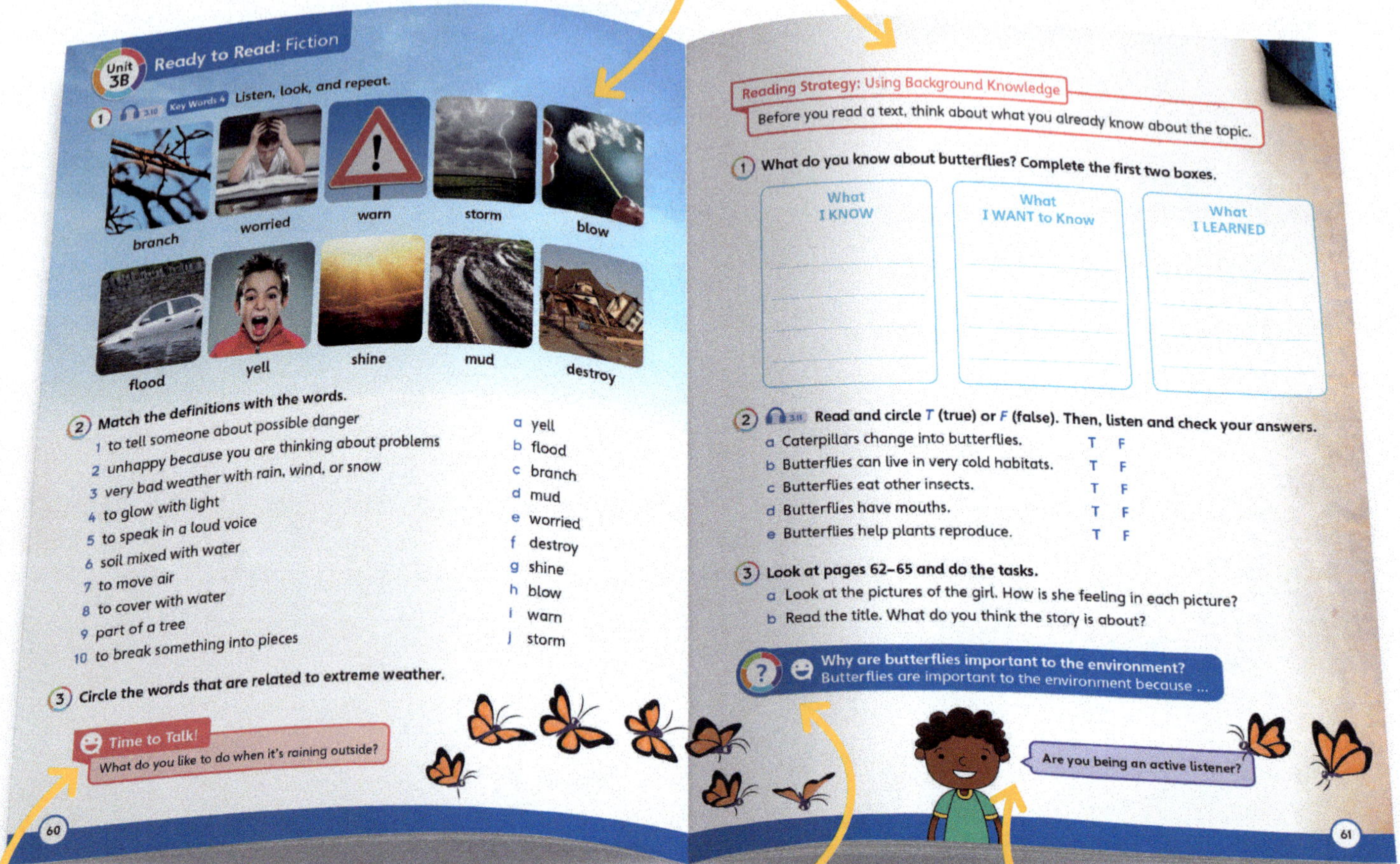

Time to Talk! helps students practice fluency by discussing kid-friendly topics. Students are encouraged to work in pairs and then switch partners for additional practice.

A **Big Question link** motivates students to think about the Big Question in the context of the fiction text.

As students discuss the Big Question link, an **Oracy Reminder** prompts them to implement the oracy skills they have been learning.

Activity Book

In another fiction text, students practice the reading strategy and Key Words 4.

Fiction Reading

The pedagogical value of stories for learning is well documented. Illustrated original and adapted **fiction stories** form the backbone of the second half of the unit. These stories motivate and engage students at an emotional level while providing rich vocabulary input and enabling them to connect to authentic, natural language.

As with the nonfiction text in the first half of the unit, students are encouraged to explore the text with critical thinking questions in the **Think prompts**. Dialogic reading prompts are included in the Teacher's Edition to promote deeper engagement with and discussions about the text.

Teacher's Edition

What are sandbags?
What was it like the next morning?
What did the storm do?
Why did Luisa yell, "They're here!"?
Was Luisa's great-grandmother right about the butterflies?
How does Luisa feel at the end of the story? Why?

Fiction Reading and Grammar

On the **Explore the Text** page, students complete a variety of comprehension tasks. These tasks go beyond literal understanding and encourage children to develop skills such as making connections, predicting, organizing information, summarizing, and inferring. This approach prepares students to become more proficient readers of complex texts.

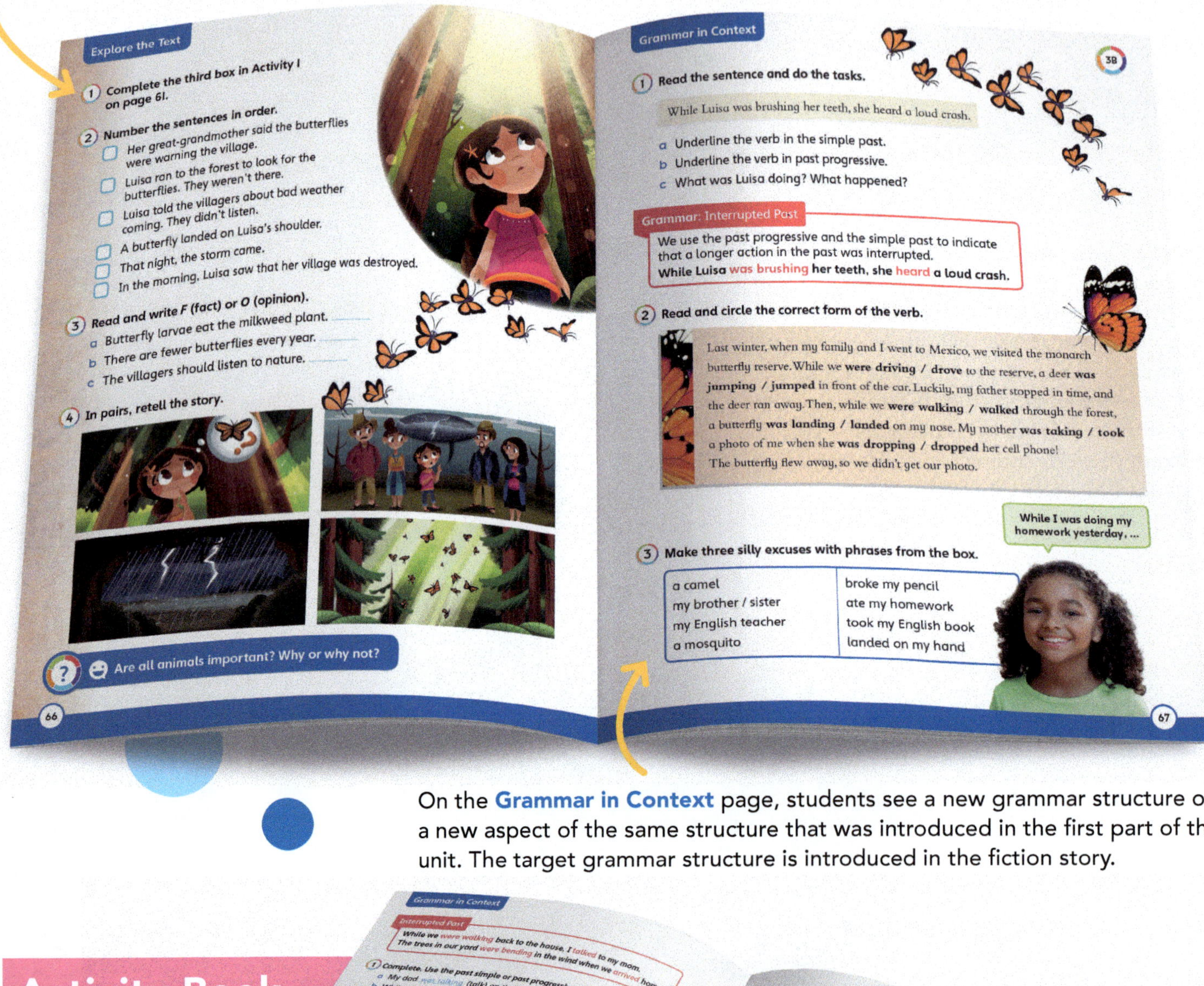

On the **Grammar in Context** page, students see a new grammar structure or a new aspect of the same structure that was introduced in the first part of the unit. The target grammar structure is introduced in the fiction story.

Activity Book

Students have two full pages of additional grammar practice. Another three pages are offered in the Grammar and Writing Workbook.

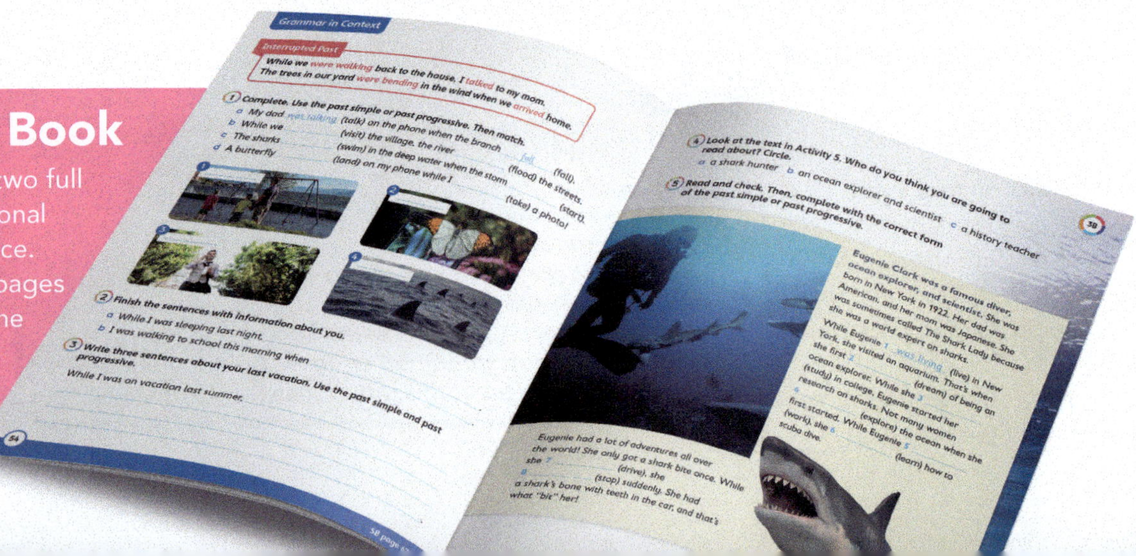

Listening and Values

The **Listening** page focuses specifically on developing listening comprehension skills, from listening for gist to listening for details, from predicting content to inferring meaning. Although students are exposed to listening activities throughout the unit, it is important to focus specifically on practicing skills that will make them stronger listeners.

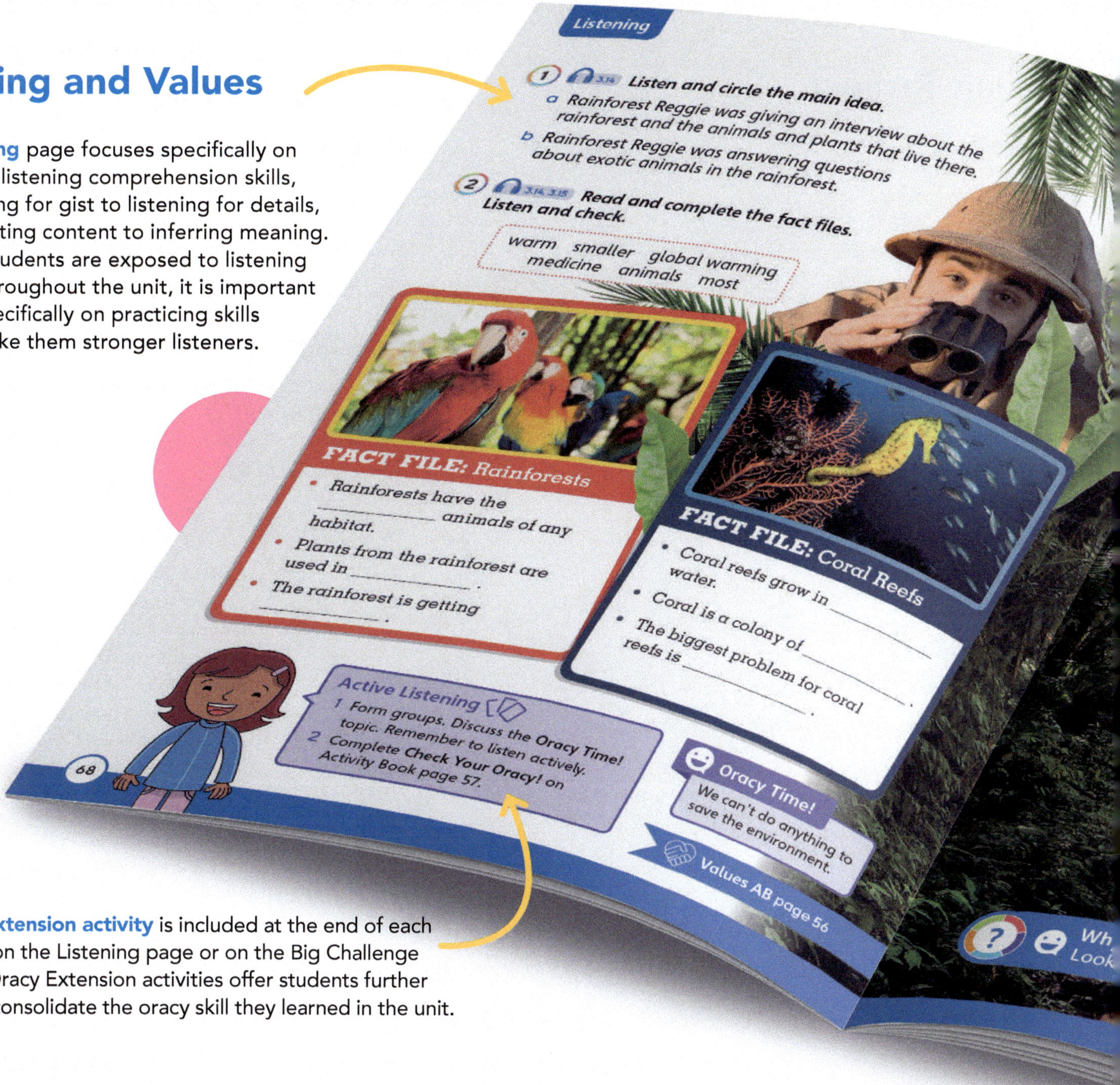

An **Oracy Extension activity** is included at the end of each unit, either on the Listening page or on the Big Challenge page. The Oracy Extension activities offer students further practice to consolidate the oracy skill they learned in the unit.

Activity Book

On the **Values** pages, students explore and reflect on universal values linked to the unit theme. Thinking about values and applying them when interacting with others is a key life competency and builds socially responsible individuals. Ideally the Value pages will be taught in class.

Unit Project

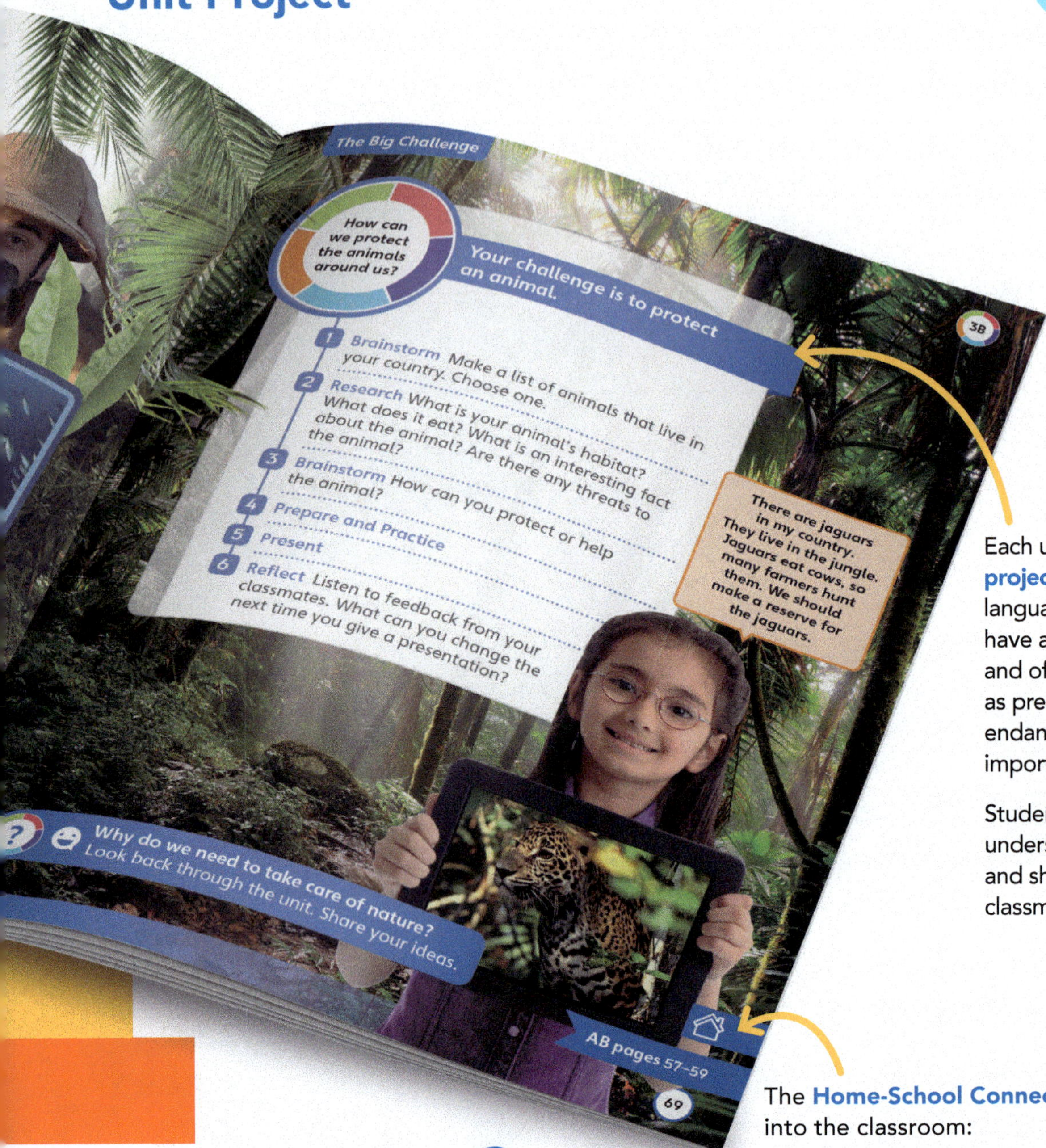

Each unit culminates in a **Big Challenge project** that brings together the language and knowledge students have acquired in a hands-on, creative, and often collaborative task, such as presenting how to protect an endangered animal or researching an important historical artifact.

Students demonstrate their understanding of the Big Question and share their knowledge with their classmates.

The **Home-School Connection** gives parents a window into the classroom:

Practice Extra is online practice that supplements classroom learning at home.

Study Guides are another key component of the Home-School Connection. These make it possible for parents to work with their children while they study for unit exams and assessments.

Monthly Blasts are activities designed specifically for parents and children to do together with the aim of practicing English at home. The Blasts are linked to the unit theme and involve tasks such as naming items to looking up a museum site online and giving the parent a tour of an exhibition.

Activity Book

Students reflect on their performance in the Big Challenge and evaluate the oracy skills linked to the Oracy Extension activity. At the end of every unit, a two-page Unit Review gives students the opportunity to revisit the target language and vocabulary covered in the unit.

Speaking

Speaking Missions are designed to build the confidence students need to speak English in real-world scenarios, such as buying a souvenir, ordering an ice cream cone, or visiting a museum in a foreign country. The focus here is on high-frequency vocabulary and functional language with a degree of repetition so that children gradually become comfortable speaking English in everyday situations. There are two Speaking Missions for every three units.

Before Your Mission presents key vocabulary to expose students to the language they will need. They also listen to an example dialogue that features the structures they will use.

During Your Mission supports students with cues and step-by-step instructions to carry out their mission.

Time to Talk! or a **Big Question link** allows students to extend the Speaking Mission topic further, with a focus on either building fluency (Time to Talk!) or strengthening discussion skills (Big Question link).

Activity Book

Students consolidate the work they did during the Speaking Mission.

Oracy

Oracy Performance Tasks enable students to apply the oracy skills they learned in the previous three units by collaborating on a communicative quest. In addition to providing students with a valuable review and reinforcement of their oracy skills, the performance task can be used to evaluate students' ongoing progress in oracy. There are three Oracy Performance Tasks per level, after Units 3, 6, and 9.

Students first review the oracy skills and language from the previous three units. Then, they are presented with the **Oracy Task**.

Oracy Performance Task 1: Collaboration

1 Which oracy skills do you remember? Read and match.

1 Active listening
2 Ground rules
3 Positive feedback

a help us remember how to behave in a discussion.
b encourages others to talk.
c is about listening and responding to others.

2 In pairs, complete the table.

Good point! That's awesome! Really? How about ... ? I see. Great idea! That's interesting. I think ...

Giving Positive Feedback	Active Listening	Giving an Opinion

YOUR TASK

You are traveling in the Arctic on a snowmobile. Your snowmobile suddenly breaks down. You have to walk for two days to the nearest shelter. You are wearing warm clothes.

Look at the pictures on page 71. You can choose five items to take with you.

Which five items will you take?

70

fishing net, pot, knife, chocolate bar, bottle of water, can of beans, sleeping bag, spoon, flashlight, sunglasses, first-aid kit, snowshoes, rope, matches

1–3

1 Form groups and circle three ground rules for the task.

- We listen to each other's ideas.
- We stand up when we speak.
- We ask each other, "What do you think?" and "Why do you think that?"
- We try to agree in the end.

2 Discuss and report your group's results to the class.

3 Talk about your talk!

- What positive feedback did you hear?
- What active listening did you observe?
- Did your group follow the ground rules?

4 Complete Check Your Oracy!

Check Your Oracy!

	☺	☺☺	☺☺☺
1 I listened actively.			
2 I followed the ground rules.			
3 I gave positive feedback.			
4 I gave an opinion.			

What I can do better next time:

71

Explicit **vocabulary** that can be used for the task is provided. Students agree on the ground rules that they will follow and then put their skills into practice by performing the task together. Results of the task are shared with the entire class.

After the task, students reflect on their talk by completing a **Check Your Oracy!** evaluation and discussing how they can improve their oracy skills in the future.

Activity Book

Students reflect on and consolidate the work they did during the Oracy Performance Task.

1 Who am I?

Literacy

Read: a nonfiction text about children who are different; a fiction text about two turtles that are different but also similar

Reading Strategies: similarities and differences; real or fantasy?

Ready to Write

Learn to Write: capital and lowercase letters: *I'm Ted.*

Getting Ready to Write: identify and trace capital and lowercase letters

Oracy

Skill: Ground Rules

Cue Card 1: 1. *This is ...*

Speaking Mission: say who you are when you are lost

Language

Key Words 1: *favorite, color, hair, girl, brown, boy*

Key Words 2: *short, long, tall, curly, straight, blond*

Key Words 3: *class, different*

Key Words 4: *old, slow, fast, tired, young, happy*

Speaking Mission Words: *yes, no, name, phone, numbers, lost*

Grammar in Context

Verb *to be*: Affirmative and Negative: *I am six years old. She isn't short.*

Verb *to be*: Affirmative and Negative: *You are young. They aren't slow.*

Phonics

The Alphabet

Listening

Dialogue: Talking About Your Things

Values

Respecting Differences

The Big Challenge

How can we talk about ourselves?
Talk about yourself to the class

Objective: to introduce the topic of who we are and how we are similar and different
Key Words 1: ***favorite, color, hair, girl, brown, boy***
Materials: Video 1.1, Audio CD 1.1, Flashcards 1.1–1.6

WHO AM I?

- Read the Big Question aloud. Have students look at the pictures. Show your book to the class, and point to one of the boys on the page. Say: *This is a boy. Boy.* Repeat to model *girl*. Then, point to a boy in the class and say: *Boy.* Do the same with a girl.
- Read the first question aloud: *Who is a boy?* Ask students to point to each boy on the page. Then, point to the pictures in your book, encouraging students to check their answers. Repeat with the next question: *Who is a girl?*
- Finally, ask the last question: *Are you similar to them?* Say: *Raise your hand if you are a boy. Stand up if you are a girl.* If necessary, model the two actions as you say them.
- 1.1 Key Words 1 Use the flashcards and audio to present Key Words 1. Hold up the *favorite* Flashcard. Say: *This is the girl's favorite toy.* Hold up three pens or pencils. Choose one, and, pantomiming enthusiasm for one over the other two, say: *This is my favorite. Favorite.* Continue with the rest of the flashcards. Hold up the flashcards again, one by one, as you play Track 1.1. Have students repeat the words.

1 1.1 Watch the video. Circle what is mentioned in the video.

Watch the first part of the video, pausing after "Let's find out!" Ask: *What is today's Big Question? (Who am I?)* Continue the video. Pause after "I have blond hair." Use the flashcards to ask comprehension questions about the presenter. For example, point to the *boy* and *girl* Flashcards. Ask: *Is the presenter a boy or a girl?* Continue the video. Pause after "She has brown eyes and brown hair." Ask questions, providing two options for students to choose from. For example, ask: *Is Ela from Turkey or China? (Turkey.)* Continue the video, repeating this procedure for Max. Finally, finish the video. Have students do Activity 1. Check answers as a class.

2 1.1 Watch again. Complete the graphic organizer in the Activity Book.

Play the video again, and have students complete Activity 1 on AB page 2. Have pairs match each picture with the correct person. Monitor, and provide support if necessary.

AB page 2

Unit 1A Ready to Read: Nonfiction

Reading Strategy: Similarities and Differences

1 1.2 Listen, point, and repeat.

eyes hair brown orange

2 1.3 Listen and number the pictures.

a 1 b 6 c 4 d 5 e 2 f 3

3 Are you similar to Larissa? Draw and color about yourself.

students' own answers

Who are you?
I'm Maria. I'm from Spain.

8

Objective: to find similarities and differences and prepare to read a nonfiction text
Key Words I: ***favorite, color, hair, girl, brown, boy***
Materials: Audio CD I.2, I.3, sample of Activity 3 about yourself; Fun Corner: large pictures of five flags from different countries, paper, crayons

1.1 **Key Words 1** Use the flashcards and audio to review Key Words I.

1 1.2 Listen, point, and repeat.

Ask students to look at the four pictures, point to each of them, and repeat the words as you play Track I.2. Say: *eyes.* Point to your eyes. Have students repeat the word and point to their eyes. Then, say: *hair.* Allow students to react on their own. It is important to give students time to make decisions without your intervention. Continue with *brown* and *orange.*

2 1.3 Listen and number the pictures.

Have students look at the six pictures in Activity 2. Ask questions, and encourage students to provide information about the girl. Ask: *Does she have brown eyes? Is she seven?* Play Track I.3, pausing after "I'm six years old." Ask: *Which picture is number two?* Give students time to identify picture 2 (the cake) and number it. Play the rest of the track. Check answers by asking students to point to the corresponding picture as you say each number.

3 Are you similar to Larissa? Draw and color about yourself.

Ask individual students questions related to the pictures, for example: *Are you six? Are you similar to or different from Larissa?* or *Is your favorite color orange? Are you similar to or different from Larissa?* Show the class the picture you prepared for Activity 3. Describe it: *I'm (Ms. Demir). I'm different from Larissa. I have (green) eyes and (brown) hair. I'm (thirty-two) years old. I'm from (Turkey).* Guide students to complete Activity 3 about themselves.

Big Question Link

Point to the Big Question Link, and read the question aloud. Point to the model answer and read it aloud. Ask individual students: *Who are you?* Guide them to answer by following the model. Then, have students form pairs and share information about themselves.

Fun Corner!

Flags

Discuss the meaning of flags with students. Explain what they represent. Ask: *What colors are on your country's flag?* Ask volunteers to draw their countries' flags on the board. Form three groups. Show a picture of a flag to the class. Give students time to visually memorize it. Then, place the picture face down on your desk. Have groups draw and color the flag. Do the same with the other four flags. Finally, ask groups to share their drawings. Check the results as a class.

Build Creativity!

Recognizing Classmates

Objective: A Different Point of View

Have a volunteer cover their eyes. The volunteer has to recognize their classmates, but without looking. Have classmates stay at their desks and, one by one, say a simple sentence. Can the volunteer tell who is speaking? Explore what information the volunteer is using to make guesses, presumably including not only voices but also the direction of the voices.

1.4 **Key Words 2** Use the flashcards and audio to pre-teach Key Words 2. Invite a student to stand next to you. Use your hands to show the height difference between you and the student. Say: *Tall, short, tall, short.* Show the *short* Flashcard. Say: *Short. (She's) short.* Do the same with the *tall* Flashcard. Teaching opposite words together will be more effective than teaching the words in isolation. Do the same with the *curly* and *straight* Flashcards. Continue with the rest of the key words. Play Track 1.4, and have students repeat each word. Even if the majority of students don't know how to read yet, lead them in identifying the highlighted words in the text on pages 9 and 10 with the help of the flashcards.

Pre-Reading

Have students look at the text on page 9. Point to the title. Say: *This is the title. The title of the text is* We Are All Different! Point to the picture of the group of children. Ask: *Who has brown hair?* Ask individual students to point to the corresponding children. Say: *Point to the children with blond hair.* Then, ask: *Are the children similar or different? (Different.)* Continue to page 10, and ask questions to help students find differences. Play Tracks 1.5 and 1.6 while students look at the pictures.

1.5 Page 9

Play Track 1.5. Ask questions:

Is Onur a boy or a girl?
Does he have brown hair?
Does he have blue eyes?
Is he short or tall?
How many boys are in the class?

Personalization

Draw seven wide columns on the board. Group the first three together and the remaining four together. At the top of each column draw and label the following pictures: brown eyes, blue eyes, green eyes, brown hair; black hair, blond hair, red hair. Say: *I have (brown) eyes. I'll draw a checkmark under the drawing of the (brown) eyes. I have (black) hair. I'll add a checkmark under the drawing of (black) hair.* Ask each student to go the board and draw a checkmark under the categories that represent them. Once everyone has drawn their checkmarks on the board, have students count the checkmarks under each category with you. This is a good activity for helping students understand the concept of being different and, at the same time, similar.

Objective: to understand that we are all different
Key Words 2: ***short, long, tall, curly, straight, blond***
Materials: Audio CD 1.4, 1.5, 1.6, Flashcards 1.7–1.12

1.6 Page 10, section 1

Have students look at the pictures, and ask: *Are the girls in the drawings similar or different? (Different.)* Play Track 1.6 through "She's tall." Then, ask questions about Emily:

Does Emily have short or long hair?
Is she short or tall?

Remember to emphasize the new words when you ask a question, to give students time to understand and recall the meaning.

1.6 Page 10, sections 2 and 3

Play the rest of Track 1.6. Ask questions using two options so that students review opposites.

Is Diane six or seven?
Does she have curly or straight hair?
Is Flora six or seven?
Is her hair brown or blond?
Is she short or tall?

Personalization

Ask: *Are you similar to or different from Onur? Are you similar to or different from Flora?*

Think

Read the question and model answer in the Think box aloud. Follow the model to provide an answer about yourself. Form pairs. Encourage them to ask and answer the question about themselves. Have students swap roles so that everyone provides an answer. Monitor, and provide support if necessary.

AB page 3

Differentiated Instruction

Below-level ★	On-level ★★	Above-level ★★★
Use Flashcards 1.7–1.12. Show the *short* Flashcard. Say: *Who is short? Emily, Diane, or Flora? (Flora.) Who has long hair? Emily, Diane, or Flora? (Emily.)* Use the rest of the flashcards to check comprehension. Allow students to look at their books.	Say the name of a girl in the text. Have volunteers say facts about her. Encourage students to try to remember the information without looking at their books.	Write and say a word or words related to one of the girls in the text: *straight hair*. Ask: *Who has straight hair?* Elicit the name. Then, ask a student to write the first letter of the girl's name next to the word or words. For example: *straight hair D (Diane)*

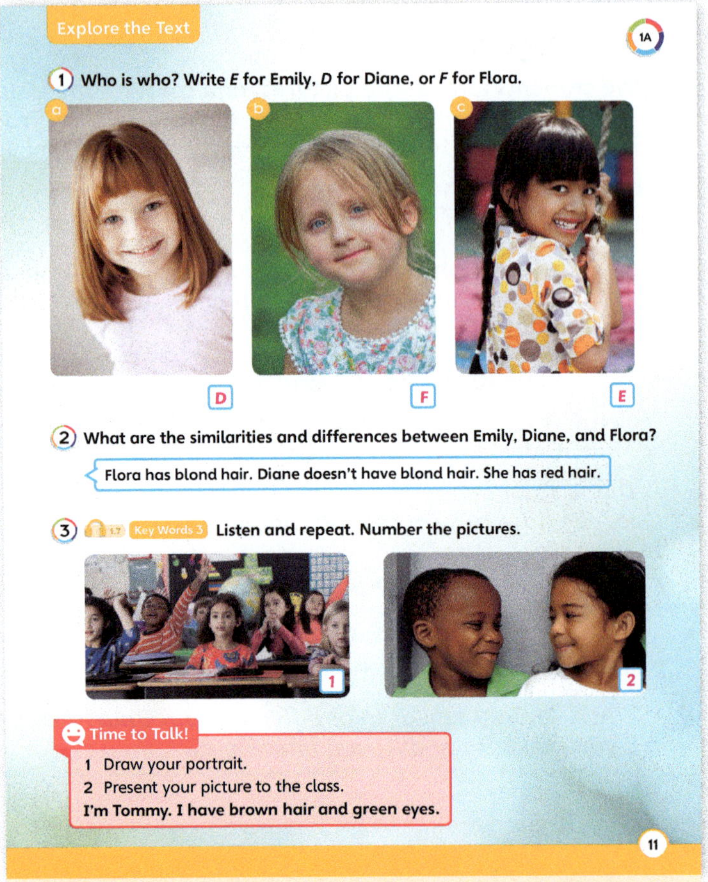
Explore the Text

1A

1 Who is who? Write *E* for Emily, *D* for Diane, or *F* for Flora.

a D b F c E

2 What are the similarities and differences between Emily, Diane, and Flora?

Flora has blond hair. Diane doesn't have blond hair. She has red hair.

3 1.7 Key Words 3 Listen and repeat. Number the pictures.

1 2

Time to Talk!

1 Draw your portrait.

2 Present your picture to the class.

I'm Tommy. I have brown hair and green eyes.

11

Objective: to recall specific information from the text and identify words in context

Key Words 3: ***class, different***

Materials: Audio CD 1.7, paper, colored pencils or crayons, drawn self-portrait of yourself

1 Who is who? Write *E* for Emily, *D* for Diane, or *F* for Flora.

Have students look at Activity 1. Ask them to look at the three photos and pay attention to the girls' eyes and hair. Then, tell students to go to page 10 and compare the drawings with the photos on page 11. Ask: *Who is Emily?* Continue with Diane and Flora. Have students label the photos.

2 What are the similarities and differences between Emily, Diane, and Flora?

Form three groups. The first group will represent Emily, the second Diane, and the third Flora. Ask the first group to describe something about Emily, for example, *Emily has long hair.* Then, ask the second group: *Does Diane have long hair? (No, she doesn't.) Are they similar? (No, they aren't.)* Continue guiding groups in this way, eliciting the similarities and differences between the three girls. Read the speech bubble on page 11 aloud, and ask volunteers to make similar comparisons between two of the three girls.

3 1.7 Key Words 3 Listen and repeat. Number the pictures.

Ask students to close their books. Play Track 1.7. Have students pronounce the words. Tell them to open their books to page 9 and point to the class. Then, ask: *Are the children different? (Yes.)* Say: *Now turn to page 11, Activity 3. Look at the two photos. Listen, and number the pictures 1 or 2.* Play Track 1.7 again. Check answers as a class.

Time to Talk!

Give each student a sheet of paper. Ask them to draw their portrait and color it using the correct colors for their hair and eyes. When all students have finished, show your self-portrait and say: *I'm (Ms. Demir). I have (brown) hair and (green) eyes.* Ask volunteers to present their self-portraits and introduce themselves following your example. Encourage them to give more information: *I'm (seven). I have (curly) hair. I'm (tall).* Model the use of negatives (*I'm not …*), and prompt students to use a negative as well: *I'm not (tall).*

Fun Corner!

Who Is Who?

Form three groups. Collect students' self-portraits, and put them facedown in a pile on your desk. Ask a student from one group to choose a portrait without showing it to the class. Guide the student in describing the portrait so that their group can guess whose portrait it is. Provide sentence frames such as: *She's (tall). She has (blond) hair. She has (curly) hair. She has (brown) eyes.* The group gets two guesses. If they don't guess correctly, the other groups can each get one guess.

Build Creativity!

Self-Portraits

Objective: A Different Point of View

Tell the class that they are going to draw their portraits again except that this time they have to do it with their eyes closed. Allow them to make one change or addition to make their portraits more recognizable.

AB pages 4–5

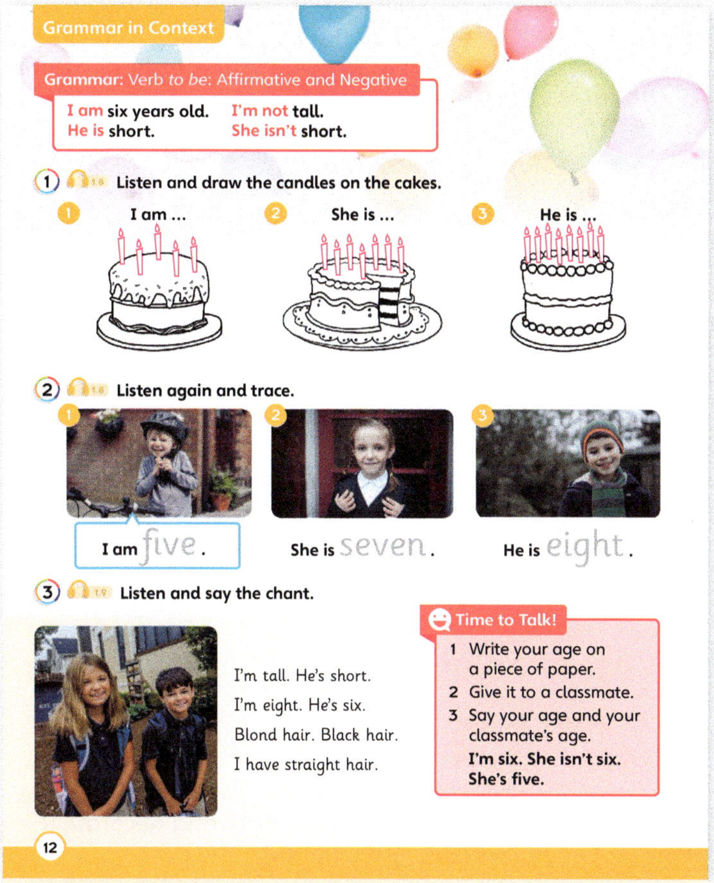
Grammar in Context

Grammar: Verb *to be*: Affirmative and Negative

I am six years old. I'm not tall.
He is short. She isn't short.

1 1.8 Listen and draw the candles on the cakes.

1 I am ... 2 She is ... 3 He is ...

2 1.8 Listen again and trace.

1 I am five. 2 She is seven. 3 He is eight.

3 1.9 Listen and say the chant.

I'm tall. He's short.
I'm eight. He's six.
Blond hair. Black hair.
I have straight hair.

Time to Talk!

1 Write your age on a piece of paper.
2 Give it to a classmate.
3 Say your age and your classmate's age.

I'm six. She isn't six. She's five.

12

Objective: to use the verb *to be* to talk about yourself

Materials: Audio CD 1.8, 1.9, paper, slips of paper

Grammar Box

Direct students' attention to the Grammar box. Ask students to focus on the words in red in the first row. Write the words on the board: *I am, I'm not.* Pronounce the words slowly as you point to them. Then, pointing to yourself, use *I am* and *I'm not* to talk about yourself: *I am (short). I'm not (six years old).* Ask volunteers to talk about themselves using *I am* and *I'm not.* Direct students' attention to the words in red in the second row. Write the words on the board. Provide examples about some of your students. Then, ask volunteers to provide more examples.

1 1.8 Listen and draw the candles on the cakes.

Draw a cake on the board. Ask a student to come to the front and draw candles on it to show how old they are. Invite the class to count the candles on the cake with you. Then, say: *(She) is (six) years old.* Explain to students that now they will draw candles on three cakes on page 12. Play Track 1.8, pausing after each age is mentioned to give students time to draw the candles. Check answers as a class.

Practice Time 1 Distribute paper to students, and ask them to draw a cake with candles on it to show their age. Invite students to sit in a big circle and share their drawings. Say: *I'm (thirty) years old.* Point to the student sitting to your right, and, looking at that student's cake, say: *(She) is (seven).* Guide students to do the same. First, they say their age. Then, they say the age of the student sitting to their right. Continue until all students have participated.

2 1.8 Listen again and trace.

Draw students' attention to the pictures in Activity 2. Play Track 1.8 again, and have students point to each child. Ask students to trace the number words. Write the numbers *5, 7,* and *8* on the board, and ask volunteers to write the number words next to them. Have students write *I am* and their age, as a number word, under their drawings of a cake they made during Practice Time. Provide support as needed.

3 1.9 Listen and say the chant.

Ask students to look at the picture of the two children in Activity 3. Lead them in describing the children and noticing their differences: *She's tall. She has long hair. He's short. He has short hair.* Play Track 1.9 once. Then, play it again, and ask students to chant along with you.

Practice Time 2 Have students work in pairs. Play Track 1.9. Ask pairs to create a chant about themselves similar to the one in the recording. Go around the class to monitor and help students if they are having difficulties using the chant as a model. For example: *I'm short. She's tall. I'm seven. She's six. Brown hair. Black hair. I have curly hair.*

Time to Talk!

Give out slips of paper, and ask students to write their age on their slips. Write your age on a slip of paper, and ask a student to give you their slip. Say: *I'm (thirty). He/She isn't (six). He/She is (seven).* Form pairs, and tell students to swap papers. Invite volunteers to tell you their age and their partner's age. Then, encourage students to go around in pairs, taking turns telling others their age and their partner's age.

AB pages 6–7

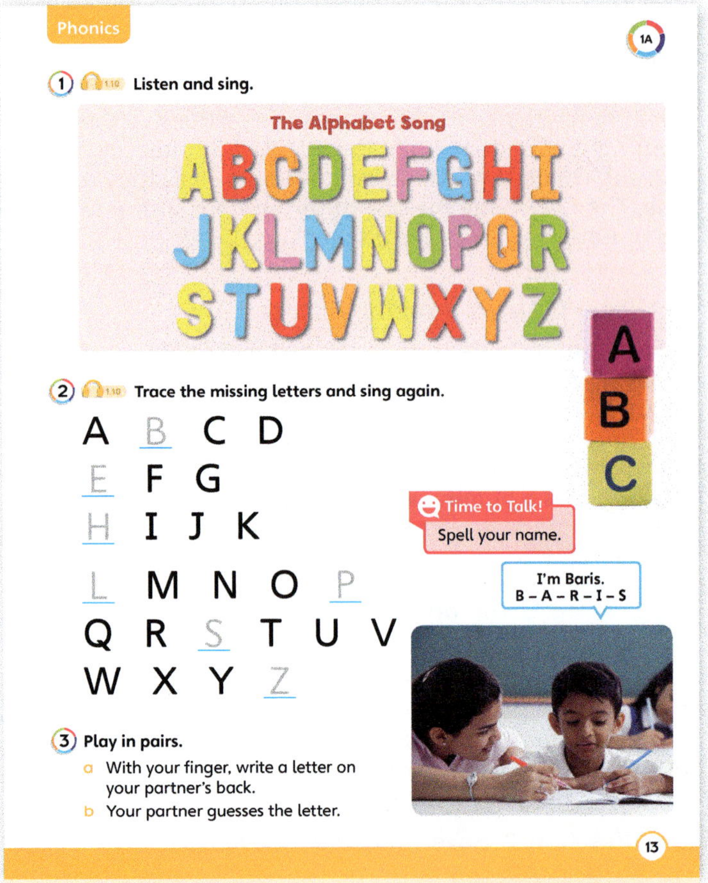

Phonics

1A

1 1.10 Listen and sing.

The Alphabet Song

ABCDEFGHI
JKLMNOPQR
STUVWXYZ

A B C

2 1.10 Trace the missing letters and sing again.

A B C D
E F G
H I J K
L M N O P
Q R S T U V
W X Y Z

Time to Talk! Spell your name.

I'm Baris. B – A – R – I – S

3 Play in pairs.

a With your finger, write a letter on your partner's back.
b Your partner guesses the letter.

13

Objective: to identify letters and say the alphabet
Materials: Audio CD 1.10; Build Creativity: paper ; Fun Corner: a soft ball

1 1.10 Listen and sing.

Write the alphabet on the board. Say: *These are letters. We use letters to make words.* Ask volunteers to point to the first letter of their name. Then, point to each letter of the alphabet in order and pronounce it slowly and clearly. Ask students to raise their hands if their name starts with that letter. Read the alphabet again, and pause after each letter for students to repeat. Play Track 1.10, pointing to each letter as it is mentioned in the song. Then, play Track 1.10 for a second time, and ask students to sing along with you. Ask volunteers to point to the letters as they sing. Alternatively, divide the class into six groups, and assign each group a part of the song:

A, B, C, D E, F, G H, I, J, K L, M, N, O, P
Q, R, S, T, U, V W, X, Y, Z

Act as an choral director, having each group in turn sing its part. Then, reassign the parts.

2 1.10 Trace the missing letters and sing again.

Play Track 1.10 again. Ask students to look at the alphabet in Activity 2 and trace the missing letters. Then, write groups of letters from the song with one or two missing letters on the board, for example: *A ____ C ____*. Have volunteers complete the sequence while singing the corresponding part of the song.

Practice Time I Write *YES* on the board. Spell it slowly and clearly. Ask a volunteer to come to the front and write a word of their choice. Help the student spell the word if needed. Repeat with other students.

3 Play in pairs.

Ask a student to come to the front and to turn their back to the class. With your finger, write a letter on the student's back. Ask: *What's the letter?* The student says the letter. Divide the class into pairs, and ask them to do the same.

Time to Talk!

Point to the boy, and read the text in the speech bubble slowly and clearly: *I'm Baris. B – A – R – I – S.* Divide the class into groups, and have the students in each group spell their names to one another. Monitor, and check pronunciation.

Build Creativity!

Choose a Letter

Objective: Focus

Hand out paper. Ask students to choose a letter of the alphabet. Have them write the letter and decorate it with drawings related to what the letter stands for. Invite the class to stand in a circle and say: *I'll sing the Alphabet Song. When you hear your letter, hold the letter up, and shake it.*

Fun Corner!

Your Turn

Have students form a circle. Say the first letter of the alphabet, and toss the ball to a student. That student says the next letter in the alphabet and tosses the ball back to you. Continue the same way until the alphabet is complete. If a student doesn't remember a letter, they can point to someone else.

AB page 8

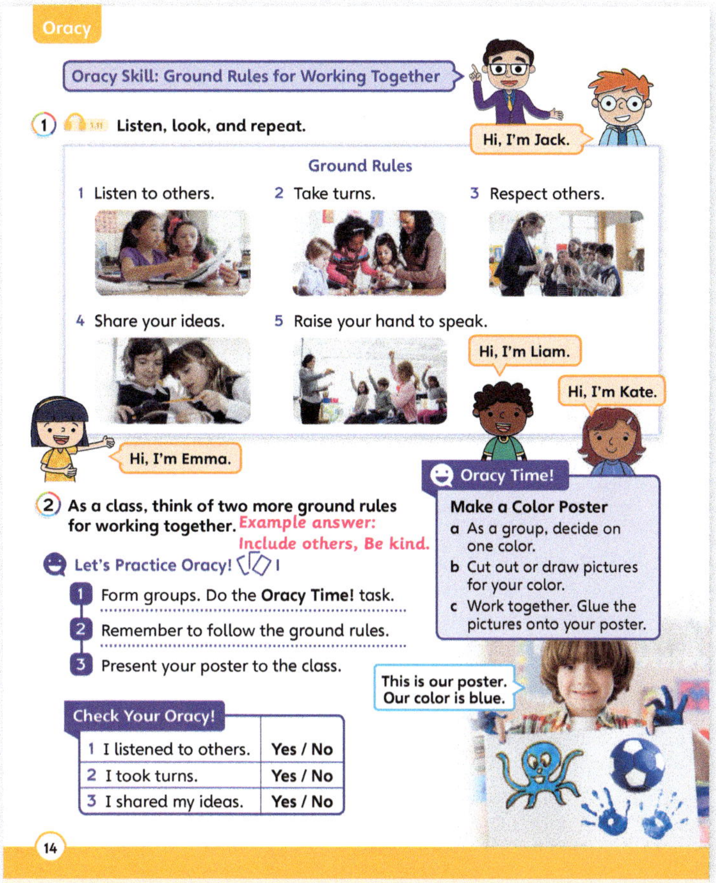
Oracy

Oracy Skill: Ground Rules for Working Together

1 Listen, look, and repeat.

Ground Rules

1 Listen to others.
2 Take turns.
3 Respect others.
4 Share your ideas.
5 Raise your hand to speak.

2 As a class, think of two more ground rules for working together. Example answer: Include others, Be kind.

Let's Practice Oracy! 1

1 Form groups. Do the **Oracy Time!** task.
2 Remember to follow the ground rules.
3 Present your poster to the class.

Oracy Time!

Make a Color Poster

a As a group, decide on one color.
b Cut out or draw pictures for your color.
c Work together. Glue the pictures onto your poster.

Check Your Oracy!

1 I listened to others.	Yes / No
2 I took turns.	Yes / No
3 I shared my ideas.	Yes / No

14

Objective: **to learn ground rules for working together**

Cue Card: **I. *This is …***

Materials: Track 1.11, Cue Card 1, poster board, pictures of objects of a single color (for example, a green ball), scissors, glue

Oracy Skill

Explain to students that it is very important to have rules in the classroom so that the class works well as a group. Introduce the oracy characters. Point to each of them, and say their names. Tell students that these characters will help them learn to be good speakers and listeners.

1 1.11 Listen, look, and repeat.

Ask students to look carefully at the photos in Activity 1. Play Track 1.11. Then, say each rule aloud while using gestures to help students understand the concepts. Encourage students to repeat the rules after you.

2 As a class, think of two more ground rules for working together.

Remind students of the ideas about helpful attitudes they came up with. Some possible ground rules are *Help others*, *Be kind*, and *Say "thank you."* Since many students don't know how to read or write, it is crucial that you use gestures to remind students of the ground rules.

Present and Practice Hold up Cue Card 1. Read the expression aloud: *This is …* Explain that every time we present information to the class, we use this expression. Hold up the Cue Card again, and say the expression for students to repeat. Display the Cue Card on the board for students to refer to during the Let's Practice Oracy! activity.

Let's Practice Oracy! 1

- **1** Form groups of about three or four students. Point to the Oracy Time! box and the list of steps. Tell students that they will make a color poster. Explain each of the steps in the Oracy Time! box. Distribute materials to the groups, and ask them to cut out or draw pictures for their color poster.
- **2** Before groups start working, remind students of the ground rules. As they work, go around the classroom to ensure that they are putting the ground rules into practice.
- **3** Invite a group of students to present its poster to the class. Remind them to use the expression on the Cue Card: *This is …* Invite other groups to present their posters.
- Optional: Record or have students record themselves as they give their presentations to share their work.
- Have students complete Check Your Oracy!

Build Creativity!

Home-school | Portfolio: Oracy

Group Sorting

Objective: **Try, Try, and Try Again**

Describe some situations and encourage students to guess good ground rules, for example: *Many kids are talking.* Then, tell students you are going to play a game that tests their use of the ground rules. Have the class stand in the middle of the room. Review some of the unit language for describing people. Say: *Let's organize ourselves into groups.* Encourage students to suggest possible groups, for example, groups based on hair color, hair length, age, or gender. As much as possible, avoid intervening, and encourage the class to sort themselves into groups. Remind students to follow their ground rules for working in groups.

AB page 8

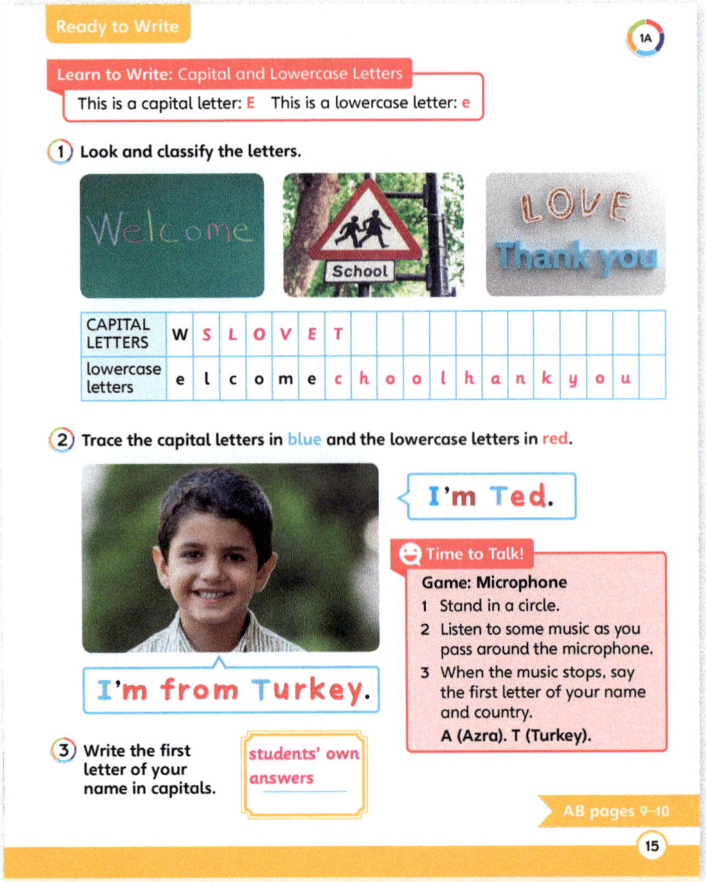

Ready to Write

1A

Learn to Write: Capital and Lowercase Letters

This is a capital letter: E This is a lowercase letter: e

(1) Look and classify the letters.

CAPITAL LETTERS	W	S	L	O	V	E	T												
lowercase letters	e	l	c	o	m	e	c	h	o	o	l	h	a	n	k	y	o	u	

(2) Trace the capital letters in blue and the lowercase letters in red.

Time to Talk!

Game: Microphone

1 Stand in a circle.
2 Listen to some music as you pass around the microphone.
3 When the music stops, say the first letter of your name and country.

A (Azra). T (Turkey).

(3) Write the first letter of your name in capitals.

students' own answers

AB pages 9–10

15

Objective: to identify capital and lowercase letters

Materials: a microphone or an object that resembles a microphone, music

Learn to Write Box

Write random capital letters on the board. Say: *These are capital letters*. Write the corresponding lowercase letters. Say: *These are lowercase letters*. Say: *Look at the red letters in the box*. Write *E* on the board, and ask a student: *Is this a capital or a lowercase letter? (Capital.)* Do the same with e.

(1) Look and classify the letters.

On the board, draw part of the table in Activity 1 without the example. Point to the first picture, and say the word: *Welcome*. Pretend you are opening the classroom door to welcome a new student. Say: *Welcome*. Students repeat: *Welcome*. Point to the first letter in the picture, and ask: *Is this* W *capital or lowercase? (Capital.)* Write *W* next to *CAPITAL LETTERS* in the table. Continue with the rest of the letters *e* and *l* in *Welcome*. Then, have students tell you the other words they see in the pictures in Activity 1. Tell them to circle the capital letters in the pictures. Then, have them complete the table with the capital and lowercase letters. Monitor, and provide support.

(2) Trace the capital letters in blue and the lowercase letters in red.

Read the text in the speech bubbles. Point to the *I* in blue, and ask: *Is this a capital or a lowercase letter? (Capital.)* Do the same with the *m*. Then, ask students to trace the capital letters in blue and the lowercase letters in red.

(3) Write the first letter of your name in capitals.

Tell students to write the first letter of their name as a capital letter in the box. Say a student's name, and ask a volunteer to write the first letter of their name as a capital letter on the board. Alternatively, write a capital letter on the board, and ask students whose names start with that letter to raise their hands.

Time to Talk!

Ask students to tell you the name of their country. Say it in English, write the English name on the board, and have students spell it. Invite students to stand in a circle. Give the microphone (real or fake) to a student. Ask: *What's the first letter of your name? What's the first letter of your country's name?* Explain to students that you will play some music while they pass the microphone around. When you stop the music, the student holding the microphone has to say the first letter of their name and of their country's name.

Fun Corner!

Name Search

Divide the class into groups of three. Remind students that names start with capital letters. Ask everyone to go to page 8 and find two names of people *(Larissa, María)*. Then, tell groups that when you say *Go!*, they should look for names in their books on pages 9 and 10. When they find a name, they have to circle it. Although each student can search in their own book, the group should circle the names in only one book. When you say *Stop*, everyone should stop searching. Then, have each group exchange their marked book with another group to check their answers. Monitor as students work. Finally, check answers as a class.

AB pages 9–10

Objective: **identifying capital and lowercase letters, tracing**
Materials: storybooks in English; pieces of paper, each with a different simple word beginning with a capital letter (for example, *Hi, Hello, Bye, No, Yes*) and written in yellow or gray for tracing over (at least two words per student), blue and red colored pencils; Differentiated Instruction: paper

Sitting and Holding a Pencil

Show students how to sit when they write. Sit straight with both feet on the floor and arms relaxed on the desk. Ask a volunteer to copy your posture. Then, model how to hold a pencil correctly. Ask students to hold their pencils, copying your hand and body position. Walk around the classroom and monitor.

1 IDENTIFY

Form groups. Give each group a storybook. Ask students to work together to search for capital letters in their storybooks. Call on a student and say: *Point to a capital letter. What letter is it?* Encourage students to say the letters out loud. Do the same with lowercase letters.

2 WRITE

Hand out the paper with tracing words to the class. Ask students to trace the words by using blue for capital letters and red for lowercase letters. Remind students about how they should sit and hold their pencils when they write.

3 EDIT

Go around the classroom and monitor as students work. If a student has not written a letter correctly, provide guidance and have the student write it again on another piece of paper.

4 FOLLOW UP

Ask students to make a poster at home with six words from the nonfiction text *We Are All Different!* Ask them to write the capital letters in blue and the lowercase letters in red. Encourage students to share their posters with the class.

Fun Corner!

Write My Code

Have students write a secret code made up of six characters. The code should include two lowercase letters, two capital letters, and two digits. For example: *Ld23eP*. Form pairs. Student A dictates their code to Student B. Student B does the same. Then students show the results to each other to see if they wrote the code accurately.

Build Creativity!

Hand Warm-Up

Objective: **Flow**

Tell students they will have a PE lesson, but for their hands! This will help them to improve their writing skills. Follow and repeat these three exercises: 1. Have students press their hands and fingers together with palms flat and stretch their fingers out wide. 2. Ask students to put their hands on the table with palms down and pretend they are playing the piano. They should lift one finger at a time. 3. Have students bend their fingers on each hand then hook them together and pull in opposite directions.

Differentiated Instruction

Below-level ★	On-level ★★	Above-level ★★★
Encourage students to make a flashcard with one of the key words from unit 1. Ask them to draw a picture representing the word and to write the first letter of the word below the picture. For example, they draw an eye and write *E* or *e*.	Encourage students to make a flashcard with one of the key words from unit 1. Ask them to draw a picture representing the word and then, below the picture, write the first letter of the word as a capital letter and a lowercase letter. For example, they draw something long and write *L* and *l*.	Encourage students to make a flashcard with one of the key words from unit 1. Ask them to draw a picture representing the word and then write the word below the picture, in all capital letters and in all lowercase letters. For example, they draw someone tall and write *TALL* and *tall*.

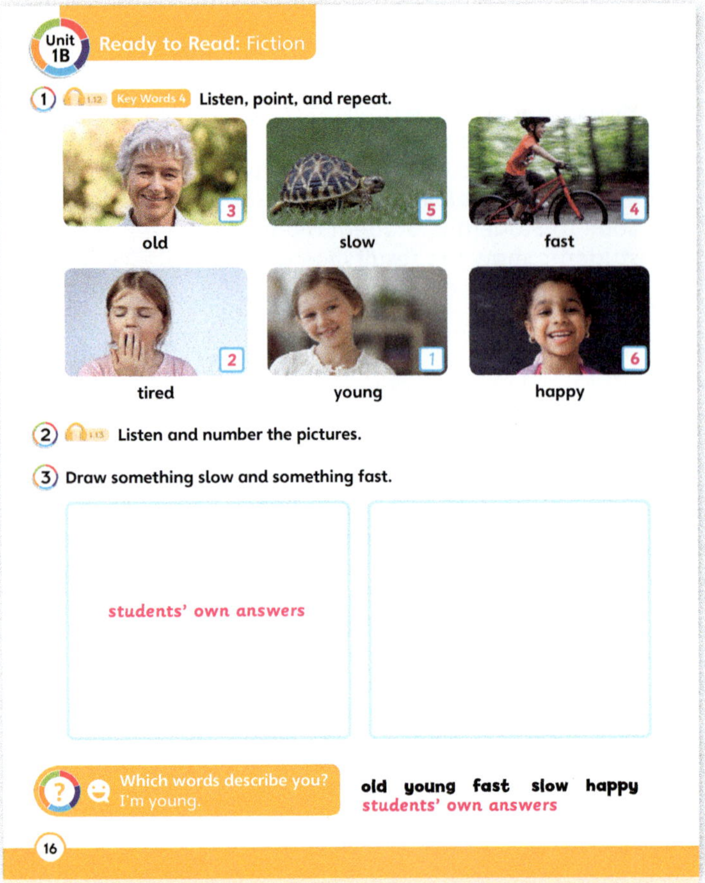
Unit 1B Ready to Read: Fiction

1 1.12 Key Words 4 Listen, point, and repeat.

old 3 | slow 5 | fast 4

tired 2 | young 1 | happy 6

2 1.13 Listen and number the pictures.

3 Draw something slow and something fast.

students' own answers

Which words describe you? I'm young.

old young fast slow happy

students' own answers

16

Objective: to introduce vocabulary from a fiction text

Key Words 4: ***old, slow, fast, tired, young, happy***

Materials: Audio CD 1.12, 1.13

1 1.12 Key Words 4 Listen, point, and repeat.

Point to the pictures in Activity 1, and say the words. Then, play Track 1.12, and ask students to point to the pictures and repeat the words.

Practice Time 1 Move in slow motion. Say: *Slow*. Move fast, and say: *Fast*. Yawn, and say: *Tired*. Smile, and say: *Happy*. Say each word again, and ask the class to pantomime it. Invite students to play a game. Say one of the words, and ask students to pantomime it until you clap. Repeat the process with the other words. Go through the words as many times as you consider necessary.

2 1.13 Listen and number the pictures.

Ask students to look at the pictures in Activity 1 again. Play Track 1.13, pausing after each word. Have students number the pictures.

Practice Time 2 Form two groups. Ask two or three volunteers who like drawing to come to the front. They will draw pictures representing the vocabulary words for the groups to guess: *old*, *slow*, *fast*, *tired*, *young*, or *happy*. For example, ask a student to draw a cake with only three candles. Allow only one group to guess the correct word. *(young)* Remind students that they should raise their hands to guess. Then, ask another student to draw a picture, and have the second group guess the word. You could, for example, ask students to draw a bed (*tired*), a smiley face (*happy*), a rabbit (*fast*), a snail (*slow*), and a face with wrinkles (*old*).

3 Draw something slow and something fast.

Have students complete Activity 3 in pairs. Then, ask pairs to show their drawings to the class and to say the words *slow* and *fast* as they show them.

Big Question Link

Read the question aloud. Point out the model answer, and read it aloud. Form pairs or small groups, and have students share their answers.

Fun Corner!

Classroom Objects

Challenge students to search the classroom to find objects that represent *old*, *slow*, *fast*, *tired*, *young*, and *happy*. Some will be easier to find than others. If necessary, encourage students to look through books for relevant pictures or let them use their classmates as examples.

AB page 11

Reading Strategy: Real or Fantasy?

Stories can be: real or fantasy.

1 Look and circle the real things in green and the fantasy things in blue.

a b c d e f g

2 Look and draw a real animal and a fantasy animal.

students' own answers

real

fantasy

Time to Talk!

What is your favorite story?

My favorite story is *Cinderella*.

Is it real or fantasy?

17

Objective: **to differentiate real from fantasy and prepare to read a fiction text**

Materials: well-known storybooks (optional); Build Creativity: white construction paper; Fun Corner: pictures of real and fantasy things, ball

1 Look and circle the real things in green and the fantasy things in blue.

Have students look at the two pictures of turtles in the Reading Strategy box. Point to each one in turn, and say: *Real, fantasy.* Ask students about the cartoons they like. Ask: *Is (...) real or fantasy? (Fantasy.)* Show objects in the classroom, and ask: *Is this real or fantasy? (Real.)*

Have students look at the pictures in Activity 1. Point to the picture of the dinosaur, and say: *The dinosaur is real. Is the dragon real or fantasy? (Fantasy.) Circle the dragon in blue.* Continue with the picture of the banana. Then, ask students to continue on their own. Check answers as a class.

2 Look and draw a real animal and a fantasy animal.

Point to the seahorse in Activity 2. Ask: *Is this animal real? (Yes.)* Do the same with the picture of the centaur. Ask students to draw a real animal and a fantasy animal. Have them share their drawings with a partner.

Time to Talk!

Have students name two or three well-known storybooks, or show several well-known storybooks to the class. Guide students to name the main characters. Tell students what your favorite storybook is: *My favorite story is (...).* Ask students about their favorite stories. Encourage them to start their sentences with *My favorite story is (...).* Ask whether the characters are real or fantasy.

Build Creativity!

Characters

Objective: **Flow**

Form groups of four students. Give each group a piece of construction paper. Ask students to invent and draw a character for a story. Encourage students to be creative. Ask them to give their characters names. Once they have finished, invite groups to introduce their characters to the class. Remind them to use *This is ...*

Fun Corner!

Go Fast!

Show pictures of real and fantasy things to the class one by one. Ask: *Is this real or fantasy?* Then, have students stand in a circle, and give one of the students a ball. The student passes the ball to another student, and, when they do, you show a picture. The student to whom the ball is passed must say whether the picture is real or fantasy. Continue, encouraging students to go faster and faster.

Objective: to learn how things can be different or similar
Materials: Audio CD 1.14, 1.15; Build Creativity: colored pencils, notecards

Pre-Reading

Ask students to look through the story and identify the main characters and their similarities and differences. Ask them to guess what the story will be about. Play Tracks 1.14 and 1.15 while they look at the pictures.

1.14 Page 18, section 1

Play Track 1.14 up to the end of the first paragraph. Pause and ask questions:

How old is Grandma Turtle? Is she old or very old?
Is your grandma 200 years old?

1.14 Page 18, section 2

Continue Track 1.14 up to the end of the second paragraph. Pause and ask questions:

Does Grandma Turtle have a small or big shell?
When you are old, you have wrinkles. Does Grandma Turtle have wrinkles?

Personalization

Ask: *Do you have wrinkles? Are you young or old?*

Think

Read the question in the Think box aloud. Ask volunteers to answer the question.

1.14 Page 19, section 1

Ask students to look at the first picture on page 19. Then, play Track 1.14 up to the end of the third paragraph. Pause and ask questions:

Is Grandma Turtle slow or fast? Why?

1.14 Page 19, section 2

Continue Track 1.14 up to the end of the fourth paragraph. Pause and ask questions:

Is Grandma Turtle alone?
Are the young turtles alone? Are they slow or fast?

1.14 Page 19, section 3

Play the rest of Track 1.14. Ask questions:

Is Grandma Turtle with the young turtles?
She is tired. Why?
Where is she?

Think

Read the question in the Think box aloud. Encourage students to provide examples.

1.14

Grandma Turtle

by Andrea González

Grandma Turtle is very **old**. She is very, very old. She is 200 years old!

Grandma Turtle has a big shell. She has many wrinkles.

Think How old is your grandma or grandpa?

18

1B

Grandma Turtle loves to surf. But she is old, so she is very **slow**.

Grandma Turtle surfs alone. Young turtles aren't slow, they are too **fast**!

At night, Grandma Turtle is **tired**, very tired. She rests alone on the beach.

Think When are you tired?

19

1.15 **Grandma Turtle**

One day, Grandma Turtle meets Young Turtle. He has a small shell. He is young, but he surfs slowly, too.

Grandma Turtle is surprised.

"You aren't old. You are young. Why do you surf slowly?" Grandma Turtle asks Young Turtle.

"I like it," says Young Turtle. "I am young, but I like to surf slowly."

Think

Is Young Turtle fast?

20

1B

The sky is yellow, orange, purple, and blue.

Grandma Turtle and Young Turtle surf together.

They are happy.

Think

Are Grandma Turtle and Young Turtle different? Are they friends?

21

1.15 Page 20, section 1

Play Track 1.15 up to the end of the first paragraph. Pause and ask questions:

Is Young Turtle's shell big or small?
Is he a slow or fast surfer?

1.15 Page 20, section 2

Continue Track 1.15 up to the end of the page. Pause and ask questions:

Is Young Turtle different from Grandma Turtle? How?
What makes them similar?

Think

Read the question in the Think box aloud, and ask a volunteer to answer it. Then, ask: *Are the other young turtles fast?*

1.15 Page 21

Play the rest of Track 1.15. Ask questions:

What color is the sky?
Is Grandma Turtle alone?
Who is happy?

Think

Read the questions in Think box aloud. Encourage students to share their answers.

Personalization

Ask: *Are you similar to your friends? How?*

Build Creativity!

Memory

Objective: Try, Try, and Try Again

Have students make cards for a game of Memory. Give each student a notecard, and have students form pairs. Assign each pair two words that are opposites to represent on their two notecards. For example, you might assign *tall* and *short*, and students can draw someone tall on one card and someone short on the other. Possible opposites or near opposites include *boy/girl*, *old/young*, *fast/slow*, *straight/curly*, *real/fantasy*, *big/small*, *capital/lowercase*. Ask each pair of students to present their notecards to the class. Encourage them to say a sentence with *This is …* and then repeat the word (for example, *This is a tall boy. Tall. This is a short boy. Short.*). After everyone has shared their drawings, collect the notecards. Tell students they will play a game of Memory. They will try to match cards with their opposites to make pairs. Shuffle the cards, and place them face down on your desk. Form four groups of students and play.

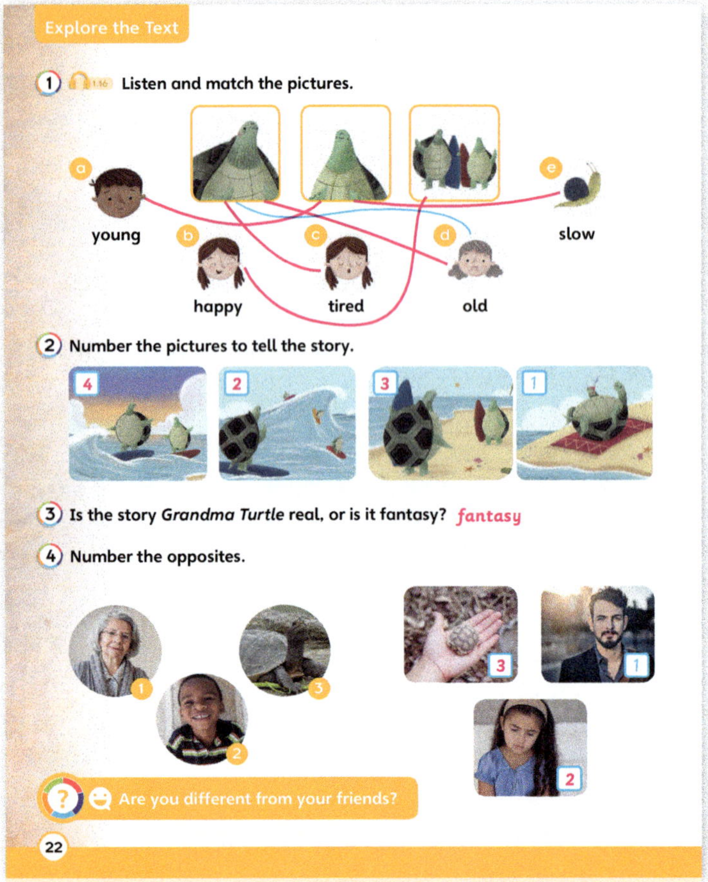
Explore the Text

1 1.16 Listen and match the pictures.

young happy tired old slow

2 Number the pictures to tell the story.

4 2 3 1

3 Is the story *Grandma Turtle* real, or is it fantasy? fantasy

4 Number the opposites.

1 2 3 3 1 2

Are you different from your friends?

22

Objective: to deepen understanding of a fiction text
Materials: Audio CD 1.16

1 1.16 Listen and match the pictures.

Point to each of the three drawings from the story. Help students identify who each character is. Then, point to the rest of the drawings and read the adjectives. Encourage students to repeat after you. Use the example to show how to do the exercise. Then, play Track 1.16, and have students do the exercise. Check answers as a class.

2 Number the pictures to tell the story.

Have students look at the four scenes in Activity 2. Point to the example, scene 1, and clarify the task. Guide students to number the scenes in order. Then, help them retell the story. (See Differentiated Instruction below.)

3 Is the story *Grandma Turtle* real, or is it fantasy?

Ask: *Are turtles real? (Yes.) Do real turtles talk? (No.) Does Grandma Turtle talk? (Yes.) Is she real or fantasy? (Fantasy.) Is the story real or fantasy? (Fantasy.)*

4 Number the opposites.

Say: *Grandma Turtle is old. You aren't old. You are …* Pause for students to provide the word *young*. Point to the picture of the woman in Activity 4. Ask: *Is she old or young? (Old.)* Then, point to the man and say: *He's young.* Guide students to number the other two opposites.

Big Question Link

Point to the Big Question Link and read the question aloud. Discuss it as a class.

AB pages 12–13

Differentiated Instruction

Below-level ★	On-level ★★	Above-level ★★★
Show the pictures from *Grandma Turtle* as you retell the story. Encourage students to repeat important words. For example, say *Grandma Turtle is old*. Then, repeat *Grandma Turtle is …* and have students complete the sentence. Allow time for students to say *old*. Continue: *She has a big shell. She has a … shell.* Retell the rest of the story in this way, using gestures to aid understanding.	Show the pictures from *Grandma Turtle* as you retell the story. Encourage students to provide some of the information. For example, say: *Grandma Turtle is …* Pause for students to say *old. She has a … shell. Grandma Turtle surfs, but she's very …* Continue in this manner, using gestures if necessary.	Show the pictures from *Grandma Turtle* one at a time and ask students to retell the story. Guide them by pointing to specific things, such as Grandma's shell. Provide sentence starters, and encourage students to continue.

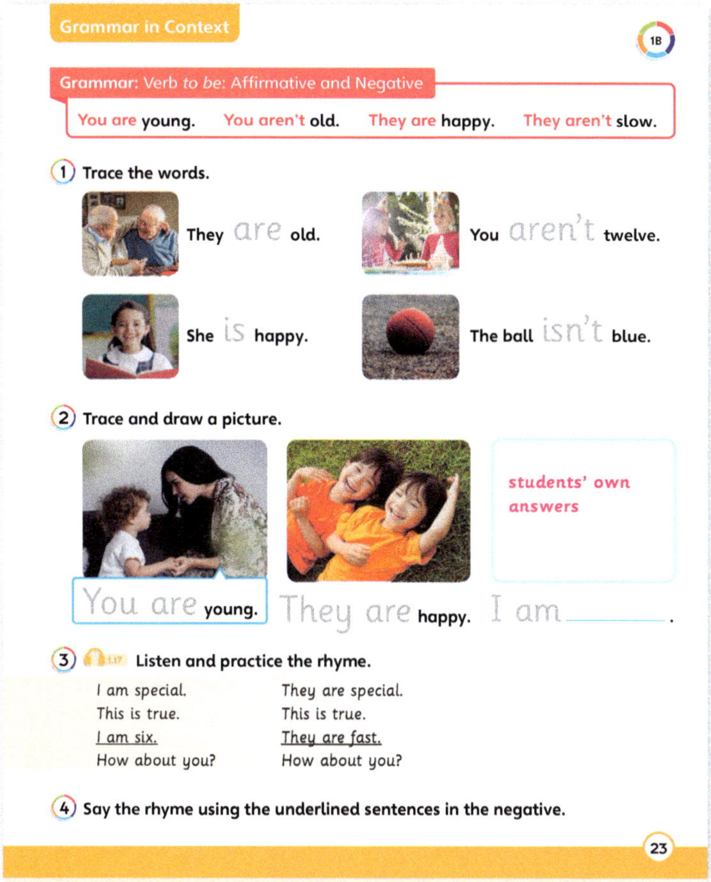

Grammar in Context 18

Grammar: Verb *to be*: Affirmative and Negative

You are young. You aren't old. They are happy. They aren't slow.

1 Trace the words.

They are old. You aren't twelve.

She is happy. The ball isn't blue.

2 Trace and draw a picture.

You are young. They are happy. I am ______.

students' own answers

3 1.17 Listen and practice the rhyme.

I am special.
This is true.
I am six.
How about you?

They are special.
This is true.
They are fast.
How about you?

4 Say the rhyme using the underlined sentences in the negative.

23

Objective: to use the verb *to be* in the affirmative and negative

Materials: Audio CD 1.17, four trays and sand or salt; Fun Corner: Flashcards 1.1–1.12

Grammar Box

Invite two girls to the front. Point to them, and say: *They are students. They aren't teachers. They are young. They aren't old. They are girls. They aren't boys.* As you say the sentences, use gestures to guide understanding. Say: *They are …, They aren't …* Invite students to repeat after you. Follow the same procedure for *You are* and *You aren't*. Write *are* and *are not* on the board. Then, show how *are not* can be shortened to *aren't*.

1 Trace the words.

Point to the first picture in Activity 1. Ask: *Are they young? (No. They aren't young.)* Say: *They are old.* Ask students to repeat after you. Have students trace the word. Repeat with the rest of the sentences.

2 Trace and draw a picture.

Point to the first picture. Say: *Is the boy old? (No.) He is young.* His mother says, "You are young." Continue with the second picture and ask students to trace the words. Then, have students draw a picture of themselves, trace the words, and complete the sentence.

Practice Time 1 Write the following on the board:

I am … I'm not … You are … You aren't … She is … She isn't … They are … They aren't …

Form four groups. Give each group a tray, and pour sand or salt into it. Say some of the words that are on the board, and have students take turns writing them in the sand or salt with their fingers. Teach students how to erase the words by gently shaking the tray. Monitor, and check answers as a class.

3 1.17 Listen and practice the rhyme.

Play Track 1.17 once. Then, say the rhyme slowly and clearly, pausing and gesturing to help students understand meaning. For example, hug yourself when you say *I'm special*, nod when you say *This is true*, and point at students when you say *How about you?* Play Track 1.17 again, and ask students to say the rhyme with you. Divide the class into two groups, and have each say a different half of the rhyme.

4 Say the rhyme using the underlined sentences in the negative.

Say the rhyme, but stop after saying *I am six*. Say: *I am six. Me? Noooo. I … six.* Encourage students to provide the negative. Continue with the rhyme, and elicit the second negative. Then, ask students to say the rhyme again with you, this time using the two new negative sentences.

Fun Corner!

Musical Statues

Use the flashcards to review some of the key words from the unit. Then, play Musical Statues. Play music, and have students dance, walk, or hop around the classroom. When you pause the music, students must mime one of the key words. Choose a student, and work with the class to guess which word the student is miming. Alternatively, challenge students to all mime the same word when you pause the music: *Everyone mime (curly).*

Build Creativity!

This Is Me

Objective: A Different Point of View

Have students form pairs. Ask each student to put three of their favorite personal belongings in front of them. Have each student present their objects to their partner. Remind them to use *This is … .*

AB pages 14–15

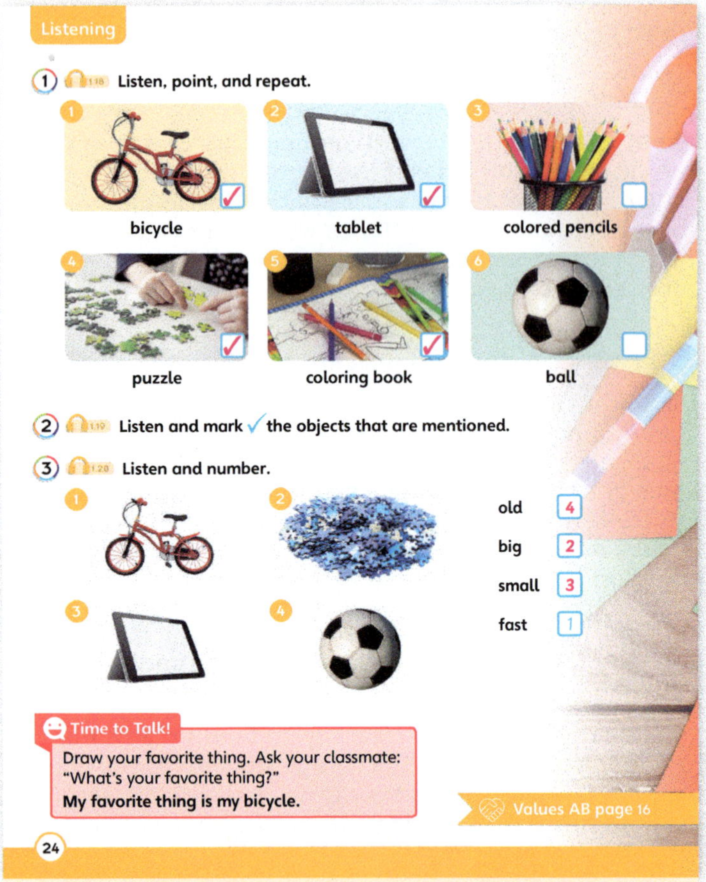
Listening

1) 1.18 Listen, point, and repeat.

1 bicycle ✓ 2 tablet ✓ 3 colored pencils
4 puzzle ✓ 5 coloring book ✓ 6 ball

2) 1.19 Listen and mark ✓ the objects that are mentioned.

3) 1.20 Listen and number.

old	4
big	2
small	3
fast	1

Time to Talk!
Draw your favorite thing. Ask your classmate: "What's your favorite thing?"
My favorite thing is my bicycle.

Values AB page 16

24

Objectives: to talk about your favorite things; to understand the value of respecting differences
Materials: Audio CD 1.18, 1.19, 1.20, paper

1) 1.18 Listen, point, and repeat.

Play Track 1.18, and ask students to point to the corresponding pictures and repeat the words. Say the words again for students to repeat.

2) 1.19 Listen and mark ✓ the objects that are mentioned.

Play Track 1.19 and have students mark the objects that are mentioned. Then, check answers as a class.

3) 1.20 Listen and number.

Point to the bicycle, and ask: *Is this bicycle old? (No.) Is it red? (Yes.)* Ask one student: *Do you have a bicycle? Is it old? Is it fast?* Read the adjectives on the right. Play Track 1.20, and pause after the first sentence. Point to the example answer. Continue with Track 1.20, and ask students to write the correct numbers. Check answers as a class.

Time to Talk!

Have each student draw their favorite thing. Ask one student: *What's your favorite thing? What color is it? Is it (...)?* Form pairs, and have students talk about their drawings. Display the drawings.

ACTIVITY BOOK PAGE 16

Values: Respecting Differences

1) Mark the children who are different ✓ with your teacher's help.

a b ✓ c ✓ d ✓

2) Match.

a He's a boy. He has short brown hair.
b She's a girl. She has straight blond hair.
c He's a boy. He has short blond hair.
d She's a girl. She has curly brown hair.

3) Draw yourself and a friend.

Are you similar? Are you different?

Students' own answers

16

SB page 24

1) Mark the children who are different ✓ with your teacher's help.

Point to the first picture in Activity 1. Ask: *Are the children similar or different? (Similar.)* Ask students to complete the activity.

2) Match.

Ask a volunteer to read the model sentences aloud. Then, read the descriptions aloud, and have students match them to the pictures. Monitor, and check answers.

3) Draw yourself and a friend.

Ask students to draw themselves and a friend. Students exchange drawings and check their classmates' work.

AB page 16

Objective: **to consolidate, extend, and personalize learning on the unit topic**

Materials: students' photos, cutouts from magazines, drawings of their favorite things, large sheets of butcher paper (or, if not available, poster board), pencils, glue

- Read the Big Challenge question and statement aloud. Point to the photos. Tell students that they are going to make a collage about themselves.
- **1** Read and explain the instructions. Elicit more ideas for things to include in the collage. Have students prepare the necessary materials for their collages at home.
- **2** Hand out large sheets of butcher paper. Demonstrate how to trace around a volunteer's body. Then, form pairs, and have them trace around each other. (Alternative: Students can use poster board and create a personalized collage by drawing a self-portrait in the middle and gluing the materials around it.)
- **3** Have students take out the materials they prepared at home. Ask them to make a collage on their traced body shape (or around their self-portrait). Provide assistance as needed.

Oracy Extension Activity

Draw students' attention to Emma, the oracy character, and read the oracy reminder aloud. Then, display Cue Card 1. Elicit the ground rules for when a classmate is talking in front of the class. After they have presented, have students complete Check Your Oracy! on page 17 of the Activity Book.

- **4** Elicit how to talk about ourselves and, in particular, what sorts of information might be included. Ask volunteers to present their collages to the class. Optional: Record or have students record one another's presentations to share their work.

Home-school | Portfolio: Big Challenge

Big Question Circle

Read the Big Question aloud. Have the class revisit the Big Question Links on pages 8, 16, and 22. Discuss what they have learned about themselves. Help with emergent language. You may want to encourage students to include ideas from their Big Challenge presentations.

- Use the following questions to help review the Big Question:

What's your name?
How old are you?
Where are you from?
Are you tall or short?
What color hair do you have?
What's your favorite color?
Are you similar to or different from your friends?

- Finally, have students turn to page 17 of their Activity Books to complete the Big Challenge self-assessment.

AB pages 17–19

Differentiated Instruction

Below-level ★	On-level ★★	Above-level ★★★
Have pairs point and say the first letter of the words for two or three of the things on their collages. For example, students can write the first letter of their name and of their favorite color.	Have students write the first letter of the words for things on their collages. For example, students can write the first letter of their name, of their favorite color, etc.	Have students write complete words for some of the things on their collages, such as the words for their favorite color, their country, their type of hair, and their eye color.

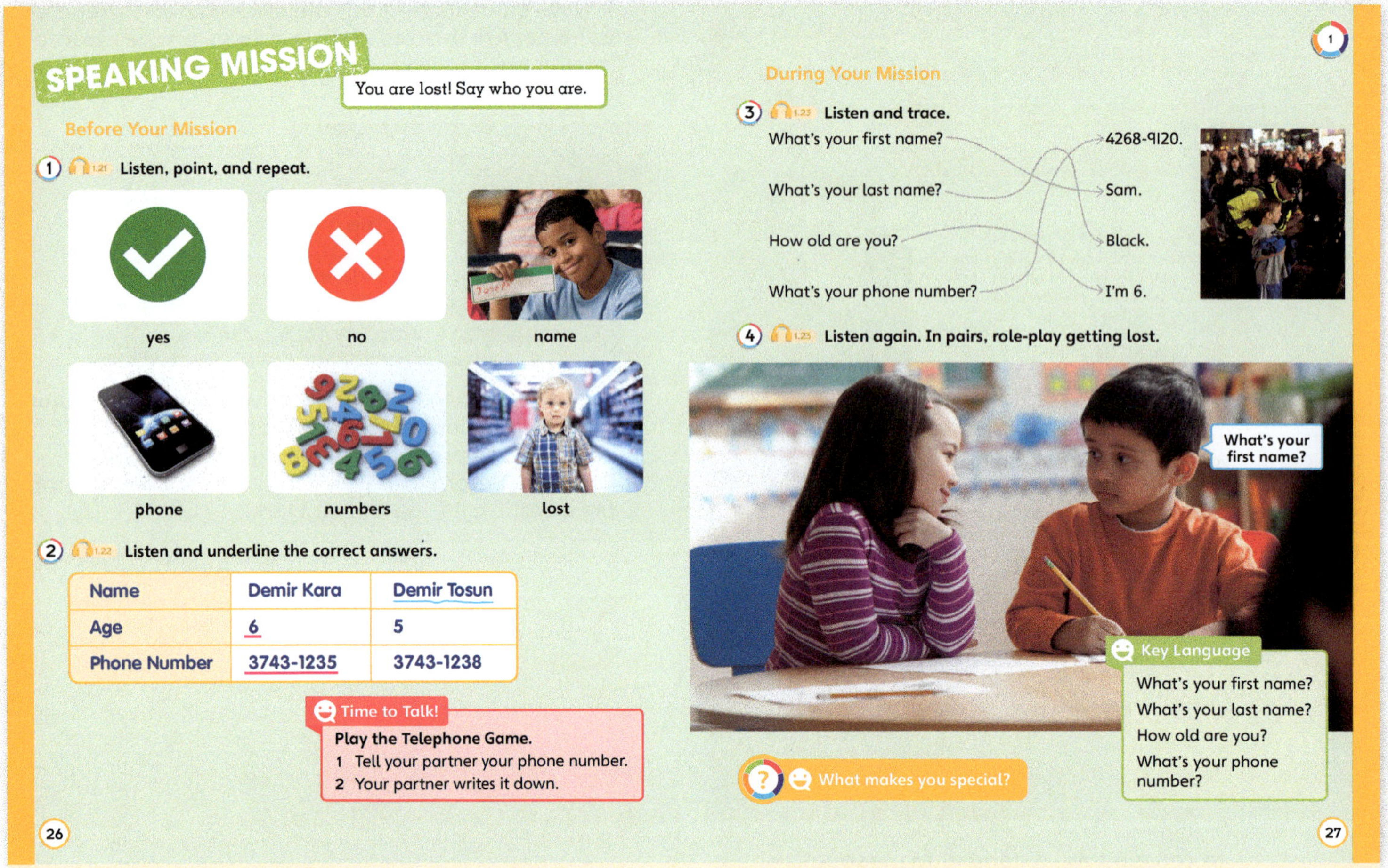

SPEAKING MISSION

You are lost! Say who you are.

Before Your Mission

1 1.21 Listen, point, and repeat.

yes | no | name | phone | numbers | lost

2 1.22 Listen and underline the correct answers.

Name	Demir Kara	Demir Tosun
Age	6	5
Phone Number	3743-1235	3743-1238

Time to Talk!

Play the Telephone Game.

1 Tell your partner your phone number.

2 Your partner writes it down.

26

During Your Mission

3 1.23 Listen and trace.

What's your first name? — 4268-9120.

What's your last name? — Sam.

How old are you? — Black.

What's your phone number? — I'm 6.

4 1.23 Listen again. In pairs, role-play getting lost.

What's your first name?

Key Language

What's your first name?
What's your last name?
How old are you?
What's your phone number?

What makes you special?

27

Objective: to say who you are if you are lost

Speaking Mission Words: *yes, no, name, phone, numbers, lost*

Materials: Audio CD 1.21, 1.22, 1.23

1 1.21 Listen, point, and repeat.

Play Track 1.21, and tell students to point to the pictures. Play the track again, and have students repeat the words.

2 1.22 Listen and underline the correct answers.

Write your complete name on the board. Point to your first name and say: *This is my first name*. Spell it. Then, do the same with you last name. Ask a volunteer to come to the front and to write, say, and spell their first and last names. Write a phone number on the board. Say: *This is my phone number*. Say it aloud. Ask a volunteer to do the same. Then, play Track 1.22, and have students complete the activity. Check answers as a class.

Time to Talk!

Form pairs. Instruct them to say their phone numbers for their partners to write down in their notebooks. Then, ask them to check the numbers.

3 1.23 Listen and trace.

Make two columns of words on the board. In the left column, write *first name, last name, phone number,* and *age*, and in the right column in random order, write *Tony, Tosun, 3743-2345*, and *6*. Read each category, and match the words. Then, go to Activity 3, and read the first question on the left aloud. Ask students to repeat it after you. Ask some students the question. Then, have students trace the line from the question to its answer. Ask a volunteer to read the answer out loud.

4 1.23 Listen again. In pairs, role-play getting lost.

Ask a volunteer to come to the front and role-play getting lost with you. Then, form pairs, and have them role-play. Provide any necessary support. Optional: Record or have students record one another's role plays to share their work.

Home-school | Portfolio: Speaking Mission

Big Question Link

Point to the Big Question Link, and read the question. Discuss with the class what makes a person special. Focus on the idea that we are all different and unique.

AB pages 20–21

2 What is school?

Literacy

Read: a nonfiction text about a boy's school; a fiction text about a boy who can't find his school objects

Reading Strategies: classifying; understanding a character's feelings

Ready to Write

Learn to Write: alphabetical order

Getting Ready to Write: write your name and put it in alphabetical order on a list

Oracy

Skill: Agreeing and Disagreeing

Cue Cards 2–3: 2. *Yes.* 3. *No.*

Speaking Mission: borrow something at school

Language

Key Words 1: *desk, teacher, classroom, gym, bathroom, playground*

Key Words 2: *library, schoolbag, pencil case, notebook, colored pencil, eraser*

Key Words 3: *classmates, apple*

Key Words 4: *story, sad, mad, hungry, lunchbox, surprised*

Speaking Mission Words: *scissors, crayon, pencil sharpener, marker, ruler, glue*

Grammar in Context

***A / an*:** *a pencil, an eraser*

Possessive Adjectives: *This is your desk. It is his first day at school. I can't find my book. Gemma shares her pencils with Max.*

Phonics

Initial Sounds: *c, p, t, n, b, h*

Listening

Song: "This Is My School"

Values

Taking Care of Your School Objects

The Big Challenge

How can we make a classroom map?
Present a classroom map to the class

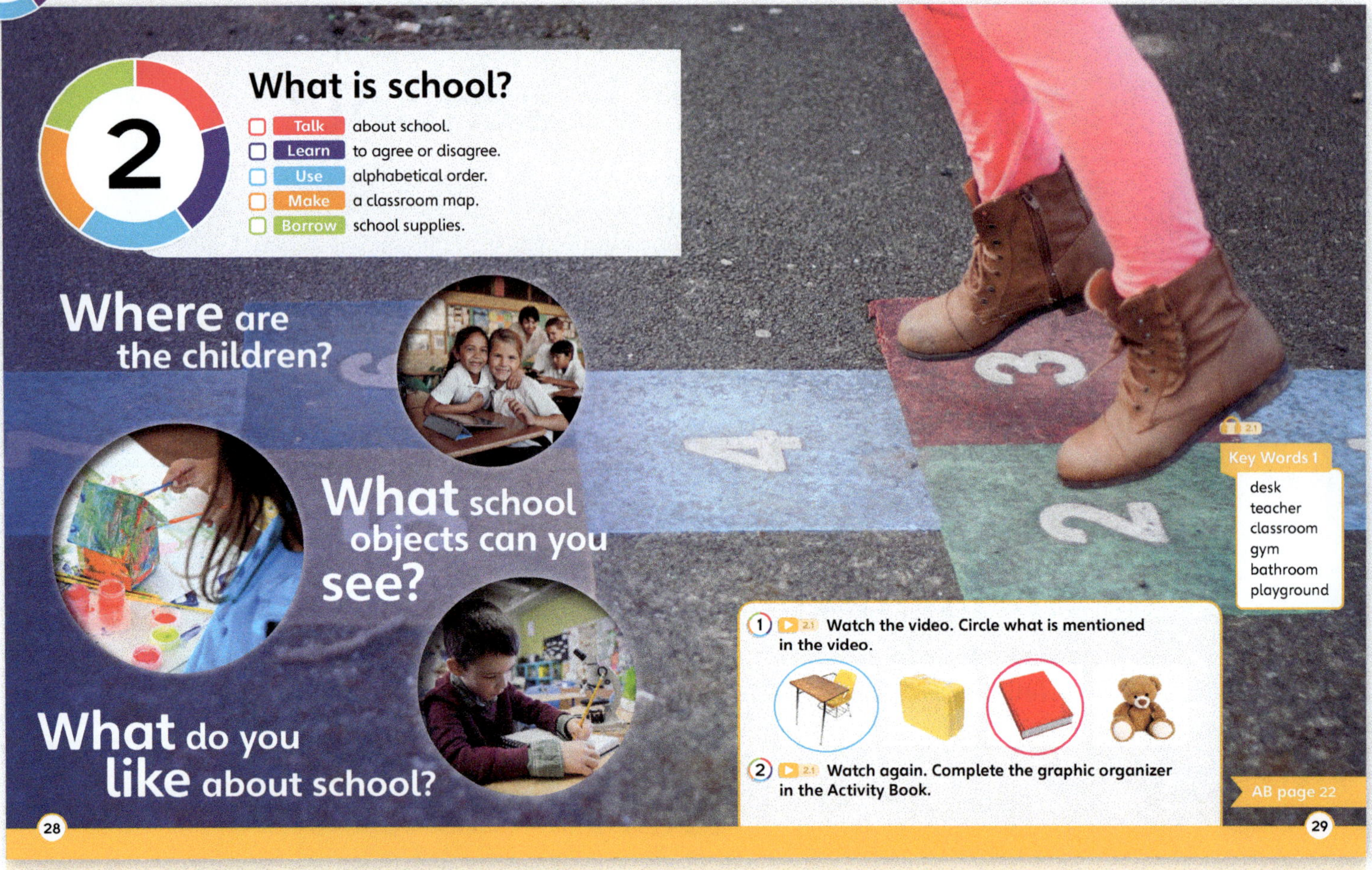

Objective: **to introduce the topic of what school is**

Key Words I: ***desk, teacher, classroom, gym, bathroom, playground***

Materials: Video 2.1, Audio CD 2.1, Flashcards 2.1–2.6; Fun Corner: paper, crayons, envelopes

WHAT IS SCHOOL?

- Read the Big Question aloud, and discuss the topic with students.
- Have students look at the pictures. Read the first question aloud: *Where are the children? (At school, in a classroom.)* Read the next question aloud: *What school objects can you see? (Paints, a tablet, a pencil, a notebook.)* Ask: *What school objects can you see in our classroom now?* Read the last question aloud: *What do you like about school? (Learning, making friends, etc.)*
- 2.1 Key Words 1 Use the flashcards and audio to present Key Words 1. Ensure that students understand the difference between the gym and the playground since some activities can be done in both places. Hold up the flashcards again as you play Track 2.1. Have students repeat the words.

1 2.1 Watch the video. Circle what is mentioned in the video.

Watch the video, pausing after "Let's find out!" Ask: *What is today's Big Question? (What is school?)* Continue the video. Pause after "Students, students, and more students!" Ask: *What can you see at school? (Books, pencils, desks, teachers, students.)* Encourage students to mention more things they see at their school. Play the rest of the video. Display the *classroom*, *gym*, *bathroom*, and *playground* Flashcards. Ask volunteers to put the flashcards in the order in which they appear in the video. Watch the video again, and ask students to circle what is mentioned.

2 2.1 Watch again. Complete the graphic organizer in the Activity Book.

Play the video again, and have students complete Activity 1 on AB page 22. Check answers as a class.

Fun Corner!

Puzzles

Give students paper and crayons. Ask them to draw and color something related to school, such as a school object or place. Then, ask them to cut their drawings into big pieces to create a puzzle. Have students put the pieces in a pile and swap piles with another student. Students complete their partner's puzzle. After the activity, have students put their puzzle pieces in an envelope for future use.

AB page 22

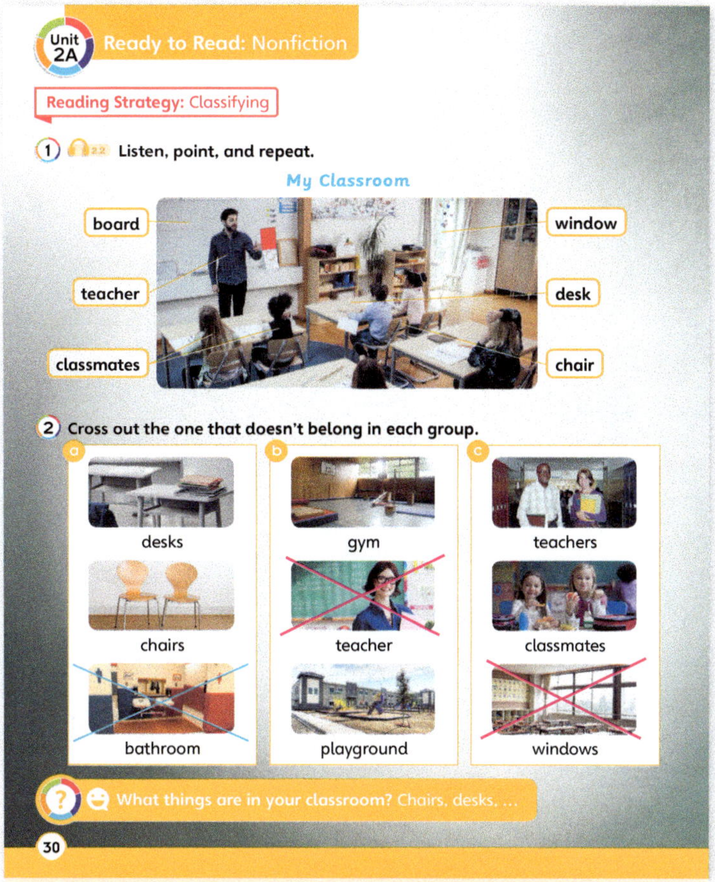

Objective: **to understand the meaning of words in context and prepare to read a nonfiction text**

Key Words I: ***desk, teacher, classroom, gym, bathroom, playground***

Materials: Audio CD 2.2, tape, Flashcards 2.1–2.6; Build Creativity: three pieces of poster board, glue, pictures or drawings of fruits, people, places, toys, drinks, animals, colors, and letters

2.1 Key Words 1 Use the flashcards and audio to review Key Words I.

1 2.2 Listen, point, and repeat.

Give students time to look at the photo in Activity I. Play Track 2.2, and ask students to listen to, point to, and repeat each word. Display all the flashcards. Write *People* on the board. Hold up the *teacher* and *classmates* Flashcards. Say: *Teachers and classmates are people*. Place those flashcards under *People*. Write *Places* on the board. Encourage students to identify the flashcards with places: *gym, bathroom, playground*. Do the same with *Things: board, window, desk, chair.*

2 Cross out the one that doesn't belong in each group.

Have students look at the pictures in Activity 2. Use the example to show how the activity works. Ask students to do the activity, and check answers as a class.

Big Question Link

Ask: *What things are in your classroom?* Invite volunteers to go to the front of the room and draw things that are in the classroom, even if they don't yet know the words in English.

Build Creativity!

Where Do They Belong?

Objective: A Different Point of View

Form three groups, and give each group a piece of poster board and glue. Tell students that they will classify pictures into categories. Mix up the pictures that you have brought in, and hand out an equal number to each group. Groups then organize them into categories and glue them on the poster board. Go around the classroom, and monitor as students work. Display the completed posters around the classroom.

2.3 **Key Words 2** Use the flashcards and audio to pre-teach Key Words 2. Play Track 2.3, and have students repeat each word. Lead students in identifying the highlighted words in the text on pages 31 and 32 with the help of the flashcards.

Pre-Reading

Have students look at the pictures on pages 31 and 32. Ask what they think the text will be about. Read the title, and remind students of the meaning of *welcome*, using gestures if needed. Hold up the *library* Flashcard, and ask a volunteer to point to the picture of the library in the text. Do the same with the rest of the flashcards. Play Tracks 2.4 and 2.5 while students look at the pictures.

2.4 Page 31, section 1

Play Track 2.4 up to the end of the first paragraph. Pause, point to the pictures, and ask questions:

What is the boy's name?
Does Tommy like school?
Is this a gym or a playground?
What can you see in the library?

2.4 Page 31, section 2

Play the rest of Track 2.4. Point to the pictures and ask questions:

What is this place?
Point to the gym. Ask: *What can you see?*
What is the teacher's name?

Personalization

Ask: *Is this school similar to or different from our school? Is this school big? Is our school big? Does this school have a playground? Does our school have a playground?*

Fun Corner!

Can You Remember?

Ask students to look at page 31 carefully for two minutes. Then, have them close their books. Form groups of four or five students, and give each group a sheet of paper. Tell them that when you say *Go!* they should draw the school objects they remember from page 31. Give groups five minutes, and then say *Stop!* Ask groups to trade papers and count how many things the other group correctly included. Have them write the total using digits. Examine the results as a class.

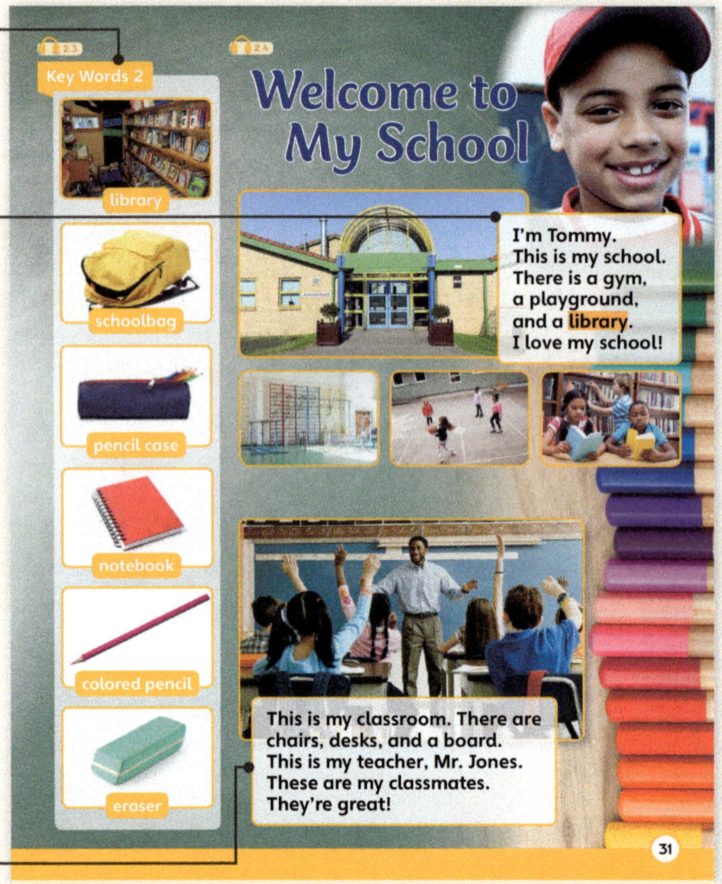

Objective: to understand the meaning of words in context and learn more about school

Key Words 2: ***library, schoolbag, pencil case, notebook, colored pencil, eraser***

Materials: Audio CD 2.3, 2.4, 2.5, Flashcards 2.7–2.12; Fun Corner: a variety of school supplies in different colors, paper, bag

2.5 Page 32, section 1

Play Track 2.5 up to the end of the first paragraph. Pause and ask questions:

What is in Tommy's schoolbag?
What color is his schoolbag?
Is the apple green?

Personalization

Ask: *What color is your schoolbag? Is there an apple in your schoolbag? Is there a book in your schoolbag?*

2.5 Page 32, section 2

Play the rest of Track 2.5. Point to the picture and ask questions:

What can you see in Tommy's pencil case?
What colors are the pencils?
How many colored pencils are there?

Personalization

Ask: *What color is your pencil case? What is in your pencil case?*

Think

Read the questions in the Think box aloud, and have volunteers answer them. Discuss what else is in your school.

Fun Corner!

Guessing Game

Display the school supplies on your desk. Hold up each object, say what it is out loud: *A red pencil.* Then, go over each object with the class: *What is this? (A green ruler.)* When you are finished, put all the objects in a bag. Reach into the bag, and grab one object. Students have to guess what you are holding by asking questions: *Is it a green ruler?* Play several times.

AB page 23

Differentiated Instruction

Below-level ★	On-level ★★	Above-level ★★★
Say one of the key words, and ask a student: *What's the first letter of (...)?* Continue with the other words.	Say one of the key words, and ask a student: *What's the first letter of (...)?* Have the student go to the board and write the letter as both a capital and lowercase letter. Continue with the other words.	Say one of the key words, and ask a student: *Can you spell (...)?* Have that student go to the board and write the word. Then, ask another student to spell the word again. Continue with the other words.

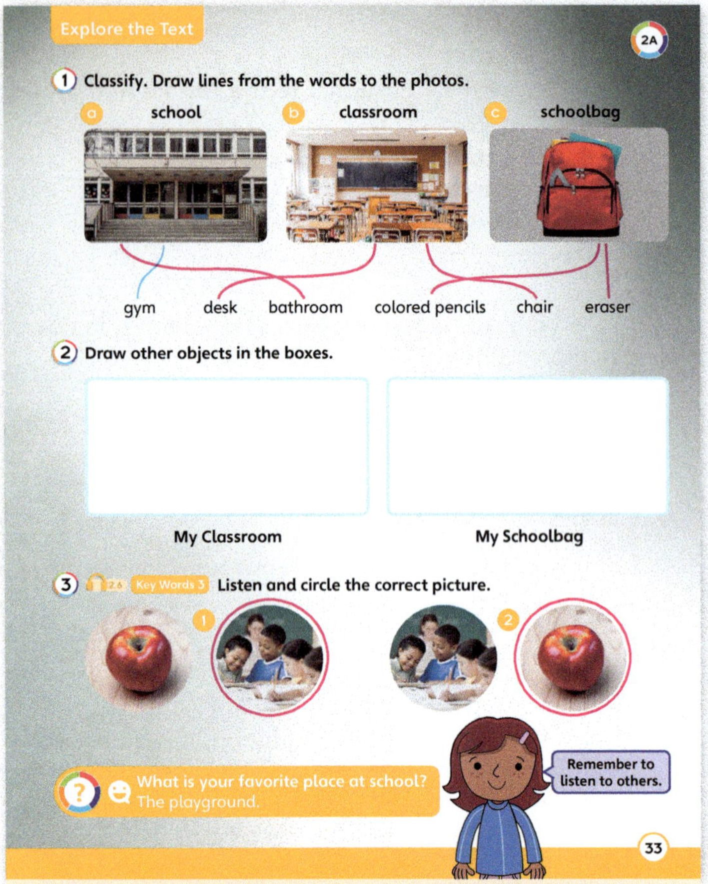

Objective: to check reading comprehension and understand words in context

Key Words 3: ***apple, classroom***

Materials: Audio CD 2.4, 2.5, 2.6; Fun Corner: paper

1 Classify. Draw lines from the words to the photos.

Point to the picture of the school. Ask: *What is this? (A school.)* Continue with the rest of the pictures. Then, point to the word *gym*. Ask: *Where is a gym? In a school, in a classroom, or in a schoolbag?* Point to the line in the example. Continue in the same way with the rest of the words, having students draw the lines.

2 Draw other objects in the boxes.

Ask: *What can you see in your classroom?* Encourage students to draw two objects in the first box. Tell them they should not use the objects from Activity 1. Do the same with the second box.

3 2.6 Key Words 3 Listen and circle the correct picture.

Ask students to tell you what they see in the two pictures in Activity 3. Tell them they should circle the correct options as they listen to Track 2.6. Check students' answers as a class.

Big Question Link

Direct students' attention to Kate, the oracy character. Read the oracy reminder in the speech bubble aloud. Then, read the question and answer aloud. Form pairs or small groups, and have students share their ideas.

Fun Corner!

Bingo

Form pairs, and give each pair one sheet of paper. Ask pairs to draw a six-square grid. Demonstrate by drawing a grid on the board. Ask pairs to draw a school object or a school place inside each square. Tell students they will play *Bingo*. You say one word, and if they have drawn what you mention, they circle the corresponding drawing on their grid. The pair that completes its grid first shouts *Bingo!* and wins.

AB pages 24–25

Differentiated Instruction

Below-level ★	On-level ★★	Above-level ★★★
Ask students to close their books and listen carefully to Track 2.4. Then, read the text yourself, stopping to provide a sentence for students to complete: *This is my school. There is a* [pause] … *(gym)*. Do the same with Track 2.5.	Ask students to close their books and listen carefully to Track 2.4. Then, read the text yourself, stopping to provide a sentence for students to complete: *This is my school. There is a* [pause] … *(gym)*. Ask volunteers to spell the missing word or to say its first letter. Do the same with Track 2.5.	Ask students to close their books and listen carefully to Track 2.4. Then, read the text yourself, stopping to provide a sentence for students to complete: *This is my school. There is a* [pause] … *(gym)*. Ask volunteers to write the missing word on the board. Do the same with Track 2.5.

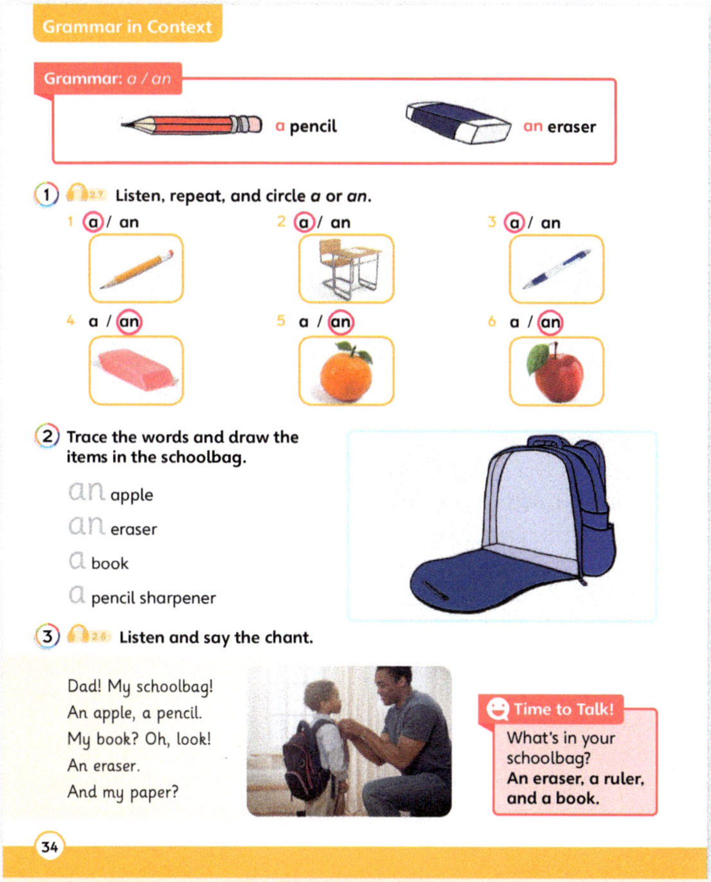

Grammar in Context

Grammar: a / an

a pencil   an eraser

1 2.7 Listen, repeat, and circle *a* or *an*.

1 a / an 2 a / an 3 a / an

4 a / an 5 a / an 6 a / an

2 Trace the words and draw the items in the schoolbag.

an apple

an eraser

a book

a pencil sharpener

3 2.8 Listen and say the chant.

Dad! My schoolbag!
An apple, a pencil.
My book? Oh, look!
An eraser.
And my paper?

Time to Talk!

What's in your schoolbag?
An eraser, a ruler, and a book.

34

Objective: to identify when to use *a* or *an*

Materials: Audio CD 2.7, 2.8, a soft ball

Grammar Box

Point to the pencil in the Grammar box. Hold up a pencil. Say: *This is a pencil, one pencil, a pencil.* Then, point to the eraser in the Grammar box and hold up an eraser. Say: *This is an eraser, one eraser, an eraser.* Emphasize the words *a* and *an*. Draw two columns on the board, and label them *a* and *an*. Write *pencil* in the *a* column and *eraser* in the *an* column. Draw each object next to its corresponding word. Draw an apple under the eraser. Say: *Apple, an apple.* Write the word *apple* next to the drawing of the apple. Follow the same process with the word *desk*. Help students deduce the use of *an* with vowel sounds by drawing a circle around the first vowel in *eraser* and *apple*.

1 2.7 Listen, repeat, and circle *a* or *an*.

Play Track 2.7 and have students choose the correct options. Check answers as a class.

Practice Time 1 Form two groups. Ask the groups to line up facing each other. A student from one group throws a soft ball to a student in the other group and names an object: *apple*. The student who catches the ball must repeat the word using *a* or *an*: *an apple*. Continue in this manner, encouraging students not to repeat words.

2 Trace the words and draw the items in the schoolbag.

Read the words in Activity 2, and ask students to repeat them. Teach the word *pencil sharpener.* Students trace the words and draw the items in the schoolbag.

3 2.8 Listen and say the chant.

Draw students' attention to the photo of the boy and his dad. Discuss with students who helps them get ready for school. Play Track 2.8. Encourage students to chant with you.

Practice Time 2 Take a ruler, a pen, and a book. Say the chant from Activity 3, but modify it slightly. Show the school objects you have chosen as you say the new version: *Mom! My schoolbag! A ruler, a pen. My book? Oh, look!* Encourage groups to invent their own versions of the chant and to share them with the class.

Time to Talk!

Read the question aloud. Point out the model answer, and read it aloud. Ask volunteers to show what they have in their schoolbags. Monitor the use of the indefinite articles *a* and *an*.

Build Creativity!

Attention, Please

Objective: A Different Point of View

Ask: *What do you do if you want to answer a question?* Elicit the idea of raising your hand. Ask: *Why don't you call out the answers?* Elicit the idea of not being disruptive and giving equal opportunity to everyone. Ask: *What can you do instead of raising your hand?* Encourage students to brainstorm as many ideas as possible. (*raise a finger, stand on one leg,* etc.) Finally, ask: *Imagine if your teacher was blind—what can you do to get his or her attention?* Have students brainstorm ideas.

AB pages 26–27

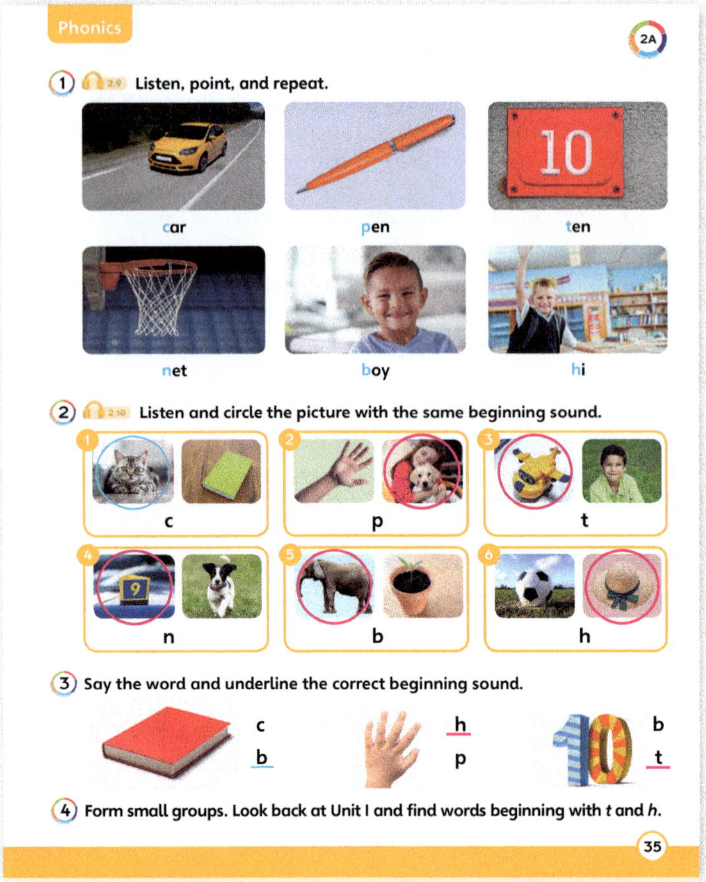
Phonics 2A

1) 2.9 Listen, point, and repeat.

car pen ten
net boy hi

2) 2.10 Listen and circle the picture with the same beginning sound.

1 c 2 p 3 t
4 n 5 b 6 h

3) Say the word and underline the correct beginning sound.

c b | h p | b t

4) Form small groups. Look back at Unit 1 and find words beginning with *t* and *h*.

35

Objective: **to identify initial sounds *c, p, t, n, b, h***
Materials: Audio CD 2.9, 2.10, paper; Build Creativity: six sheets of posterboard, each with a letter representing a sound written at the top—*c, p, t, n, b, h*

1) 2.9 Listen, point, and repeat.

Play Track 2.9, and have students repeat the sounds and the words. Pronounce each word in isolation, exaggerating the initial sound. Emphasize how air is released when pronouncing *p* and *t* by holding a slip of paper an inch or so in front of your mouth and showing how it moves when you pronounce them. Also, demonstrate to students how they should put their lips together to pronounce *p* and *b*. Taking as much time as necessary to teach the correct sounds is crucial for getting good results in the long run.

2) 2.10 Listen and circle the picture with the same beginning sound.

Focus students' attention on the example. Then, guide them to complete the activity.

Practice Time 1 Write the letters *c, p, t, n, b,* and *h* on the board. Say: *Ten. What's the first letter in* ten? Give three options from the letters on the board for students to choose from: *c, p, or t? (t)* Words you could continue with, even if students do not know their meanings, include *can, cut, cot, pan, pink, pet, tan, tin, ton, not, nut, nap, bell, Ben, Bob, he, his,* and *how*. The objective of this activity should only be to discriminate initial sounds.

3) Say the word and underline the correct beginning sound.

Point to each object, and say what it is. Have students repeat the word. Then, have them underline the correct letters.

4) Form small groups. Look back at Unit 1 and find words beginning with *t* and *h*.

Form small groups. Have students go back to unit 1 and search for words with the initial sound *t* or *h*. Ask students to write the words down on a sheet of paper. Point out that students will need to avoid words in which an initial *t* is followed by *h*, such as *this*, because this combination makes a different sound. Words they will find in unit 1 include *tall, tired, turtle, Tommy, Ted, Turkey, take turns, tablet, happy, hair, has,* and *hand*. Assign a set time for the search, and then say *Stop!* Check words as a class. Count how many correct words each group has found.

Build Creativity!

Wall Charts

Objective: Focus

Form six groups, and give each group one of the sheets of posterboard with a letter at the top. Have the groups draw objects whose names start with the letter written on their sheet. Go around the classroom, monitoring students' work. The long-term objective is to have wall charts for all the sounds that will be taught throughout the year. Display students' work on the classroom walls.

AB page 28

Objective: **to learn to agree and disagree**
Cue Cards: **2. *Yes*. 3. *No*.**
Materials: Video 2.2, Audio CD 2.11, Cue Cards 2–3

Oracy Skill

Remind students that we are all different and special. Discuss the importance both of listening to other people's opinions and of having and expressing our own opinions. Ask students if they like all the same things. Then, express some opinions and ask for agreement or disagreement. For example, you could say: *Orange is a great color! Do you agree?* Have students say *Yes* or *No* out loud if they agree or disagree with what you say. Tell students that when we agree we say *Yes*, and when we disagree we say *No*.

1 2.2 2.11 Watch and circle the answers to the questions.

Ask: *Is school fun?* Have students agree or disagree. Then, play V2.2 up to "When you agree, you say 'Yes.'" Ask students: *Does Emma agree with Liam? (Yes.)* Direct students' attention to Activity 1, and ask them to circle the correct answer. Follow a similar process with the second scene in the video, between Kate and Jack. Then, play the first part of the third scene about the library. Ask: *Do they agree? (No.)* Continue with the final part of the third scene.

Present and Practice Display Cue Cards 2 and 3. Ask a volunteer to go to the front and hold the two Cue Cards.

Say: *This classroom is big. Do you agree?* The student should answer by putting up a Cue Card. Continue with more volunteers and more examples such as: *My desk is small. Your classmates are old. This school is great!*

Let's Practice Oracy! 2, 3

- **1–2** Look at your students and say: *Books are great! Do you agree?* Listen to students' opinions.
- Ask students to think about their opinions on books and the other three topics shown in the pictures on page 36. Explain that, this time, you will be the one who agrees or disagrees.
- When students are ready, have volunteers give their opinions. Use the Cue Cards to agree or disagree.
- Optional: Record or have students record themselves as they give their opinions to share their work.
- Have students complete Check Your Oracy!

Home-school   Portfolio: Oracy

Fun Corner!

Mini Dialogues

Form pairs to perform for the class. One student gives an opinion, and the other agrees or disagrees. Remind students to use *Do you agree?*

Build Creativity!

How Many?

Objective: **Try, Try, and Try Again**

Ask: *How many desks are in the classroom?* Encourage students to guess, and then ask them how they can find out the answer: *count them*. Count the desks together. Help with higher numbers as needed. Repeat with some other common classroom objects.

AB page 28

Ready to Write

2A

Learn to Write: Alphabetical Order

(1) 2.12 Listen and say the alphabet.

A B C D E F G
H I J K L M N
O P Q R S T
U V W X Y Z

(2) Write your name in your notebook and spell it out loud.

(3) Look and write the words next to the correct beginning letters.

girl boy her cat

a	ant	d	desk	g	g i r l
b	b o y	e	eight	h	h e r
c	c a t	f	fish	i	iguana

Time to Talk!

What's the next letter?

1 Stand in a circle.
2 Take turns saying the letters in alphabetical order.

AB pages 29–30

37

Objective: **to put words in alphabetical order**
Materials: Audio CD 2.12, paper; Fun Corner: construction paper, each with a letter of the alphabet

Learn to Write Box

Tell students that they will learn how to put words in alphabetical order. After introducing the concept, discuss with students the usefulness of alphabetical order—for instance, when you want to search for a name on a list or a word in a dictionary.

(1) 2.12 Listen and say the alphabet.

Have students say the alphabet to check how much they remember. Monitor, and check pronunciation. Play Track 2.12, and ask students to say the alphabet again. Call on individual students to say successive parts of the alphabet out loud.

(2) Write your name in your notebook and spell it out loud.

Ask students to do Activity 2. Like the first activity, this will review learning done in unit 1.

(3) Look and write the words next to the correct beginning letters.

Review the example, then ask students to do the activity on their own. Check answers on the board with the help of volunteers. Point out that the words are in alphabetical order.

Time to Talk!

Have students look at the picture of the classroom. Ask: *What letters of the alphabet can you see? Are they in alphabetical order? (Yes.)* Ask students to get in a circle and take turns saying the letters in alphabetical order. Continue with this activity as many times as you feel necessary. You could also ask students to do the same in small groups.

Fun Corner!

Alphabet Scramble

Hand out the letters of the alphabet in random order. Give students more than one letter if necessary. Invite the class to tape the letters on the wall in the correct order. Monitor, and provide assistance as needed.

AB pages 29–30

Objective: make a class list in alphabetical order

Materials: one note card per student and some extras (big enough to write a name on that is visible from a distance), construction paper with one letter of the alphabet at the top of each piece, glue, colored pencils; Fun Corner: a balloon

First and Last Letter in a Word

Write the word *desk* and the letter *d* on the board. Ask a volunteer to point to the letter and, then, to the word. Have students provide examples of letters and words. Ask them how they know where a word ends. Write a simple sentence, and help students isolate words. Have them tell you the first and last letter in each word.

1 IDENTIFY

Ask volunteers to tell you what the first and last letters of their first names are. Ask other volunteers for the first and last letters of their last names. Tell students they will make a class list. Remind them why lists in alphabetical order are useful.

2 WRITE

Give each student a note card and colored pencils. Have students write their first name on the card. Remind them that the first letter in a name must be a capital letter. Encourage students to use different colors for each letter and to write their names big enough so that they will be visible from a distance. Go around the classroom and help students. (See Differentiated Instruction.)

3 EDIT

Ask students to form pairs and swap cards. One student spells their name aloud, and the other checks that the name has been written correctly. When pairs have finished, if any names are incorrect, give those students a new card so they can write their names again.

4 FOLLOW UP

Display the construction paper with the letters of the alphabet in order. The paper should be positioned so that it is low enough for students to work on and everyone can see it. Explain that you will say each letter of the alphabet and that, when you say a letter, those students whose names start with it should go to the front and glue their name cards below the letter there. You may need more than one piece of construction paper for some letters. Use this class list for further activities. For example, you could ask students to bring pictures of their favorite things and glue them next to their names or have them write their birthdays there.

Fun Corner!

Balloon in the Air

Have students stand in a circle. Hit the balloon into the air gently. Have students continue hitting the balloon gently to keep it in the air. Then, take the balloon and say the letter *a*. Hit the balloon into the air. Have the next person who hits the balloon say the next letter. If a student says the wrong letter, stop the game, have them say the correct letter and hit the balloon into the air. Continue through the whole alphabet.

Build Creativity!

Upside Down Letters

Objective: Focus

Write each letter of the alphabet on a separate sheet of paper. Put the letters face down on your desk in random order. Divide the class into four groups. Flip a letter upside down and show it to one group for them to identify. Continue with the rest of the letters and the rest of the groups.

Differentiated Instruction

Below-level ★	On-level ★★	Above-level ★★★
Write students' first names on the cards in yellow so that students can trace over them.	Ask students to write their first names on the cards, as in the *Write* section.	Ask students to write their first names and last names on the cards.

Objective: **to learn vocabulary related to a fiction text**
Key Words 4: ***story, sad, mad, hungry, lunchbox, surprised***
Materials: Audio CD 2.13, 2.14; Build Creativity: construction paper

1 2·13 Key Words 4 Listen, point, and repeat.

Play Track 2.13. Have students listen and look at the pictures. Play the track again for students to repeat the words. Then, smile, and say: *I'm happy*; yawn, and say: *I'm tired*. Next, introduce the new emotions: *sad, mad, surprised*. Ask the class to act out the different emotions as you mention them. Then, focus your attention on the word *story*. Say: Grandma Turtle *is a story. Tell me about your favorite stories*. As students mention stories, ask: *Is it a happy story or a sad story?*

Practice Time 1 Ask volunteers to draw an emoticon on the board for each of the emotions they know from unit 1 and each new one (*happy, tired, sad, mad, hungry, surprised*). When all of the emoticons are on the board, call on individual students, and say an emotion: *Sad*. The student you call on goes to the board and points to the corresponding emoticon.

2 2·14 Listen and draw the school object inside the schoolbag.

Have students listen and draw the school object inside the schoolbag. Then, ask them to color the schoolbag.

Build Creativity!

Concentration Game

Objective: **Focus**

Form groups of four students. Give each group two sheets of construction paper. Ask students to draw a big schoolbag on each piece of paper. Have students draw six school objects inside one of the schoolbags. Allow students to color their drawings, and then have them place the drawings facedown. Ask two groups to work together. The two groups hold up their drawings of the schoolbag with school objects for one minute. When you say *Stop!*, the groups put their drawings facedown. Groups must draw all the objects they remember inside the other group's empty schoolbag. Monitor results, and say who the winners are.

AB page 31

Objective: to understand a character's feelings and prepare to read a fiction text
Materials: Audio CD 2.15; Build Creativity: storybooks that illustrate characters showing various emotions, cutouts of people showing happiness, sadness, surprise, anger (at least five pictures per emotion), four sheets of paper big enough to glue five of the pictures on, glue

1 2.15 Listen and repeat.

Discuss with students how they feel in different situations (when they go to a birthday party, when their parents yell at them, when they get mad at a friend, etc.). Have students look at the picture in the Reading Strategy box. Ask: *Is he happy? (No, he is sad.)* Then, play Track 2.15, and ask students to repeat the words.

2 How do these children feel?

Point to the pictures in Activity 2, and ask students to tell you how each child feels.

Big Question Link

Read the question aloud. Point out the model answer, and read it aloud. Ask volunteers to tell you how they feel at school.

Build Creativity!

Emotions

Objective: Focus

Ask students to say the names of the characters from their favorite stories. Ask them about those characters' emotions in different parts of the stories. Hold up the storybooks, and point out the characters' expressions. Ask about their emotions: *How do they feel? Are they happy?* Then, form four groups. Hand out paper and glue. Assign each group an emotion, and ask them to draw the corresponding emoticon at the top of their sheet of paper. Write the word for each emotion on the board, and guide each group to copy the word for their emotion below their emoticon. Place the cutouts on your desk, and ask one student per group to go to your desk and take a cutout that shows the emotion they were assigned. Continue this way until there are no more cutouts. Have students glue the cutouts to the paper. Display students' work around the classroom.

Objective: to understand a character's feelings and learn more about school
Materials: Audio CD 2.16, 2.17

Pre-Reading

Read the title aloud. Then, pretend you are searching for something, and say: *I can't find my (pencil).* Show the object you were searching for, and sigh. Repeat with a different object. Read the title again. Ask students to look through the story and guess what it will be about.

2.16 Page 40, section 1

Play Track 2.16 up to the end of the second sentence. Pause and ask questions:

What is the teacher's name?
What is the new boy's name?

Digging Deeper

Direct students' attention to Max. Ask: *Who is new at school? How do you think Max feels? Is he sad?*

Personalization

Ask: *Is there a new student at your school?*

2.16 Page 40, section 2

Continue Track 2.16 to the end of the page. Pause and ask questions:

Point to Max's desk. Ask: *What is this?*

Is Max happy?

Point to the girl sitting next to Max, and ask: *Is she happy?*

Think

Read the question in the Think box aloud. Accept all answers. Encourage students to guess what happens next in the story.

2.16 Page 41

Play the rest of Track 2.16. Ask questions:

Point to the book the teacher is holding, and ask: *What is this?*

Point to Max in the second scene, and ask: *Is Max happy?*

Point to Gemma, and ask: *What is her name?*

Encourage students to guess: *Where is Max's book?*

Think

Read the question in the Think box aloud, and have students answer it.

2.16

I Can't Find My Things!

by Silvia Zapiain

"Good morning, children," says Miss Brown.
"This is Max. It's his first day at school."

"Max, this is your desk,"
says Miss Brown.
Max sits down. He is happy.

Think
Why do you think Max is happy?

40

"Let's read a story!"
says Miss Brown.

"Max, what's wrong?" asks Miss Brown.
"I'm sad. I can't find my book!"
"That's OK. You can read with Gemma."

Think
Who helps Max?

41

2.17 **I Can't Find My Things!**

"Let's draw a picture!" says Miss Brown.
"Max, what's wrong?" asks Miss Brown.
"I'm mad. I can't find my colored pencils!"
Gemma shares her pencils with Max.

"Lunchtime!" shout the children.
"Max, what's wrong now?" asks Miss Brown.
"I'm hungry. I can't find my lunchbox!"

Think
Why is Max mad? Why is he hungry?

42

2B

Miss Brown is surprised.
"Max, show me your schoolbag, please," says Miss Brown.

"Oh, dear! Look out the window! Your book, your pencils, and your lunchbox are all on the playground!"

Think
Why are Max's things on the playground?

43

2.17 Page 42, section 1

Have students look at the first scene carefully before you play the audio. Encourage students to guess what is going on in the classroom. Play Track 2.17 through "Gemma shares her pencils with Max." Pause and ask questions:

How does Max feel now? Is he happy?
What can't he find?
Who helps Max?

2.17 Page 42, section 2

Continue Track 2.17 to the end of page 42. Pause and ask questions:

What time is it now?
How does Max feel now?
What can't Max find?

Personalization

Ask: *Are your colored pencils in your schoolbag? Is your lunchbox in your schoolbag?*

Think

Read the questions in the Think box aloud. Help students provide answers by saying: *Max is mad because he can't find …* Pause and give students time to provide the missing information. Do the same with the second question.

2.17 Page 43

Play the rest of Track 2.17. Ask questions:

Are Max's things in the classroom?
Where are they?
Is Miss Brown mad?

Think

Read the question in the Think box aloud. Encourage students to guess what may have happened.

Fun Corner!

Performance

Focus students' attention on expressions in the second part of the story. Teach *What's wrong? Lunchtime! Show me your… , please.* and *Oh, dear!* After making sure students understand the expressions, play Track 2.17 up to the end. Have students work in small groups to perform a short version of the second part of the story. Monitor, and provide support as needed.

Explore the Text

1 Look at the story. Number the pictures in order.

4 3 2 1

2 Mark ✓ the things that Max can't find.

book notebook colored pencils lunchbox ruler

3 How do they feel? Circle the correct answers.

a Max is mad / sad.

b Max is mad / hungry.

c The teacher is happy / surprised.

d Max is sad / mad.

What makes you happy about school? English class!

44

Objective: to deepen understanding of a fiction text

Materials: Fun Corner: paper, colored pencils, scissors, envelopes

1 Look at the story. Number the pictures in order.

Have students look at the pictures in Activity 1. To help students identify the sequence of events, provide some relevant sentences from the text. For example, you could say *This is your desk.* for the first scene and *I can't find my colored pencils.* for the second scene.

2 Mark ✓ the things that Max can't find.

Elicit the names of each of the objects in Activity 2. Have students mark the things that Max can't find. Check answers by saying *Max can't find ...* and calling on individual students.

3 How do they feel? Circle the correct answers.

If you still have the emotion posters on the wall (page 59, Build Creativity!), ask volunteers to point to and read the emotions. The objective is for everyone to be able to identify the words in Activity 3. Have students choose the correct options to complete the sentences, providing support as needed.

Big Question Link

Point to the Big Question Link, and read the question and the sample answer aloud. Discuss with students what makes them happy about school.

Fun Corner!

Hot and Cold

Have students put five of their possessions on their desks. Ask a volunteer to leave the room. The rest of the class then hides one of the volunteer's possessions. When the volunteer returns, have them check their things. Encourage them to say: *I can't find my (ruler).* The volunteer then searches the classroom while their classmates give clues: *cold, very cold, hot, very hot.*

AB pages 32–33

Differentiated Instruction

Below-level ★	On-level ★★	Above-level ★★★
Form two groups. Tell students that they must mention as many objects and emotions as they can remember from *I Can't Find My Things!* Groups must take turns and not repeat words.	Form pairs or small groups. Tell students that when you say *Go!* they must draw as many school objects as they can remember from *I Can't Find My Things!* When you say *Stop!* they must exchange papers with another pair or group who will count the correct answers and write the total number on the paper.	Form pairs or small groups. Tell students that when you say *Go!* they must write as many school and emotion words as they can remember from *I Can't Find My Things!* When you say *Stop!* they must exchange papers with another pair or group who will count the correct answers and write the total number on the paper.

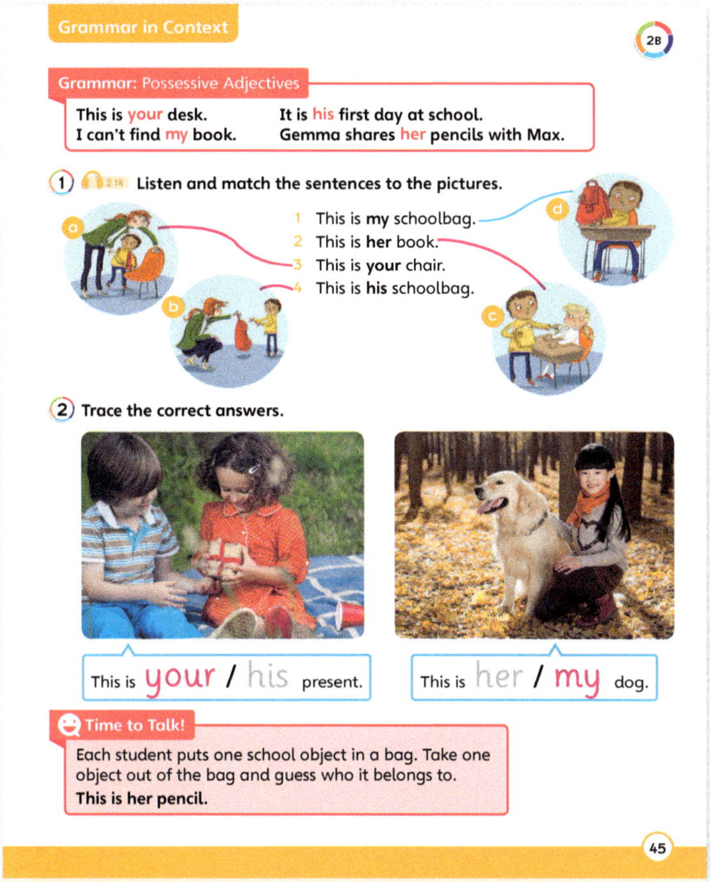

Grammar in Context

28

Grammar: Possessive Adjectives

This is your desk. I can't find my book.
It is his first day at school. Gemma shares her pencils with Max.

1 2.18 Listen and match the sentences to the pictures.

1 This is **my** schoolbag.
2 This is **her** book.
3 This is **your** chair.
4 This is **his** schoolbag.

a b c d

2 Trace the correct answers.

This is your / his present.

This is her / my dog.

Time to Talk!

Each student puts one school object in a bag. Take one object out of the bag and guess who it belongs to.
This is her pencil.

45

Objective: **to understand and use possessive adjectives**
Materials: Audio CD 2.18, big bag (non-transparent)

Grammar Box

Ask one boy and one girl to come to the front, each with something that belongs to them. Take one thing that belongs to you. Put the three objects on your desk. Pretend you are a bit absent-minded. Take the object that belongs to the boy, and, without looking at him, say: *This is my (...). Oh, no, no. This is his (...).* Point to the boy. Repeat the process with the girl and her object, this time saying: *This is her (...).* Then, show your object, and say: *This is my (...).* Give the students back their objects, and say: *Thank you. This is your (...).* Have them sit down.

Practice Time I Write the possessive adjectives in lowercase letters on the board. Point to each of the adjectives, say it, and have students repeat it after you.

1 2.18 Listen and match the sentences to the pictures.

Have students look at the pictures in Activity 1 carefully. Have them identify the possessive adjectives in the text. Play Track 2.18, and pause after the first sentence. Point to the example, and explain how to do the exercise. Continue with the rest of the track.

2 Trace the correct answers.

Have students look at the pictures carefully. Read the sentences, and ask students to trace the correct words to complete them.

Time to Talk!

Read the instructions in the Time to Talk! box aloud. Have five students come to the front, each with one of their school supplies. Pass a bag around, and ask each student to hold up their object, say what it is, and put it inside the bag. Then, pass the bag around the class. Each student takes an object, points, and says: *This is (her) (pencil).* Repeat the activity with five other students. (See *Fun Corner!* for an alternative.)

Fun Corner!

Oh, Dear!

Use the bag with the school supplies from *Time to Talk!* The bag should have an object from each student. Ask students to stand in a circle. Say: *Close your eyes.* Put one object on the floor behind each student. Also, put an object that belongs to you on the floor next to you. Ask students to open their eyes. Look at the object next to you, and say: *Oh, dear!* Pick up the object, and say: *This is my (pencil)!* Ask students to look behind them, pick up the object they see, and guess who it belongs to. Encourage students to say: *Oh, dear! This is my (ruler)* or, alternatively, to say: *Oh, dear! This is (his/her) (ruler),* pointing to the object's owner. At the end of the game, students return the object they have to its owner, saying: *This is your (ruler).* If your class is large, this activity can be done in two or three groups.

AB pages 34–35

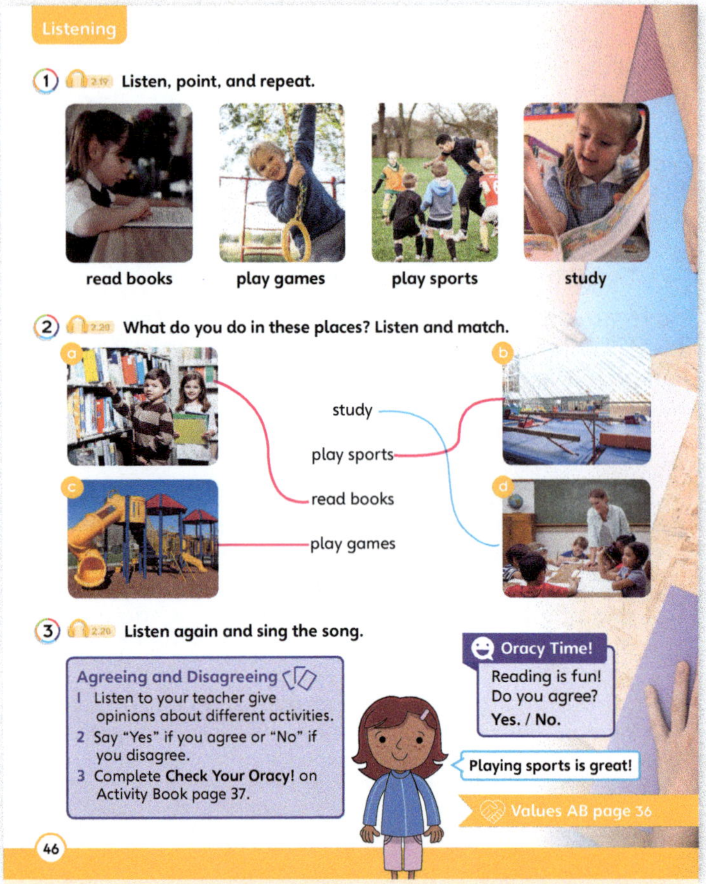

Listening

1 2.19 Listen, point, and repeat.

read books | play games | play sports | study

2 2.20 What do you do in these places? Listen and match.

study
play sports
read books
play games

3 2.20 Listen again and sing the song.

Agreeing and Disagreeing
1 Listen to your teacher give opinions about different activities.
2 Say "Yes" if you agree or "No" if you disagree.
3 Complete **Check Your Oracy!** on Activity Book page 37.

Oracy Time!
Reading is fun! Do you agree?
Yes. / No.

Playing sports is great!

Values AB page 36

46

Objectives: to talk about the things you do at school; to learn to take care of your school objects
Materials: Audio CD 2.19, 2.20, Cue Cards 2, 3

1 2.19 Listen, point, and repeat.

Discuss with students the things they do at school. Have them look at the pictures and tell you what the children are doing. Play Track 2.19. Ask students to point and repeat.

2 2.20 What do you do in these places? Listen and match.

Have students tell you the names of the places in Activity 2. Read the first example as you follow the line with your finger. Read the rest of the actions. Then, play Track 2.20 and have students complete the activity. Check answers as a class.

3 2.20 Listen again and sing the song.

Play Track 2.20 again. Then, sing the song, and pause at some parts to encourage students to complete what is missing. For example: *This is my school. It's so … (cool).*

Oracy Extension Activity

Read the steps in the Oracy Extension activity aloud. Display the Cue Cards, and have students do the activity with you. Ask students to complete Check Your Oracy! on page 37 of their Activity Books.

Portfolio: Oracy

ACTIVITY BOOK PAGE 36

Values: Taking Care of Your School Objects

1 Circle 🙂 or ☹.

2 Mark ✓.

I take care of my school objects.

3 Draw yourself in school.

I take care of my school objects.

Students' own answers

36

SB page 46

1 Circle 🙂 or ☹.

Have students turn to page 36 of their Activity Books. Discuss with students the importance of taking care of their school objects. Talk about the importance of taking care of other people's objects as well. Ask them to look at the pictures and tell you which ones don't illustrate the value. Do the activity as a class.

2 Mark ✓.

Have students look at the pictures. Then, have them complete the activity. Monitor, and provide support if necessary. Check answers as a class.

3 Draw yourself in school.

Ask students about their favorite school object, and ask if they take care of it. Then, have students draw themselves in school with their favorite school object.

AB page 36

The Big Challenge

28

How can we make a classroom map?

Your challenge is to present a classroom map to the class.

1. Brainstorm in small groups. Name all the things you can find in your classroom.
2. Work together to draw the shape of the classroom on a large sheet of paper.
3. Cut out colored paper shapes to represent different objects.
4. Make a key. See the example in the picture.
5. Glue the shapes on the map.
6. Display your classroom map on the wall.
7. Present your classroom map to other groups.

What is school? Look back through the unit. Share your ideas.

AB pages 37–39

47

Objective: to consolidate, extend, and personalize learning on the unit topic

Materials: construction paper (one sheet for each small group of students), paper of different colors, scissors, glue

- Read the Big Challenge question and statement aloud.
- Draw a simple map of the classroom on the board. Ask students to guess what the map represents.
- **1** Form small groups. Ask them to name and count the things in the classroom. Monitor groups' work.
- **2** Show students the sample map on the page, and tell them they will be making a classroom map. Hand out the materials. Ask groups to draw the shape of the classroom.
- **3** Have students decide what they will include in their classroom. Point out to students that maps should be easy to understand, so, in making their map, they should focus on important objects in the classroom. Students then work together and cut out shapes for each object. Go around the classroom, monitoring students' work.
- **4** Explain to students what a key is. Focus their attention on the sample key.
- **5** Once groups have decided on the classroom layout and on how they will make the key, have students glue the shapes to the paper.
- **6–7** Display the maps on the wall at children's eye level. Ask each group to present their map. Remind them that they should use *This is …* Optional: Record or have students record one another's presentations to share their work.

Home-school | Portfolio: Big Challenge

Big Question Circle

Read the Big Question aloud. Have the class revisit the Big Question Links on pages 30, 33, 39, and 44. Discuss what they have learned about school. Help with emergent language.

- Use the following questions to help review the Big Question:

  What school objects can you name?
  What school places can you name?
  What is your favorite place?
  What activities do you do in school?
  How do you feel at school?
  Do you take care of your school objects?
  What is in your classroom?

- Finally, have students turn to page 37 of their Activity Books to complete the Big Challenge self-assessment.

AB pages 37–39

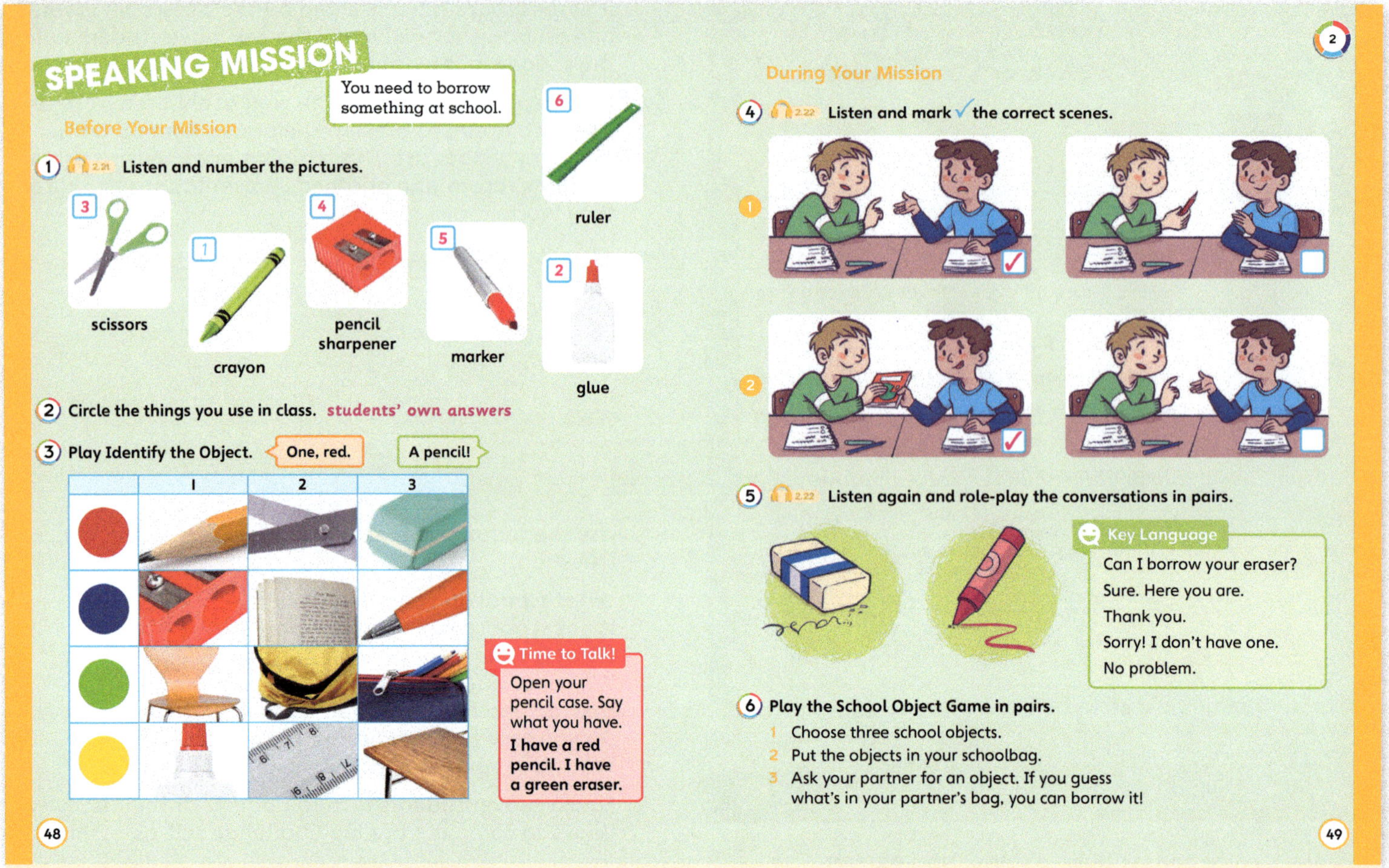

SPEAKING MISSION

You need to borrow something at school.

Before Your Mission

1 2.21 Listen and number the pictures.

3 scissors
1 crayon
4 pencil sharpener
5 marker
6 ruler
2 glue

2 Circle the things you use in class. students' own answers

3 Play Identify the Object. One, red. A pencil!

Time to Talk! Open your pencil case. Say what you have. I have a red pencil. I have a green eraser.

48

During Your Mission

4 2.22 Listen and mark ✓ the correct scenes.

5 2.22 Listen again and role-play the conversations in pairs.

Key Language
Can I borrow your eraser?
Sure. Here you are.
Thank you.
Sorry! I don't have one.
No problem.

6 Play the School Object Game in pairs.
1 Choose three school objects.
2 Put the objects in your schoolbag.
3 Ask your partner for an object. If you guess what's in your partner's bag, you can borrow it!

49

Objective: to borrow something at school
Speaking Mission Words: *scissors, crayon, pencil sharpener, marker, ruler, glue*
Materials: Audio CD 2.21, 2.22

1 2.21 Listen and number the pictures.

Have students look at the pictures. Play Track 2.21, and encourage students to number the pictures. Play the track again for students to repeat the words.

2 Circle the things you use in class.

Have students look at the objects in Activity 1 and circle the ones they use in class.

3 Play Identify the Object.

Draw students' attention to the chart. Point to the numbers at the top of the chart, and count: *one, two, three*. Then, elicit the colors. Form pairs. Have them play the game by pointing to the chart and reading the text in the speech bubbles. Go around the classroom and monitor work.

Time to Talk!

Read the directions and example in the Time to Talk! box aloud. Form pairs, and have them do the activity. Flip the light switch off and on, and have students form new pairs. Repeat several times. Monitor, and provide support if necessary.

4 2.22 Listen and mark ✓ the correct scenes.

Draw students' attention to the scenes in Activity 4. Play the first conversation of Track 2.22. Guide students to choose the correct scene. Continue with the second conversation.

5 2.22 Listen again and role-play the conversation in pairs.

Play Track 2.22 again, and ask a pair of students to come to the front with a crayon and an eraser and perform the two dialogues from the track. Then, ask other pairs to do the same. Focus on correcting pronunciation and intonation of questions, which in this case should be a rising intonation. Optional: Record or have students record one another's role plays to share their work.

Home-school | Portfolio: Speaking Mission

6 Play the School Object Game in pairs.

Review the steps in the game with students. Monitor students as they play.

AB pages 40–41

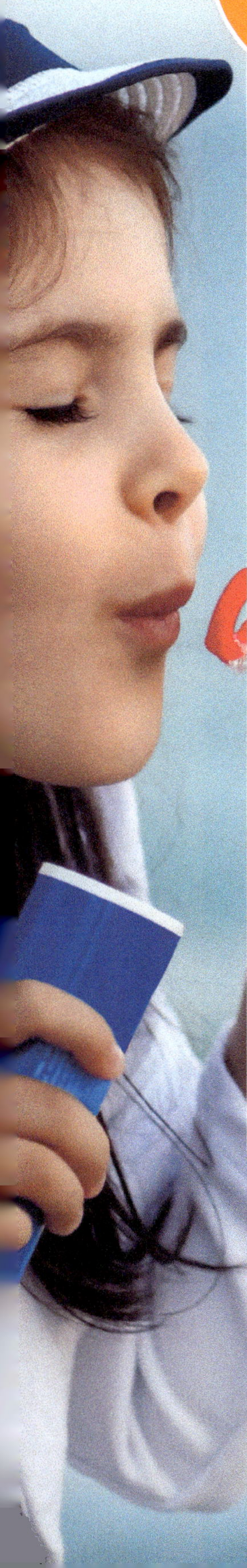

3 What is a toy?

Literacy

Read: a nonfiction text about children's toys; a fiction text about two friends learning to share

Reading Strategies: classifying words; ordering story events

Ready to Write

Learn to Write: complete sentences: *The ball is blue.*

Getting Ready to Write: write a sentence using drawings

Oracy

Skill: Active Listening

Cue Card 4: 4. *Please repeat that.*

Oracy Performance Task I:

Collaboration: agree on buying a toy

Language

Key Words I: *toy, box, house, paper, airplane, tablet*

Key Words 2: *robot, fun, dollhouse, tent, train, jump rope*

Key Words 3: *children, jump*

Key Words 4: *monkey bars, bike, car, action figure, dinosaur, spaceship*

Oracy Performance Task Words: *please, here you go, thank you*

Grammar in Context

Commands: *Listen! March! Stop! Stand! Sit! Jump!*

Negative Commands: *Don't touch my cars! Don't run!*

Phonics

Ending Sounds: -*at*,-*en*

Listening

Dialogue: Playing a Game

Values

Sharing

The Big Challenge

How can we make a toy?
Make a toy

Objective: to introduce the topic of what a toy is
Key Words I: ***toy, box, house, paper, airplane, tablet***
Materials: Video 3.I, Audio CD 3.I, Flashcards 3.I–3.6

WHAT IS A TOY?

- Read the Big Question aloud. Ask students what their favorite toys are. Read the first question, and ask students to point to the toys they can see.
- Ask the second question. Have students point to each toy and say what color or colors it is.
- Finally, ask the last question. Discuss with students whether the toys in the pictures are fun. Elicit examples of other toys they have at home, and ask whether these are all fun.
- 3.1 Key Words 1 Use the flashcards and audio to present Key Words I. Hold up the flashcards as you play Track 3.I. Have students repeat the words. Put the flashcards face down on your desk. Lift one at a time, and have students say the words. Lift the flashcards faster in random order, pointing to individual students to say the words.

1 3.1 Watch the video. Circle the toys from the video.

Watch the video, pausing after "Let's find out!" Ask: *What is today's Big Question? (What is a toy?)* Continue the video, pausing after "… yellow." Guide students in providing information. Say: *Toys are big and … They are blue, red, green, and …* Continue the video, pausing after "And this piece of paper … is a bird!" Have volunteers go to the board. Ask them to draw as many toys made from boxes as they can remember from the video. Then, have other volunteers draw the toys made from paper. Finally, finish the video, and have students complete Activity I. Check answers as a class.

2 3.1 Watch again. Complete the graphic organizer in the Activity Book.

Form pairs. Play the video again, and have students complete Activity I on AB page 42.

AB page 42

Unit 3A Ready to Read: Nonfiction

Reading Strategy: Classifying Words

1 3.2 Listen and follow along.

This is **Tim**.
He has a **car**.
The car is **blue**.

Tim car blue

2 Match the words.

1 name a car
2 toy b blue
3 color c Tim

What colors are your toys?

52

Objective: to classify words and prepare to read a nonfiction text

Key Words 1: ***toy, box, house, paper, airplane, tablet***

Materials: Audio CD 3.1, 3.2, Flashcards 3.1–3.6, *colors* Flashcard from unit 1; Fun Corner: paper

3.1 Key Words 1 Use the flashcards and audio to review Key Words 1.

1 3.2 Listen and follow along.

Draw three columns on the board. Write your name at the top of the first column, place the *toys* Flashcard at the top of the second one, and place the *colors* Flashcard from unit 1 at the top of the third. Play Track 3.2 as students look at the pictures in Activity 1. Then, ask: *Is Tim a name, a toy, or a color?* Point to each column as you mention the categories. Write *Tim* under your name. Continue with *car* and *blue*, but represent them with drawings instead of writing the words. Leave the activity as it is on the board.

1 Match the words.

Guide students to complete Activity 2. Read the words. Include the numbers and letters to help students identify each word.

Big Question Link

Point to the Big Question Link, and read the question aloud. Elicit answers from students. Then, call on individual students to tell you their favorite toy including its color, for example: *My favorite toy is (a blue car).* Model this example for students.

Fun Corner!

Classify

Form groups of three students. Hand out a sheet of paper to each group. Tell students they will draw things under categories as you did on the board. They have to draw two columns. Ask them to draw a happy face at the top of the first column and a pen at the top of the second. When you say *Go!*, groups must draw emoticons that represent the emotions they have learned in the first column and school objects in the second. When you say *Stop!*, groups exchange papers and count the other group's correct drawings.

Build Creativity!

Which One Doesn't Belong?

Objective: Focus

Ask students to prepare an activity to do at home. They should draw three circles, each one on a separate sheet of paper. Inside each circle, students have to draw three things, two of which must belong to the same category. For example, in one circle they could draw a splotch of blue, a book, and a pencil. Ask students to bring their work to class. Have each student trade circles with a classmate. Students must cross out the drawing that does not belong. Continue the activity with the other circles.

3.3 Key Words 2 Use Flashcards 3.7–3.12 and the audio to pre-teach Key Words 2. Show each flashcard as students listen to Track 3.3. Have students repeat each word. Then, take out the *toys* Flashcard (Key Words 1), and place it at the top of the board. Place other Key Words 1 and Key Words 2 flashcards on the board below it to show that *toys* is a category and that the rest of the flashcards belong in this category. Ask volunteers to come to the board and draw other toys they can think of. Leave the cards and drawings on the board.

Pre-Reading

Have students look at the nonfiction text on pages 53 and 54. Ask: *How many toys can you see? (Five.)* Read the title. Say the name of each of the toys in random order, and have students point to the toy you mention. Then, play Tracks 3.4 and 3.5 while students look at the pictures.

3.4 **Page 53, section 1**

Play Track 3.4 through "It's fun!" Pause and ask questions:

What's the boy's name?
What is Lucas's favorite toy?
What does the robot say?

3.4 **Page 53, section 2**

Play the rest of Track 3.4. Ask questions:

What's the girl's name?
What is Olivia's favorite toy?
What color is the dollhouse?

Personalization

Say: *Look at the board. What is your favorite toy on the board?*

Fun Corner!

Mirror Image

Have students line up in two rows so that each student faces a partner. Tell pairs that one student is the mirror and the other has to make faces and do actions for the mirror to imitate. Encourage the "non-mirrors" to think of how to make the actions as hard as possible for the mirror. For example, if they hold up their left hand, the mirror needs to figure out that they have to hold up their right hand. And if they walk away from the mirror, can the mirror figure out how to make the reflection get smaller?

Objective: to understand that we like different things

Key Words 2: ***robot, fun, dollhouse, tent, train, jump rope***

Materials: Audio CD 3.3, 3.4, 3.5, Flashcards 3.1–3.6, 3.7–3.12; Differentiated Instruction: tape; slips of paper, each with *robot, dollhouse, tent, jump rope*, or *train* written in large letters

3.5 **Page 54**

Play Track 3.5. Ask questions:

What is the boy's name?
What is his favorite toy?
What color is the tent?
What is Emma's favorite toy?
What color is the jump rope?
What is Angie's favorite toy?
What color is the train?
What is similar about the jump rope and the train?
Which toy has zigzags?

Personalization

Ask: *What toys from the text do you have at home?*

Think

Read the question in the Think box aloud. Form pairs. Have students ask their partners this question and answer it about themselves. Monitor answers.

AB page 43

Differentiated Instruction

Below-level ★	On-level ★★	Above-level ★★★
Draw a robot on the board. Ask a volunteer to come to the front and draw the next toy that appears in the text *Top Five Toys* below your drawing. Continue so that all toys from the text are drawn in the order in which they appear in the text. You could repeat the activity, this time going from the last toy to the first one.	Show students the slips of paper with the words for the five toys written on them. Read the words aloud, and ask students to repeat them after you. Tape one slip on the board, and say the word. Then, ask a student to come to the board. Read another word, and ask the student to tape the word above or below the one you taped so that the words are in the order in which they appear in the text. You can repeat the activity as many times as you consider necessary for other students to participate.	Show students the slips of paper with the words for the five toys written on them, Read the words aloud, and ask students to repeat them after you. Tape one slip on the board, and say the word. Then, ask a student to come to the board. Read another word, and ask the student to tape the word above or below the one you taped so that the words are in the order in which they appear in the text. You can repeat the activity as many times as you consider necessary for other students to participate. Ask students to copy the words in the same order in their notebooks.

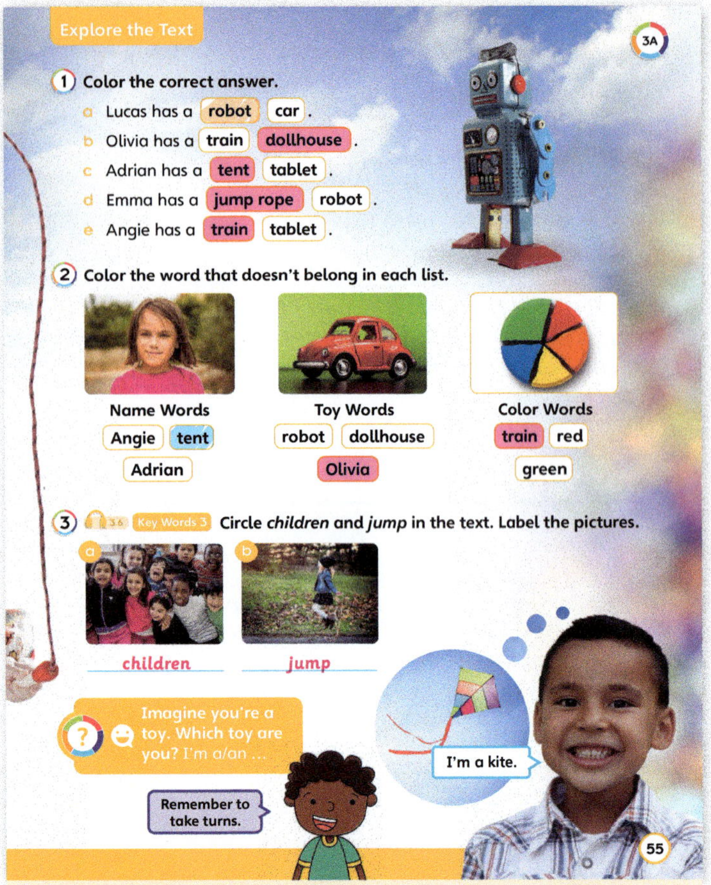

Explore the Text

3A

1 Color the correct answer.

a Lucas has a robot car.
b Olivia has a train dollhouse.
c Adrian has a tent tablet.
d Emma has a jump rope robot.
e Angie has a train tablet.

2 Color the word that doesn't belong in each list.

Name Words	Toy Words	Color Words
Angie, tent, Adrian	robot, dollhouse, Olivia	train, red, green

3 3.6 Key Words 3 Circle *children* and *jump* in the text. Label the pictures.

a children
b jump

55

Objective: to recall specific information from the text and identify words in context

Key Words 3: *children, jump*

Materials: Audio CD 3.6, *gym* Flashcard from unit 2, students' favorite toys from home

1 Color the correct answer.

Read sentence *a* as an example. Continue with the rest of the sentences, guiding students in coloring the correct words.

2 Color the word that doesn't belong in each list.

Place two flashcards of toys on the board, for example, the *airplane* and *tablet* Flashcards. Then, place the *gym* Flashcard next to them. Say each of the words aloud. Ask: *Which one doesn't belong? (Gym.)* Remove the *gym* Flashcard. Guide students in applying this same process to Activity 2, where they color the word that does not belong.

3 3.6 Key Words 3 Circle *children* and *jump* in the text. Label the pictures.

Write the words *children* and *jump* on the board. Say each word as you write it. Ask students to find and circle the two words in the text *Top Five Toys*. Monitor students' work. Then, play Track 3.6 as you point to the words on the board. Have students label the pictures in Activity 3. Form pairs, and ask them to swap books to check answers.

Big Question Link

Direct students' attention to Liam, the oracy character. Read the oracy reminder in the speech bubble aloud. Then, ask students to close their eyes. Read the Big Question prompt aloud. Then, have students open their eyes and draw and color the toy in their notebooks. Ask volunteers to come to the front. Ask: *Which toy are you?* Guide students to answer: *I'm a/an …*

Fun Corner!

Classify

Ask each student to show you the toy they brought from home. Identify features that the toys could have in common and could therefore be used to categorize toys—size, color, material, use, etc. Tell students you will mention a category (e.g., *soft toys*) and those who have a toy that fits in that category should stand up and come to the front. Continue with as many categories you can think of. As a follow-up for this activity, you could ask specific students to come to the front with their toys and have them say which toy does not belong to the group.

AB pages 44–45

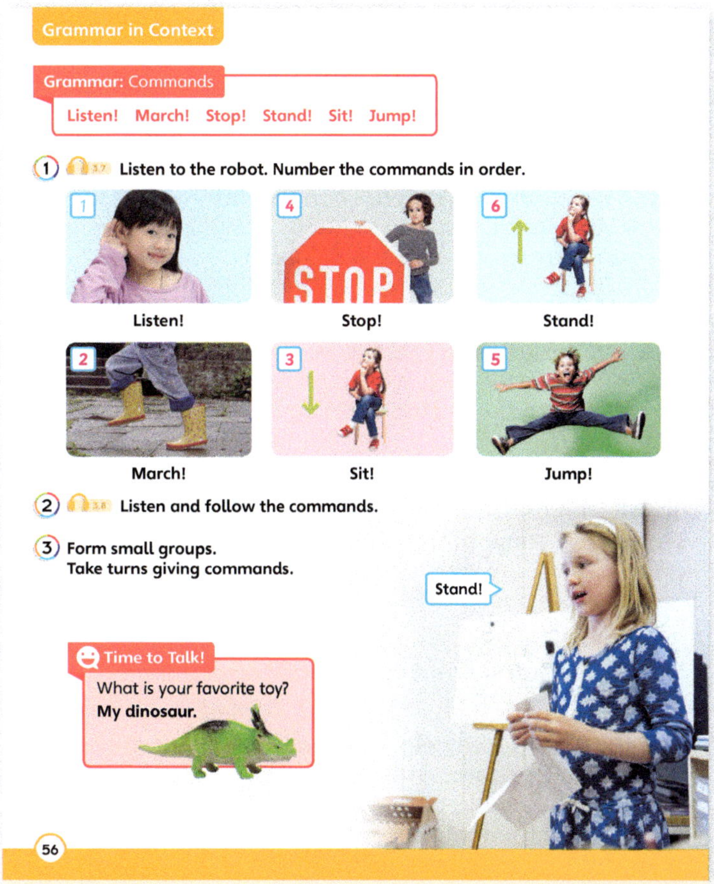

Grammar in Context

Grammar: Commands

Listen! March! Stop! Stand! Sit! Jump!

1 3.7 Listen to the robot. Number the commands in order.

1 Listen! 4 Stop! 6 Stand!

2 March! 3 Sit! 5 Jump!

2 3.8 Listen and follow the commands.

3 Form small groups. Take turns giving commands.

Stand!

Time to Talk!

What is your favorite toy?

My dinosaur.

56

Objective: to use commands

Materials: Audio CD 3.7, 3.8

Grammar Box

Give some classroom commands: *Sit down! Listen! Stand up!* Ask students when they think people give commands (*when you see someone is in danger, when parents are angry with you, when you train a pet, when you give game instructions*, etc.). Say the commands from the Grammar box, and do the actions. Guide students to identify the exclamation points. Explain why they are used at the end of commands.

1 3.7 Listen to the robot. Number the commands in order.

Ask students to look at the pictures in Activity 1. Help them identify each command. Then, play Track 3.7, and ask students to listen and to number the commands in order. To check answers, say the numbers in order and pause after each one for students to provide the answer.

Practice Time 1 Form pairs. One student points to one of the pictures in Activity 1, and the other says the command. Students should repeat the procedure faster and faster. Then, have pairs swap roles.

2 3.8 Listen and follow the commands.

Ask two students to come to the front. Play Track 3.8, and have them follow the commands. Then, ask the class to stand up, and play Track 3.8 again for all students to follow the commands.

3 Form small groups. Take turns giving commands.

Ask students to work in groups. In each group, assign a student to be the first to give commands. When you say *Go!* students start the activity. When you say *Stop!* students stop and another student in the group gives the commands when you resume the activity.

Time to Talk!

Read the question in the Time to Talk! box aloud. Ask students to draw their favorite toy on a piece of paper. Then, form pairs, and have them talk about their favorite toys. Encourage students to ask each other more questions, such as *What color is your toy? Is it (big)?* Form new pairs as many times as you feel necessary.

Fun Corner!

Simon Says

Children love playing this well-known game, and it works perfectly for teaching commands. In addition to using the commands taught in this lesson, you can teach and use new ones or review and use those you regularly use in class (*open/close your books, write, walk, dance, sing, touch your desk*, etc.). As an alternative to the usual way of playing, you can say two commands (e.g., *jump, listen*) and do the actions, and then ask students to do the actions in the order you did them. When they do, you start again but add another command, and ask students to do the three actions in the order you did them. Continue by adding more commands. This activity provides the kind of practice that can help students improve their memory.

AB pages 46–47

Phonics

3A

1 3.9 Listen, point, and repeat.

bat cat hat

pen hen ten

2 3.10 Listen and circle the correct word.

1 cat bat

2 pen hen

3 bat hat

3 Play in pairs. Point to a word. Your partner says the word.

cat	pen	hat
hen	bat	ten

57

Objective: to identify the ending sounds ***-at*** **and** ***-en***

Materials: Audio CD 3.9, 3.10; Differentiated Instruction (On-level): cards with letters written on them (*at* on six cards; *en* on six cards; two cards each with *b, c, p, t;* four cards with *h*)

1 3.9 Listen, point, and repeat.

Have students look at the pictures in Activity 1. Ask if they know the word for any of them. Play Track 3.9, and ask students to point and repeat. Say: *bat, cat, hat.* Guide students to identify sounds that are similar. Do the same for the words ending in *-en*. Then, concentrate on the beginning sounds. Remind students of how to pronounce the sounds from unit 2: *c, t, p, b,* and *h*.

2 3.10 Listen and circle the correct word.

Have students look at the pictures in Activity 2. Play Track 3.10, pausing after each word and reading the words below each picture to guide students to do the activity.

Practice Time 1 Write *-at* and *-en* on the board, and say the sounds out loud. Say *cat,* and point to *-at*. Ask a volunteer to come to the board and point to the correct ending as you say words. For example, you say *hen,* and the volunteer points to *-en*. Continue with other volunteers.

3 Play in pairs. Point to a word. Your partner says the word.

Form pairs. With the help of a volunteer, demonstrate how to play the game. After doing the previous activities, students will be able to read the words. If they have trouble, read them aloud, and ask individual students to repeat after you.

AB page 48

Differentiated Instruction

Below-level ★	On-level ★★	Above-level ★★★
Tell students that you will say words and they will have to draw the corresponding objects in their notebooks. Say: *cat.* Give students time to draw a cat. Continue with the words from the phonics page until students have drawn all six. This exercise can help improve students' understanding of sounds.	Form two groups. Distribute the cards so that the groups have identical letters. (See Materials.) Have groups put the letters in order so that they form the six words from the phonics page. Then, have students write the words in their notebooks and illustrate them.	Tell students that you will dictate six words and they have to write them in their notebooks. If you see that your students find it difficult to write the words, spell them out loud as they write.

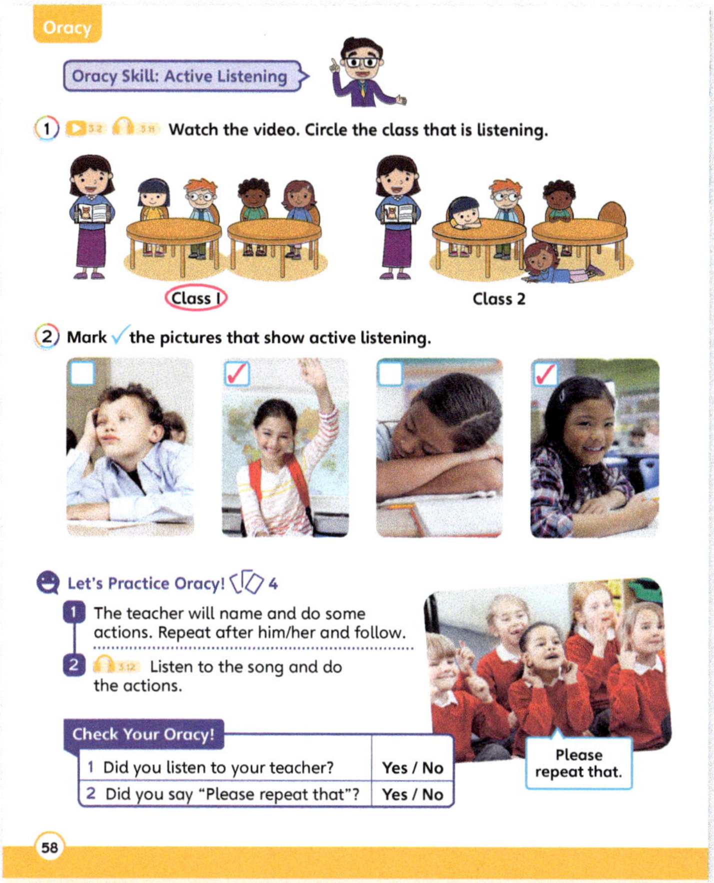

Oracy

Oracy Skill: Active Listening

1 3.2 3.11 Watch the video. Circle the class that is listening.

Class 1 Class 2

2 Mark ✓ the pictures that show active listening.

Let's Practice Oracy! 4

1 The teacher will name and do some actions. Repeat after him/her and follow.

2 3.12 Listen to the song and do the actions.

Check Your Oracy!

1 Did you listen to your teacher?	Yes / No
2 Did you say "Please repeat that"?	Yes / No

Please repeat that.

58

Objective: to listen actively

Cue Card: ***4. Please repeat that.***

Materials: Video 3.2, Audio CD 3.11, 3.12, Cue Card 4

Oracy Skill

Discuss with students how important it is to listen to someone who is speaking. Ask students to show you what a person does when not listening. To help them with ideas, you could pretend to be looking out a window and daydreaming or to be looking for something in your bag.

1 3.2 3.11 Watch the video. Circle the class that is listening.

Ask students to look at the two scenes in Activity 1. Remind them who each oracy character is. Also, have them guess who the woman is. (*The teacher.*) Introduce Class 1 by pointing to the first scene. Then, play V3.2, pausing after the part about Class 1. Ask simple questions to check basic understanding. Play the rest of the video. Then, ask basic questions. Discuss which class is listening to the teacher, and have students circle the correct scene in Activity 1. Note that the video must be shown to model this oracy skill.

2 Mark ✓ the pictures that show active listening.

Have students look at the four pictures in Activity 2 and mark the ones that show active listening.

Present and Practice Hold up Cue Card 4. Read the sentence aloud: *Please repeat that.* Talk about the importance of asking for repetition when you don't understand something that someone says. Leave the Cue Card on the board. Ask students to watch and listen carefully as you play V3.2 again. Tell them that when they hear the expression from the Cue Card, they should raise their hands. Encourage students to repeat the expression. Ensure they use the correct intonation.

Fun Corner!

Act It Out!

Form three groups. One of the members of each group should act as the teacher, and the others as the class. With the help of volunteers, provide a short example for groups to follow:

Teacher: *Let's read a story.* (The student acting as the teacher shows the pages corresponding to *Grandma Turtle.*) *Are you ready?*

Student 1: *Yes.*

Teacher: *This is Grandma Turtle. Grandma Turtle is old.*

Student 2: *Please repeat that.*

Provide the same example but with minor changes to show that the class is not listening actively. Groups perform the two versions in front of the class.

Let's Practice Oracy! 4

- **1** Ask students to move with you. Say: *Jump!* Start jumping, and encourage students to jump with you. Do the same with *run* and *dance.*
- **2** 3.12 Play Track 3.12 as you sing and do the actions. Encourage students to follow you. Tell them that, if they don't understand, they should use *Please repeat that.*
- Optional: Record or have students record themselves as they practice oracy.
- Have students complete Check Your Oracy!

Home-school Portfolio: Oracy

AB page 48

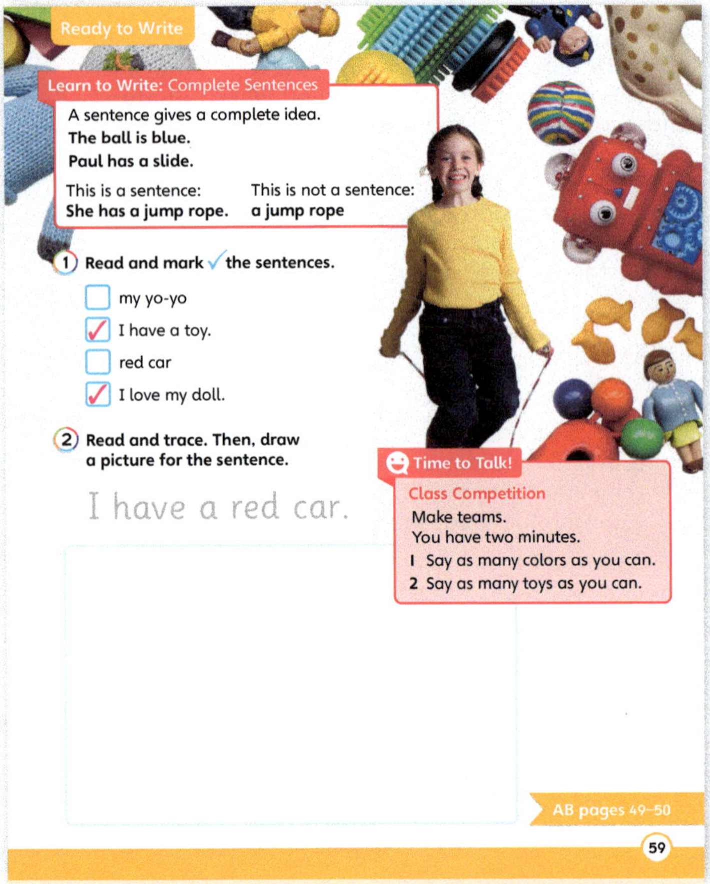
Ready to Write

Learn to Write: Complete Sentences

A sentence gives a complete idea.
The ball is blue.
Paul has a slide.

This is a sentence: **She has a jump rope.**
This is not a sentence: **a jump rope**

1 **Read and mark ✓ the sentences.**

- [ ] my yo-yo
- [x] I have a toy.
- [ ] red car
- [x] I love my doll.

2 **Read and trace. Then, draw a picture for the sentence.**

I have a red car.

Time to Talk!
Class Competition
Make teams.
You have two minutes.
1 Say as many colors as you can.
2 Say as many toys as you can.

AB pages 49–50

59

Objective: **to identify complete sentences**

Materials: Differentiated Instruction: (Below-level) simple sentences including capital letters and periods, simple incomplete sentences; (On-level) simple sentences with no capital letters or periods (one per pair of students); (Above-level) simple sentences with no capital letters or periods, cut up into three pieces (one per student)

Learn to Write Box

Write a sentence on the board, and read it aloud: *I have a big bag.* Ask a volunteer to come to the front, and say: *Point to a letter.* Then, have the volunteer say and circle the letter. Ask students to mention other letters they see in what you have written. Make reference to the alphabet. Ask for a different volunteer and say: *Point to a word.* Then, have the student underline the word. Tell students that a written word is made up of letters. Guide students to identify spaces between words. Ask students to count the number of words in the sentence you wrote. *(Five.)* Finally, circle the sentence, and say: *This is a sentence—a group of (…) that give a complete idea.* Encourage students to provide the missing words. Point to the first letter in the sentence, and ask: *Is this a capital or a lowercase letter? (Capital.)* Tell students that a sentence starts with a capital letter. Guide them to identify the period at the end of the sentence, and explain that many simple sentences end with a period. Draw students' attention to the Learn to Write box. Read the examples as you point to them. Ask students if they are sentences or not.

1 Read and mark ✓ the sentences.

Help students complete Activity 1. Guide them to identify capital letters and periods.

2 Read and trace. Then, draw a picture for the sentence.

Read the sentence in Activity 2, and ask: *Is this a sentence? (Yes.)* Help students identify the capital letter at the beginning of the sentence and the period at the end. Then, have students trace the sentence and draw a picture to illustrate it.

Time to Talk!

Form two teams, and ask each team to stand in a line. (In this way, all students will participate.) Ask a team to say as many colors as they can in two minutes. The first student in line says a color and then moves to the end of the line. Have the other team follow the same procedure but name toys. You could continue the exercise with other categories—school objects, names, letters, words, sentences, etc.

AB pages 49–50

Differentiated Instruction

Below-level ★	On-level ★★	Above-level ★★★
Form pairs. Distribute one simple sentence and one incomplete sentence to each pair. Tell students to identify which is a complete sentence.	Form pairs. Distribute the sentences you have prepared, one to each pair. Tell students to correct the sentences to make them complete. They will need to capitalize the first word and add a period.	Distribute the sentences you prepared, one to each student. Students have to put the pieces in the correct order, and capitalize the first word and add a period, to make complete sentences.

Objective: **to write sentences using drawings**

Materials: sheets of paper with the following: a smiley face, a picture of a boy, a picture of a girl, your age in digits; tape; poster with information about yourself in large writing and pictures:

My favorite color is (splotch of your color).
This is my (drawing of a school supply).
I have (splotch of the color) hair.
Don't touch my (drawing of any object)!
I'm (emoticon that shows an emotion).

Build Creativity: toys (one per student, brought from home)

Providing Examples

In everyday life, children need examples and learn by following them. This is equally true in the classroom. It is important to provide examples of how an exercise works. At this level especially, scaffolding is crucial as well. When you scaffold, you give support to students so that they have the tools to progressively reach independence in the learning process. In the activities below, scaffolding is used.

1 IDENTIFY

Write *I'm* _________ . on the board three times. Point to the first one. Say: *I'm ...* , while showing a picture of a happy face, and say: *happy*. Say the complete sentence again, pointing to the text and then showing the picture: *I'm happy*. Do the same showing your age in digits and then a picture of a girl or a boy. Say: *I'm happy. I'm (your age). I'm a (girl or boy)*. Tape the three drawings to the board to make three sentences.

2 WRITE

Ask students to write *I'm* in their notebooks and then write their age in digits or draw a cake with candles to represent their age. Then, help them complete sentences corresponding to the other two examples you provided on the board. (See Differentiated Instruction.)

3 EDIT

Tell students that they have written sentences. Elicit the use of a period at the end of each sentence. Ask students to swap notebooks with a partner to check they have used capital letters at the beginning of the sentences and periods at the end.

4 FOLLOW UP

Tape the poster you have made about yourself on the board. Read the first sentence, and when you reach the picture, encourage students to say the corresponding word. Do the same with the rest of the sentences. With this activity, you are supporting students in becoming independent writers and readers.

Fun Corner!

No Smiling!

Discuss which game the class would like to play. Some options are Musical Chairs, Statues, and What's the Time, Mr. Wolf? Tell the class to play the game, but without smiling or laughing. If they do, they're out until the next round.

Build Creativity!

Name the Toy

Objective: **Focus**

Ask students to take a small toy to class. Students take turns showing their toys to the class and saying a short sentence about it. Provide examples, such as: *This car is blue*, *This is a jump rope*, *The doll has curly hair*, etc.

Differentiated Instruction

Below-level ★	On-level ★★	Above-level ★★★
Provide students with sheets of paper with *I'm* written on them three times. Ask students to follow the examples on the board to complete the sentences.	Do Activity 2 as stated above.	Extend Activity 2 as described above by guiding students to also provide examples that use other sentence frames, such as *I have*, *This is*, and *My favorite toy is*. Complete these sentences on the board first, and then have students complete them in their notebooks.

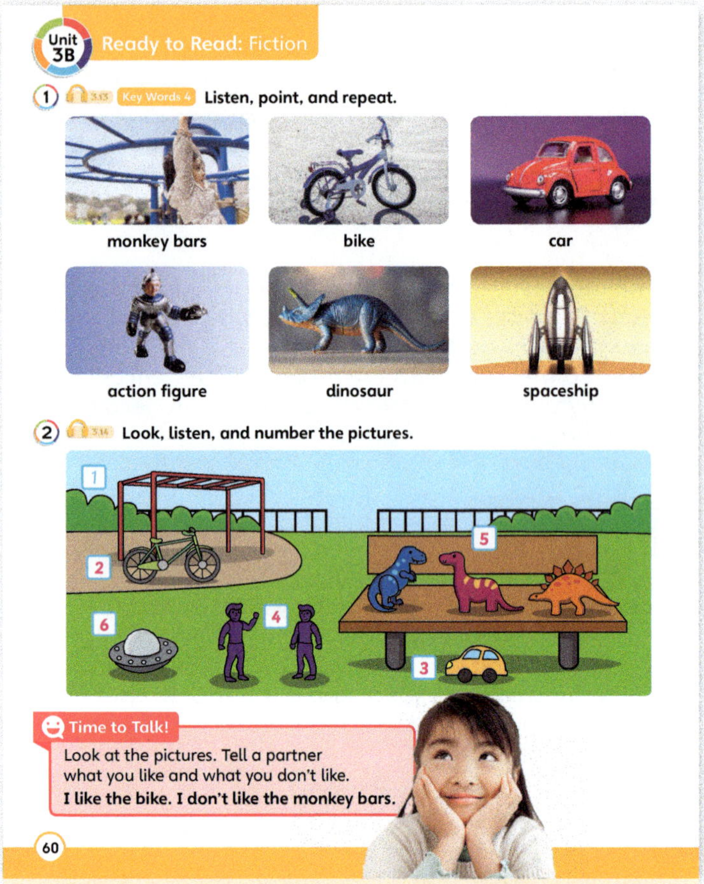

Unit 3B Ready to Read: Fiction

1 3.13 Key Words 4 Listen, point, and repeat.

monkey bars | bike | car

action figure | dinosaur | spaceship

2 3.14 Look, listen, and number the pictures.

Time to Talk!
Look at the pictures. Tell a partner what you like and what you don't like.
I like the bike. I don't like the monkey bars.

60

Objective: **to introduce vocabulary from a fiction text**

Key Words 4: ***monkey bars, bike, car, action figure, dinosaur, spaceship***

Materials: Audio CD 3.13, 3.14, colored pencils

1 3.13 Key Words 4 Listen, point, and repeat.

Point to the pictures in Activity 1 and say the words. Then, play Track 3.13, and ask students to point and repeat.

Practice Time 1 Tell students you will say the first part of the words they have just listened to and they have to complete them. For example, say: *bi … (bike), space … (spaceship)*. If necessary, play Track 3.13 again. Say the words in random order as many times as you consider necessary. You could also say the last part of words: *… ship*.

2 3.14 Look, listen, and number the pictures.

Ask students to look at the pictures in Activity 2. Form pairs. One student points to a toy, and the other names it. Then, students swap roles. Play Track 3.14, and have students number the toys. Check answers as a class.

Practice Time 2 Show colored pencils to review colors. Teach color names that students may not know, such as *gray*. Form pairs. Have one student say the color(s) of one toy in Activity 2 and the other guess the toy. For example, Student A says: *Green and gray*, and Student B guesses: *Bicycle*. Have students swap roles.

Time to Talk!

Hold up a colored pencil, and say: *I like (green)*. Then, hold up a different pencil, and say: *I don't like (purple)*. Use gestures to communicate the concepts "like" and "dislike." Ask volunteers to use colored pencils to do the same. Then, point to the toys in the book one at a time, and talk about which ones you like and which ones you dislike. Form pairs. Have students talk about which toys in Activity 2 they like and which they dislike. Go around the classroom to monitor that students say *the*: *I like the bike.*

Fun Corner!

Color Dictation

Ask a student to name a color. Draw a circle in that color on the board. Ask another student to name a different color. Draw a circle in that color next to the first. Continue until there are four colored circles in a row on the board. Tell students that you will dictate four colors and they have to draw a circle in each color in their notebooks. Check answers as a class. Then, form pairs. Student A dictates four colors to Student B, and Student A checks that they are correct. Have pairs swap roles.

Build Creativity!

Toys Play with Toys

Objective: A Different Point of View

Show pictures of common toys, such as a teddy bear, a doll, a soccer ball, and a toy car. Ask: *What toys do toys like to play with?* For example, the teddy bear might like to ride the toy car, and the doll might like to play soccer. Encourage students to be creative and to think of reasons for their answers.

AB page 51

Reading Strategy: Ordering Story Events

1 3.15 Listen and number the story events in order.

2 3.15 Listen again and number the sentences.

3 Thank you, mom.
1 I'm hungry.
2 I'm sad.
4 I'm so happy!

What toys do you and your friends play with at school?
We play with ...

61

Objective: to put story events in order and prepare to read a fiction text

Materials: Audio CD 3.15; Build Creativity: three sheets of paper showing a sequence of events in a simple story (e.g., an egg, the egg cracking, and a chick hatching), paper, tape

1 3.15 Listen and number the story events in order.

Have students look at the pictures in Activity 1. Tell them that they are scenes from a story. Guide students to identify the characters and the toys. Discuss with students what they think the order of the story events is. Then, play Track 3.15, and have students number the events in order. Play Track 3.15 again, and stop after each scene to check answers as a class.

2 3.15 Listen again and number the sentences.

Go through each of the sentences in Activity 2, and pantomime them. Then, play Track 3.15 again, and have students number the sentences.

Big Question Link

Discuss with students what they play with in the school playground. Guide them to start their answers with *We play with ...*

Build Creativity!

Tell Your Story

Objective: A Different Point of View

Show students the three sheets you prepared with scenes from a story in random order. Tell them that the scenes are events in a story. Ask students which scene comes first, which second, and which third. Tape the scenes in order to the board. Then, form groups of three students, and give three sheets of paper to each group. Tell students they should think of a story and three scenes from the story and then draw the scenes in order. Provide ideas to help students—for example, a person fishing, a fish, a plate with a fish on it; a child eating breakfast, brushing their teeth, and then going to school; a baby, the boy the baby has become, the adolescent the boy has become. It is important to give students examples for this activity. When students are ready, each group comes to the front and shows the three scenes in random order. Another group puts the scenes in order and tapes them to the board.

Build Creativity!

A Box Toy

Objective: Try, Try, and Try Again

Show students a box. Challenge them to think of as many different ways it could be used as a toy. Have students work individually, then in pairs, and then in small groups. Groups share their ideas with the class, and the class votes on the best ideas.

Objective: **to understand the importance of sharing**
Materials: Audio CD 3.16, 3.17; Fun Corner: two toys (if possible, toys mentioned in the fiction story)

Pre-Reading

Ask students to touch their hair. Then, say: *Don't touch your hair!* Use gestures. Repeat with other actions such as *Touch your desk*, *Don't touch your desk*, etc. Then, point to the story title, and read it. Have students go through the story pages, and elicit information about the characters and where the story takes place.

3.16 Page 62, section 1

Play Track 3.16 up to the end of the first paragraph. Pause and ask questions:

What's the girl's name?
What's the boy's name?
Where are they?

3.16 Page 62, section 2

Continue Track 3.16 up to the end of the second paragraph. Pause and ask questions:

What can you see in the park?
Are Hiro and Olivia happy?

Personalization

Ask: *Do you like parks? Why?*

3.16 Page 63, section 1

Play Track 3.16 up to the end of the first paragraph. Pause and ask questions:

Are Hiro and Olivia on the swings?
What can you see on the grass?
What toys can you see?

3.16 Page 63, section 2

Play the rest of Track 3.16. Ask questions:

Are Hiro and Olivia happy now?

Olivia says: Don't touch my … And don't touch my … Encourage students to provide the answers. Do the same for what Hiro says.

Think

Discuss with students how they feel when their friends or siblings do not share their toys with them. Remind students of the story from unit 2, *I Can't Find My Things!* Discuss whether Gemma shared her things with Max.

Personalization

Ask: *How do you feel when you share your things?*

3.16

Don't Touch!

By Irma Calvo

Hiro and Olivia are friends.
They are at the park.

They play on the monkey bars. They play on the swings. They ride their bikes. They have lots of fun.

62

3B

Then, they sit on the grass. They open their backpacks. The backpacks are full of toys.

There's a problem. Hiro and Olivia don't want to share their toys.
"Don't touch my cars!" says Hiro. "They're mine!"
"Don't touch my action figures!" says Olivia. "They're mine!"
"And don't touch my dinosaur," says Hiro.
"And don't touch my spaceship," says Olivia.

Think
Your friend says, "Don't touch my toys!" Does it make you feel happy or sad?

63

3.17 Page 64, section 1

Teach what *bored* means. Then, play Track 3.17 up to the end of the first paragraph. Pause and ask questions:

Is Hiro mad?
Is Olivia mad?
Who is bored?

3.17 Page 64, section 2

Continue Track 3.17 up to the end of the page. Pause and ask questions:

Are the children bored now?
Do they share their toys?
Do they agree?

Think

Discuss with students why they think Hiro and Olivia get bored.

3.17 Page 65

Play the rest of Track 3.17. Ask questions:

Do Hiro and Olivia have fun?
Where are the toys now?

Teach the meaning of *tomorrow*; tell students Hiro and Olivia will play the following day.

Think

Read the question in the Think box aloud. Encourage students to share their answers.

Personalization

Ask: *Where do you have fun with your friends?*

Fun Corner!

Performance

Call on a girl and a boy to play Olivia and Hiro. Ask them to bring their backpacks to the front. Give a toy to each of them. While you tell the story, guide students to play their parts. Simplify the story.

You: *Hiro and Olivia are at the park. They ride their bikes. Hiro and Olivia open their backpacks. They don't want to share.*

Hiro: *Don't touch my (car).*

Olivia: *Don't touch my (dinosaur).*

You: *The children are mad. The children are bored.*

Hiro: *Can I play with your (dinosaur)?*

Olivia: *OK.*

You: *Hiro and Olivia are happy.*

Hiro: *Bye, Olivia.*

Olivia: *See you tomorrow.*

Explore the Text

1 Look at the story. Number the pictures in order.

3 5 4 1 2 6

2 Look at Activity 1 and number the sentences in order.

2 They play on the swings.
5 They play together. They have lots of fun.
3 "Don't touch my action figures!"
1 Olivia and Hiro are at the park.
4 "Can I play with your spaceship?"
6 "Let's play again tomorrow."

Remember to listen to others.

Do you like to share your toys? Why or why not?

66

Objective: **to deepen understanding of a fiction text**
Materials: Fun Corner: sheets of paper, each with a large drawing or picture of the following: two backpacks, swings, a park, children laughing, a dinosaur, a child who is angry, two cars

1 Look at the story. Number the pictures in order.

Form pairs, and ask students to look carefully at the scenes in Activity 1. Have them number the scenes in order. Check answers as a class.

2 Look at Activity 1 and number the sentences in order.

Read each of the sentences in Activity 2, and have students write the number of the scene in Activity 1 it belongs to.

Big Question Link

Draw students' attention to Emma, the oracy character, and read the oracy reminder aloud. Then, point to the Big Question Link, and read the questions aloud. Discuss them with the class.

Fun Corner!

Oral Pictogram

Remind students about the sentences they wrote by using words and drawings. Tell them you will say some sentences from the story and they have to complete them by pointing to pictures that you will tape on the board. Take out the sheets of paper with the drawings or pictures, and tape them in random order on the board. Elicit the words they represent (*backpacks, swings, park, fun, dinosaur, mad, cars*). Then, ask a volunteer to come to the board. Say: *Hiro and Olivia are at the …* The student must complete the sentence by pointing to the picture of the park and saying the word. Continue with other sentences following the order in the story. Ask different students to come to the board and point to the drawings:

They play on the … (swings).

They have lots of … (fun).

They open their … (backpacks).

Don't touch my … (dinosaur).

The children are … (mad).

Can I play with your … (cars)?

Build Creativity!

Artistic Diversity

Objective: **A Different Point of View**

Discuss with students how artists can draw the same object but use different colors, shapes, sizes, styles, etc. Ask students to draw three of the toys from the story on different sheets of paper at home. Encourage students to draw their own versions of the toys and decorate them. The following class, have students present their drawings. Tape the same toys next to each other to show students how different other people's interpretations of a toy can be.

AB pages 52–53

Differentiated Instruction

Below-level ★	On-level ★★	Above-level ★★★
Review the fiction stories from units 1 and 2 using the same procedure as in the Fun Corner! activity on this page.	Review the fiction stories from units 1 and 2 using the same procedure as in the Fun Corner! activity on this page. Then, ask students to retell the stories by looking at the pictures on the board.	Review the fiction stories from units 1 and 2 using the same procedure as the Fun Corner! activity on this page. Ask students to retell the stories by looking at the pictures on the board. Then, have them invent their own versions of the stories. Provide a model if needed.

Grammar in Context

3B

Grammar: Negative Command

Don't touch my cars!

Don't run!

1 3.18 Listen and number. Then, listen again, point, and repeat.

4 3 Don't talk! 2 1

2 Look at the pictures and give commands.

Don't touch the ...

spider plant scissors

3 Play a game with a partner.

You and your partner are robots. Give your partner commands.

Don't run! Sit down!

67

Objective: to use negative commands
Materials: Audio CD 3.18

Grammar Box

Ask students to look at the pictures in the Grammar box. Point to the first picture, and read the sentence. Remind students of the reasons people use commands. Point to the second picture, and elicit the sentence.

1 3.18 Listen and number. Then, listen again, point, and repeat.

Ask students to look closely at each of the scenes in Activity 1. Elicit commands they would use in each situation. Play Track 3.18, and ask students to number the scenes. Check answers as a class. Play Track 3.18 again, and ask students to point and repeat.

2 Look at the pictures and give commands.

Discuss with students what is dangerous to touch (a wild animal, electrical outlets, hot water, etc.). Ask students to look at the pictures in Activity 2. Elicit sentences using *Don't touch*.

Practice Time | Tell students that you will give commands and they have to say them in the negative. Say: *Sit!* Elicit the negative using gestures: *Don't sit!* Do the same with these commands: *Jump! Touch my hair! Run! Stop! Stand! March! Listen! Open your books! Write your name! Read!*

3 Play a game with a partner.

Form pairs. One student is a robot that gives commands, and the other is a robot that follows them. Encourage students to use a robot-like voice. Have pairs switch roles.

Build Creativity!

Signs

Objective: Why, Why, Oh Why?

Direct students' attention to the sign in the Grammar box that represents *Don't run*. Guide them to explain to you what the diagonal line means. *(Don't.)* Ask students how they would draw the action *touch*. They will probably mention a hand. If students do not come up with an answer, help them to do so. Continue with other actions. Some options could be: *listen (ear), write (pencil), read (book), sit (chair), speak (mouth).* Have students work at home to draw and decorate signs (one per student) similar to the one in their books. Demonstrate how to go about the activity by drawing a big circle on the board, a hand inside, and a diagonal line. Say: *Don't touch!* The following class, students show their signs, and the rest of the class has to come up with the corresponding negative commands.

AB pages 54–55

Listening

1 3.19 Listen and circle.

a The children are playing a game.

b The children are reading a book.

2 3.19 Listen again and circle the two toys.

3 Play the game with a partner.

Oracy Time!

Do you like (action figures)?

Yes. / No.

Please repeat that.

Active Listening

1 Choose a toy.

2 Walk around. Ask the Oracy Time! question about the toy.

3 Listen actively and answer the questions.

4 Complete Check Your Oracy! in the Activity Book on page 57.

Values AB page 56

68

ACTIVITY BOOK PAGE 56

Values: Sharing

1 Who is sharing? Mark ✓.

2 Circle what we share.

3 Draw yourself.

What do you share with a friend?

Students' own answers

56

SB page 68

Objectives: to play a game; to understand the value of sharing

Materials: Audio CD 3.19, Cue Cards 2–4

1 3.19 Listen and circle.

Play Track 3.19. Read the two sentences in Activity 1, and ask students what the correct situation is. Have them circle it.

2 3.19 Listen again and circle the two toys.

Have students look at the toys in Activity 2. Elicit the name of each one. Play Track 3.19 again, and guide students to identify the two toys and circle them.

3 Play the game with a partner.

Practice with the class how to play the game in Activity 2. Form pairs to play the game. Go around the classroom to monitor performance.

Oracy Extension Activity

Read the steps in the Oracy Extension activity aloud. Ask students to choose a toy from Activity 2. Have them walk around and ask other students: *Do you like (robots)?* Remind students how active listening works. Tape Cue Cards 2 (*Yes.*), 3 (*No.*), and 4 (*Please repeat that.*) on the board, and have students use them to answer the questions. Ask students to complete Check Your Oracy! on page 57 of their Activity Books.

1 Who is sharing? Mark ✓.

Talk about how important it is to share. Ask students what they usually share with friends. Point to the pictures in Activity 1, and guide students to mark the pictures that involve sharing.

2 Circle what we share.

Help students identify the items. Then, guide them to circle the things they would share with a friend.

3 Draw yourself.

Ask students to draw a picture of themselves with something they usually share with a friend.

Fun Corner!

Now You See It, Now You Don't

Gather a collection of items on a table, ideally toys. Work as a class to name each of the objects, and then cover them. Ask students to make a list, in drawings, of all the objects. Then, have students compare lists in pairs. Two variations of this game are: Lay out the items in a certain order, then ask students to recall the order; Show the items, cover them, and take one away. Then, ask students to say which one is missing.

AB page 56

The Big Challenge

38

How can we make a toy?

Your challenge is to make a toy with recycled materials.

1 Work in small groups. Talk about your favorite toys.

2 Bring clean recycled materials to class.

3 Work together to make a toy.

4 Present your toy to the class.

5 Play with all the toys you made.

This is a car.

What is a toy? Look back through the unit. Share your ideas.

AB pages 57–59

69

Objective: to consolidate, extend, and personalize learning on the unit topic

Materials: clean recycled materials from home, tape, scissors; Differentiated Instruction: paper, materials to decorate students' toys

- Read the Big Challenge question and statement aloud. Point to the photo of the boy at the bottom of the page. Tell students that they are going to make a toy.
- **1** Read and explain the instruction. Form small groups, and encourage students to talk about their favorite toys. First, elicit expressions to use: *My favorite toy is … ; I like/don't like … ; My (car) is (blue); I have (ten) (cars).*
- **2** Ask each student to think of a toy they would like to make and to bring to class clean recycled materials to make that toy.
- **3** Form small groups, and ask students to make toys. Remind students that sharing materials and helping each other is very important.
- **4** Ask groups to present their toys to the class. Encourage students to use *This is …* (See Differentiated Instruction.) Optional: Record or have students record one another's presentations to share their work.
- **5** Tell students they can now play with the toys they made with other groups.

Home-school　Portfolio: Big Challenge

Big Question Circle

Read the Big Question aloud. Have the class revisit the Big Question Links on pages 52, 55, 61, and 66. Discuss what they have learned about what a toy is.

- Use the following questions to help review the Big Question:

  Can a box be a toy?
  What colors can toys be?
  What's your favorite toy?
  Do you like all your toys?
  Do you share your toys?

- Finally, have students turn to page 57 of their Activity Books to complete the Big Challenge self-assessment.

AB pages 57–59

Differentiated Instruction

Below-level ★	On-level ★★	Above-level ★★★
Ask students to decorate their toys. Then, have them categorize the toys by putting them together in groups; for example, cars should be together. With the help of students, create a paper label for each toy. Display the toys in the classroom, or organize an art exhibition.	Ask students to decorate their toys. Then, have them categorize the toys by putting them together in groups; for example, cars should be together. Have students each create a label with the name of their toy. Display the toys in the classroom, or organize an art exhibition.	Ask students to decorate their toys. Have them categorize the toys by putting them together in groups; for example, cars should be together. Have students each create a label for their toy using *This is* with the name of the toy and its color. (*This is a blue car.*) Display the toys in the classroom, or organize an art exhibition.

Oracy Performance Task 1: Collaboration

1-3

1 Look and match.

Listening to others | Agreeing and disagreeing | Ground rules

1 Take turns
2 Listen
3 Respect

Please repeat that.

Do you agree?

No.

YOUR TASK

a In pairs, choose three toys on page 71. Agree or disagree with your partner. *Students circle the photo of the soccer ball on page 71.*

Let's buy a jump rope. Do you agree?

Yes.

b 3.20 Listen and circle the correct toy on page 71.

A ball, please.

Here you go.

Thank you.

c Play Store with your partner. Remember your ground rules.

yo-yo | play dough | boat | board game

bike | action figure | jump rope | soccer ball

doll | dinosaur | jigsaw puzzle | dollhouse

Check Your Oracy!

	☺	☺☺	☺☺☺
1 I listened.			
2 I agreed and disagreed.			
3 I took turns.			

70 71

Objective: to apply oracy skills by doing a collaborative task
Oracy Performance Task Words: ***please, here you go, thank you***
Materials: Audio CD 3.20, three toys with labels with their prices on them

1 Look and match.

Remind students of the oracy skills that they have learned in units 1–3. Read each of the categories in Activity 1, and guide students to match the categories to the pictures. Read the text in the pictures as well to help students with the matching.

YOUR TASK

Place the three toys with price labels on your desk, and tell students that your desk is now a toy store. Ask a volunteer to join you. Point to one of the toys, and say: *Let's buy (a car). Do you agree?* Perform the same scene with other volunteers to elicit examples both of agreement and of disagreement. Leave the toys on your desk. Direct students' attention to the toys on page 71. Go over each of the toys, and have students repeat after you. Mention the toys in random order, and ask students to point to them. Tell students they should imagine the toys belong to the same toy store.

- **a** Form pairs. Ask students to choose three toys, using *Let's …* and *Do you agree?* Monitor students' work.
- **b** 3.20 Ask a volunteer to come to your desk. Act as the seller, and guide the student to act as the buyer. Provide set expressions for the student to follow: … , *please.* and *Thank you.* Teach *Here you go.* by using gestures. Then, play Track 3.20, and have students circle the correct toy on page 71.
- **c** Tell students they will be playing Store with a partner. This time, they will buy toys from page 71. Remind students of the importance of taking turns. Optional: Record or have students record one another's role plays to share their work.

Home-school | Portfolio: Oracy Performance

AB pages 60–61

4 What makes a home?

Literacy

Read: a nonfiction text about different children's homes; a fiction text about a snail trying to find its home

Reading Strategies: comparing; identifying plot and setting

Ready to Write

Learn to Write: nouns

Getting Ready to Write: make a pictionary

Oracy

Skill: Taking Turns

Cue Cards 5–6: 5. *It's my turn.* 6. *It's your turn.*

Speaking Mission: describe an object you lost

Language

Key Words 1: *home, family, dining room, living room, bedroom, kitchen*

Key Words 2: *apartment, room, water, garden, stove, bed*

Key Words 3: *roof, stairs*

Key Words 4: *snail, ladybug, forest, spider, butterfly, mouse*

Speaking Mission Words: *socks, T-shirt, hat, jacket, skirt, glasses*

Grammar in Context

Prepositions: *It's in the kitchen. It's on the roof. It's under the tree house.*

Verb *to be*: *Yes/No* Questions (Singular): *Is Mouse under a tree? No, he isn't. Is Spider under the leaf? Yes, he is.*

Phonics

Ending Sounds: *-ut, -ig*

Listening

Poem: "My Home!"

Values

Helping Others

The Big Challenge

How can I describe my home?
Make your home and describe it to the class

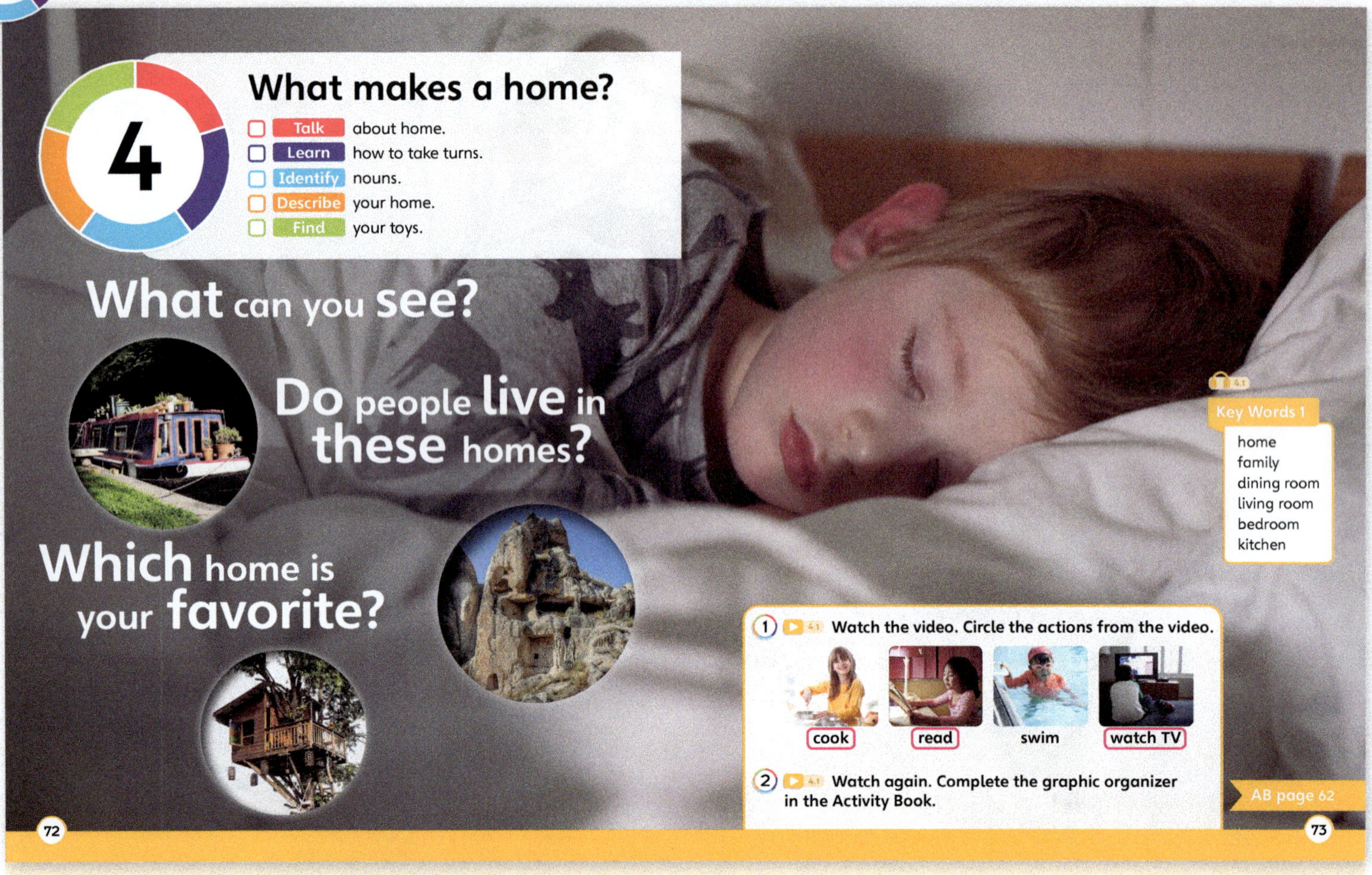

Objective: to introduce the topic of what makes a home
Key Words I: ***home, family, dining room, living room, bedroom, kitchen***
Materials: Video 4.I, Audio CD 4.I, Flashcards 4.I–4.6

WHAT MAKES A HOME?

- Ask students to open their books to page 72. Read the Big Question aloud. Encourage students to share if they live in a house or in another type of home. Read the first question, and have students say what they can see.
- Ask the second question, and encourage students to say whether they know of any other types of homes.
- Finally, ask the last question. Have students vote to see which home is the winner.

4.1 Key Words 1 Use the flashcards and audio to present Key Words I. Hold up the flashcards as you play Track 4.I. Have students repeat the words. Put the flashcards facedown on your desk. Show them one at a time, and have the class say the words. Then, call on individual students to say the words.

1 4.1 Watch the video. Circle the actions from the video.

Watch the video, and pause after "Let's find out!" Ask: *What is today's Big Question? (What makes a home?)* Continue the video. Pause after "… or small?" Invite volunteers to answer the question and to say how many family members live with them. Continue the video. Pause after "Home is where all your things are." Encourage students to recall the places and activities mentioned. Finally, play the rest of the video. Have students do Activity I. Check answers as a class.

2 4.1 Watch again. Complete the graphic organizer in the Activity Book.

Form pairs. Play the video again, and have students complete Activity I on AB page 62.

AB page 62

Objective: to compare and prepare to read a nonfiction text

Key Words 1: ***home, family, dining room, living room, bedroom, kitchen***

Materials: Audio CD 4.1, 4.2, 4.3, Flashcards 4.1–4.6; Build Creativity: paper, crayons

4.1 **Key Words 1** Use the flashcards and audio to review Key Words 1.

1 4.2 Listen, point, and repeat.

Have students look at the picture in Activity 1 and identify each room in the house. Play Track 4.2, and encourage students to repeat the words. Ask individual students to say the words to check pronunciation.

1 4.3 Listen and circle the correct answers.

Call on individual students, and encourage them to talk about their bedrooms by asking questions: *Is your bedroom big or small? What color is it? What toys do you have in your bedroom?* Introduce the children in the photos to students, and ask questions about the pictures, such as: *What color is this bedroom? What are these toys?* Play Track 4.3, and pause after Ahmet's response. Have students circle the corresponding pictures. Continue with Sabita. Check answers as a class.

Big Question Link

Point to the Big Question Link, and read it aloud. Ask volunteers to compare their bedrooms to the children's bedrooms.

Fun Corner!

Which Room?

Draw six columns on the board, and label each with a word for a room in the house in Activity 1. Read the words out loud. In each column, draw something that is found in the room. For example, draw a fork under *kitchen* and a bar of soap under *bathroom*. Divide the class into three groups, and assign two rooms to each. Ask each group to form a line. When you say *Go!*, a student from each group goes to the board and draws an object that is found in either of the group's two assigned rooms. Continue until all students have drawn something. Then, as a class, evaluate whether the drawings are each in the correct room.

Room Charades

Play Charades with the class. Review the names of the rooms in a home. Mime an action that would be typical of each room. For example, pretend you are cooking. Students have to guess the action and say which room you are in. The first person to guess correctly performs the next mime.

Build Creativity!

My Bedroom

Objective: Focus

Ask students to draw a big bed in their notebooks or on a sheet of paper. Tell them that the bed represents their bedroom, and ask them to make it the color of their room. Then, inside the bed, have students write "BIG" or "SMALL" and draw a toy they have in their bedrooms. When they have finished, have students talk about their bedrooms in pairs: *My bedroom is (blue). It's (big). I have (cars) in my bedroom.*

4.4 **Key Words 2** Use Flashcards 4.7–4.12 and the audio to pre-teach Key Words 2. Hold up each flashcard as students listen to Track 4.4. Have students repeat each word. Ask which rooms in a home the *stove* and *bed* Flashcards belong to.

Pre-Reading

Have students look at pages 75 and 76. Ask: *How many kinds of homes can you see? (Four.)* Ask students if any of the homes on these pages are similar to the ones on page 72. Display Flashcards 4.1–4.6 on the board. Ask students to search in the text for the words on the flashcards. Have them circle the words. Ask: *How many words from the flashcards are in the text? (Five.) Which word is not in the text? (Family.)* Have students count the times the word *home* is repeated. Then, ask a volunteer to come to the front. Ask the class to search for numbers in the text and dictate them to the volunteer. Play Tracks 4.5 and 4.6 while students look at the pictures.

4.5 Page 75, section 1

Play Track 4.5 up to "... and three bedrooms." Pause and ask questions:

What's the girl's name?
What kind of home is Lisa's home?
How many rooms does Lisa's home have? Six, seven, or eight?
How many bedrooms does is have? One, two, or three?

Personalization

Ask: *How many rooms does your home have? How many bedrooms does it have? How many bathrooms does it have?*

4.5 Page 75, section 2

Play the rest of Track 4.5. Ask questions:

What is Lisa's favorite room in her home?
Where is Lisa's cat?

Personalization

Ask: *What is your favorite room in your home?*

Objective: to learn that there are different kinds of homes

Key Words 2: ***apartment, room, water, garden, stove, bed***

Materials: Audio CD 4.4, 4.5, Flashcards 4.1–4.12

Build Creativity!

My Favorite Place

Objective: Why, Why, Oh Why?

Have students close their eyes and imagine they are standing outside their front door. Before they open the door, ask: *How do you feel about arriving home? When you open the door, where are you going to go? Think about all the rooms in your home. Which is your favorite room? Go to that room. What's your favorite place in that room? Go and sit there.* Invite volunteers to describe their favorite place and say why they like it.

All Kinds of Homes

This is Akila's home. It's a houseboat. It floats on **water**. It has a kitchen, a living room, a bathroom, and two bedrooms.

Look! It has a **garden**, too. Where is it? It's on the roof.

This is Pablo's home. It's a tree house. You climb stairs to get inside. It has four rooms—a kitchen, a living room, and two bedrooms.

Where's the bathroom? It's under the tree house.

This is Kallic's home. It's an igloo. It has one big room. It has a **stove** and a big **bed**.

Think

Which house is your favorite?

76

4.6 Page 76, section 1

Play Track 4.6 through "It's on the roof." Pause and ask questions:

What's the girl's name?
What's Akila's home?
Where is it?
How many rooms does it have?
What is on the roof?

4.6 Page 76, section 2

Play Track 4.6 through "It's under the tree house." Pause and ask questions:

What's the boy's name?
What's Pablo's home?
How many rooms does it have?
Where is the bathroom?

4.6 Page 76, section 3

Play the rest of Track 4.6. Ask questions:

What's the boy's name?
What's Kallic's home?
How many rooms does it have?
What's inside the igloo?

Personalization

Have students compare their homes to Akila's, Pablo's, and Kallic's homes.

Think

Read the question in the Think box aloud. Form pairs. Encourage students to ask and answer the question. Monitor, and provide support.

AB page 63

Differentiated Instruction

Below-level ★	On-level ★★	Above-level ★★★
Ask students to draw their favorite home from the text in their notebooks. Ask them to write the word for the kind of home under their drawing.	Ask students to draw their favorite home from the text in their notebooks. Ask them to write the word for the kind of home under their drawing along with other words related to that home. For example, they could write *four rooms* for the tree house.	Ask students to draw their favorite home from the text in their notebooks. Ask them to write the word for the kind of home under their drawing along with two sentences about the home. For example, they could write *This is Pablo's home.*

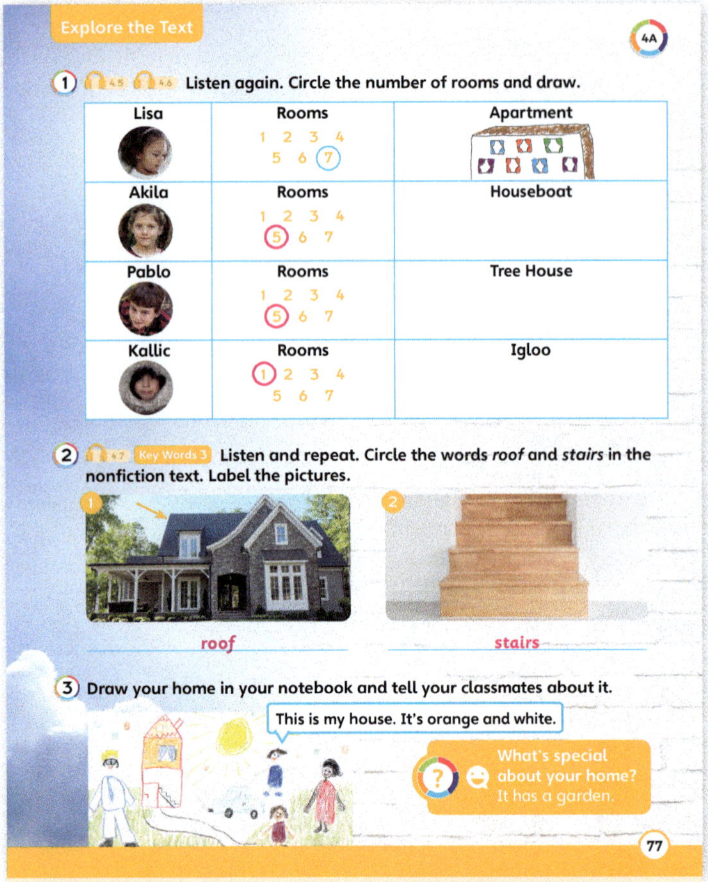
Explore the Text

4A

1 4.5 4.6 Listen again. Circle the number of rooms and draw.

Lisa	Rooms 1 2 3 4 5 6 (7)	Apartment
Akila	Rooms 1 2 3 4 (5) 6 7	Houseboat
Pablo	Rooms 1 2 3 4 (5) 6 7	Tree House
Kallic	Rooms (1) 2 3 4 5 6 7	Igloo

2 4.7 Key Words 3 Listen and repeat. Circle the words *roof* and *stairs* in the nonfiction text. Label the pictures.

1 roof 2 stairs

3 Draw your home in your notebook and tell your classmates about it.

This is my house. It's orange and white.

What's special about your home? It has a garden.

77

Objective: to recall specific information from the text and identify words in context

Key Words 3: ***roof, stairs***

Materials: Audio CD 4.5, 4.6, 4.7; Build Creativity: pictures of different homes around the world (caves, stilt houses, lighthouses, etc.), paper

1 4.5 4.6 Listen again. Circle the number of rooms and draw.

Use the example about Lisa to guide students to do Activity I while they listen to the nonfiction text again. Play Tracks 4.5 and 4.6. Then, check answers as a class.

2 4.7 Key Words 3 Listen and repeat. Circle the words *roof* and *stairs* in the nonfiction text. Label the pictures.

Guide students to identify the key words in the nonfiction text. Ask two volunteers to come to the board and write the two words. Then, ask students to label the pictures in their books. Go around the classroom and check spelling.

3 Draw your home in your notebook and tell your classmates about it.

Draw your home on the board. Describe it in terms of color and size. Say how many rooms it has and what the rooms are. Mention distinctive features—a garden, stairs, etc. Have students draw the outside of their home. Then, form small groups, and ask students to describe their homes to the rest of the group.

Big Question Link

Tell students what is special about your home. Then, ask them to tell you what is special about theirs.

Build Creativity!

Imaginary Houses

Objective: A Different Point of View

Tell students about special homes around the world. Explain to them that some people live in caves, stilt houses, and lighthouses, among other types of homes. Show the class pictures of different types of homes so that students get familiar with them. Hand out the paper. Ask students to pretend they are an architect and create an imaginary home—for example, a floating home, a home made of ice, a home inside a big tree, or a spaceship home. Students draw their homes at home and then present them to the class. Encourage them to think about special features for their homes and about the number of rooms they have.

Fun Corner!

Sad Man

Form two groups, Group A and Group B. Ask each group to choose ten words from the nonfiction text and write them on a piece of paper without letting the other group see them. Group A goes to the front and writes a blank line for each letter in a word. Group B makes guesses: *Is there a p in the word?* If group B guesses a letter, Group A fills in the corresponding blank. If Group B does not guess, Group A draws a circle for the head of the sad man. For every wrong guess, Group A draws another part of the man—a vertical line for the body, two arms, two legs, two eyes, and a frowning mouth. If the word is guessed before the mouth is drawn, Group B wins a point. The winner is the group that gets the most points.

AB pages 64–65

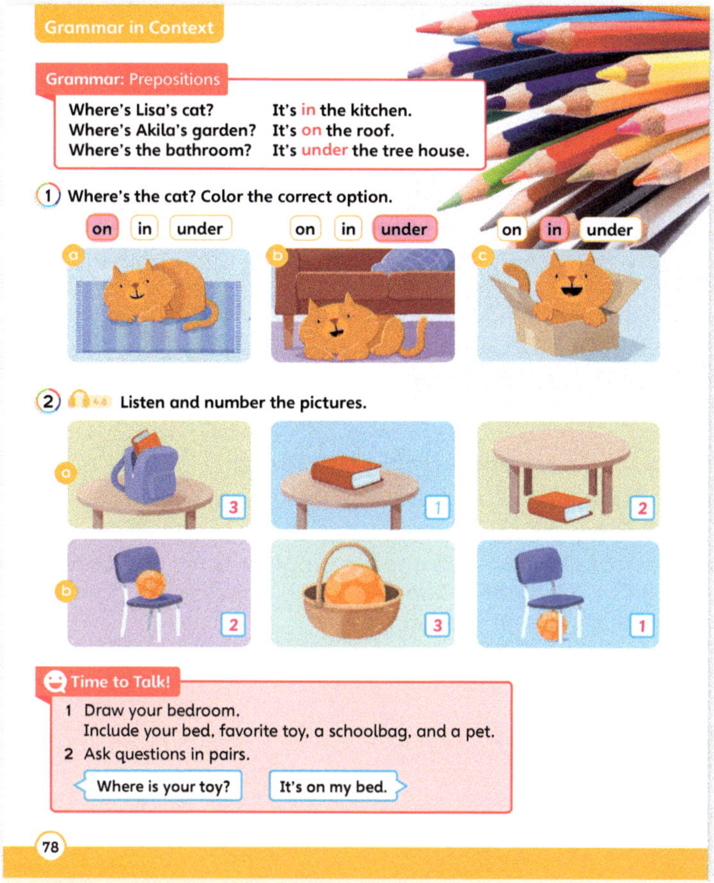

Objective: **to use prepositions**

Materials: Audio CD 4.8, paper; Fun Corner: tape, four big sheets of butcher paper—two with identical drawings of a kitchen, two with identical drawings of a bedroom (the rooms should only include basic furniture, e.g., the kitchen could have a stove, chairs, a table, an open refrigerator, and a cabinet)

Grammar Box

Ask questions about the nonfiction text as you point to the pictures on pages 75 and 76: *Where is Lisa's cat? Is it in the bedroom or in the kitchen?* As you ask the questions, use your hands to indicate what each preposition means. Continue by asking questions about school objects in the classroom.

1 Where's the cat? Color the correct option.

Ask students to look at the pictures in Activity 1. Guide them to do the activity.

Practice Time 1 Draw a chair on the board. Draw a cat under it, and ask: *Where is the cat?* Call on a volunteer to answer the question. Draw other pictures to practice *on* and *in*. Then, ask volunteers to come to the board to draw similar pictures and to ask questions about their pictures with *Where's … ?* for other students to answer.

2 4.8 Listen and number the pictures.

Play Track 4.8, and do Activity 2 as a class.

Time to Talk!

Explain to students how the activity works. Form pairs, and go around the classroom to monitor performance. Then, have students change partners.

Fun Corner!

How Similar Are They?

Form two teams, and have them work as far away from each other as possible. Give a drawing of the bedroom to one team and a drawing of the kitchen to the other. Review the name of each piece of furniture as needed. On the board, draw objects that students are familiar with, such as school objects and toys. Ask teams to draw the objects on, in, and under the furniture in their pictures. Once the teams have finished, tape the other drawings of the kitchen and bedroom on the board. Ask one team to go to the front and the other to dictate where their objects are in their drawing. For example, the team with the drawing of the kitchen may say: *The ball is on the stove.* The other team draws the ball on the stove. Then, the teams switch roles. Finally, compare the original drawings with the ones on the board. The team whose drawing is the most similar to the original drawing wins.

Build Creativity!

Bedroom Visualization

Objective: **A Different Point of View**

Have students stand up, making sure there is plenty of space between them so they won't bump into each other. Tell them to close their eyes and imagine they are standing in their bedrooms. Say: *Point to your bed. Now walk over to your bed. What is on your bed? Get on your knees, and look under your bed. What can you see?* Continue in this way with other areas of the room, such as the closet or the bedside table. As they are "looking," call on individual students to describe what they see.

AB pages 66–67

Phonics

4A

1 4.9 Listen, point, and repeat.

nut cut hut

big wig dig

2 4.10 Listen and underline the correct words.

a cut hut
b wig big
c but nut
d big fig

3 4.11 Listen and sing the songs.

Look at this chick.
His name is Stig.
He has a wig,
A big, big wig!
He likes to dig,
With his big wig.
His name is Stig.

Nuts, nuts,
I love nuts.
A nut in a hut.
Big nuts,
Peanuts,
Any kind of nut.
I love nuts!

79

Objective: to identify the ending sounds *-ut* and *-ig*

Materials: Audio CD 4.9, 4.10, 4.11

1 4.9 Listen, point, and repeat.

Ask students to look at the pictures in Activity 1. Play Track 4.9, and ask students to point and repeat. Then, point to the pictures in random order, and ask individual students to repeat after you.

2 4.10 Listen and underline the correct words.

Before doing Activity 2, point to the picture of the hut. Say: *Is this a cut or a hut?* This way, students will first concentrate on the sounds, rather than on the spelling. Do the same with the rest of the pictures. Then, play Track 4.10, and have students underline the correct words, providing help as needed.

3 4.11 Listen and sing the songs.

Tell students they will be listening to a song about a chick with a wig. Play the first song on Track 4.11. Then, sing the song, pausing for students to complete the lyrics: *Look at this ... His name is Stig. He has a ...* Follow the same procedure for the second song.

AB page 68

Differentiated Instruction

Below-level ★	On-level ★★	Above-level ★★★
Review the ending sounds from unit 3, and practice the new ones from this unit: Draw a cat and say the word, emphasizing the ending sounds. Encourage students to recall words that end with the same sound. Ask individual students to come to the board and illustrate the words they recall next to the drawing of the cat. Do the same with words ending in *-en*, *-ut*, and *-ig*.	Review the ending sounds from unit 3, and practice the new ones from this unit: Write *-at*, *-en*, *-ut*, and *-ig* in columns on the board. Pronounce the sound *-at*, and encourage students to recall words from unit 3 that end with this sound. Ask individual students to illustrate the words they mention. For example, they draw a cat in the *-at* column. Continue with the rest of the ending sounds.	Review the ending sounds from unit 3, and practice the new ones from this unit: Write *-at*, *-en*, *-ut*, and *-ig* in columns on the board. Pronounce the sound *-at*, and encourage students to recall words from unit 3 that end with this sound. Ask individual students to write the words they mention. For example, they write *cat* in the *-at* column. Continue with the rest of the ending sounds.

Oracy

Oracy Skill: Taking Turns

1 4.2 4.12 Watch and answer the questions.

a Are they playing a game or doing their homework? *They are playing a game.*
b What does Jack say at the end? *Good job!*
c Are they taking turns? *Yes, they are.*

Let's Practice Oracy! 5, 6

1 Form pairs. Play Tic-Tac-Toe.
2 Remember to take turns.

Check Your Oracy!	
1 I played.	Yes / No
2 I took turns.	Yes / No
3 I spoke in English.	Yes / No

80

Objective: to learn how to take turns
Cue Cards: 5. ***It's my turn.*** 6. ***It's your turn.***
Materials: Video 4.2, Audio CD 4.12, Cue Cards 5–6, paper; Fun Corner: simple games (brought to class by students)

Oracy Skill

Discuss with students how important it is to take turns in certain situations, such as when you play board games. With students, brainstorm other situations that require taking turns.

1 4.2 4.12 Watch and answer the questions.

Give students time to look at the drawings in Activity 1. Then, play V4.2, and have students answer the questions. Check answers as a class.

Present and Practice Hold up Cue Cards 5 and 6. Read the sentences out loud, and ask students to repeat after you. Leave the Cue Cards on the board. Ask students to watch and listen carefully as you play the video again. Then, ask a volunteer to come to the board and play Tic-Tac-Toe with you. Explain the rules of the game to the class to make sure everyone understands the game. Guide the student to use the expressions from the Cue Cards as well as *I win!* and *Good job!* Repeat the game with another volunteer.

Let's Practice Oracy! 5, 6

- **1** Ask students to form pairs to play Tic-Tac-Toe.
- **2** Go around the classroom, and check if pairs are taking turns and using the expressions correctly. You could organize a Tic-Tac-Toe class competition and give prizes to the three best players.
- Optional: Record or have students record themselves as they practice oracy.
- Have students complete Check Your Oracy!

Home-school Portfolio: Oracy

Fun Corner!

Time to Take Turns!

Ask students what (non-digital) games they have at home. Possibilities include checkers, dominoes, card games for kids, puzzles, and board games. Assign individual students to bring a game to class. Avoid complicated games that would take too much class time. The main objective of this activity is to practice the oracy skill of taking turns and the related expressions. Before playing the games, review the expressions used by the oracy characters in Activity 1.

AB page 68

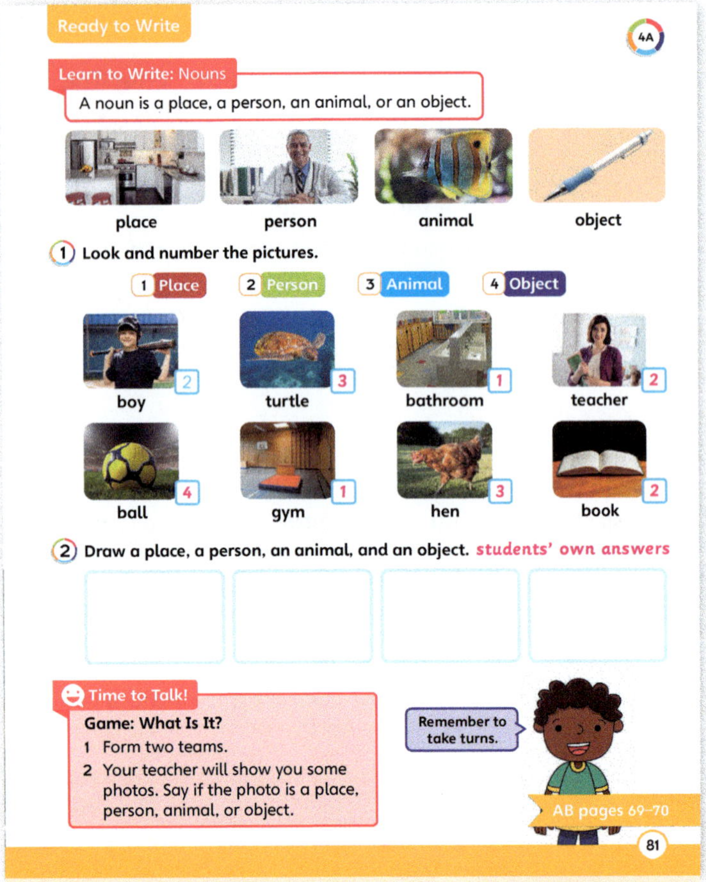

Ready to Write

4A

Learn to Write: Nouns

A noun is a place, a person, an animal, or an object.

place | person | animal | object

1 Look and number the pictures.

1 Place | 2 Person | 3 Animal | 4 Object

boy 2 | turtle 3 | bathroom 1 | teacher 2

ball 4 | gym 1 | hen 3 | book 2

2 Draw a place, a person, an animal, and an object. students' own answers

Time to Talk!

Game: What Is It?

1 Form two teams.

2 Your teacher will show you some photos. Say if the photo is a place, person, animal, or object.

Remember to take turns.

AB pages 69–70

81

Objective: to identify nouns

Materials: units 1, 2, 3, and 4 Flashcards (nouns only), photos of animals

Learn to Write Box

Tape three flashcards to the board, each one representing a different category: place, person, and object. Then, draw an animal. Explain that the pictures are examples of nouns. As you point to each picture, say: *A place is a noun. A person is a noun. An object is a noun. An animal is a noun. They are all nouns.* Leave the flashcards on the board. Have students look at the pictures below the Learn to Write box. Read the definition of a noun as you point to each picture.

1 Look and number the pictures.

Tell students that all the things in the pictures in Activity 1 are nouns. Read each of the categories, and guide students to complete the activity with you.

2 Draw a place, a person, an animal, and an object.

Have students do Activity 2. Then, form pairs, and ask them to say a sentence about each drawing and which category each drawing belongs to: *This is a living room. It's a place.*

Time to Talk!

Before students play the game, draw their attention to Liam, the oracy character. Remind them of the expressions they can use to make sure they are taking turns. Then, take out units 1, 2, and 3 Flashcards and the photos of animals. Form two teams, and play the What Is It? game.

AB pages 69–70

Differentiated Instruction

Below-level ★	On-level ★★	Above-level ★★★
Say a simple sentence that contains one noun, for example, *I have a dog.* Help students identify the noun, *dog*. Ask students to draw a dog in their notebooks. Continue with other sentences, such as *I'm a girl. My school is fun. My teacher is tall.* For each, ask students to draw the noun in their notebooks.	Write a simple sentence that contains one noun on the board, for example, *I have a dog*. Read the sentence out loud, and ask a volunteer to come to the board and circle the noun. Continue with more sentences, such as *I'm a girl. My school is fun. My teacher is tall. Turtles are slow. My colored pencils are new.*	Write a simple sentence that contains one noun on the board, for example, *I have a dog*. Read the sentence out loud, and ask a volunteer to come to the board and circle the noun. Continue with more sentences, such as *I'm a girl. My teacher is tall. Turtles are slow.* Then, ask students to write all the nouns from the board in their notebooks and draw them.

Objective: **to make a pictionary in groups**

Materials: paper, glue, cards with four different categories: place, person, animal, object; small pictures or drawings of places, people, animals, and objects students can name in English (brought to class by students)

Categorizing

Why is categorizing so important? Ask students to tell you some things they categorize and how they categorize them. They may mention examples such as putting socks in one drawer and shirts in another or putting toys in a box and books on a shelf. Encourage students to provide as many examples as possible. Elicit reasons for categorizing, for example, *It helps us to find things more easily.*

1 IDENTIFY

Form small groups. Show the cards with categories to the class, and read them aloud. Then, hold up a card, and ask groups to show pictures that match the category. Do the same with the rest of the categories.

2 WRITE

Ask groups to put their pictures or drawings into categories (place, person, animal, object). Guide them to write the name of each category at the top of a sheet of paper. Have them start with one category, glue the corresponding pictures/drawings to the paper, and label each picture with an erasable pencil. For example, they write *girl* under the picture of a girl. Have them continue with the rest of the categories. (See Differentiated Instruction.)

3 EDIT

Ask groups to exchange their pictionaries with other groups. Ask groups to check if the words that have been written under the pictures are correct and are spelled correctly. If they are not, ask groups to mark the incorrect words with an erasable pencil so that students can edit and finalize their own work.

4 FOLLOW UP

Have students paste one picture per category in their notebooks and label them.

Fun Corner!

Hot and Cold

Take some kitchen utensils to class. Place the *kitchen* Flashcard on the board. Invite students to pretend they are in a kitchen. Teach the words *cold, very cold, hot,* and *very hot.* Form pairs. Give a utensil to each pair and guide them to play Hot and Cold. One student in each pair goes outside the classroom while their partner hides the utensil. Students return to the classroom and search for the utensils as their partners guide them by saying *cold, warm,* or *hot.*

Build Creativity!

Choose the Location

Objective: Focus

Give each student a piece of paper. Ask them to choose and draw one object that belongs in the bedroom, the kitchen, the bathroom, or the garden. Place the *bedroom, kitchen, bathroom,* and *garden* Flashcards in different places around the classroom and place a bag next to each flashcard. Collect students' drawings and place them face down on a desk. Ask students to form a line. The first student chooses a drawing, puts it in its corresponding bag, and takes their seat, allowing the next student to play. Review the results as a class. Note that there may be objects that belong to two different places, such as a chair.

Differentiated Instruction

Below-level ★	On-level ★★	Above-level ★★★
Simplify the writing task for Activity 2. Instead of asking students to write the word, ask them to write its first letter—for example, *g* under the picture of a girl.	Do Activity 2 as stated above.	Modify the last part of Activity 2 by asking students to arrange and then glue the pictures in alphabetical order.

Unit 4B Ready to Read: Fiction

1 4.13 Key Words 4 Listen, point, and repeat.

snail ladybug forest

spider butterfly mouse

2 Match the animals with their homes.

3 In your notebook, draw an animal inside its home.

Do you have a pet at home?

82

Objective: to introduce vocabulary from a fiction text

Key Words 4: ***snail, ladybug, forest, spider, butterfly, mouse***

Materials: Audio CD 4.13; Fun Corner: thick yarn, scissors

1 4.13 Key Words 4 Listen, point, and repeat.

Point to the pictures in Activity 1, and ask students if they can name the animals and place in the pictures. Ask questions about the color of each animal and what other colors these animals can be. Then, play Track 4.13, and have students point and repeat. Correct pronunciation.

Practice Time 1 Write the first two or three letters of each key word on the board. Ask students to provide the rest of the letters to complete each word. Then, ask individual students to spell the words orally and others to come to the board and write them.

2 Match the animals with their homes.

Guide students to identify the animal homes. Ask them why homes are also important to animals. Then, have students match the animals to their homes.

Practice Time 2 Using the pictures in Activity 2, teach two words from the fiction text: *hole* and *shell*. Draw a big shell on the board, and encourage students to think about what animals live in shells (e.g., turtles and crabs). Ask students to draw an animal inside the shell on the board. Do the same with a drawing of a big hole. Elicit animals that might live there (e.g., mice, rabbits, and foxes). Encourage students to mention other homes animals live in (e.g., caves, tunnels, hives, and nests).

3 In your notebook, draw an animal inside its home.

Ask students to choose an animal they like and to draw it inside its home.

Big Question Link

Ask students if they have pets at home. Encourage volunteers to share what types of pets they have. Brainstorm with students what types of pets other people around the world have.

Fun Corner!

The Web

Make a "web" of yarn on the floor. Form three teams, and ask them to stand in lines. One at a time, students must cross the web without stepping on the yarn. The team whose members touched the web the fewest times wins the game.

Build Creativity!

Homes on Our Backs

Objective: A Different Point of View

Talk about animals that carry their homes on their backs. How many can students think of? (snails, turtles, some crabs, etc.) Then, say: *Imagine your home is on your back. What do you carry? Do you carry only things you need, or do you also carry things you want? Where do you sleep?* Brainstorm as a class things we need, such as clothes, and things we want, such as toys. Have students work individually to answer the question of what they would carry and then compare answers with a partner. You may wish to make the task more difficult by telling students they can carry no more than ten items.

AB page 71

Reading Strategy: Plot and Setting

Plot: What is the story about?
A girl and two lambs.
Setting: Where does the story take place?
On a farm.

1 **Look at the book cover. Circle the correct answer.**

a Plot: What is the story about?
Friends. **Homes.**
b Setting: Where does the story take place?
On the beach. **In the forest.**

Time to Talk!
Think of your favorite story.
What is it about?
Where does it take place?

83

Objective: **to introduce the terms *plot* and *setting* and prepare to read a fiction text**
Materials: Build Creativity: paper

1 Look at the book cover. Circle the correct answer.

Talk to students about well-known storybooks. Ask what the stories are about and where they take place. Use these examples to explain plot and setting. Have students look at the picture next to the Reading Strategy box. Introduce the words *lamb* and *farm*. Read the questions and answers in the Reading Strategy box aloud. Then, have students focus on the book cover in Activity 1. Ask questions about the cover to help understanding. Complete the activity as a class.

Time to Talk!

Ask a volunteer the questions in the box. If students need help with ideas, remind them of stories discussed in Activity 1 and mention other stories they are likely to know.

Build Creativity!

Book Covers

Objective: A Different Point of View

Before doing this activity, brainstorm places where a story could take place. Draw them on the board with the help of volunteers. For example, you could draw a house, a school, a beach, a park, a store, a forest, a castle, and a farm. Teach any new words to students so that they can talk about the settings later on. Do the same with people or animals that could be the protagonists of a story. This vocabulary will help students to define and discuss the plot of their stories. Then, have students work individually to create a book cover for a story, such as the cover in Activity 1. Remind them to show the setting and characters. Have them think of a very simple plot for their story. Form pairs, and give students time to show their book covers to their partners and tell them about the plot. They will probably use their native language because students at this age often find summarizing difficult. (See Differentiated Instruction.)

Differentiated Instruction

Below-level ★	On-level ★★	Above-level ★★★
Have students draw the book cover to show to the class, but do not ask them to explain the plot of their story.	Do the Build Creativity! activity as described above.	After doing the Build Creativity! activity as described above, ask students to tell the plot of their story in a sentence with the words *is a story about*. Provide examples such as: Grandma Turtle *is a story about an old turtle and a young friend.* I Can't Find My Things *is a story about a new student at school.*

Objective: to understand the importance of helping others
Materials: Audio CD 4.14, 4.15

Pre-Reading

Read the title of the story and the name of its author aloud. Ask students to go through the story and identify the setting and the characters. Then, ask students to guess what the plot is. Write the prepositions *on*, *in*, and *under* on the board, and have students circle the words in the text. Teach the expression *What's the matter?* before listening to the story.

4.14 Page 84

Play Track 4.14 through "So, off they go into the forest." Pause and ask questions:

Who are the characters?
Who is sad?
What can't Snail find?
Where do Snail and Ladybug go?

Think

Ask the question in the box. Guide students to use *because* in their answers.

Personalization

Ask: *When are you sad?*

4.14 Page 85

Play the rest of Track 4.14. Ask questions:

What animals are in the forest?
How many animals help?
Is Snail's home under a leaf?

Think

Ask the question in the box. Point out that the animals are helping Snail. Emphasize the importance of helping others.

4.14

Snail Finds His Home

by Silvia Zapiain

"My home! My home!" says **Snail** sadly.
"What's the matter?" asks **Ladybug**.
"I can't find my home!"
"Let's go and find it!"

So, off they go into the **forest**.

Think Why is Snail sad?

84

48

They see Spider.
"Hey! What's the matter?" asks **Spider**.
"I can't find my home," says Snail.
"Let's go and find it!"

They see Butterfly.
"What's the matter?" asks **Butterfly**.
"I can't find my home," says Snail.
"Is it under a leaf?" asks Butterfly.
"No, it isn't," says Snail.

Think Are Snail, Ladybug, Spider, and Butterfly friends?

85

4.15 Snail Finds His Home

They see Mouse.

"Hey! What's the matter?" asks Mouse.

"I can't find my home," says Snail.

"Let's go and find it!"

Suddenly, there is a loud noise.

"What's that?" asks Mouse.

"It's a storm!" says Ladybug. "Let's find a place to hide from the rain!"

Think What makes a loud noise in a storm?

4B

Where is Butterfly? She's under the tree on a rock.

Where is Mouse? Is he under a tree?

No, he isn't. He's in a hole.

And Ladybug? She's under a leaf.

Is Spider under the leaf, too? Yes, he is.

"Eek!" says Snail. It starts to rain. He goes inside his shell.

"It's really warm in here," says Snail. "This is my home!"

Think Do you think Snail is happy now? Why?

4.15 Page 86

Play Track 4.15 through "'Let's find a place to hide from the rain!'" Pause and ask questions:

Who is the new friend?
What's the problem?

Teach new vocabulary to aid understanding of the problem in the story: *loud, noise, storm, hide, rain.*

Think

Ask students if they know what makes a loud noise in a storm. Discuss thunder and lightning.

4.15 Page 87, section 1

Play Track 4.15 through "Yes, he is." Pause and ask questions:

Where is Butterfly?
Is Mouse under a tree?
Who is under a leaf?

4.15 Page 87, section 2

Play the rest of Track 4.15. Ask questions:

Where is Snail now?
Where is his home?

Think

Read the questions in the Think box aloud. Encourage students to answer using *because*.

Personalization

Ask: *Do you hide when it rains? Where?*

Fun Corner!

Act It Out!

Assign roles to a group of students to act out a short version of the story.

Snail: *My home! My home!*

Ladybug: *What's the matter?*

Snail: *I can't find my home.*

Ladybug: *Let's go and find it!*

Narrator: *So, off they go into the forest.*

Repeat, replacing Ladybug with Spider, Butterfly, and Mouse.

The narrator makes a loud noise.

Ladybug: *It's a storm!*

The characters hide, and the narrator asks: *Where is Butterfly?* Help students answer the question using a preposition. Repeat for the other animals.

Snail: *It's really warm in here. This is my home!*

Explore the Text

1 Circle the answers.

a Plot: What is the story about?

Snail and Butterfly. | Snail finds a home.

b Setting: Where does the story take place?

In the park. | In the forest.

2 Color the answers.

a Ladybug is under in on Snail's shell.

b The friends are under in on the tree.

c Snail is under in on his shell.

3 Number the pictures and retell the story.

88

Objective: to deepen understanding of a fiction text

Materials: Build Creativity: paper, crayons

1 Circle the answers.

Read each question and answer option aloud. Complete the activity as a class.

2 Color the answers.

Ask students to focus their attention on picture *a*. Guide students to color the correct word to complete each sentence. Do the same with the other two pictures.

3 Number the pictures and retell the story.

Form pairs, and ask them to number the pictures in order. Then, guide the class to retell the story by providing sentences to complete orally. For example:

1 Snail can't find his _____. (home)
2 Snail and his friend go to the _____. (forest)
3 A storm! Let's _____! (hide)
4 Snail hides in his _____. (shell)

Then, write the incomplete sentences on the board. Ask students to copy them into their notebooks. Ask volunteers to come to the board and provide the missing words with their classmates' help. Correct spelling as a class, and have students complete the sentences in their notebooks.

Fun Corner!

Spirals and More Spirals

Talk about the shape of a snail's shell. Have students draw spirals in the air. Then, have them draw spirals of as many different sizes as possible on a piece of paper. Encourage them to experiment by drawing from the outside in and vice versa. How many spirals can they draw without stopping? Which is their best spiral? Why?

Build Creativity!

A New Setting

Objective: A Different Point of View

Ask students to draw a setting in their notebooks—for example, a classroom, a park, a bedroom, or a farm. Have them draw the five characters from the story in different parts of the setting so that each is in, on, or under something. You could ask students to do this activity at home. The following class, form pairs, and ask students to present their drawings to their partners and describe where each character is: *Ladybug is (under) (a tree)*. Then, ask students to label their drawings with the corresponding prepositions. (See Differentiated Instruction.) Students will be using these drawings for an activity on Teacher's Edition page 103.

AB pages 72–73

Differentiated Instruction

Below-level ★	On-level ★★	Above-level ★★★
Have students describe their drawings using the prepositions, but don't ask them to write them.	Do the Build Creativity! activity as described above.	After students have labeled the prepositions, ask them to write at least two sentences about their drawings.

Grammar in Context 4B

Grammar: Verb *to be*: Yes/No Questions

Is Mouse under a tree?
No, he isn't. He's in a hole.

Is Spider under the leaf?
Yes, he is.

1 4.16 Where is the red marker? Listen and circle the correct answer.

a b c

2 Match the questions to the correct answers and trace.

1 Is the mouse on the chair? — a No, it isn't.
2 Is the mouse under the chair? — b Yes, it is.

Time to Talk!

1 Two classmates leave the classroom.
2 Hide a small ball somewhere in the classroom.
3 The two classmates come back in and guess where the ball is.
Is it under the teacher's desk?
No, it isn't.

89

Objective: to use *yes/no* questions with the verb *to be*
Materials: Audio CD 4.16, ball

Grammar Box

Ask students to look at the pictures in the Grammar box. Point to the first picture, and ask the question in the box. Give students time to answer the question. Do the same with the second picture.

1 4.16 Where is the red marker? Listen and circle the correct answer.

Ask students to pay close attention to each of the scenes in Activity 1. Ask: *Where is the red marker?* Have students listen to Track 4.16 and then answer the question.

2 Match the questions to the correct answers and trace.

Read the questions and answers in Activity 2 aloud. Then, guide students to do the activity.

Practice Time 1 Write *Yes, it is.* and *No, it isn't.* on the board, and read the sentences out loud. Ask a volunteer to come to the board. Ask the class *yes/no* questions about where things are in the classroom—for example: *Is my bag on the desk?* Students answer, and the volunteer points to the corresponding answer. Leave the answers on the board.

Time to Talk!

Explain to students how this activity works. When the two classmates return to the classroom, encourage them to ask different students questions so as many students as possible have a chance to practice.

Practice Time 2 Ask students to go back to page 87. Tell them that you will ask questions about the first scene and they have to write the answers to each question in their notebooks. Point to the two possible answers on the board (*Yes, it is. No it isn't.*). Give an example. Say: *One. Is Butterfly under a leaf?* (Make sure you number your questions.) Write the answer on the board: *No, she isn't.* Give students time to write the example answer in their notebooks. Continue with three more questions. Say: *Two. Is Ladybug under a leaf? (Yes, she is.) Three. Is Mouse in a hole? (Yes, he is.) Four. Is Snail in his shell? (No, he isn't.)*

Fun Corner!

Do You Remember?

Ask students to take out their drawings from the Build Creativity! activity on Teacher's Edition page 102 (A New Setting) and put them face down. Form pairs. Have two pairs work together so that there are two teams. Team A shows a drawing to Team B to memorize. When you say *Stop*, Team A puts the drawing away. Team B asks *yes/no* questions to demonstrate what they remember about the drawing, for example, *Is Ladybug under the chair?* Teams can ask five questions per drawing. Teams count how many affirmative answers they get, and the team with the most is the winner.

AB pages 74–75

Listening

1 4.17 Listen to the poem. Circle the correct answer.

What is the poem about?

A person. An animal. A place. An object.

2 4.17 Listen again. Point to the actions in the order you hear them.

I eat. I draw. I sleep. I get love.

I paint. I read. I am myself. I play.

Taking Turns

1 Draw what home means to you in the frame.

2 In groups, take turns showing your drawing. Remember to say, "It's your turn."

3 Complete **Check Your Oracy!** on Activity Book page 77.

Home is …

Values AB page 76

90

Objectives: to listen to a poem about what home means; to understand the value of helping others

Materials: Audio CD 4.17, Cue Cards 5,6

1 4.17 Listen to the poem. Circle the correct answer.

Read the question and answer options in Activity 1. Then, play Track 4.17, and answer the question as a class.

2 4.17 Listen again. Point to the actions in the order you hear them.

Go through the drawings in Activity 2, and elicit the word for each action. Ask students to pantomime the actions with you. Then, play Track 4.17 again, and have students point to the pictures.

Oracy Extension Activity

Read the steps in the Oracy Extension activity aloud. Display the Cue Cards, and have students do the activity with you. Ask students to complete Check Your Oracy! on page 77 of their Activity Books.

ACTIVITY BOOK PAGE 76

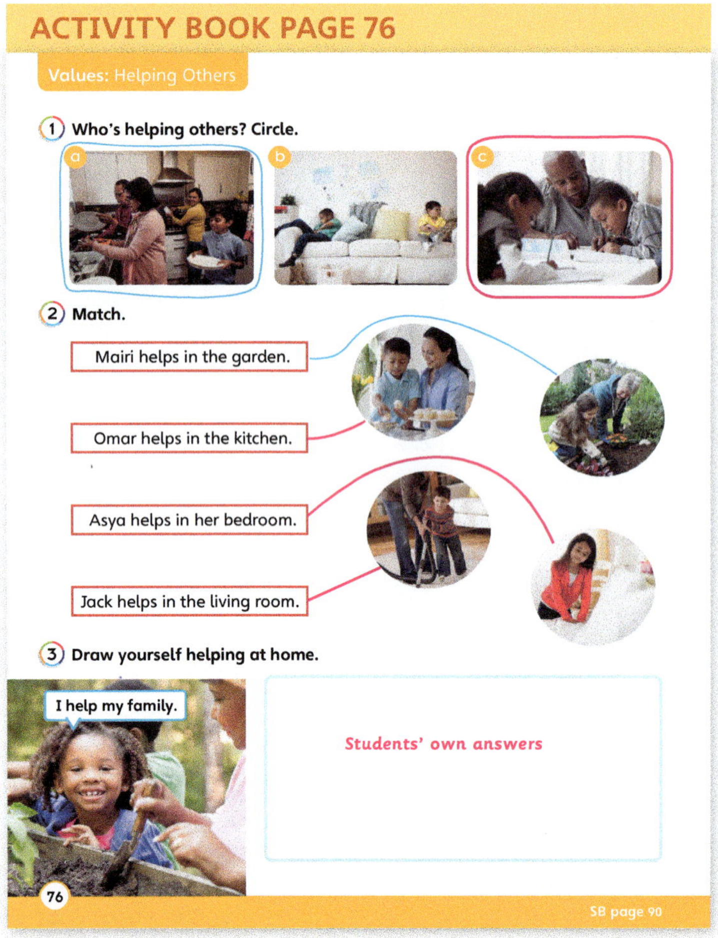
Values: Helping Others

1 Who's helping others? Circle.

a b c

2 Match.

Mairi helps in the garden.

Omar helps in the kitchen.

Asya helps in her bedroom.

Jack helps in the living room.

3 Draw yourself helping at home.

I help my family.

Students' own answers

76

SB page 90

1 Who's helping others? Circle.

Ask the class: *Do you help your family? When? Do you help your friends?* Talk about the importance of helping others and how students feel when they give and receive help. Go through the pictures in Activity 1, and ask students to circle the scenes in which people are helping others.

2 Match.

Ask students to look at the pictures carefully. Then, read the sentences one by one, and ask students to match them with the pictures. Check answers as a class.

3 Draw yourself helping at home.

Ask students to draw themselves helping at home.

AB page 76

Objective: **to consolidate, extend, and personalize learning on the unit topic**

Materials: construction paper, paper, colored pencils

- Read the Big Challenge question and statement aloud. Point to the photos of the girl at the bottom of the page. Tell students that they are going to make a big envelope and drawings to go in it.
- **1** Ask students to use construction paper to make a big envelope at home with the help of their parents or caregivers.
- **2** Explain to students that they have to draw the outside of their homes on one side of the envelope. Encourage them to decorate their drawings.
- **3** Ask students what about their homes makes them feel happy. On separate pieces of paper, have them draw their family, pet, favorite things, and rooms in the house. They can also draw themselves doing an activity they love doing at home.
- **4** Have students put their drawings inside their envelopes.
- **5** Students will present their drawings of their home and describe what home is to them. If your class is big, form two groups. Use the text in the speech bubble on the page as an example for students to follow. Optional: Record or have students record one another's presentations to share their work.

Home-school | Portfolio: Big Challenge

Big Question Circle

Read the Big Question aloud. Have the class revisit the Big Question Links on pages 74, 77, and 82. Discuss what students have learned about what makes a home.

- Use the following questions to help review the Big Question:

How many types of homes can you think of? What are they?
What's your favorite room in your home?
What makes your home special?
Do you have any pets? What pets do you have?
How do you feel at home?
What can you do at home?

- Finally, have students turn to page 77 of their Activity Books to complete the Big Challenge self-assessment.

AB pages 77–79

Differentiated Instruction

Below-level ★	On-level ★★	Above-level ★★★
As a follow-up to the Big Challenge, ask students to draw the inside of their homes on the other side of their envelopes. Have students describe their homes to the class: *This is my bedroom. It's small.*	As a follow-up to the Big Challenge, ask students to draw the inside of their homes on the other side of their envelopes. Have students label the rooms and things in the home. Then, ask them to describe their homes to the class.	As a follow-up to the Big Challenge, ask students to draw the inside of their homes on the other side of their envelopes. Have students label the rooms and things in the house. Then, ask them to write three complete sentences about their homes.

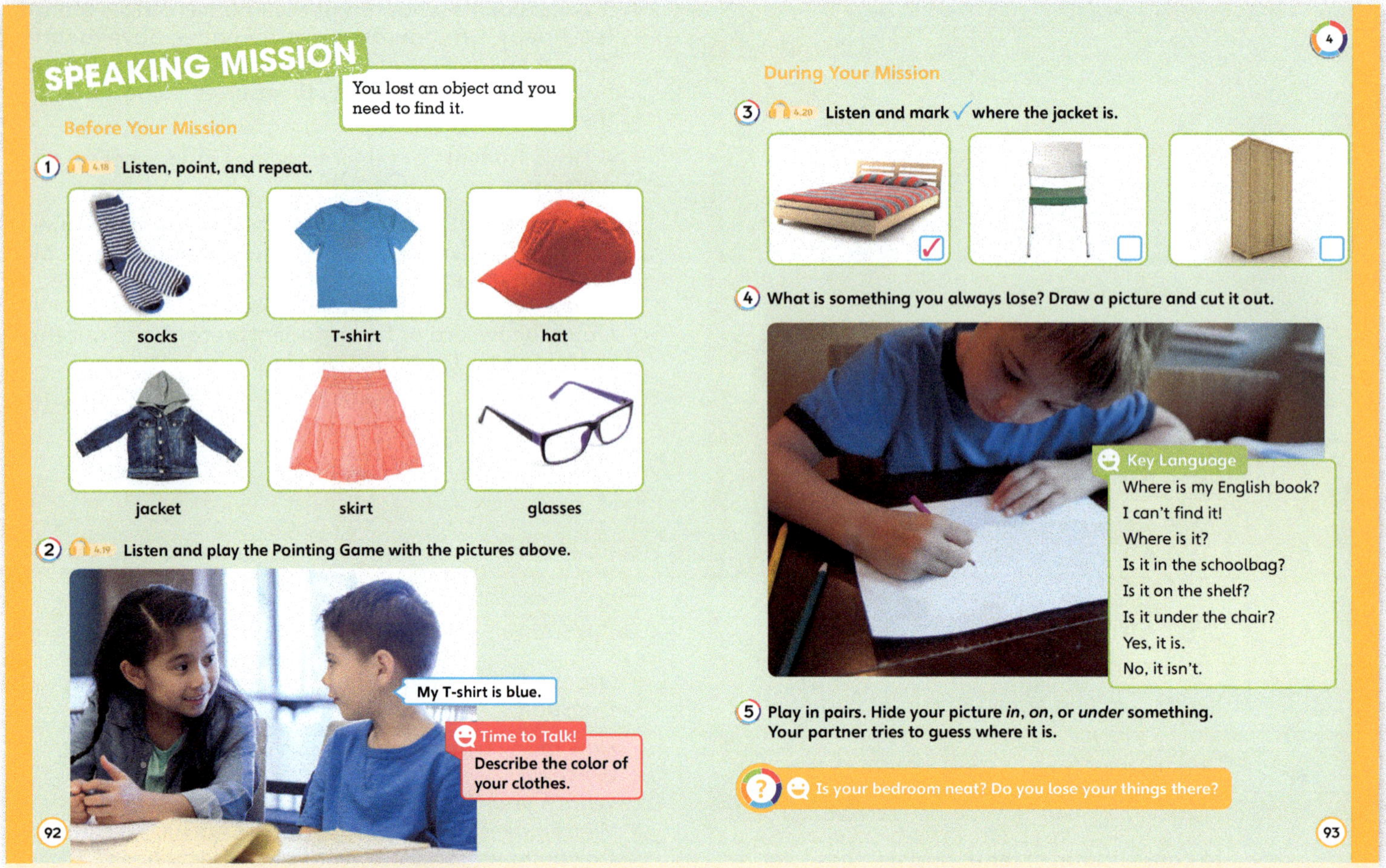
SPEAKING MISSION

You lost an object and you need to find it.

Before Your Mission

1 4.18 Listen, point, and repeat.

socks | T-shirt | hat

jacket | skirt | glasses

2 4.19 Listen and play the Pointing Game with the pictures above.

My T-shirt is blue.

Time to Talk!
Describe the color of your clothes.

92

4

During Your Mission

3 4.20 Listen and mark ✓ where the jacket is.

4 What is something you always lose? Draw a picture and cut it out.

Key Language
Where is my English book?
I can't find it!
Where is it?
Is it in the schoolbag?
Is it on the shelf?
Is it under the chair?
Yes, it is.
No, it isn't.

5 Play in pairs. Hide your picture *in*, *on*, or *under* something. Your partner tries to guess where it is.

Is your bedroom neat? Do you lose your things there?

93

Objective: to describe something you lost
Speaking Mission Words: ***socks, T-shirt, hat, jacket, skirt, glasses***
Materials: Audio CD 4.18, 4.19, 4.20, paper

1 4.18 Listen, point, and repeat.

Have students look at the pictures in Activity 1. Play Track 4.18 for students to point to and repeat the words.

2 4.19 Listen and play the Pointing Game with the pictures above.

Tell students that they will play a game in which they have to point to the pictures in Activity 1 at the same pace as the audio. Form groups of three students. Assign one student per group to do as the audio says. The other students have to check how accurate the student is by counting the mistakes. Play Track 4.19, and have students play the game. Play two more times for the other two students to take a turn. The winner is the student who makes the fewest mistakes.

Time to Talk!

Read the text in the Time to Talk! box aloud. Form pairs to do the activity.

3 4.20 Listen and mark ✓ where the jacket is.

Play Track 4.20, and have students mark the correct option.

4 What is something you always lose? Draw a picture and cut it out.

Ask students about something they always lose at home or at school. Ask them to draw it and cut it out to be used in Activity 5.

5 Play in pairs. Hide your picture *in*, *on*, or *under* something. Your partner tries to guess where it is.

Explain to students how the game works. Read the key language aloud. Then, with a volunteer, act out a scene using the key language so that students have an example to follow. Have students play the game. Remind students not to look as their partner hides the drawing. Check performance. Optional: Record or have students record one another's presentations to share their work.

Home-school | Portfolio: Speaking Mission

Big Question Link

Point to the Big Question Link, and read the questions. Ask volunteers to share their answers with the class. Discuss why it is helpful to keep our things neat.

AB pages 80–81

5 Where do wild animals belong?

Literacy

Read: a nonfiction text about wild animals; a fiction text about a rabbit and a snake

Reading Strategies: visualizing; predicting from pictures

Ready to Write

Learn to Write: questions and exclamations

Getting Ready to Write: write a card

Oracy

Skill: Participating Actively

Cue Card 7: 7. *Let's ...*

Speaking Mission: play a board game

Language

Key Words 1: *zebra, land, elephant, octopus, ocean, dolphin*

Key Words 2: *teeth, tail, beak, jungle, claw, fur*

Key Words 3: *feathers, insects*

Key Words 4: *rabbit, moon, snake, tongue, sun, stars*

Speaking Mission Words: *board game, dice, game piece, square, lose, win*

Grammar in Context

Verb *to be*: *Wh-* Questions: *What color are they? What are they?*

Verb *to be*: *Yes/No* Questions (plural): *Are Ketzi and the little rabbit near the stars?*

Phonics

Initial Sounds: *q, s, f, j, g, r*

Listening

Guessing Game: Identifying Wild Animals

Values

Taking Care of Animals

The Big Challenge

How can we describe a wild animal?
Make a mask and describe a wild animal

5 Where do wild animals belong?

- Talk about wild animals.
- Learn to participate actively.
- Identify questions and exclamations.
- Make animal masks.
- Play a board game.

Where do these animals live?

What are their favorite foods?

Which one is your favorite?

1 5.1 Watch the video. Number the animals in the order they appear.

2 elephant, 1 zebra, 4 dolphin, 3 octopus

2 5.1 Watch again. Complete the graphic organizer in the Activity Book.

5.1 Key Words 1

zebra
land
elephant
octopus
ocean
dolphin

AB page 82

94 95

Objective: **to introduce the topic of where wild animals belong**
Key Words I: ***zebra, land, elephant, octopus, ocean, dolphin***
Materials: Video 5.I, Audio CD 5.I, Flashcards 5.I–5.6; Build Creativity: music, pictures of common animals

WHERE DO WILD ANIMALS BELONG?

- Teach the word *wild*. Ask students to mention as many wild animals as they can think of. Read the Big Question aloud, and ask students where wild animals live. You may want to introduce the expressions *on land* and *in the ocean* so that students become familiar with this vocabulary from the opening video.
- Have students look at the pictures, and ask them if they know the names of the animals in English and know where they live. Continue with the rest of the questions.

5.1 Key Words 1 Use the flashcards and audio to present Key Words I. Hold up the flashcards as you play Track 5.I. Have students repeat the words.

1 5.1 Watch the video. Number the animals in the order they appear.

Watch the video, and pause after "Let's find out!" Ask: *What is today's Big Question? Where can wild animals live?* Continue the video through the part about the zebra. Ask comprehension questions such as: *Where do zebras live? What's their favorite food? What colors are they?* Continue the video, pausing after each animal is described. Ask comprehension questions. Watch the video again, and ask students to do Activity I. Check answers as a class. You could do the same activity by placing the four animal flashcards in random order on the board and asking students to put them in order.

2 5.1 Watch again. Complete the graphic organizer in the Activity Book.

Play the video again, and have students complete Activity I on AB page 82.

Build Creativity!

Animal Imitations

Objective: **Take a Break**

Play some background music, and have the class walk or dance around the classroom. When you pause the music, hold up a picture of an animal, and have students imitate that animal. For example, they can trumpet like an elephant, slither like a snake, hop like a rabbit, snore like a bear, or waddle like a penguin.

AB page 82

Objective: to learn how to visualize and prepare to read a nonfiction text

Key Words I: ***zebra, land, elephant, octopus, ocean, dolphin***

Materials: Audio CD 5.1, 5.2, 5.3, 5.4, 5.5, Flashcards 5.1–5.6; Build Creativity: tape, a large Venn diagram drawn on butcher paper, glue, students' animal cutouts

5.1 Key Words 1 Use the flashcards and audio to review Key Words I.

1 5.2 Listen, point, and repeat.

Give students time to look at the photos in Activity I. Play Track 5.2, and ask students to listen, point, and repeat each word.

2 5.3 Listen to three animal sounds. Guess the animals.

Ask students to tell you if they know how to make animal sounds. Ask volunteers to make sounds for the rest of the class to guess the animals they belong to. Play Track 5.3, and pause after each sound. Have students guess which animal each sound belongs to. If necessary, provide clues, such as the animal's habitat and color.

3 5.4 Listen and visualize the animal. What is it?

Tell students that they will listen to the description of an animal and they have to guess which one it is. You could provide an example of another animal first, such as: *It lives on land. It has big ears. (Elephant.)* Then, play Track 5.4, and do Activity 3 as a class.

4 5.5 Listen, visualize the animal, and draw it.

Play Track 5.5, and ask students what animal is described. Have students draw it in the box below the instruction.

Big Question Link

Draw students' attention to Emma, the oracy character, and read the oracy reminder aloud. Then, ask the question from the Big Question Link box. Ask students if any of these wild animals can be pets.

Build Creativity!

Venn Diagram

Objective: Focus

Draw a large Venn diagram on the board. Show how this type of graphic organizer works by using the flashcards. Tape the *elephant* Flashcard in the circle on the left and the *dolphin* Flashcard in the circle on the right. Ask: *Which animal lives on land? (The elephant.)* Write *Land* at the top of the circle. Do the same for *Water*. Then, draw a crocodile in the overlapping section. Ask: *Where does the crocodile live? (On land and in water.)* Label the section *Land and Water*. Ask volunteers to tape the remaining flashcards in the corresponding parts of the diagram. Have other volunteers add the animals on page 96 by drawing them. As homework, ask students to bring pictures or drawings of wild animals that belong to each of the three categories. The following class, tape the butcher paper with the Venn diagram to a wall and label the sections: *Land, Land and Water, Water*. Ask students to glue their animals to the correct sections of the diagram. Then, ask volunteers to write the names of the animals they already know in English next to the corresponding pictures. As students learn about new animals, ask volunteers to add them to the diagram.

5.6 **Key Words 2** Use the flashcards and audio to pre-teach Key Words 2.

Pre-Reading

Ask students what their favorite animals are. Introduce the safari guide. Ask students to look at pages 97 and 98 to see what his top five wild animals are. Point out that #1 is his favorite animal. Compare them with the class results. Have students focus on each animal in the nonfiction text, and ask about their habitats. Write the habitats on the board, and say them out loud: *ocean, jungle, forest.*

5.7 **Page 97, section 1**

Play Track 5.7 up to the end of the first paragraph. Pause, point to the pictures, and ask questions:

Where do crocodiles live?

Ask students to complete sentences: *They have big … They have a long …*

What are their favorite foods?

5.7 **Page 97, section 2**

Play the rest of Track 5.7. Point to the pictures and ask questions:

Which animal is number four?
What do parrots have?
What are their favorite foods?
Where do they live?
What color are they?

Personalization

Ask: *Do you like crocodiles? Do you like parrots? Why or why not?*

Fun Corner!

What's Missing?

Form two teams, and have students close their books. Tell students you will write incomplete words from pages 95 and 97. Ask two or three students from each team to come to the board to complete the words. Write *b ___ ___ k (beak)*, and ask students from one team to complete the word and then spell it out loud to get a point. Based on the size of your class, decide how many words you will assign per team. The winning team is the one with the most points. Alternatively, provide the words for students to unscramble: *e a k b (beak).*

Objective: to understand the meaning of words in context and learn more about wild animals

Key Words 2: ***teeth, tail, beak, jungle, claw, fur***

Materials: Audio CD 5.6, 5.7, 5.8, Flashcards 5.7–5.12

5.8 Top Five Wild Animals

#3 Blue Whale

Blue whales live in the ocean. They're very, very, very big—as big as three school buses!

But this giant has no teeth!

#2 Brown Bear

Brown bears live in the forest. Their favorite foods are plants and small animals.

They have long claws.

claws

#1 Panda

This is my number one wild animal, the giant panda! Giant pandas are bears, too! But their favorite food is bamboo. Pandas have black and white fur. They live in the forest.

fur

bamboo

What are they?

They're baby pandas. They're so cute.

Think

Which animals walk on four legs?

98

5.8 Page 98, section 1

Play Track 5.8 through "They have long claws." Pause and ask questions:

Which animal is number two?
Which animal lives in the ocean?
How big are blue whales?
What are the brown bear's favorite foods?
Who doesn't have teeth?

Personalization

Ask: *Do you prefer the whale or the bear? Would you like to live in the ocean or in the forest?*

5.8 Page 98, section 2

Play the rest of Track 5.8. Ask questions:

What is the giant panda's favorite food?
What color is the fur of giant pandas?
Where do they live?

Personalization

Ask: *Why do you think the panda is the man's number one wild animal?*

Think

Read the question in the Think box aloud, and have volunteers answer it.

Build Creativity!

Animal Sounds

Objective: A Different Point of View

Have individuals make animal noises, and encourage the class to guess the animal. After a few examples, encourage students to think about the noises "silent" animals make. For example, ask: *What noise does a rabbit or a fish make?* Make it even more challenging by asking: *How does (an elephant) laugh/cry/yawn/ask for ice cream?*

AB page 83

Differentiated Instruction

Below-level ★	On-level ★★	Above-level ★★★
As a follow-up activity to the nonfiction text, draw a crocodile, a parrot, a whale, a bear, and a panda at the top of five columns on the board. Write words on the board: *land, water, long tail, fish, beak, fruit, feathers, jungle, forest, ocean, no teeth, claws, fur, bamboo.* Point to and say each word. Ask volunteers to come to the board and point to the animal or animals that the word relates to. Write the words in the corresponding columns.	As a follow-up activity to the nonfiction text, draw a crocodile, a parrot, a whale, a bear, and a panda at the top of five columns on the board. Ask students to do the same in their notebooks. Write words on the board: *land, water, long tail, fish, beak, fruit, feathers, jungle, forest, ocean, no teeth, claws, fur, bamboo.* Point to and say each word. Make sure that students remember what they mean. Tell students that you will say each word and they have to tell you which of the five animals it relates to. Some words, such as *forest*, will relate to more than one animal. Students write the words in the same columns in their notebooks as you do on the board.	Do this activity as it is described in the On-level section, but, instead of writing the words on the board yourself, ask volunteers to write them.

Explore the Text

5A

1 Match the animals to their homes.

a brown bear

b blue whale

c parrot

forest

ocean

jungle

2 5.7 5.8 Read and listen to the text again. Mark ✓ the correct answer.

a teeth		b fur	
✓			✓

3 5.9 Key Words 3 Listen and repeat. Label the pictures *F* (feathers) or *I* (insects).

a F

b I

4 Visualize an imaginary animal made up of two wild animals. Draw it and name it.

panda + penguin = panguin

It's a panda and a penguin. It's a panguin!

Where does your favorite wild animal live?

99

Objective: to check reading comprehension and understand words in context

Key Words 3: *feathers, insects*

Materials: Audio CD 5.7, 5.8, 5.9, paper

1 Match the animals to their homes.

Have students look at the animals and their homes. Ask volunteers to say the name of each animal and each home. Then, have students do Activity 1. Check answers as a class.

2 5.7 5.8 Read and listen to the text again. Mark ✓ the correct answer.

Ask volunteers to read the words in the chart: *teeth, fur.* Ask: *Who has teeth, the crocodile or the whale? Who has fur?* Then, have students listen to the nonfiction text again to confirm their answers.

3 5.9 Key Words 3 Listen and repeat. Label the pictures *F* (feathers) or *I* (insects).

Ask students to tell you what they see in the two pictures in Activity 3. Play Track 5.9, and have students repeat the words. Then, ask students to label the pictures.

4 Visualize an imaginary animal made up of two wild animals. Draw it and name it.

Have students look at the drawing of the "panguin," and ask them which two animals they think make up this animal. Ask a volunteer to read aloud what the girl says. Have students think of two wild animals, and give them time to visualize an imaginary animal made from them. Ask students to draw their imaginary animal. Finally, ask them to write the names of each of the two animals and then put the words together so that a new name is formed. (See Differentiated Instruction.)

Big Question Link

Read the question aloud, and have students answer it. Invite volunteers to share their answers with the class.

Build Creativity!

Animal Combinations

Objective: A Different Point of View

Review the names of the animals from the unit. Talk about the special characteristics of each one. Encourage students to recall what they learned. Then, have students explore more strange animal combinations, for example: *What happens if you put together a whale and an elephant?* Have students draw pictures.

AB pages 84–85

Differentiated Instruction

Below-level ★	On-level ★★	Above-level ★★★
As a follow-up to Activity 4, ask students to present their imaginary animal to the class by following this structure: *This is a (panda) and a (penguin). It's a (panguin). It has (a long nose). It's (black and white).*	As a follow-up to Activity 4, ask students to present their imaginary animal to the class. They can mention its home, its favorite food, its color, and special features, such as a long tail. Then, guide students to write about their animals in their notebooks by completing these sentences: *This is a … and a … It's a … It lives … Its favorite food is … It has …*	As a follow-up to Activity 4, use the procedure in the On-level section, but let students talk and write as much as they want about their imaginary animals.

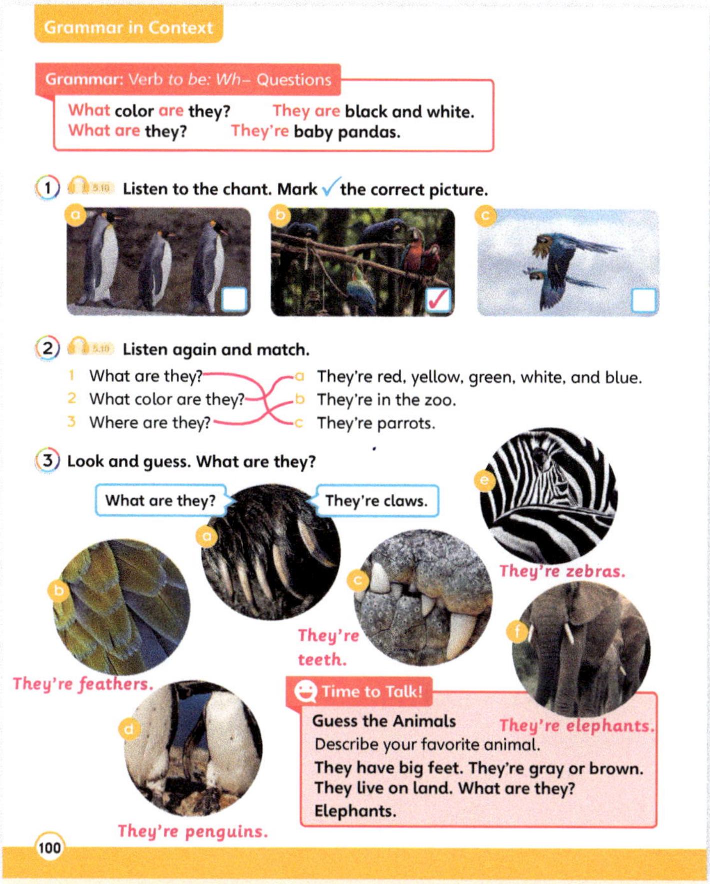
Grammar in Context

Grammar: Verb *to be*: *Wh–* Questions

What color are they? They are black and white.
What are they? They're baby pandas.

1 5.10 Listen to the chant. Mark ✓ the correct picture.

a b c

2 5.10 Listen again and match.

1 What are they? a They're red, yellow, green, white, and blue.
2 What color are they? b They're in the zoo.
3 Where are they? c They're parrots.

3 Look and guess. What are they?

What are they? They're claws.

a b c d e f

They're feathers. They're teeth. They're zebras. They're elephants. They're penguins.

Time to Talk!
Guess the Animals
Describe your favorite animal.
They have big feet. They're gray or brown. They live on land. What are they?
Elephants.

100

Objective: to make *Wh-* questions with *to be* in the plural

Materials: Audio CD 5.10, paper, slips of paper with half a sentence on each (e.g., *Crocodiles live / on land. Crocodiles have / big teeth. Parrots have / beaks. Parrots live / in the jungle. Blue whales live / in the ocean. Brown bears live / in the forest. Giant pandas are / bears. Bears have long / claws. What are / they? What color / are they?*)

Grammar Box

Ask questions about the classroom using *What* and the plural form of *to be*, *are*. For example: *What color are the desks?* Point to objects in the classroom, and ask: *What are they?* Ask students to look at the Grammar box, and read the questions. Ask volunteers to read the answers. Remind students how they would ask the questions if they were talking about only one animal: *What color is it? It's ...* Emphasize the use of the plural *are* and *they* to talk about more than one animal.

1 5.10 Listen to the chant. Mark ✓ the correct picture.

Ask questions about the animals in the pictures in Activity 1: *What are they? What color are they? Where are they?* Play Track 5.10, and have students choose the correct option.

2 5.10 Listen again and match.

Read the questions, and ask volunteers to read the answers. Play Track 5.10 again, and have students match the questions with the answers. Check answers as a class.

Practice Time 1 Distribute a slip of paper to each student. (See Materials.) Tell students that they have to find the half that completes their sentence. Provide an example. Give students time to find their match. Then, ask pairs to stand in a line and take turns reading their complete sentence. Ask volunteers to say if the sentences are correct.

3 Look and guess. What are they?

Ask students to look at the pictures carefully. Review the example, and then move on to the rest of the pictures. Focus students' attention on the pronunciation of *they're*.

Practice Time 2 Form pairs. Ask students to write the question *What are they?* in their notebooks and then write the answer for all the pictures in Activity 3. Pairs check each other's answers.

Time to Talk!

Explain to students how the activity works. Read the example, and ask students to follow it to describe their favorite animal. Then, form two teams. Each team makes guesses about the other team's descriptions. The winner is the one that makes the most correct guesses.

Fun Corner!

Sleeping Lions

Discuss what students would do if a lion walked into the classroom. The majority would probably try to run away. Tell students that some animals, such as frogs and snakes, when in danger, pretend to be dead. Can students think of reasons why animals might do that? Play Sleeping Lions. Have most of the class lie down on the floor and pretend to be sleeping lions. Have one or two students walk around the classroom, trying to make the lions laugh (without touching them). Any lions that wake up join their classmates in trying to make the remaining sleeping lions laugh.

AB pages 86–87

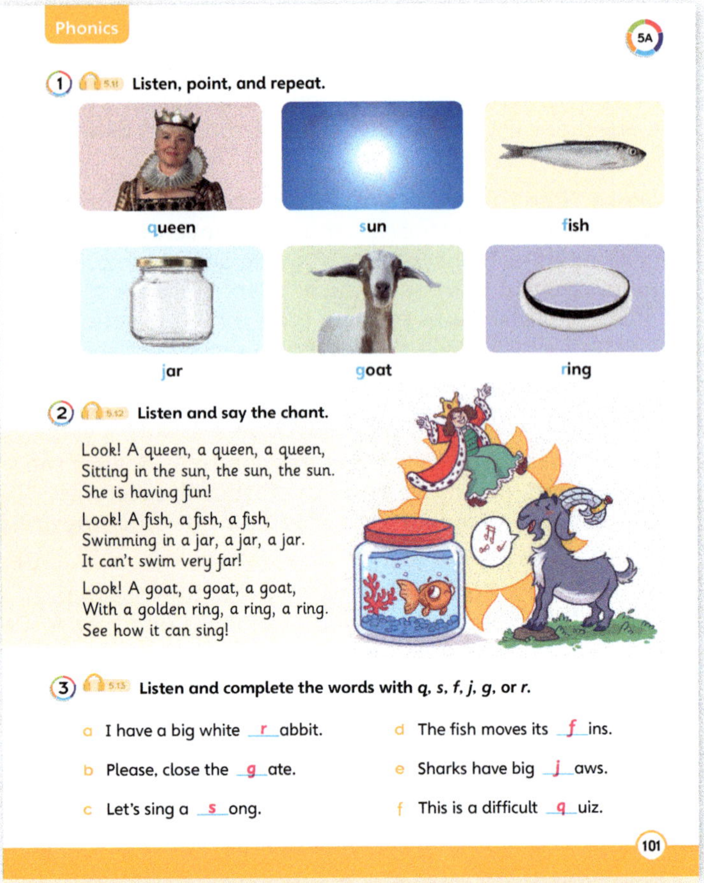

Phonics

5A

1 5.11 Listen, point, and repeat.

queen sun fish

jar goat ring

2 5.12 Listen and say the chant.

Look! A queen, a queen, a queen,
Sitting in the sun, the sun, the sun.
She is having fun!

Look! A fish, a fish, a fish,
Swimming in a jar, a jar, a jar.
It can't swim very far!

Look! A goat, a goat, a goat,
With a golden ring, a ring, a ring.
See how it can sing!

3 5.13 Listen and complete the words with *q, s, f, j, g,* or *r*.

a I have a big white _r_abbit.
b Please, close the _g_ate.
c Let's sing a _s_ong.
d The fish moves its _f_ins.
e Sharks have big _j_aws.
f This is a difficult _q_uiz.

101

Objective: to identify initial sounds ***q, s, f, j, g, r***

Materials: Audio CD 5.11, 5.12, 5.13, construction paper

1 5.11 Listen, point, and repeat.

Ask students if they know the English words for each of the pictures in Activity 1. Play Track 5.11, and have students repeat the words. Pronounce each word in isolation, and ask individual students to repeat after you.

2 5.12 Listen and say the chant.

Focus students' attention on the pictures, and ask general questions: *Where is the queen? Is she happy? Where is the fish? Is it happy? What does the goat have?* Play Track 5.12, and pause after each verse. Encourage students to say the chant with you.

Practice Time 1 Form two groups. Guide students to complete the chant as you say part of it. Point to one group and then the other so that they take turns. Say: *Look! A queen, ...* Encourage one group to continue: *a queen, a queen.* Continue: *Sitting in ...* Encourage the other group to continue: *the sun, the sun, the sun.* Continue with the rest of the chant in the same manner.

2 5.13 Listen and complete the words with *q, s, f, j, g,* or *r*.

Read sentence *a*, and encourage students to complete the word *rabbit*. Play Track 5.13, and guide students to complete the rest of the sentences.

Build Creativity!

Wall Charts

Objective: Focus

This activity was done in unit 2 with the objective of having wall charts for the sounds taught throughout the year. Repeat the activity with the new sounds. Form six groups, and give each a sheet of construction paper. Assign one of the initial sounds to each group. Have groups write the sound at the top of the sheet and draw the items whose names start with that sound. Monitor students' work. Display students' work on the classroom walls.

AB page 88

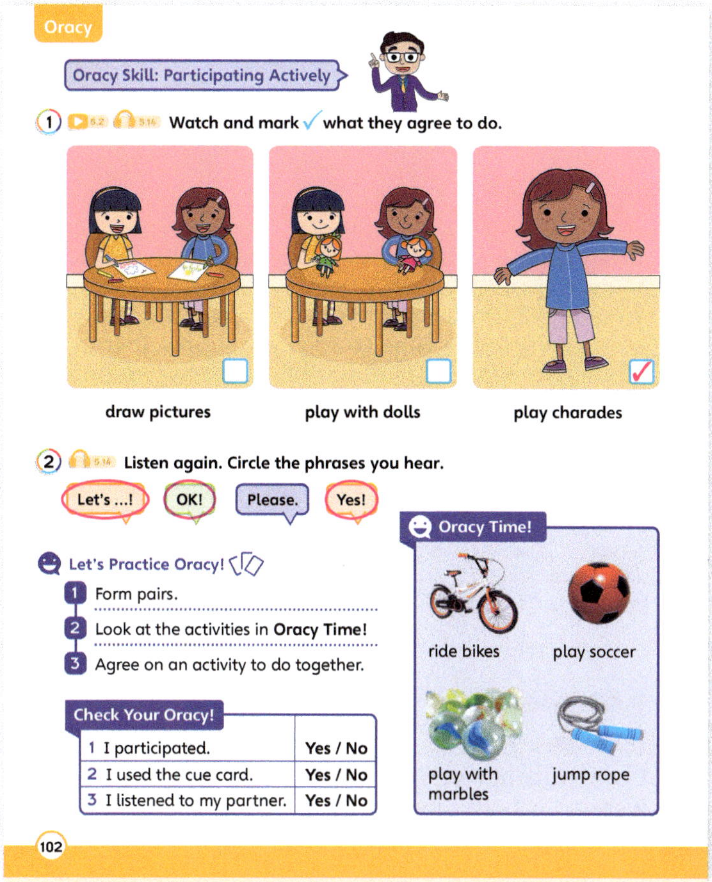
Oracy

Oracy Skill: Participating Actively

1 5.2 5.14 Watch and mark ✓ what they agree to do.

draw pictures	play with dolls	play charades ✓

2 5.14 Listen again. Circle the phrases you hear.

Let's ...! OK! Please. Yes!

Let's Practice Oracy!

1 Form pairs.

2 Look at the activities in **Oracy Time!**

3 Agree on an activity to do together.

Oracy Time!

ride bikes, play soccer, play with marbles, jump rope

Check Your Oracy!

1 I participated.	Yes / No
2 I used the cue card.	Yes / No
3 I listened to my partner.	Yes / No

102

Objective: to learn to participate actively
Cue Card: *7. Let's ...*
Materials: Video 5.2, Audio CD 5.14, Cue Card 7

Oracy Skill

Tell students that they will be learning how to participate actively. Ask them how they usually suggest an idea to friends, for example, when they want to play together. Students already know the expression *Let's ...* from the fiction story *I Can't Find My Things!* Elicit the expression by making reference to the story.

1 5.2 5.14 Watch and mark ✓ what they agree to do.

Have students look at the three scenes, and ask general questions such as: *What are these? (Dolls.)* Read the actions below each picture. Play the video, and have students do Activity 1.

Present and Practice Display Cue Card 7 on the board. Have students suggest what to do in class by using the expression *Let's ...* Give an example: *Let's read!* Students can come up with ideas such as: *Let's have lunch! Let's go to the playground!*

2 5.14 Listen again. Circle the phrases you hear.

Ask a volunteer to read the phrases in Activity 2. Have students complete Activity 2 while listening to Track 5.14. Ask students what Emma and Kate say when they do not agree on a game: *No, that's boring!* You could teach *Yes, that's great!* and have them incorporate the two expressions in the Let's Practice Oracy! activity.

Let's Practice Oracy! 7

- Ask volunteers to identify the activities in the Oracy Time! box.
- **1–2** Form pairs, and have students agree on one of the activities. Tell them that they will create a dialogue similar to the one between Emma and Kate. With a volunteer, model a possible dialogue. Use all the expressions from the video and the ones taught in Activity 2.
- **3** Go around the class, and monitor the dialogues.
- Optional: Record or have students record each other's dialogues to share their work.
- Have students complete Check Your Oracy!

Home-school   Portfolio: Oracy

Fun Corner!

What Am I Thinking?

With the help of the class, brainstorm ideas on the board. Write: *Let's eat ...* Ask volunteers to come to the board and draw food below your incomplete sentence. Do the same with: *Let's draw ... , Let's go to ... ,* and *Let's play ...* Form two teams. Without letting students know, choose one of the things on the board for each category. For example, you could choose *pizza* for the *Let's eat ...* category. Teams have to guess what you have chosen by suggesting options: *Let's eat (apples)!*

AB page 88

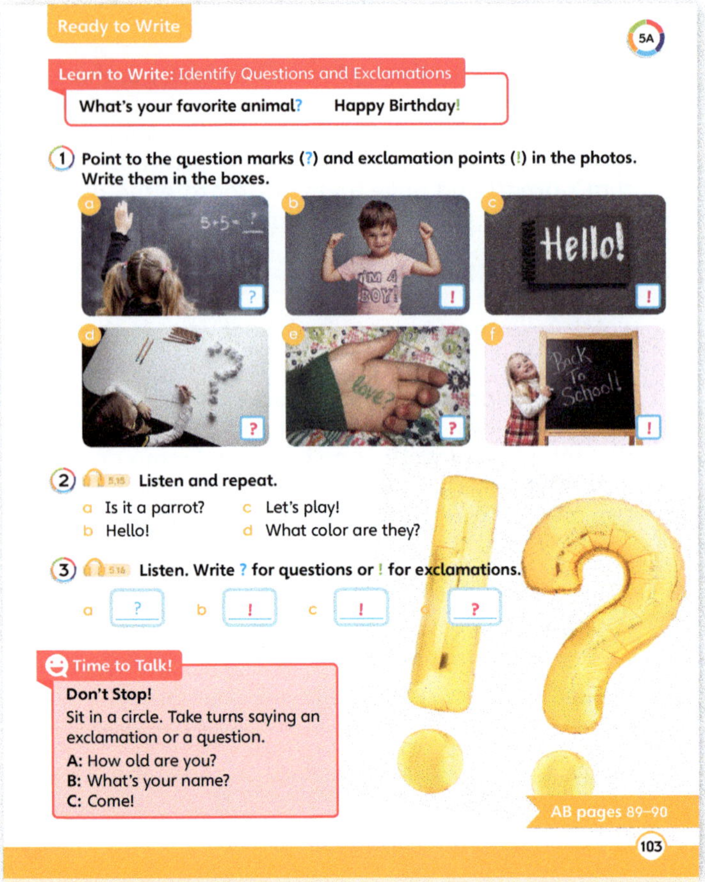
Ready to Write

5A

Learn to Write: Identify Questions and Exclamations

What's your favorite animal? Happy Birthday!

1 Point to the question marks (?) and exclamation points (!) in the photos. Write them in the boxes.

a ? b ! c ! d ? e ? f !

2 5.15 Listen and repeat.

a Is it a parrot?
b Hello!
c Let's play!
d What color are they?

3 5.16 Listen. Write ? for questions or ! for exclamations.

a ? b ! c ! d ?

Time to Talk!

Don't Stop!

Sit in a circle. Take turns saying an exclamation or a question.

A: How old are you?
B: What's your name?
C: Come!

AB pages 89–90

103

Objective: to identify questions and exclamations

Materials: Audio CD 5.15, 5.16

Learn to Write Box

Write a question mark and an exclamation point on the board. Ask students if they know what the punctuation marks are used for. Ask volunteers to write the marks next to yours. Read the question and exclamation in the box, emphasizing their intonation. Have students repeat them after you. Say more questions and exclamations for students to identify.

1 Point to the question marks (?) and exclamation points (!) in the photos. Write them in the boxes.

Ask volunteers to look for question marks and exclamation points in the photos and point to them. Then, ask the class to write them in the boxes. Have students swap books with a classmate and check their partner's work.

2 5.15 Listen and repeat.

Play Track 5.15, and ask students to repeat. Then, focus on the rising and falling intonation of questions. Ask a *yes/no* question with a rising intonation, and draw an arrow pointing up on the board. Ask students to repeat the question. Ask a *Wh-* question with falling intonation, and draw an arrow pointing down on the board. Have students identify intonation by asking more questions and having volunteers point to the corresponding arrow on the board.

3 5.16 Listen. Write ? for questions or ! for exclamations.

Ask students to listen and write the corresponding punctuation marks in the boxes.

Time to Talk!

Brainstorm questions and exclamations from previous units, such as personal questions and commands from unit 3. Have the class sit in a circle. Explain how the activity in the Time to Talk! box works. Instruct students that they should not repeat the question or exclamation of the student who spoke before them. When a student cannot come up with an example or makes a mistake, they stand next to you and help you monitor the other students' performance. The winner of this game is the last student sitting on the floor.

Build Creativity!

T-Shirt Designs

Objective: Flow

Draw students' attention to the picture of the boy wearing a T-shirt in Activity 1. Tell students they will create a T-shirt design, such as the one on the boy's T-shirt. They have to include a question mark or an exclamation point in their designs. Provide examples, such as: *Are you happy? Let's play! Ready? Run!* Ask students to make their designs at home and decorate them. You could also ask students to make their designs on a T-shirt made of paper. Have students present their designs to the class.

AB pages 89–90

Objective: **make a card**
Materials: paper; Build Creativity: objects that can be squeezed, such as sponges, squishies, or anti-stress balls (brought from home by students)

Purpose and Audience

Lead students in understanding that we write for a particular reason and for a particular audience. Ask students if they have sent cards to friends or relatives and if they have received cards. Tell them that when people send a card or letter to another person, they do so with a purpose in mind, to say something. For example, they may want to wish the person a happy birthday. Elicit more examples from students. Discuss how, in writing for a particular reason, we are also writing to a particular person or particular people. Ask students to tell you to whom they usually send cards.

1 IDENTIFY

Ask students to tell you what celebrations they are most interested in. On the board, write basic text that could be included in a card, such as *Happy … ! Have a great … !* Also, mention other reasons for writing a card, such as to say *thank you* or *sorry*. Provide example text: *Thank you! I love you! Sorry!* Leave the text on the board.

2 WRITE

Tell students they will write a card. Ask them to decide what they would like to say in their cards and to whom they would like to write. Instruct students to include text such as: *To (Mary); From, (Anna).* Have students write the text in their notebooks first. (See Differentiated Instruction.)

3 EDIT

Form pairs, and ask students to swap notebooks and check their partner's work. They should check for correct use of punctuation marks (question marks, exclamation points, periods) and capital letters. Go around the classroom, and monitor students' work.

4 FOLLOW UP

Have students make their cards at home and write the edited text on them. Encourage students to decorate their cards. You may wish to discuss what children can draw for different cards. Ask them to bring their cards to class and show them to their classmates.

Build Creativity!

Sensory Squeeze

Tell students they will play a game to help them relax. Ask them to take out their squeezable objects. Then, have students form a circle. Play music. Stop the music and ask students to squeeze their objects. Play the music again and ask students to pass the objects to their right. Continue as long as you think necessary. This activity can be adapted using other objects and textures.

Mystery Writers

Objective: **Flow**

Write each students name on a slip of paper and randomly distribute them to students, ensuring that nobody receives their own name. Ask students to make a card at home and put it in an envelope with the assigned name written on it. Tell students that they will be mystery writers and they shouldn't write their names on the card. However, have them write their names on a folded slip of paper and put it in the envelope. Ask students to give you their cards and hand them out to their recipients. Students open the envelopes and guess who the mystery writer is. Then, have them check if their guesses were correct by looking at the slips of paper. Ask students to raise their hands if they guessed correctly.

Differentiated Instruction

Below-level ★	On-level ★★	Above-level ★★★
To simplify the task, choose a type of card for the class—for example, a birthday card—and ask students to follow a set text.	Do the writing task as stated above.	Encourage students to include more sophisticated sentences, such as: *I wish you … I hope you …*

Unit 5B Ready to Read: Fiction

1 5.17 Key Words 4 Listen, point, and repeat.

rabbit 2	moon 1	snake 6
tongue 5	sun 3	stars 4

2 5.18 Listen and number the pictures.

3 Draw suns, stars, flowers, and hearts on the animals.

Time to Talk!
In pairs, give each other instructions.
Draw two hearts.

Remember to take turns.

104

Objective: to learn vocabulary related to a fiction text

Key Words 4: ***rabbit*, *moon*, *snake*, *tongue*, *sun*, *stars***

Materials: Audio CD 5.17, 5.18, paper

1 5.17 Key Words 4 Listen, point, and repeat.

Play Track 5.17. Have students listen and look at the pictures. Play the track again for students to repeat the words.

2 5.18 Listen and number the pictures.

Have students listen to Track 5.18 and number the pictures in Activity 1 based on the descriptions. Then, help students to reproduce the descriptions.

Practice Time 1 Have students add to the descriptions of the pictures in Activity 1. For instance, they could add this information about the rabbit: *It lives on land. It has long ears. It's brown and white. Its favorite food is grass.*

3 Draw suns, stars, flowers, and hearts on the animals.

Ask students to tell you the names of the animals in Activity 3. Have them decorate the animals with small drawings, as shown in the example.

Time to Talk!

Ask volunteers to give you instructions similar to the one in the Time to Talk! box. Draw what they instruct you to draw on the board. Then, draw students' attention to Kate, the oracy character, and read the reminder aloud. Form pairs, and have students tell their partners what to draw in their notebooks. Later, have students include colors in their instructions: *Draw two green hearts.*

Build Creativity!

Word Search

Objective: Focus

Draw a ten-by-ten grid on the board, and teach students how to make a word search. First, write five words in random order horizontally and vertically. Complete the empty squares with letters. Form pairs, and ask students to create word searches that include five key words that are words for animals, homes, or body parts. Have pairs swap word searches and solve them. (See Differentiated Instruction.)

Fun Corner!

Guess!

Form pairs, and ask students to draw with their fingers any of the shapes from Activity 3 (suns, stars, flowers, hearts) on their partner's back. Students must guess the shape and say it. Alternatively, ask students to draw a number and then a shape for their partner to guess: *Ten suns!*

AB pages 91

Differentiated Instruction

Below-level ★	On-level ★★	Above-level ★★★
Have students make their word searches just with words that are written horizontally.	Students do their word searches as stated above.	Encourage students to make their word searches with words that share a letter. For example, they write *parrot* horizontally and *forest* vertically so that they share the letter *o*.

Reading Strategy: Predicting from Pictures

1 Look at the picture. Which animal comes in next? *the elephant*

2 Look at the pictures. What comes next? Draw a picture.

a

b

Students draw a pot with a red flower in full bloom.

105

Objective: **to predict from pictures and prepare to read a fiction text**

Materials: Build Creativity: butcher paper, paper, tape

1 Look at the picture. Which animal comes in next?

Focus students' attention on the picture in Activity I. Ask: *What is behind the door? (An elephant.) How do you know? (We can see part of the elephant.)* Tell students that pictures tell a lot about stories and that they can use them to predict what will happen next. Show a book to the class. Tell students to predict what will happen next. Students can make various predictions. For example, they could say that you will start reading or that you will ask them to read. Accept all predictions.

2 Look at the pictures. What comes next? Draw a picture.

Focus students' attention on the first sequence in Activity 2. Ask them to tell you what happens in the first picture that helps them guess what comes next. Guide students to guess what comes next in the second sequence, and ask them to draw it in the space provided.

Build Creativity!

What Comes Next?

Objective: Flow

In a column, draw the following on a piece of butcher paper before class, leaving space to the right of each drawing: yellow and blue splotches of paint, a drinking glass on the edge of a table, a rabbit looking at a leaf, a boy walking toward an anthill, a ball bouncing toward a window, an egg with cracks. Next to the drawing of the yellow and blue splotches of paint, draw an arrow to show sequence and, then, a green splotch. Lead students to understand why the splotch is green: *Yellow and blue make green.* If possible, show how, by mixing the two colors, you get green. With the class, draw what comes next after the drawing of the glass on the edge of a table—a broken glass on the floor. Form pairs, and have them draw what could happen next in the rest of the cases. Have students use one sheet of paper per drawing. Once students have finished their drawings, ask pairs to tape their drawings next to the corresponding drawings on the butcher paper. With students, talk about how similar or different predictions can be.

Cloud Animals

Objective: Focus

If possible, take the class outside. Have them lie on the ground and look up at the clouds. Encourage them to look in one spot and relax their eyes. Say: *What animals can you see?* Students might see multiple animals in the clouds and may even be able to tell a story about the animals they see. If you cannot go outside, consider showing a picture of clouds, or simply having students stare up at the ceiling. If students really focus, they will soon see patterns and shapes everywhere.

Objective: **to understand how to predict from pictures and to learn more about wild animals**
Materials: Audio CD 5.19, 5.20

Pre-Reading

Read the title and the name of the author. Ask students to look at the pictures and tell you who they think the main characters in the story are. Ask why they think the snake has a tongue full of paint. Ask if they think the snake and the rabbit are friends.

5.19 Page 106, section 1

Play Track 5.19 up to the end of the first paragraph. Pause and ask questions:

What is the snake's name?
What does Ketzi do?
What is her paintbrush?
What color is her tongue?

Personalization

Ask: *Do you know of any animal that can make art?*

5.19 Page 106, section 2

Continue Track 5.19 up to the end of the second paragraph. Pause and ask questions:

What does Ketzi paint?
Where does she paint?
What colors are the hearts, flowers, and suns?

5.19 Page 107, section 1

Play Track 5.19 through "'Eat my carrot.'" Pause and ask questions:

Where is Ketzi?
Who is she with?
What's the problem?
What does the rabbit have?

5.19 Page 107, section 2

Play the rest of Track 5.19. Ask questions:

What is Ketzi's favorite food?
What color is the rabbit?
Does the snake eat the rabbit? Why not?

Think

Read the questions in the Think box aloud, and have students answer them.

5.19

The Rabbit on the Moon

by Andrea González

Ketzi is a snake. She is an artist. Her tongue is her paintbrush! Her tongue is green, yellow, and orange.

Look at her pictures! Yellow hearts on the frogs, green flowers on the birds, and orange suns on the fish.

106

5B

One day, Ketzi is under a tree. A little rabbit is with her, too.
"I'm hungry!" says Ketzi.
"Here you are! Eat my carrot."

"No, thank you. My favorite food is white," Ketzi says.
"White food? Mmm … I'm white. Eat me!" the rabbit says.
"No! You're only a little rabbit, and you are so cute."

Think

What are rabbits' favorite foods?
What are snakes' favorite foods?

107

The Rabbit on the Moon

"Hug me, little rabbit! Let's fly!"

Are Ketzi and the little rabbit near the **stars**? Yes, they are!

They dance around the moon.

Think

Why do Ketzi and the rabbit dance?

108

Look! Ketzi is drawing on the moon!

That's a picture of the little rabbit!

Now, Ketzi and the little rabbit are friends forever.

Look at the full moon at night. A picture of the little rabbit is on the moon.

Think

Can you see a little rabbit on the moon?

109

5.20 Page 108

Play Track 5.20 up to the end of page 108. Pause and ask questions:

Where do Ketzi and the rabbit go?
What are they close to?
What do they do around the moon?

Personalization

Ask: *Would you like to go to the moon?*

Think

Read the question in the Think box aloud. Help students provide answers.

5.20 Page 109

Play the rest of Track 5.20. Ask questions:

What does Ketzi draw?
Where does she draw the rabbit?
What can we see at night?

Think

Read the question in the Think box aloud. You may want to explain what a legend is to avoid students' thinking there is really a drawing of a rabbit on the moon.

Build Creativity!

New Version

Objective: Try, Try, and Try Again

Form pairs. Have students invent a new version of the story by changing the two main characters and the setting. Have them draw new pictures of the characters, the decorated setting, the two characters going to the moon, and the moon with the drawing on it. As a follow-up activity, you could write a simple summary on the board for students to complete. Splitting the work between them, pairs write the summary under their four scenes. For example:

Scene 1:

(Joanne) is a (tiger). (Her) (tail) is (her) paintbrush. A (monkey) is with (her).

Scene 2:

Look at (her) pictures! (Yellow) hearts on the (elephants).

Scene 3:

(Joanne and the monkey) go to the moon.

Scene 4:

A picture of the (monkey) is on the moon. (Joanne and the monkey) are friends forever.

Explore the Text

1 Number the pictures in order. Retell the story with a partner.

2 Circle *T* (true) or *F* (false).

a Ketzi is a snake. (T) F
b The rabbit is hungry. T (F)
c Ketzi's favorite food is yellow. T (F)
d Ketzi eats the rabbit. T (F)

3 What comes next? Imagine and draw.

Which wild animals are not good friends?

110

Objective: **to deepen understanding of a fiction text**
Materials: paper

1 Number the pictures in order. Retell the story with a partner.

Form pairs, and ask them to number the scenes in Activity I. Correct the numbering as a class. Then, assign a scene to each pair. Since there are only six scenes, depending on the size of the class, some pairs will be assigned the same scene. Have the pairs who were assigned the first scene retell that part of the story. Continue the same way with the rest of the scenes.

2 Circle *T* (true) or *F* (false).

Have students do Activity 2 on their own. Then, check answers as a class. Call on volunteers to correct the sentences that are false.

3 What comes next? Imagine and draw.

Ask students general comprehension questions about the picture in Activity 3. Then, ask them to predict what will happen next and draw it.

Big Question Link

Point to the Big Question Link and read the question. Have volunteers answer the question.

Fun Corner!

Third Scene

After doing Activity 3, ask students to draw a third scene that would come after the one they have drawn.

Build Creativity!

Animal Categories

Objective: Try, Try, and Try Again

Write a category of animals on the board, and read it aloud. Give students thirty seconds to think of animals that fit in that category. Ask students to share the animals they came up with. Write them on the board. Then, repeat with other categories of animals. Possible categories include brown animals, scary animals, animals with two legs, animals with horns, etc. Have students compare each of their lists with a partner to see if they can add examples.

AB pages 92–93

Differentiated Instruction

Below-level ★	On-level ★★	Above-level ★★★
On the board, write ten *yes/no* questions with *is* about the fiction story and read them aloud—for example: *Is Ketzi a snake? Is her tongue white?* Form pairs. One student reads a question from the board, and the other student answers. Then, they swap roles until all the questions have been answered. Go around the class, monitoring performance.	Write these *yes/no* questions and answers on the board as you read them aloud: *Is Ketzi a snake? Yes, she is. Is her tongue white? No, it isn't.* Form four groups. Give groups time to think of five other *yes/no* questions they could ask about the fiction story. Ask students to follow the examples on the board. When students are ready, the groups take turns asking each other their questions. Check answers as a class.	Do the activity as described in the On-level section but have students write the *yes/no* questions. When students are ready, ask them to give their questions to another group to answer in writing.

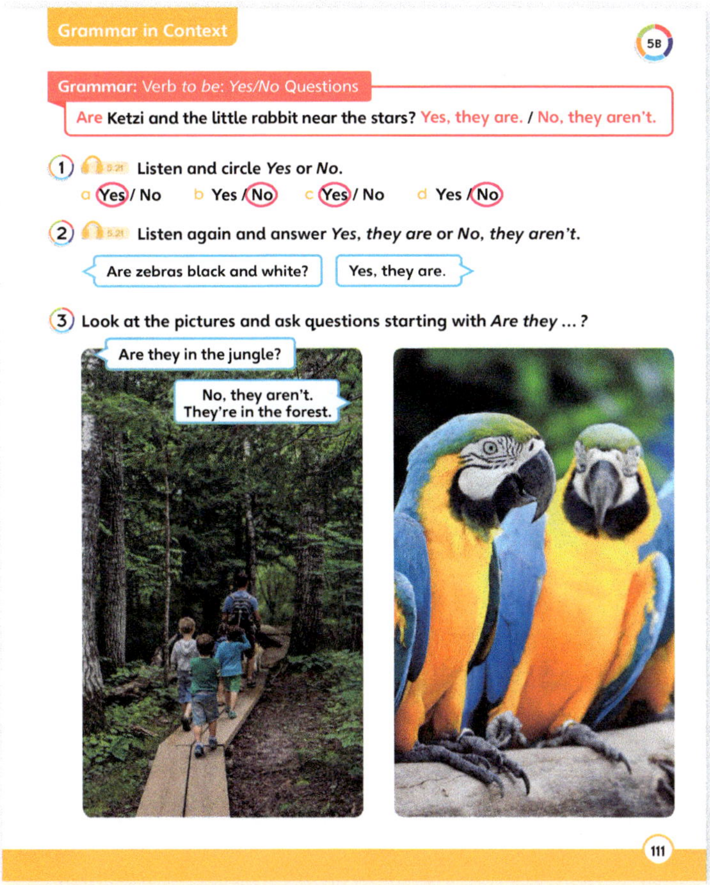

Grammar in Context

5B

Grammar: Verb *to be*: Yes/No Questions

Are Ketzi and the little rabbit near the stars? Yes, they are. / No, they aren't.

1 5.21 Listen and circle *Yes* or *No*.

a Yes / No b Yes / No c Yes / No d Yes / No

2 5.21 Listen again and answer *Yes, they are* or *No, they aren't*.

Are zebras black and white? Yes, they are.

3 Look at the pictures and ask questions starting with *Are they ...* ?

111

Objective: to use the verb ***to be*** in the plural in ***yes/no*** questions

Materials: Audio CD 5.21

Grammar Box

Write and say this aloud: *Is Ketzi an artist? Yes, she is.* Then, write and say this aloud: *Are Ketzi and the rabbit friends? Yes, they are.* Circle Ketzi in the first question and say: *One.* Then, circle Ketzi and the rabbit in the second question, and, as you point to the words, say: *One, two.* Focus students' attention on the use of *is* and *are* in the questions and answers. Read the example in the Grammar box aloud.

Practice Time I Ask *yes/no* questions with to be in the singular and plural about things in the classroom—for example: *Are the windows big? Is the door old?*

1 5.21 Listen and circle *Yes* or *No*.

Tell students that they will listen to some questions and that they will have to circle the correct answer, *yes* or *no*. Play Track 5.21, and check answers as a class.

2 5.21 Listen again and answer *Yes, they are* or *No, they aren't*.

Have students listen to Track 5.21 again and provide the answers after each question they hear.

3 Look at the pictures and ask questions starting with *Are they ... ?*

Have students look at the pictures in Activity 3. Read the example question and answer. Encourage students to provide more questions starting with *Are*. Write them on the board. Possible questions: *Are they a family? Are the children friends? Are the trees tall? Are the children tired? Are the children classmates?* Do the same with the second picture.

AB pages 94–95

Differentiated Instruction

Below-level ★	On-level ★★	Above-level ★★★
Write *yes/no* questions with the verb *to be* in the plural about the fiction story on the board and read them aloud. For example: *Are Ketzi and the rabbit in the jungle? Are the colors on Ketzi's tongue green, yellow, and red? Are there green flowers on the fish? Are Ketzi and the rabbit hungry?* Form pairs. One student reads a question from the board, and the other student answers. Then, they swap roles until all the questions have been answered. Go around the classroom, monitoring performance.	On the board, write a *yes/no* question with *to be* in the plural and read it aloud: *Are Ketzi and the rabbit in the jungle?* Form four groups. Give groups time to think of five other *yes/no* questions in the plural about the fiction story. Ask students to follow the example on the board. When students are ready, the groups take turns asking each other their questions. Check answers as a class.	Do the activity as described in the On-level section, but have the students write their *yes/no* questions. When students are ready, ask them to give their questions to another group to answer.

Objectives: to talk about wild animals; to learn to take care of animals
Materials: Audio CD 5.22, 5.23, Cue Card 7

1 5.22 Listen, point, and repeat.

Play Track 5.22, and have students point and repeat. Ask students if they can recognize which animal each body part belongs to.

2 Which animals can you see in the pictures? Guess.

Ask volunteers which animal they see in each picture.

3 5.23 Listen and number the animals.

Ask students to describe the animals in Activity 2 in terms of color, size, home, body parts, etc. Then, play Track 5.23, and have students number the animals. Check answers.

Oracy Extension Activity

Read the steps in the Oracy Extension activity aloud. Display the Cue Card, and have students do the activity with you. Ask students to complete Check Your Oracy! on page 97 of their Activity Books.

Big Question Link

Point to the Big Question Link, and read the question and answer aloud. Complete the activity as a class.

ACTIVITY BOOK PAGE 96

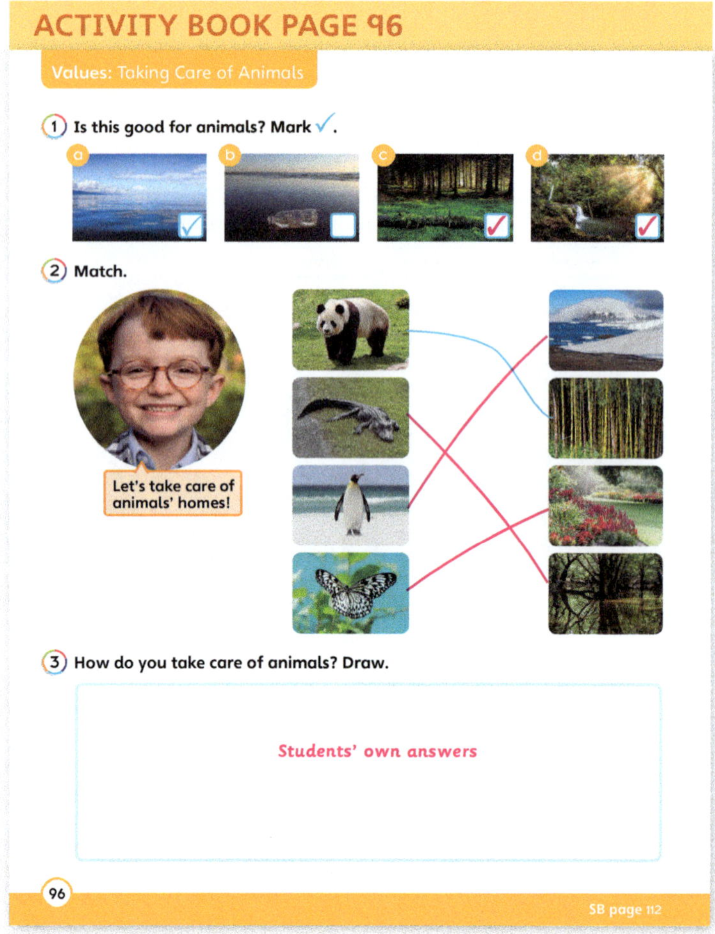

1 Is this good for animals? Mark ✓.

Have students turn to page 96 of their Activity Books. Ask them to look at the pictures and mark what is good for animals.

2 Match.

Have students look at the pictures. Focus on the example to make sure students understand the activity. Monitor, and provide support if necessary. Check answers as a class.

3 How do you take care of animals? Draw.

Ask students what animals need and what people do to help them. Have students tell you what they do to take care of animals. Lead them to draw based on the text in the speech bubble in Activity 2.

AB page 96

Objective: **to consolidate, extend, and personalize learning on the unit topic**

Materials: a mask of a wild animal, scissors, glue, boxes, colored paper, paint, recycled material from home

- **1** Ask students to choose their favorite wild animal and write its name in their notebooks.
- **2** Take out the wild animal mask, and show it to the class. Tell students they will make masks of their favorite animal at home. Read the Big Challenge question and statement aloud. Show students the pictures of the children wearing masks. Provide ideas to help students imagine the mask they will create. Give students a reasonable amount of time to do the masks at home.
- **3** Ask students whose favorite wild animals are the same to get together in a group in class and think about their animal and the things they could say about it. On the board, write a structure for students to follow: *I'm a … I have … I live …* Have students complete the sentences and add more ideas—the animal's color, its favorite food, etc. Monitor students' work.
- **4** Establish a day for students to present their work to the class. Optional: Record or have students record one another's presentations to share their work.
- As a follow-up, hold an art exhibition of the masks. You could also organize a play.

Home-school | Portfolio: Big Challenge

Big Question Link

Read the Big Question aloud. Have the class revisit the Big Question Links on pages 96, 99, 110, and 112 and discuss what they have learned about wild animals. Help with emergent language.

- Use the following questions to help review the Big Question:

  Where do wild animals live?
  What do wild animals eat?
  What's your favorite wild animal?
  Where does it live?
  What does it eat?
  Which wild animals don't you like?
  Which animals can be friends?
  Name animals that live in the jungle.
  Name animals that live in the ocean.
  Name animals that have a tail.
  Name animals that have four legs.
- Finally, have students turn to page 97 of their Activity Books to complete the Big Challenge self-assessment.

AB pages 97–99

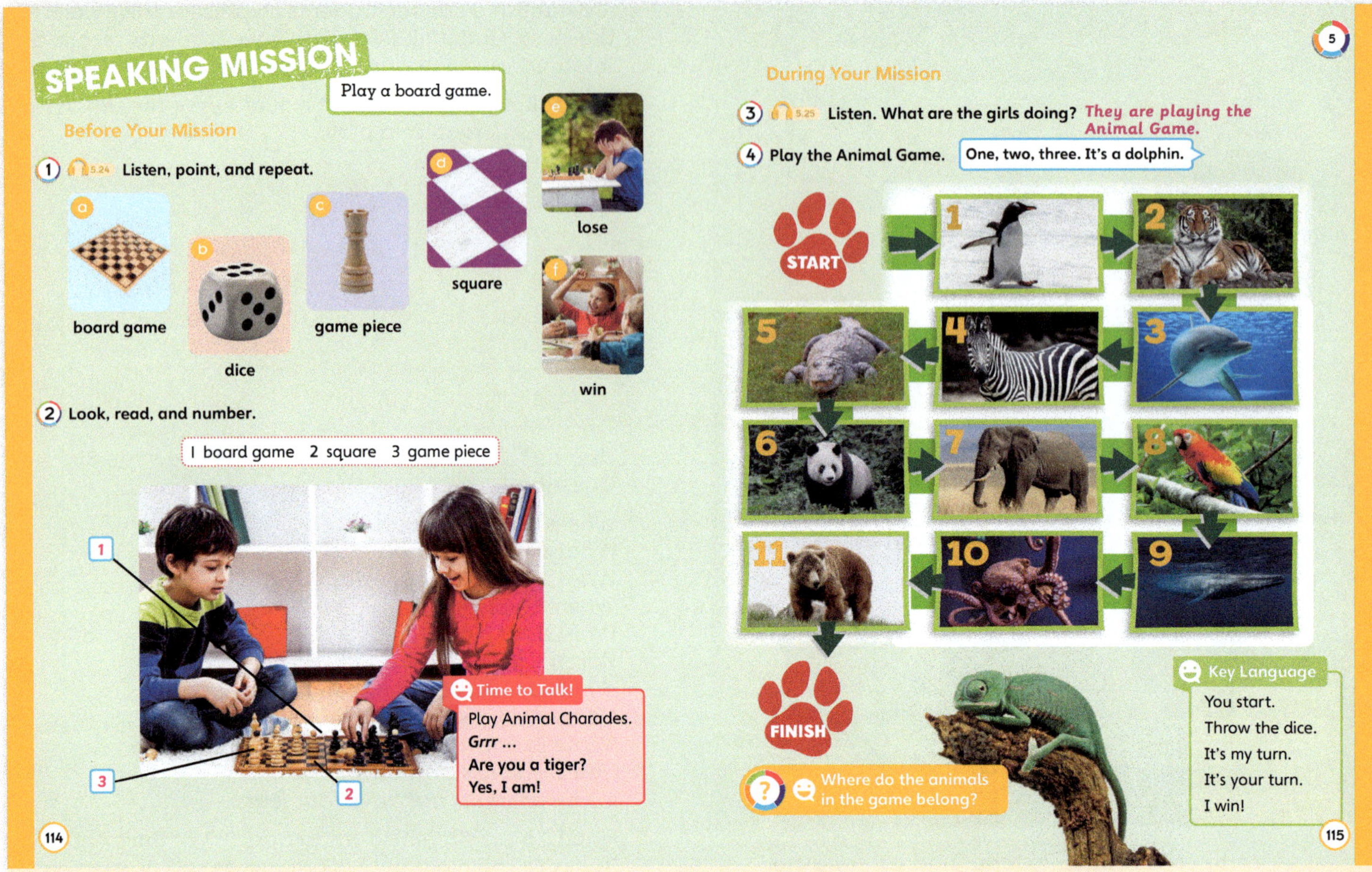

SPEAKING MISSION

Play a board game.

Before Your Mission

1 5.24 Listen, point, and repeat.

a board game
b dice
c game piece
d square
e lose
f win

2 Look, read, and number.

1 board game 2 square 3 game piece

Time to Talk!
Play Animal Charades.
Grrr ...
Are you a tiger?
Yes, I am!

114

5

During Your Mission

3 5.25 Listen. What are the girls doing? They are playing the Animal Game.

4 Play the Animal Game. One, two, three. It's a dolphin.

START 1 2 3 4 5 6 7 8 9 10 11 FINISH

Where do the animals in the game belong?

Key Language
You start.
Throw the dice.
It's my turn.
It's your turn.
I win!

115

Objective: to play a board game
Speaking Mission Words: ***board game, dice, game piece, square, lose, win***
Materials: Audio CD 5.24, 5.25, dice and tokens (paperclips, coins, and other small objects)

1 5.24 Listen, point, and repeat.

Have students look at the pictures. Play Track 5.24, and encourage students to point and repeat the words.

2 Look, read, and number.

Have students look at the pictures in Activity 2, read the words, and number the pictures.

> **Time to Talk!**
>
> Read the text and examples in the Time to Talk! box aloud. Demonstrate how to play the game. Form pairs and have them play the game.

3 5.25 Listen. What are the girls doing?

Play Track 5.25, and ask: *What are the girls doing?* Invite volunteers to answer the question.

4 Play the Animal Game.

Play Track 5.25 again, and ask students if they remember what the girls said while they were playing. Then, read the key language aloud. Ask volunteers to repeat, and monitor pronunciation. Have students take out the dice and tokens.

Ask students to play the Animal Game in pairs or in groups of four. Explain how the game works: Students take turns rolling the dice and moving along the board. Participants have to mention the animal they land on. To win the game, a participant has to land exactly on FINISH. If the roll takes them past FINISH, the game piece is moved backwards the extra number of space and the participants continue playing until someone finally lands on FINISH. Remind students to use the key language while they are playing. Monitor performance. Optional: Record or have students record one another to share their work.

Home-school Portfolio: Speaking Mission

> **Big Question Link**
>
> Point to the Big Question Link, and ask the question. Have volunteers answer.

AB pages 100–01

6 What can people do?

Literacy

Read: a nonfiction text about children with amazing abilities; a fiction text about a girl who learns how to persevere

Reading Strategies: predicting from titles; identifying cause and effect

Ready to Write

Learn to Write: verbs

Getting Ready to Write: make a mind map

Oracy

Skill: Asking for Agreement

Cue Cards: 2–3, 8: 2. *Yes.* 3. *No.* 8. *Do you agree?*

Oracy Performance Task 2: Discussion: agree on a game to play

Language

Key Words 1: *ability, paint, run, skate, play basketball, talk*

Key Words 2: *see, ride, climb, say, spell, swim*

Key Words 3: *blind, backwards*

Key Words 4: *music, love, dancer, practice, read, puppy*

Oracy Performance Task Words: *charades, tag, musical chairs, freeze dance, hopscotch, hide-and-seek, board games, marbles, telephone*

Grammar in Context

***I can / I can't*:** *I can ride a horse. I can't walk.*

***Yes/No* Questions with *can* and *can't*:** *Can Hanna dance well? Yes, she can. No, she can't.*

Phonics

Initial Sounds: *h, t, p, m, b, d*

Listening

Dialogue: Asking for Help

Values

Perseverance

The Big Challenge

What different things can we do?
Make a spinner

What can people do?

- [ ] Talk about your abilities.
- [ ] Learn to agree or disagree.
- [ ] Identify an action verb.
- [ ] Make a spinner.
- [ ] Agree on what to play together.

What can the children do?

Can you do these things?

Can everyone do the same things?

6.1 Key Words 1

ability
paint
run
skate
play basketball
talk

1 6.1 Watch the video. Mark ✓ the actions you see.

dance ✓	draw ☐	swim ☐
paint ✓	play basketball ✓	

2 6.1 Watch again. Complete the graphic organizer in the Activity Book.

AB page 102

116 117

Objective: to introduce the topic of what people can do
Key Words I: ***ability, paint, run, skate, play basketball, talk***
Materials: Video 6.I, Audio CD 6.I, Flashcards 6.I–6.6

WHAT CAN PEOPLE DO?

- Ask students to open their books to page II6. Read the Big Question aloud. Ask the first question on page II6, and elicit the actions in the pictures.
- Ask the second question. Point to the girl jumping rope, and ask a volunteer: *Can you jump rope?* Do the same with the rest of the pictures.
- Have students decide which of the activities in the pictures they think is the most difficult for them. You could mention an activity and ask students to put their hands up if they think it is the most difficult. Check results as a class.
- Finally, ask the last question. Say: *Raise your hand if you can play the violin. Raise your hand if you can ride a bike.* This way, you can help students see that not everyone can do the same things.

6.1 Key Words 1 Use the flashcards and audio to present Key Words I. Hold up the flashcards as you play Track 6.I. Have students repeat the words. Then, show the flashcards one at a time, and have students say the words.

1 6.1 Watch the video. Mark ✓ the actions you see.

Watch the video, pausing after "Let's have a look!" Ask: *What is today's Big Question? (What can people do?) What can and can't the presenter do?* Continue the video. Pause after "Her mom is teaching her." Then, ask comprehension questions about Nadia, Javier, the boy and his dog, and Jane. Continue the video. Pause after "She can talk in sign language," and ask comprehension questions. Then, say: *Can you use sign language?* If anybody in the class knows how, let them teach some words in sign language. Continue with the rest of the video. Finally, have students do Activity I. Check answers as a class.

2 6.1 Watch again. Complete the graphic organizer in the Activity Book.

Form pairs. Play the video again, and have students complete Activity I on AB page I02.

AB page 102

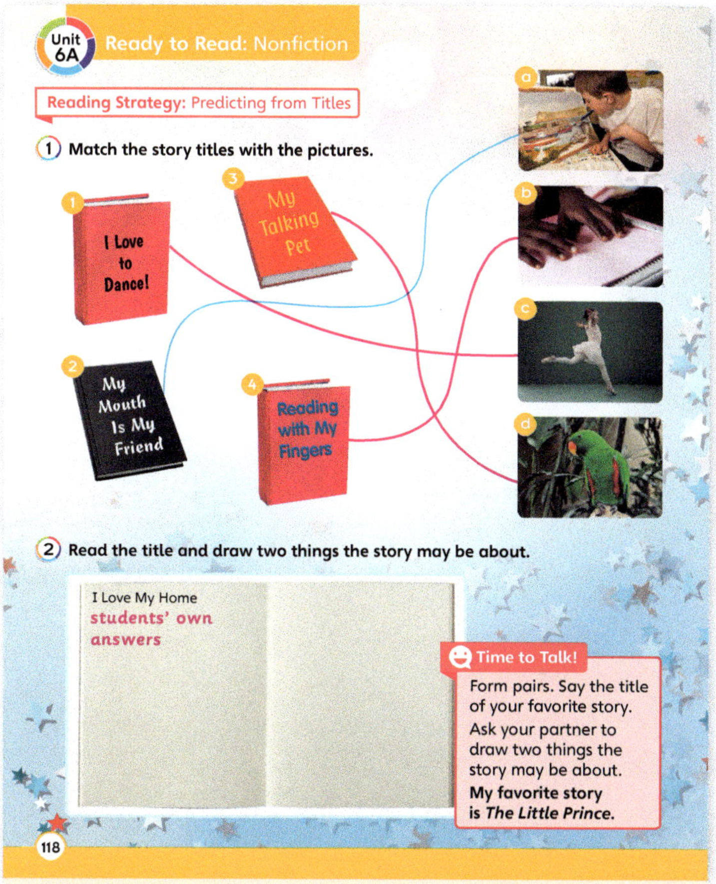
Unit 6A Ready to Read: Nonfiction

Reading Strategy: Predicting from Titles

1 Match the story titles with the pictures.

1 I Love to Dance!
2 My Mouth Is My Friend
3 My Talking Pet
4 Reading with My Fingers

a b c d

2 Read the title and draw two things the story may be about.

I Love My Home
students' own answers

Time to Talk!
Form pairs. Say the title of your favorite story. Ask your partner to draw two things the story may be about.
My favorite story is *The Little Prince*.

118

Objective: to predict from titles and prepare to read a nonfiction text

Key Words 1: ***ability, paint, run, skate, play basketball, talk***

Materials: storybooks, paper; Fun Corner: three pictures that can represent different storybook covers (e.g., a picture of a girl in a park, a picture of a pet, a picture of friends); Build Creativity: timer

6.1 Key Words 1 Use the flashcards and audio to review Key Words 1.

1 Match the story titles with the pictures.

Ask students what they used in unit 5 to predict what comes next in a story. *(Pictures.)* Tell students that story titles can also help us predict what a story is about. Show the class the cover of one of the storybooks you have, and read the title on it. Ask students what they think the story is about. Do the same with the other storybooks. Then, have students look at the book covers and pictures in Activity 1. Read each of the book titles, and ask students to match them with the pictures. Check answers as a class.

2 Read the title and draw two things the story may be about.

Lead students in doing Activity 2. Once they have completed it, ask volunteers to show the class their drawings. Write the words for the things students have drawn: *family, bedroom,* etc. Analyze which words come up the most often.

Time to Talk!

Have the class form two lines with an equal number of students. Ask students to take their notebooks and pencils with them. Have the first student in the two lines pair up. Do the same with the rest of the students. Then, ask pairs to do the Time to Talk! activity together.

Fun Corner!

Book Titles

Form three groups. Tape three pictures on the board, and tell students that these represent book covers of different stories. Ask groups to come up with simple titles made up of two or three words for each picture. Provide examples (*My Pet, Happy Girl,* etc.). When students are ready, write the groups' titles under each picture and compare them.

Build Creativity!

Guess the Number

Objective: Try, Try, and Try Again

Think of a challenge with movements that are easy to count, such as hopping on one leg. Ask students to guess how many times they can do it in a certain amount of time. Then, set a timer, and have students do the movement and count. How close were their guesses to the reality? Have them repeat the process. Their guesses should be more accurate the second time around. You can then repeat, specifying a different amount of time.

My Story

Objective: Flow

Ask students to do this activity at home. Have them make a book cover that includes a title and a drawing. Encourage students to use thick paper and to decorate their work. As a follow-up, you can ask students to take three sheets of paper and draw a simple picture story based on the book title. These can then be stapled behind the cover.

6.2 **Key Words 2** Use Flashcards 6.7–6.12 and the audio to pre-teach Key Words 2. Show each flashcard as students listen to Track 6.2. Have students repeat each word. Tape the flashcards on the board, and leave them there.

Pre-Reading

Read the title, and teach the word *amazing*. Ask students if they know a person with an amazing ability or if they have special abilities themselves. Then, ask if they know a person who cannot do something that they can do. Have students look at pages 119 and 120. Encourage them to guess what amazing abilities the kids have.

6.3 **Page 119, section 1**

Play the part of Track 6.3 about Sven. Teach the word *clap*. Pause and ask questions:

What's the boy's name?
How old is he?
What can he do?

Set the clock for students to see how long a minute is. Tell them the world record for clapping is more than 1,000 times in a minute!

6.3 **Page 119, section 2**

Play the rest of Track 6.3. Ask questions:

What's the boy's name?
What can't he do?
What can he do?

Personalization

Say: *Can you do any of the things Sven and Ethan can do?*

Objective: to learn about some kids' amazing abilities
Key Words 2: *see, ride, climb, say, spell, swim*
Materials: Audio CD 6.2, 6.3, 6.4, Flashcards 6.7–6.12

6.4 Page 120, section 1

Play the part of Track 6.4 about Sharie. Pause and ask questions:

What is the girl's name?
What can she say?
What is TAC?

Ask volunteers to spell some easy short words in their language backwards. Then, try with simple three-letter words in English.

6.4 Page 120, section 2

Play the part of Track 6.4 about Buassi. Pause and ask questions:

What's the boy's name?
How old is he?
Where can he swim?
What can he do underwater?

Personalization

Ask: *What happens to your eyes when you open them in the ocean?*

6.4 Page 120, section 3

Play the rest of Track 6.4. Ask questions:

What's the boy's name?
What can't he do?
What can he do?

Personalization

Ask: *Whose ability would you like to have?*

Think

Ask the question in the Think box. Discuss what makes other people amazing.

AB page 103

Differentiated Instruction

Below-level ★	On-level ★★	Above-level ★★★
Hold an abilities contest. Form three groups. Call on one student from each group, and have them do the same task in a set amount of time. The student who performs best gets a point for their group. Repeat with other students and tasks. Possible activities: Name as many animals as possible in thirty seconds. Memorize objects in a picture in one minute. Solve a simple math problem. Sing a song. Dance.	Hold an abilities contest, and, to the abilities mentioned in the Below-level description, add: Write the alphabet. Put letters in alphabetical order.	Hold the abilities contest, but make the activities more challenging. For example: Spell words from previous units. Spell words backwards. Write as many toy names as possible. Put key words in alphabetical order.

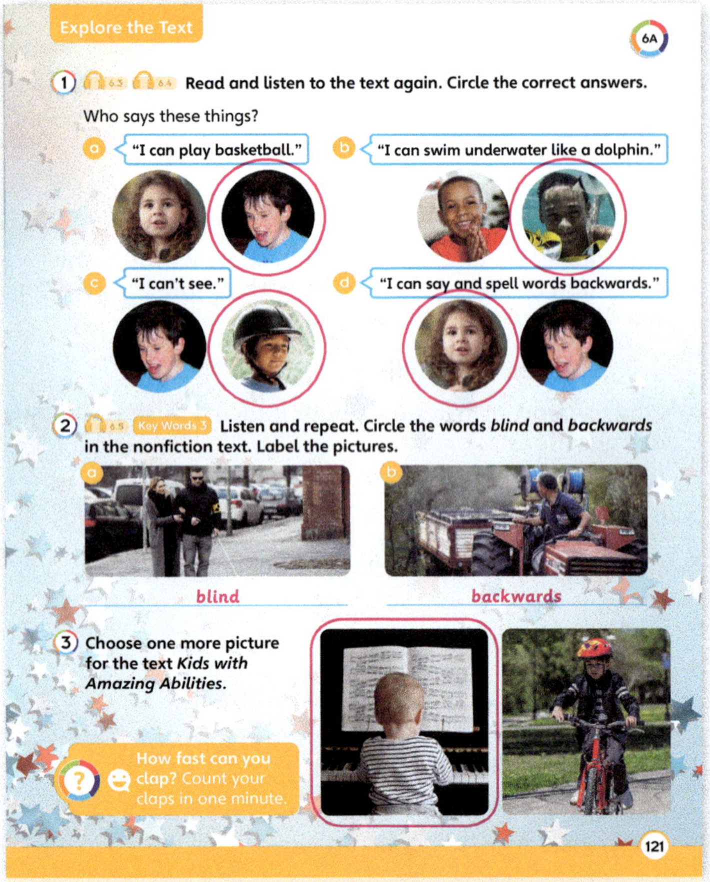

Explore the Text

6A

1 6.3 6.4 Read and listen to the text again. Circle the correct answers.

Who says these things?

a "I can play basketball."

b "I can swim underwater like a dolphin."

c "I can't see."

d "I can say and spell words backwards."

2 6.5 Key Words 3 Listen and repeat. Circle the words *blind* and *backwards* in the nonfiction text. Label the pictures.

a blind

b backwards

3 Choose one more picture for the text *Kids with Amazing Abilities.*

How fast can you clap? Count your claps in one minute.

121

Objective: to recall specific information from the text and identify words in context

Key Words 3: ***blind, backwards***

Materials: Audio CD 6.3, 6.4, 6.5, timer

1 6.3 6.4 Read and listen to the text again. Circle the correct answers.

Ask students to follow the text as you play Tracks 6.3 and 6.4. Then, ask volunteers to read the text in the speech bubbles in Activity 1, and have students circle the child who says those words.

2 6.5 Key Words 3 Listen and repeat. Circle the words *blind* and *backwards* in the nonfiction text. Label the pictures.

Play Track 6.5, and ask students to repeat. Then, tell them to circle the words in the nonfiction text. Have students label the pictures in Activity 2. Form pairs, and ask them to swap books to check spelling.

3 Choose one more picture for the text *Kids with Amazing Abilities.*

Ask volunteers to tell you what the kids in the pictures in Activity 3 can do. Ask: *Who has an amazing ability? (The baby who plays the piano.)*

Big Question Link

Ask a volunteer to go to the front. Set a timer for one minute. Ask the student to clap for one minute while two other students count the number of claps. Then, let other students do the same. Depending on the size of your class, you could hold a contest to see who is the fastest clapper. Another possibility is to ask students to work in pairs and then share their results.

Build Creativity!

Quiz

Objective: Try, Try, and Try Again

Form four groups. Tell them they will make a five-item quiz for another group to answer. Guide students by providing examples, such as an addition problem *(5 + 9)*, a sentence with a word to complete *(I can play b________l.)*, an instruction to draw *(Draw a feather.)*, jumbled letters to make a word *(u s m i c)*, and a sentence to capitalize and punctuate correctly *(i don't like soup)*. If you think your class will find this activity difficult, write an example five-item quiz on the board, and ask students to model their five items on the five items in your quiz:

5 + 6 =

I can ride a h ___ ___ ___ ___.

Draw a pencil case.

s h c o l o (school)

i can swim (capitalize I, add period)

Monitor groups' work. Then, ask groups to exchange quizzes and complete them.

AB pages 104–05

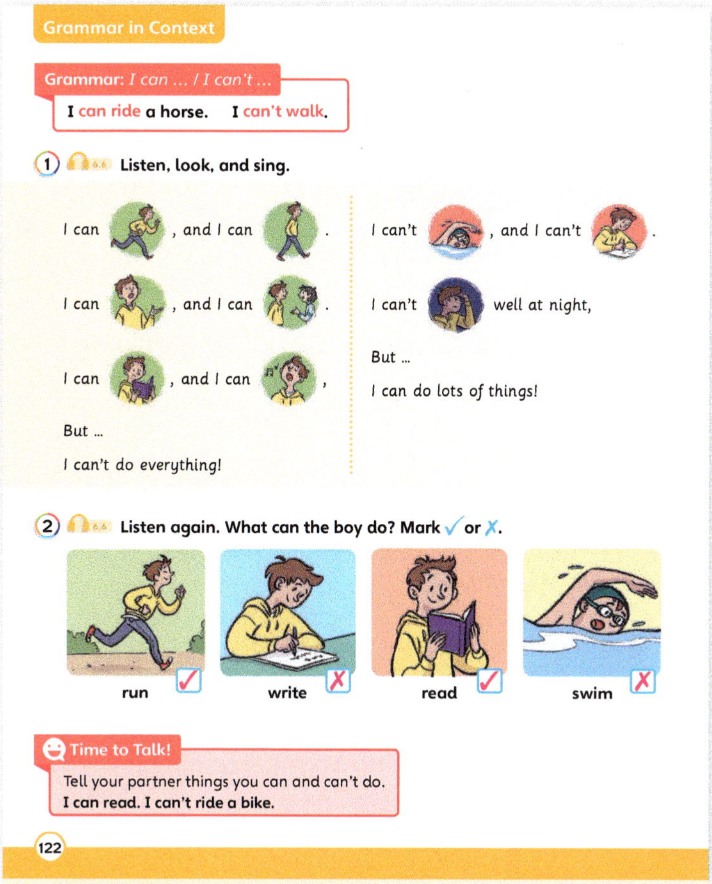

Grammar in Context

Grammar: *I can … / I can't …*

I can ride a horse. I can't walk.

1 6.6 Listen, look, and sing.

I can , and I can .

I can , and I can .

I can , and I can ,

But …

I can't do everything!

I can't , and I can't .

I can't well at night,

But …

I can do lots of things!

2 6.6 Listen again. What can the boy do? Mark ✓ or ✗.

run ✓ write ✗ read ✓ swim ✗

Time to Talk!

Tell your partner things you can and can't do.

I can read. I can't ride a bike.

122

Objective: to use *can* and *can't*

Materials: Audio CD 6.6

Grammar Box

Ask a volunteer to read the sentences in the Grammar box aloud. Have other students provide similar examples.

1 6.6 Listen, look, and sing.

Read the text in the song, stopping wherever there is a drawing. Encourage students to guess the verb each drawing represents. Then, play Track 6.6 through "I can't do everything!" Ask volunteers to go to the front and mime the actions as you sing and play the song, for example, to run when they hear *I can run*. Then, play the second part of Track 6.6, sing, and ask other volunteers to mime the actions. Finally, play the complete song as the class sings with you and mimes.

2 6.6 Listen again. What can the boy do? Mark ✓ or ✗.

Read each of the verbs in Activity 2, and have students mark what the boy can and can't do.

Practice Time I As a class, brainstorm other verbs that can be used with *can/can't*. Write them on the board. Examples include: *ride (a horse/a bike), say, spell, clap, play (soccer/ the drums), draw, paint, dance, skate,* and *jump*. Keep the words on the board for the *Fun Corner!* activity.

Time to Talk!

Form pairs, and ask them to do the activity in the Time to Talk! box.

Fun Corner!

Our Song

Form groups of four or five students. Have them invent their own version of the song in Activity I by using the verbs that are on the board or any others they can think of. For example, their first part might be: *I can draw, and I can paint. I can dance, and I can jump. I can skate, and a can ride a bike. But … I can't do everything!* Students sing their song, miming the actions.

Build Creativity!

Quiz

Objective: Try, Try, and Try Again

Give students one minute, and challenge them to write as many things that they can do as possible. You may want to encourage them to write complete sentences, such as: *I can play the piano.* Have students compare answers in small groups and see if they can add to their lists. Repeat with *can't*, but allow them less time. Have groups discuss what things in their *can't* lists they would like to be able to do.

AB pages 106–07

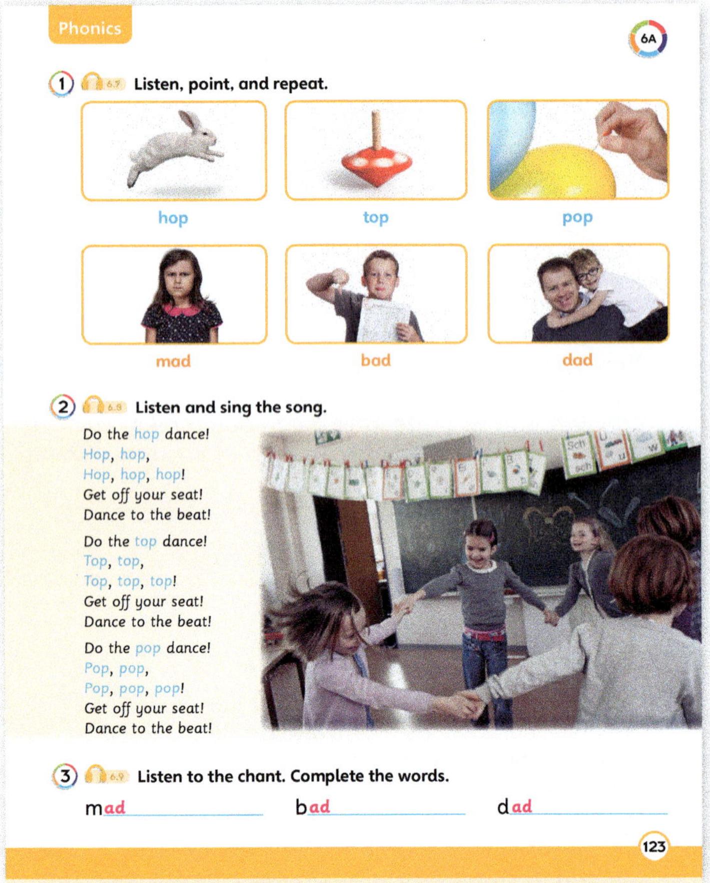

Phonics

6A

1 6.7 Listen, point, and repeat.

hop top pop

mad bad dad

2 6.8 Listen and sing the song.

Do the hop dance!
Hop, hop,
Hop, hop, hop!
Get off your seat!
Dance to the beat!

Do the top dance!
Top, top,
Top, top, top!
Get off your seat!
Dance to the beat!

Do the pop dance!
Pop, pop,
Pop, pop, pop!
Get off your seat!
Dance to the beat!

3 6.9 Listen to the chant. Complete the words.

mad ______ bad ______ dad ______

123

Objective: to identify the initial sounds *h, t, p, m, b, d*

Materials: Audio CD 6.7, 6.8, 6.9, paper

1 6.7 Listen, point, and repeat.

Have students look at the pictures in Activity 1. Play Track 6.7, and ask students to point and repeat. Correct pronunciation as needed.

2 6.8 Listen and sing the song.

Ask students to stand up and hop with you. Then, ask them to move as if they were tops. Finally, ask them to pretend to pop like a balloon. Ask students to get in one or two circles (depending on the size of your class). Tell them that you will play a song, and invite them to dance with you using their new moves.

3 6.9 Listen to the chant. Complete the words.

Ask students to say as many words in English as they remember that start with *m*. Do the same with *b* and *d*. Play Track 6.9, and give students enough time to complete each word in Activity 3.

Fun Corner!

Freeze Dance

Play Freeze Dance with children. Play Track 6.8. and ask everyone to dance. Whenever you pause the song, students have to freeze. If they don't, they are out of the game.

Alphabet Words

Write __*ad* on the board. As a class, work through the whole alphabet and see how many different words you can make simply by changing the first letter: *had*, *mad*, etc. Repeat with __*op*.

Build Creativity!

Give Me a ... !

Objective: **Flow**

Form three groups, and ask them to write a list of five words with the pattern consonant–vowel–consonant (CVC), such as the words they learned in Activity 1 (*hop*, *mad*, etc.). The words can have any vowel. Go around the classroom, providing support. Tell students they can search for words on previous phonics pages in the book. They will encounter CVC words such as *hen*, *ten*, *mom*, *pan*, *man*, *pen*, *bed*, and *pin*.

Have students follow the chant from Activity 3 to create chants with the words they have written. Ask one group to go to the front and chant:

Give me (an M. M)!

Give me (an A. A)!

Give me (a D. D)!

What does that spell?

The other groups should say what the word is: *(Mad)*. The group at the front continues with the chant: *Say it three times. (Mad! Mad! Mad!)* Continue the same way with the rest of the words and groups.

AB page 108

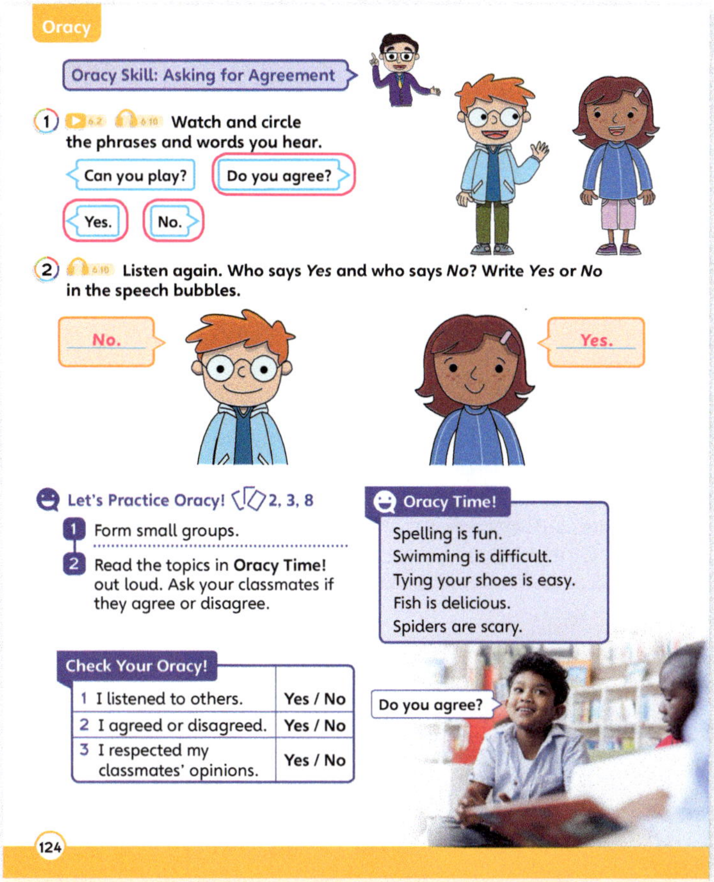

Oracy

Oracy Skill: Asking for Agreement

1 6.2 6.10 Watch and circle the phrases and words you hear.

Can you play? | Do you agree?

Yes. | No.

2 6.10 Listen again. Who says *Yes* and who says *No*? Write *Yes* or *No* in the speech bubbles.

No. | Yes.

Let's Practice Oracy! 2, 3, 8

1 Form small groups.

2 Read the topics in **Oracy Time!** out loud. Ask your classmates if they agree or disagree.

Oracy Time!

Spelling is fun.
Swimming is difficult.
Tying your shoes is easy.
Fish is delicious.
Spiders are scary.

Check Your Oracy!

1	I listened to others.	Yes / No
2	I agreed or disagreed.	Yes / No
3	I respected my classmates' opinions.	Yes / No

Do you agree?

124

Objective: to ask for agreement
Cue Cards: 2. *Yes.* 3. *No.* 8. *Do you agree?*
Materials: Video 6.2, Audio CD 6.10, tape, Cue Cards 2–3, 8; Fun Corner: puppets or stuffed animals

Oracy Skill

Remind students of the two words they have been using to agree and disagree. (*Yes. No.*)

1 6.2 6.10 Watch and circle the phrases and words you hear.

Ask students to look at the oracy characters, and have them tell you who they are. *(Jack and Kate)* Ask a volunteer to read the text in the speech bubbles in Activity 1. Have students watch V6.2 and circle what they hear.

2 6.10 Listen again. Who says *Yes* and who says *No*? Write *Yes* or *No* in the speech bubbles.

Play Track 6.10, and ask students to complete the speech bubbles.

Present and Practice Hold up Cue Card 8. Read the question aloud: *Do you agree?* Tape the Cue Card to the board. Ask students to watch and listen carefully as you play V6.2 again. Tell them that, when they hear the expression on the Cue Card, they should raise their hand. Encourage students to repeat the expression with rising intonation.

Let's Practice Oracy! 2, 3, 8

- **1** Ask students to form small groups.
- **2** Ask a volunteer to read the sentences in the Oracy Time! box and check that everyone understands. Then, ask groups to make short dialogues using them. Encourage students to use *I think …* .
- Optional: Record or have student record themselves as they perform their dialogues to share their work.
- Have students complete Check Your Oracy!

Home-school | Portfolio: Oracy

Fun Corner!

Act It Out!

Ask a volunteer to come to the front and tell you something they do not like, for example, broccoli. Take out the puppets or stuffed animals, and give one to the volunteer. Guide them to make a dialogue with you and perform it in front of the class. Use *I think* … followed by the Cue Card question. Encourage the volunteer to use *I don't like …* and *I think …*

You: *I think broccoli is delicious. Do you agree?*

Student: *No, I don't like broccoli. I think …*

Form pairs, and ask them to think of a dialogue similar to yours and perform it in front of the class.

AB page 108

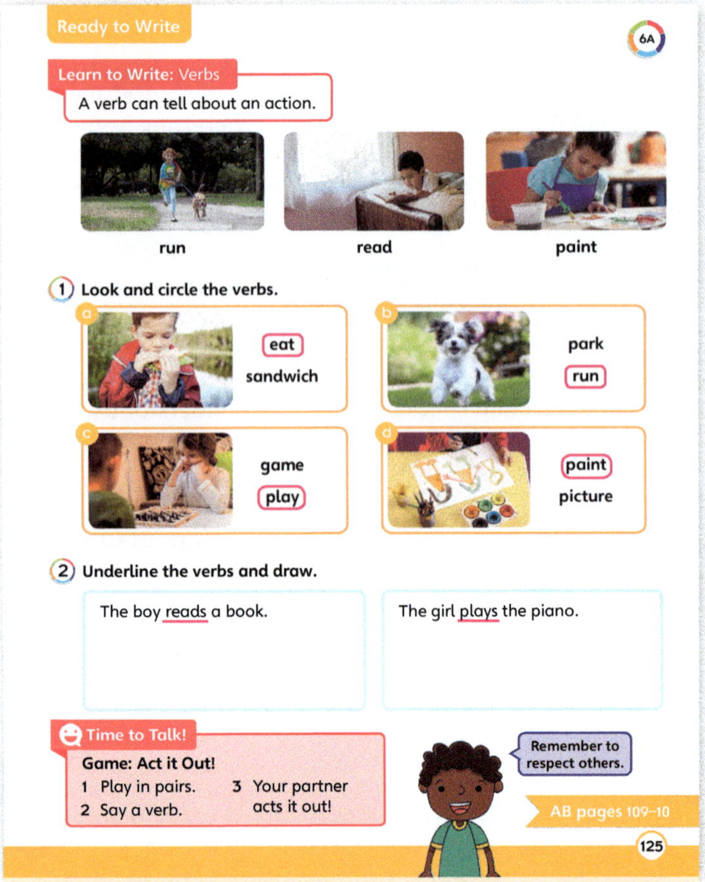

Ready to Write

6A

Learn to Write: Verbs

A verb can tell about an action.

run read paint

1 Look and circle the verbs.

a eat / sandwich

b park / run

c game / play

d paint / picture

2 Underline the verbs and draw.

The boy reads a book.

The girl plays the piano.

Time to Talk!

Game: Act it Out!

1 Play in pairs.
2 Say a verb.
3 Your partner acts it out!

Remember to respect others.

AB pages 109–10

125

Objective: to identify verbs

Materials: paper

Learn to Write Box

Read the sentence in the Learn to Write box aloud. Have students look at the pictures under the box. Ask what the children are doing. Tell the class that the things the children are doing are all actions. Explain that action words are called *verbs*. Ask students to give you examples of verbs they learned in the text *Kids with Amazing Abilities*.

1 Look and circle the verbs.

Pretend you are eating. Say: *I'm eating.* Eat *is an action. It's a verb. Is* sandwich *an action? (No.)* Have students circle the verb *eat*. Then, give students time to work on their own. Correct answers as a class.

2 Underline the verbs and draw.

Read the sentences in Activity 2, and ask students to identify the verbs and underline them. Then, have students draw the actions.

Time to Talk!

Before students play the game, draw their attention to Liam, the oracy character. Read the reminder aloud. Guide two volunteers to demonstrate how the game is played for the rest of the class. Then, form pairs, and have them play.

Fun Corner!

Guess!

Form two teams. Assign ten verbs per team. Hold a guessing competition. A member of Team A acts out a verb, and Team B has two chances to guess the action. Team B gets two points if they guess correctly on the first attempt and one point if they guess correctly on the second. If they don't guess correctly, then they perform an action, and Team A gets two chance to guess. The winning team is the one with the most points. Possible verbs to perform include: *play (basketball/the piano), dance, draw, eat, read, swim, sing, write, clap, climb, talk, skate, ride (a horse/a bike), tie (shoelaces), sit, see, jump rope, touch, paint, run*, etc.

AB pages 109–10

Differentiated Instruction

Below-level ★	On-level ★★	Above-level ★★★
Write words that are nouns, adjectives, and verbs on the board. Invite students to come to the board and draw a red circle around the verbs. Students learned what a noun is in unit 4. You could also ask them to circle the nouns in another color. Tell students that some words on the board are neither verbs nor nouns.	Form three groups of students. Ask them to make a list of words that are verbs and another list of words that are not. Then, have them swap lists with another group, and instruct students to circle the list with the actions. Have them check that all of the words are verbs. Students learned what a noun is in unit 4. You could also ask them to circle the nouns from the second list in another color.	Write complete sentences on the board. Ask students to copy them into their notebooks and circle the verbs in them. Students learned what a noun is in unit 4. You could also ask them to circle the nouns in another color. Have pairs of students swap notebooks and correct each other's work.

Objective: **to make a spider diagram**
Materials: Optional: examples of creative graphic organizers, paper

Graphic Organizers

Graphic organizers are simple yet effective visual learning tools to help students organize ideas. They help as a pre-writing strategy to show students how to plan out their writing in a fun way. There are various types of organizers, such as spider diagrams, Venn diagrams, and tables. Use the one that best suits your class and the task you have in mind.

1 IDENTIFY

Write *run* in the center of the board. Ask: *Is this a noun or a verb? (A verb.)* Ask students what objects they associate with the action of running. Students may come up with *sneakers, shorts, a bottle of water,* etc. Teach students how to make a spider diagram by drawing pictures of these objects around the verb *run*.

2 WRITE

Ask students to choose one of the verbs they learned in the unit and make a spider diagram for it. Guide them to make a creative spider diagram on their own. (See Differentiated Instruction.)

3 EDIT

Have students swap spider diagrams to check their work. Encourage students to suggest more ideas for the spider diagrams, if possible. Have students edit their work, if necessary.

4 FOLLOW UP

Write the word *verbs* on the board. Then, ask some students to give you their spider diagrams. Tape them on the board around the word *verbs*, and draw lines from the spider diagram to the word to make a big spider diagram.

Fun Corner!

Word Chains

Write a word on the board; for example: *run*. Ask students to think of a word that starts with the last letter in *run*, such as *nut*. Divide the class into two groups and continue the activity until you consider it should be over.

Build Creativity!

Just Doodle

Objective: **Flow**

Give a piece of paper to each student. Play music and ask students to doodle. Then, stop the music and have students pass the paper to another student. Start the music again and ask students to doodle. Continue as long as you think necessary.

Differentiated Instruction

Below-level ★	On-level ★★	Above-level ★★★
Instead of making the spider diagram individually, students can make it in small groups.	Do Activity 2 as described above.	As homework, ask students to find out the English word for each of the things they included in their spider diagrams and to write each word under the appropriate drawing.

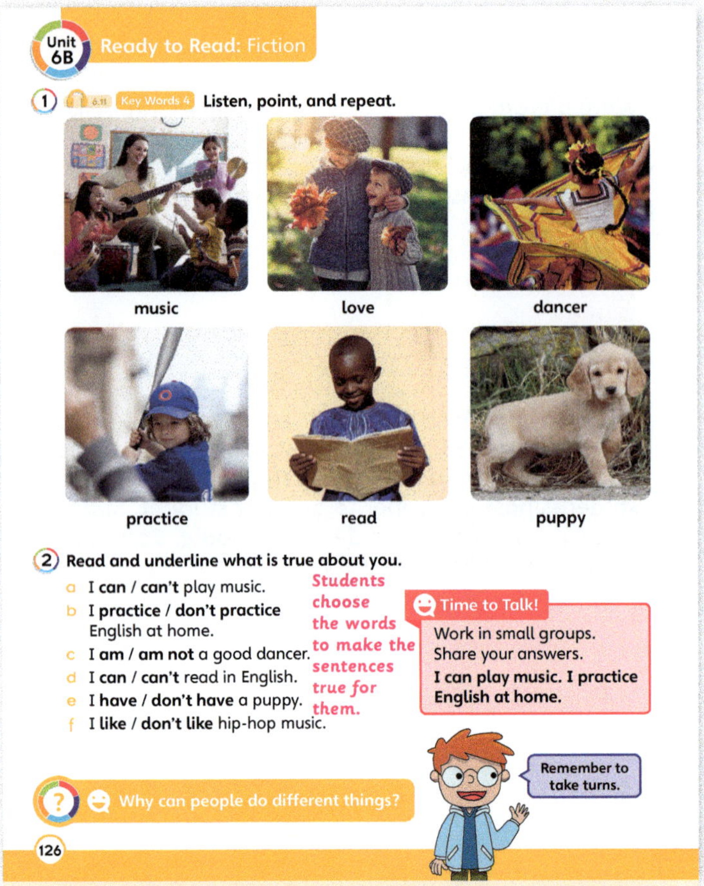

Unit 6B Ready to Read: Fiction

1 6.11 Key Words 4 Listen, point, and repeat.

music love dancer

practice read puppy

2 Read and underline what is true about you.

a I can / can't play music.
b I practice / don't practice English at home.
c I am / am not a good dancer.
d I can / can't read in English.
e I have / don't have a puppy.
f I like / don't like hip-hop music.

Students choose the words to make the sentences true for them.

Time to Talk!
Work in small groups. Share your answers.
I can play music. I practice English at home.

Remember to take turns.

Why can people do different things?

126

Objective: to introduce vocabulary from a fiction text
Key Words 4: ***music, love, dancer, practice, read, puppy***
Materials: Audio CD 6.11; Fun Corner: music of various genres for students to identify (rock, classical, hip-hop, jazz, Latin, country, etc.)

1 6.11 Key Words 4 Listen, point, and repeat.

Play Track 6.11, and ask students to point and repeat. Have students tell you which words under the pictures are verbs. Point out that the words *love* and *practice* can be both verbs and nouns.

Practice Time 1 Teach students how to make a simple crossword puzzle with the key words in Activity 1. Write the key word *practice* vertically on the board. Write *puppy* horizontally using the *p* in *practice*. Then, demonstrate how to add *music* by using the *i*. Have students use the rest of the key words to complete the crossword puzzle. They can repeat words.

2 Read and underline what is true about you.

Read each sentence aloud, first with the two choices and then with the choice that makes it true for you. For each sentence, ask a volunteer to tell you what is true for them. Have students do Activity 2 in their books.

Practice Time 2 On the board, write three of the sentences from Activity 2, and underline a word in each: *I can't play music; I can read English; I don't like hip-hop music.* Encourage students to complete the sentences with other options. For example, instead of *I can't play music*, they could write *I can't play tennis*. Invite volunteers to come to the board and write the new alternatives.

Time to Talk!

Form small groups, and ask students to share their answers with their classmates. Make sure they take turns.

Big Question Link

Before students discuss the Big Question Link, draw their attention to Jack, the oracy character, and read the reminder aloud. Then, discuss with students why people have different abilities. Relate it to the fact that people have different hobbies and preferences.

Fun Corner!

Move to the Rhythm

Ask students if they know the names of different styles of music. Elicit as many styles as they can think of. Tell them that you will play music and they should identify what style it is. Then, tell students that you will say a verb and they have to do the action in a way that matches the style of the music you play. For example, if you say *swim*, they may swim frantically when they listen to rock or swim slowly when they listen to classical music. Let students choose the verbs if they want to. Possible verbs include: *dance, paint, clap, play the guitar, walk, eat,* etc.

AB page 111

Reading Strategy: Cause and Effect

Cause → Effect

1 Look and match the cause with the effect.

Cause:

Effect:

2 Look at the cause and draw the effect.

Example answer: Students draw a broken chair and the elephant on the floor.

When you can't do something, what do you do?

127

Objective: to identify cause and effect and prepare to read a fiction text

Materials: Build Creativity: paint or food coloring (yellow, blue, red), water, two bowls, a balloon

1 Look and match the cause with the effect.

Ask students to look at the pictures in the Reading Strategy box. Have students tell you what the children in the first picture are doing. Lead them to see the cause-and-effect relationship between the two pictures. Ask students about daily situations that show cause and effect. For example, ask what may happen if they touch a hot stove or if they do not tie their shoes. Then, give students time to focus on the pictures in Activity I. Have them match the causes with the effects.

2 Look at the cause and draw the effect.

Ask: *Is the elephant big or small? (Big.) And the chair? (Small.)* Ask students what the effect of an elephant standing on a small chair will be. Have students draw the effect in the box and share their drawings with the rest of the class.

Big Question Link

Ask students the question in the Big Question Link box. Discuss some activities students may find difficult—for example, reading, writing, getting dressed alone, swimming, or playing a sport. Encourage students to come up with possible ways of dealing with their difficulties.

Build Creativity!

Experience the Effect

Objective: Why, Why, Oh Why?

One of the most effective ways to learn something is to do an experiment. Place two bowls with water on your desk. Add some yellow paint or food coloring to each bowl. Ask students what color they see. Then, ask what will happen if you add blue to one of the bowls. Add blue to a bowl, and show students how the two colors turn into green. Do the same with red in the other bowl so that you get orange. Use this experiment as an example of cause and effect.

Show the balloon, and ask students what the effect will be if you blow into it. Blow into the balloon. Then, ask what will happen if you do not tie the balloon. Release the balloon for students to see another cause-and-effect example. Blow the balloon up again, and tie it. Rub it back and forth against your hair for ten seconds. Pull the balloon away so that students see that your hair is pulled up by the balloon.

Tell students you would like to see more cause-and-effect experiments. As homework, ask them to think of an experiment and prepare to show it to the class.

Objective: to understand how important it is to practice when you want to improve

Materials: Audio CD 6.12, 6.13; Build Creativity: pictures of people dancing different dance styles (e.g., tango, merengue, ballet, rock and roll, hip-hop, contemporary)

Pre-Reading

Read the title of the story. Ask students what "hip-hop" is. Have them mention other styles of music. Ask questions about the pictures in the story: *Look at the picture on pages 128 and 129. Why do you think Hanna is sad?* Point to the storybook that Hanna's mom is holding on page 129, and ask: *What do you think the story is about?* Refer to cause and effect by asking why Hanna is sad at the beginning of the story and why she is happy at the end.

6.12 Page 128, section 1

Play Track 6.12 up to the end of the first paragraph. Pause and ask questions:

What's the girl's name?
What does she love?
What class does she go to?

6.12 Page 128, section 2

Continue Track 6.12 up to the end of the second paragraph. Pause and ask questions:

Who can dance very well?
Why is Hanna sad?
Teach the words trip *and* fall down.

Personalization

Ask: *What styles of music do you like?*

6.12 Page 129, section 1

Play Track 6.12 up to the end of the first paragraph. Pause and ask questions:

Why doesn't Hanna want to dance?
Is Hanna a terrible dancer?
What's the solution to Hanna's problem?

Think

Discuss the questions with students.

6.12 Page 129, section 2

Play the rest of Track 6.12. Ask questions:

Who reads a story?
Who is in the story?
What can't the puppy do?
How does the puppy feel?

Personalization

Ask: *How do you feel when you make mistakes?*

6.12 **Hip-hop Hanna**
by Irma Calvo

Hanna loves music. She loves dance movies. She wants to dance. She's in a hip-hop dance class.

The other girls are good. They can dance very well. Can Hanna dance very well? No, she can't. She trips and falls down. She makes mistakes. Hanna is sad.

128

6B

"Mom, I don't want to dance," she says. "I'm a terrible dancer."

"You are not a terrible dancer," says Mom. "You need to practice."

Think
Do you agree with Hanna's mom? Why?

That night, Mom and Hanna read a story about a puppy. The puppy can't run. He trips and falls down. He makes mistakes. The puppy is sad.

129

Hip-hop Hanna

A horse shows the puppy how to run. The puppy practices and practices and practices. In the end, he can run *very* fast.

The teacher shows Hanna how to dance. Hanna practices and practices and practices.

Think
What happens next to Hanna?

130

One day, there's a school show.

In the show, Hanna dances *very* well.

Mom says, "Look at Hanna! She can dance really well now."

Everyone claps hard. They are clapping for Hanna!

Think
Why can Hanna dance so well now?

131

6.13 Page 130, section 1

Play Track 6.13 up to the end of the first paragraph. Pause and ask questions:

Who teaches the puppy how to run?
What does the puppy do?
What happens in the end?

6.13 Page 130, section 2

Continue Track 6.13 up to the end of the page. Pause and ask questions:

Who helps Hanna?
What does Hanna do?

Think

Ask students to guess what the effect of Hanna's attitude will be.

6.13 Page 131

Play the rest of Track 6.13. Ask questions:

Where does Hanna dance?
What does Hanna's mom say?
Why are people clapping?

Think

Discuss the question with the class.

Personalization

Ask: *Are there dance shows at your school?*

Build Creativity!

Dance Styles

Objective: A Different Point of View

Ask students if they have ever danced and what styles of music they have danced to. Show them the pictures of different dance styles (ballet, tango, etc.), telling them what each style is called. Ask students to search for pictures of dance in different styles in books or magazines or on the Internet at home with a caregiver's help. Have them bring to class one picture of people dancing in a style they like. Ask students to write the name of the dance style on their picture. Students show their picture to the class and say what the dance style is. Have students who chose the same style get together, and see which dance style was chosen the most.

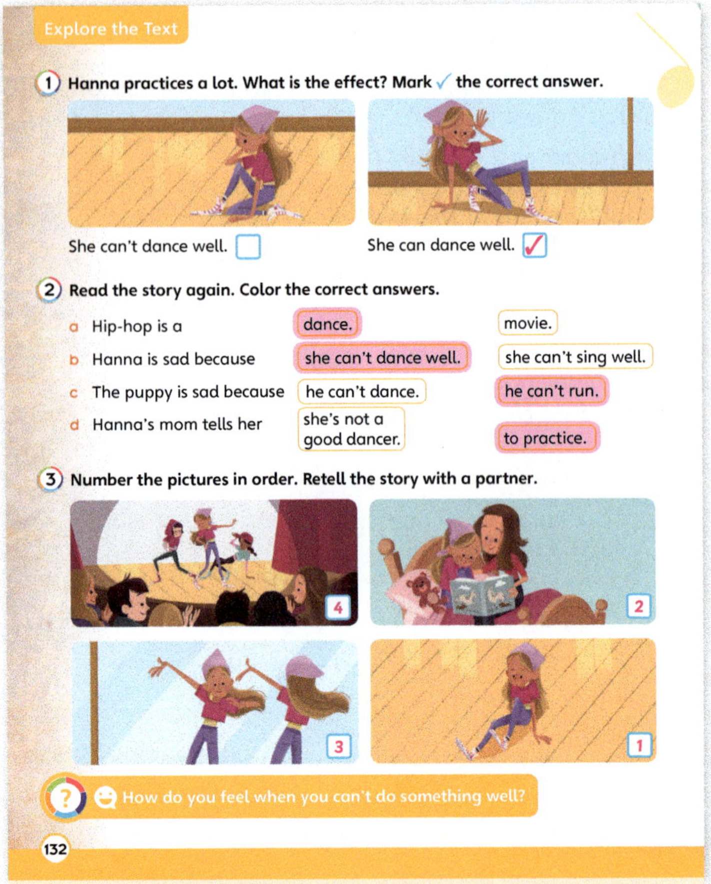

Explore the Text

1 Hanna practices a lot. What is the effect? Mark ✓ the correct answer.

She can't dance well. ☐ She can dance well. ☑

2 Read the story again. Color the correct answers.

a Hip-hop is a dance. / movie.

b Hanna is sad because she can't dance well. / she can't sing well.

c The puppy is sad because he can't dance. / he can't run.

d Hanna's mom tells her she's not a good dancer. / to practice.

3 Number the pictures in order. Retell the story with a partner.

4 2 3 1

How do you feel when you can't do something well?

132

Objective: to deepen understanding of a fiction text

Materials: paper

1 Hanna practices a lot. What is the effect? Mark ✓ the correct answer.

Have students look at the two pictures of Hanna. Ask general questions such as: *Is Hanna sad or happy in this picture?* Read the instructions for the activity and the two answer options aloud. Complete the activity as a class.

2 Read the story again. Color the correct answers.

Ask a student to read aloud the first paragraph of *Hip-hop Hanna*. Then, have another student read the second paragraph. Continue in this manner through the end of the story. If students find it hard to read a complete paragraph, have them read sentences instead. Then, do Activity 2 as a class.

3 Number the pictures in order. Retell the story with a partner.

Ask students to number the pictures in Activity 3. Check answers as a class. Then, form four groups, one for each scene in Activity 3. Give students time to think about what they can say about their scene. Hand out one piece of paper per group. Groups should write down at least two sentences for their scene. Then, have the group that has scene 1 retell their part by reading the sentences they have written. Continue with the rest of the groups. (See Differentiated Instruction.)

Big Question Link

Point to the Big Question Link, and read the question aloud. Discuss it with the class.

Build Creativity!

Yes, You Can!

Objective: Try, Try, and Try Again

As a class, make a list on the board of things some students can't do (*I can't stand on my head, I can't swim,* etc.). Have students choose three things from the list and write them in their notebooks. Say: *Soon you're going to say you can do these things.* Challenge students to set goals for themselves to achieve each of the actions they chose. Discuss what they need to do in order to be able to achieve their goals. You may wish to have students put their challenges on the wall. Check in with the students from time to time to see how they're progressing.

AB pages 112–13

Differentiated Instruction

Below-level ★	On-level ★★	Above-level ★★★
In Activity 3, instead of asking groups to think of sentences for their scene, provide sentence frames for them to complete in writing. For example, for scene 1: *Hanna loves … (music/hip-hop/dancing). She can't … (dance) well.* After all groups have completed their sentences, have them retell the story.	Do Activity 3 as described above.	Do Activity 3 as described above, but have individual students also write a sentence for each of the scenes they were not assigned.

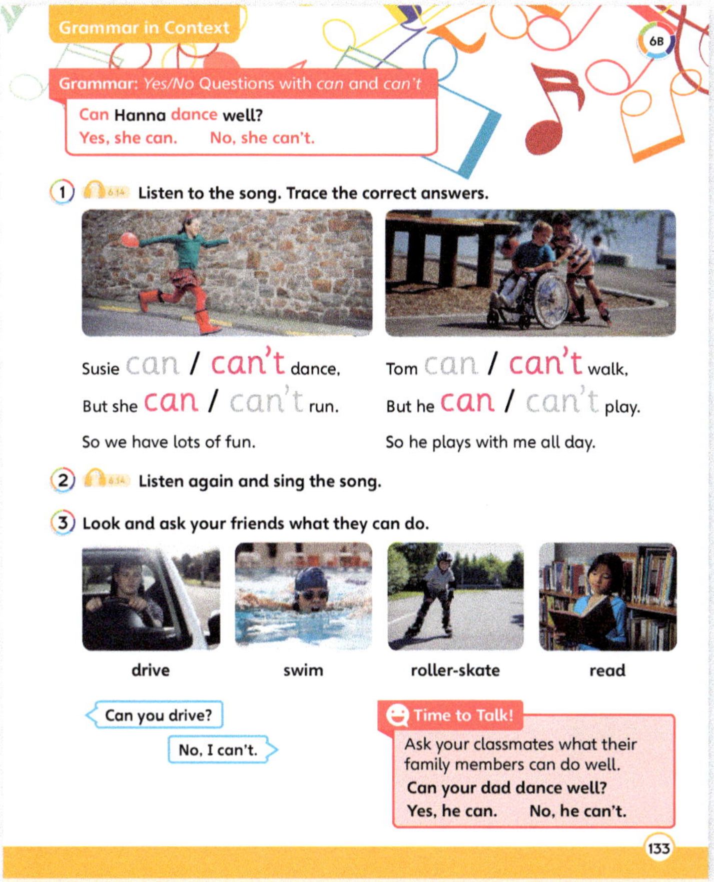

Grammar in Context

6B

Grammar: *Yes/No* Questions with *can* and *can't*

Can Hanna dance well?

Yes, she can. No, she can't.

1 6.14 Listen to the song. Trace the correct answers.

Susie can / can't dance,
But she can / can't run.
So we have lots of fun.

Tom can / can't walk,
But he can / can't play.
So he plays with me all day.

2 6.14 Listen again and sing the song.

3 Look and ask your friends what they can do.

drive swim roller-skate read

Can you drive?

No, I can't.

Time to Talk!

Ask your classmates what their family members can do well.

Can your dad dance well?

Yes, he can. No, he can't.

133

Objective: to use *yes/no* questions with *can* and *can't*
Materials: Audio CD 6.14, Flashcards 6.1–6.12 (only *paint, skate, play basketball, ride, spell, swim*), tape

Grammar Box

Read the question and answers in the Grammar box aloud. Use gestures to indicate affirmative and negative. Have students repeat the question and answers. Then, tape the flashcards to the board. Call a volunteer to come to the front, and ask them questions about the flashcards: *Can you (skate)?* Leave the flashcards on the board.

1 6.14 Listen to the song. Trace the correct answers.

Play Track 6.14 without asking students to look at the book. After playing the track, ask: *What's the girl's name? What can she do? What can't she do?* Ask questions about Tom as well. Then, do Activity 1 as a class.

2 6.14 Listen again and sing the song.

Sing the song yourself, modeling gestures and movements that you and the students will use when you sing the song together: Shake and nod your head to communicate *can* and *can't*, and do the actions mentioned in the song. Then, play Track 6.14 again, and sing the song with the gestures and movements as a class.

Practice Time 1 Ask students to write their own version of a verse of the song in their notebooks. What they write should be true—for example, *I can't (swim), but I can (skate). So I have lots of fun.* Ask volunteers to sing their songs to the class.

3 Look and ask your friends what they can do.

Form small groups, and explain how to do Activity 3. Monitor, and provide support.

Time to Talk!

Form two circles, and have students ask the question in the Time to Talk! box to the classmate next to them going clockwise. Tell them to model their questions and answers on the example in the box. You may need to teach the name of some family members.

Fun Corner!

The Biggest Team

Return to the flashcards on the board to go through them and add information below them. Pointing to the *paint* Flashcard, say: *You can paint pictures*. Write *pictures* under the flashcard. Repeat this process with *skate* (*fast*), *ride* (*a horse, a bike*), *spell* (*words in English*), and *swim* (*in the ocean*). Ask two volunteers to come to the front for each to be the leader of a team. The leader of Team 1 asks a question of any student in the class using the vocabulary on the board: *Can you paint pictures?* If the answer is affirmative (*Yes, I can.*), the student who answered becomes a member of Team 1. The team with the most members at the end is the winner. You may wish to rotate leaders.

Build Creativity!

Group Challenge

Objective: Try, Try, and Try Again

Have students think of challenges for their classmates, for example: *Can you stand on one leg for thirty seconds?* Have students work in groups of four. Each student asks a question to challenge their group. Tell students to encourage each other by saying things like *You can do it!* and *Keep going!*

AB pages 114–15

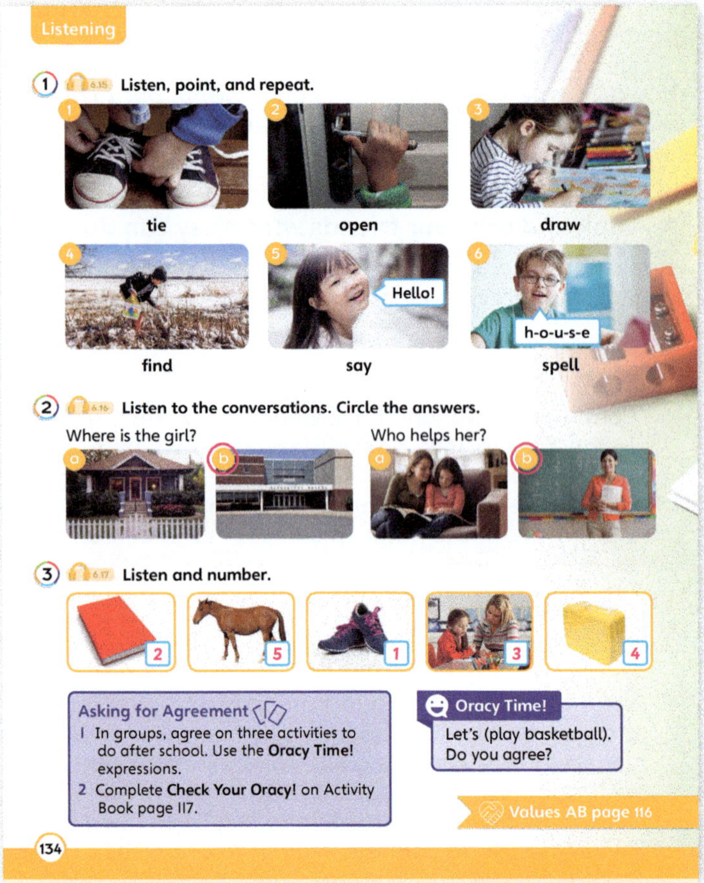

Listening

1 6.15 Listen, point, and repeat.

1 tie 2 open 3 draw
4 find 5 say 6 spell

2 6.16 Listen to the conversations. Circle the answers.

Where is the girl? a b
Who helps her? a b

3 6.17 Listen and number.

2 5 1 3 4

Asking for Agreement
1 In groups, agree on three activities to do after school. Use the **Oracy Time!** expressions.
2 Complete **Check Your Oracy!** on Activity Book page 117.

Oracy Time!
Let's (play basketball). Do you agree?

Values AB page 116

134

Objectives: to learn how to ask for help; to understand the importance of persevering
Materials: Audio CD 6.15, 6.16, 6.17, Cue Card 8

1 6.15 Listen, point, and repeat.

Play Track 6.15, and do Activity 1 as a class. Have students tell you which words are verbs. *(All of them.)*

2 6.16 Listen to the conversations. Circle the answers.

Guide students to identify what each picture in Activity 2 represents. Then, play Track 6.16, and do the activity as a class.

3 6.17 Listen and number.

Ask students what each picture in Activity 3 represents. Play Track 6.17, and have students number the pictures. Check answers as a class. Then, make short dialogues with volunteers, encouraging students to say: *Teacher, I can't (open my lunchbox). Can you help me, please?*

Oracy Extension Activity

Read the steps in the Oracy Extension activity aloud. Display Cue Card 8, and have students use *Do you agree?* in their dialogues. Ask students to complete Check Your Oracy! on page 117 of their Activity Books.

ACTIVITY BOOK PAGE 116

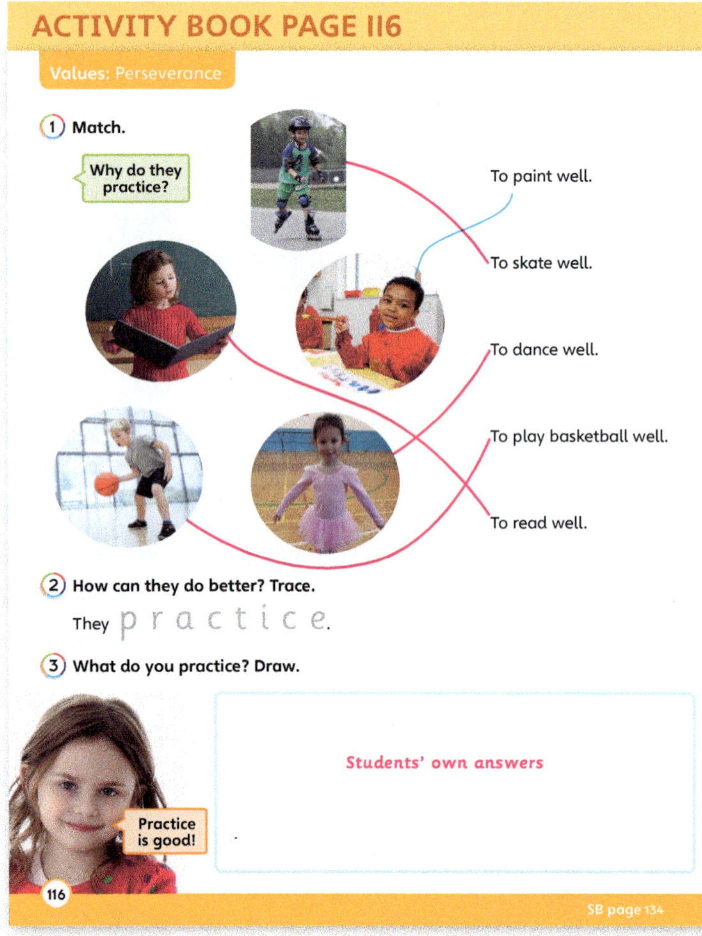

Values: Perseverance

1 Match.

Why do they practice?

To paint well.
To skate well.
To dance well.
To play basketball well.
To read well.

2 How can they do better? Trace.

They practice.

3 What do you practice? Draw.

Students' own answers

116

SB page 134

1 Match.

Ask students what each child is practicing in the pictures in Activity 1. Ask why they are practicing, and guide students to match the pictures to the text.

2 How can they do better? Trace.

Talk about the importance of persevering at an activity in order to do it better. Read the sentence, and ask students to trace.

3 What do you practice? Draw.

Ask various volunteers to tell you what they like practicing. Then, ask students to draw themselves practicing an activity they enjoy.

AB page 116

The Big Challenge

6B

What different things can we do?

Your challenge is to say what different abilities you have.

1 Think of three things you can do and three things you can't do.

2 Make a spinner. Draw a circle on paper. Divide it into six parts and write one action in each section.

3 Draw a picture next to each action.

4 Cut the circle out and glue it onto cardboard. Cut it out again.

5 Draw a small arrow on the cardboard. Cut it out and attach it to the spinner with a butterfly clip.

6 Play in pairs. Spin your partner's spinner and say if you can or can't do the action.

What can people do? Look back through the unit. Share your ideas

AB pages 117–119

135

Objective: **to consolidate, extend, and personalize learning on the unit topic**

Materials: paper, cardboard, butterfly clips, glue, scissors

- Read the Big Challenge question and statement aloud. Point to the picture at the bottom right of the page, and tell students they will make a spinner.
- **1** Give students time to think about the things that they can and can't do. Ask students to draw a happy face and a sad face in their notebooks. Students already know what a spider diagram is, so guide them to write three things they can do coming from the happy face and three they can't do coming from the sad face. (See Differentiated Instruction.)
- **2** Tell students that they should work at home to make the first part of their spinner. They have to draw a circle on a piece of paper with the help of an adult and then divide the circle into six parts by using a ruler. Tell students that they should then write the actions they wrote in their notebooks in separate sections of the spinner. Remind students that they should leave space for the drawings.
- **3** At home, students draw each action in the appropriate section.
- **4** Guide students to cut the circle, glue it on cardboard, and recut it with the cardboard backing.
- **5** Students draw and cut an arrow on cardboard with the help of an adult and attach it to the spinner with a butterfly clip.
- **6** Form pairs, and show students how to play with the spinners. Optional: Record or have students record one another to share their work.

Home-school | Portfolio: Big Challenge

Big Question Circle

Read the Big Question aloud. Have the class revisit the Big Question Links on pages 121, 126, 127, and 132. Discuss what they have learned about what people can do.

- Use the following questions to help review the Big Question:

  What can you do?
  What can't you do?
  Can people all do the same things?
  What amazing things can some people do?
  How can you do something well?

- Finally, have students turn to page 117 of their Activity Books to complete the Big Challenge self-assessment.

AB pages 117–19

Differentiated Instruction

Below-level ★	On-level ★★	Above-level ★★★
Instead of asking students to write words on the mind maps, ask them to draw the things, for example, a guitar on the spider diagram of the happy face. Omit the writing in step 2, and just have students do the drawings in step 3.	Students make the spinner as explained above.	As a follow-up to the Big Challenge, ask students to choose two actions from their partner's spinner and write sentences about themselves using *can* or *can't*.

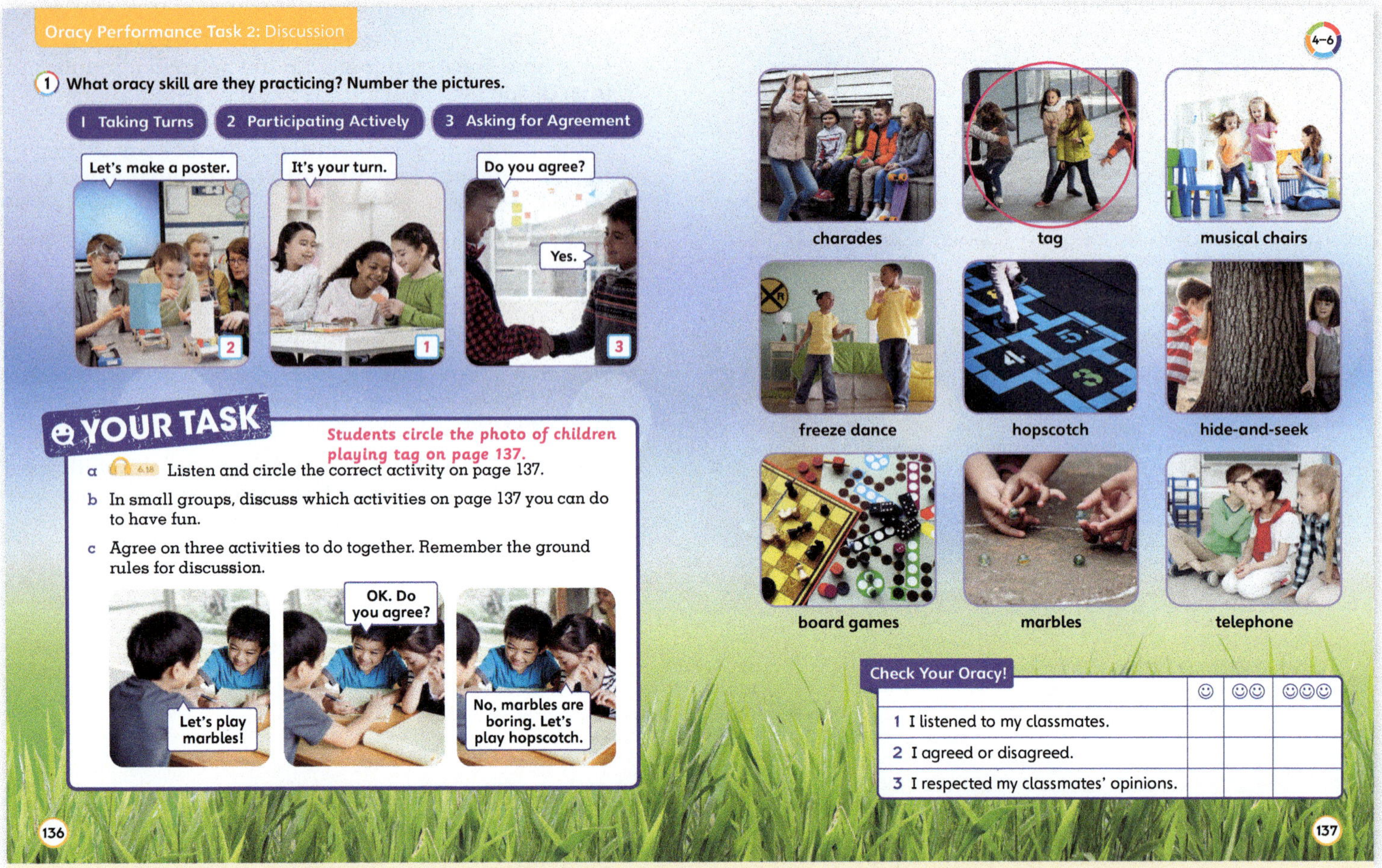

Oracy Performance Task 2: Discussion

4–6

1 What oracy skill are they practicing? Number the pictures.

1 Taking Turns | 2 Participating Actively | 3 Asking for Agreement

YOUR TASK

Students circle the photo of children playing tag on page 137.

a 6.18 Listen and circle the correct activity on page 137.

b In small groups, discuss which activities on page 137 you can do to have fun.

c Agree on three activities to do together. Remember the ground rules for discussion.

charades | tag | musical chairs

freeze dance | hopscotch | hide-and-seek

board games | marbles | telephone

Check Your Oracy!

	☺	☺☺	☺☺☺
1 I listened to my classmates.			
2 I agreed or disagreed.			
3 I respected my classmates' opinions.			

136 137

Objective: to apply oracy skills in discussions

Oracy Performance Task Words: ***charades, tag, musical chairs, freeze dance, hopscotch, hide-and-seek, board games, marbles, telephone***

Materials: Audio CD 6.18

1 What oracy skill are they practicing? Number the pictures.

Remind students of the oracy skills they learned in units 4–6. Read each of the categories in Activity 1, and guide students to associate the categories with the pictures.

YOUR TASK

- Ask students what games they play at home and in the school playground. Go through all the games on page 137, and say their names. Have students tell you if they play them and what they are called in their language.
- **a** 6.18 Play Track 6.18, and ask students to circle the correct activity on page 137.
- **b** Form small groups. Have students tell each other which of the games on page 137 they like the most.
- **c** Ask groups to agree on three activities by using the expressions in the speech bubbles: *Let's … ! Do you agree?* Optional: Record students' discussions to share their work.

Home-school | Portfolio: Oracy Performance

Fun Corner!

Play Time!

Say: *Let's play Telephone! Do you agree?* Have students raise their hands if they agree, and count how many students raise their hands. Ask in the same way about Charades and Freeze Dance, which are also games that can be played in the classroom. Play the game that gets the most votes. You may want to practice verbs if you play Telephone or Charades, or you may want to play the different styles of music you worked with in previous lessons if you play Freeze Dance.

AB pages 120–121

7 Is all food healthy?

Literacy

Read: a nonfiction text about snacks from around the world; a fiction text about a boy who doesn't like broccoli

Reading Strategies: identifying similarities and differences; identifying the main idea

Ready to Write

Learn to Write: adjectives

Getting Ready to Write: make a memory game

Oracy

Skill: Giving and Responding to Positive Feedback

Cue Cards 9–10: 9. *Good job!* 10. *Thank you.*

Speaking Mission: buy groceries

Language

Key Words 1: *fruit, banana, grapes, vegetable, spinach, sugar*

Key Words 2: *juice, water, oil, yogurt, tomato, rice*

Key Words 3: *fried, freezer*

Key Words 4: *broccoli, fish, French fries, chocolate, soup, muffin*

Speaking Mission Words: *bread, cookies, lollipop, potato chips, tomato, corn*

Grammar in Context

like/don't like: *I like peanut butter sandwiches. I don't like cheese sandwiches.*

Yes/No* Questions with *like: *Do you like broccoli now? Yes, I do. No, I don't.*

Phonics

Ending Sounds: *x, m, b*

Listening

Song: "Please Eat Your Greens"

Values

Healthy Eating

The Big Challenge

How can we make a healthy dessert?
Present your recipe to the class

Objective: **to introduce the topic of what people eat**
Key Words 1: ***fruit, banana, grapes, vegetable, spinach, sugar***
Materials: Video 7.1, Audio CD 7.1, Flashcards 7.1–7.6

? IS ALL FOOD HEALTHY?

- Read the Big Question aloud. Explain that *healthy* food is good for your body. Ask students to give you examples of healthy foods.
- Have students look at the pictures. Read the first question aloud: *What are the children eating? (a carrot, a popsicle, a burger, pizza)* Read the other two questions aloud for students to give their opinion.

7.1 Key Words 1 Use the flashcards and audio to present Key Words 1. Hold up the flashcards again, and have students repeat the words. Ask students if the food on the flashcards is healthy.

1 7.1 Watch the video. Circle the food you see.

Play the video, and pause after "Let's find out!" Ask: *What is today's Big Question? (Is all food healthy?)* Continue the video. Pause after "Let's have a look!" Write the words *fruits* and *vegetables* on the board. Ask volunteers to go to the board and write the fruits and vegetables that are mentioned in the first part of the video. Ask students if they know what vitamins and minerals are. You may want to mention that grapes have vitamin C and spinach has the mineral iron. Continue the video to the end. Then, write the word *sugar* on the board, and ask volunteers to write foods that contain sugar underneath it. Complete Activity 1 as a class.

2 7.1 Watch again. Complete the graphic organizer in the Activity Book.

Play the video again, and have students complete Activity 1 on AB page 122. Form pairs, and have them compare answers.

AB page 122

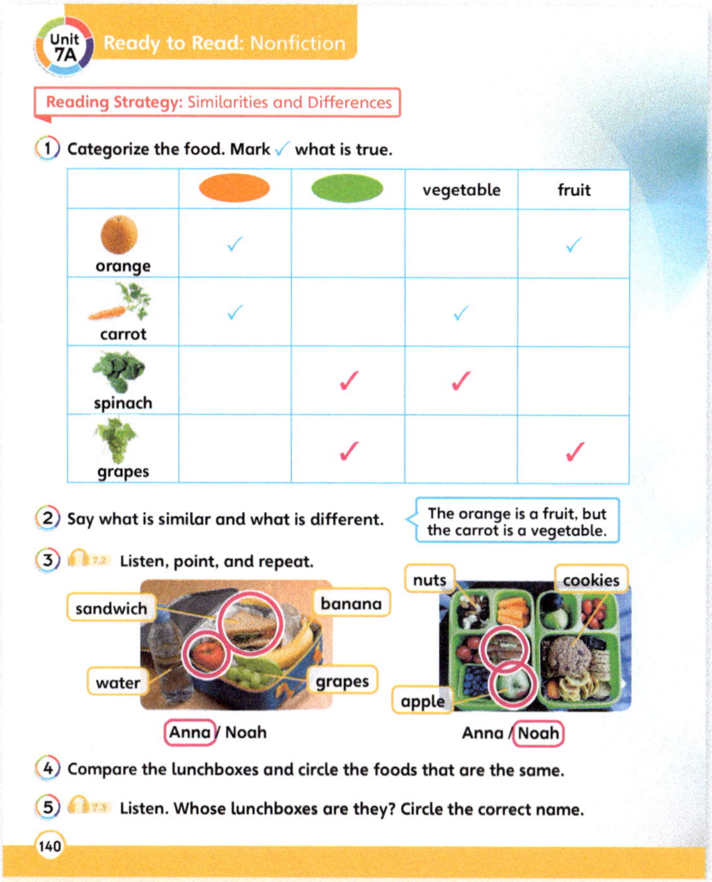

Unit 7A Ready to Read: Nonfiction

Reading Strategy: Similarities and Differences

1 Categorize the food. Mark ✓ what is true.

	(orange)	(green)	vegetable	fruit
orange	✓			✓
carrot	✓		✓	
spinach		✓	✓	
grapes		✓		✓

2 Say what is similar and what is different. The orange is a fruit, but the carrot is a vegetable.

3 7.2 Listen, point, and repeat.

Anna / Noah   Anna / Noah

4 Compare the lunchboxes and circle the foods that are the same.

5 7.3 Listen. Whose lunchboxes are they? Circle the correct name.

140

Objective: to identify similarities and differences and prepare to read a nonfiction text

Key Words I: ***fruit, banana, grapes, vegetable, spinach, sugar***

Materials: Audio CD 7.2, 7.3; Fun Corner: paper plates or paper; Build Creativity: cut fruits and vegetables

NOTE: Be aware of any food allergies your students may have.

7.1 Key Words 1 Use the flashcards and audio to review Key Words I.

1 Categorize the food. Mark ✓ what is true.

Have students look at the chart. Point out the foods on the left. Point out the colors and words on the top. Read the words and help with meaning. Then, say: *Look at the orange. What color is it, orange or green?* Point to the checkmark under orange. Ask: *Is it a vegetable or a fruit?* Point to the checkmark under fruit. Do the same with *carrot*. Then, form pairs and have them classify the other foods by color and type. Monitor, and provide support. Check answers as a class.

2 Say what is similar and what is different.

Read the text in the speech bubble, and emphasize the word *but*. Have students focus on differences first, and lead them in using the word *but*. Then, ask about similarities.

3 7.2 Listen, point, and repeat.

Play Track 7.2, and have students point and repeat. Encourage students to identify the other foods that are in the two lunchboxes.

4 Compare the lunchboxes and circle the foods that are the same.

Students are already familiar with Venn diagrams. Draw one on the board, and write *Lunchbox I* and *Lunchbox 2* above the circles. Have students focus on the similarities and differences between the two lunchboxes in Activity 3. Ask volunteers to come to the front and draw the foods in the corresponding sections of the diagram. Once the diagram is complete, ask students to do Activity 4.

5 7.3 Listen. Whose lunchboxes are they? Circle the correct name.

Play Track 7.3, and have students circle the correct name under each photo in Activity 3.

Fun Corner!

What I Eat

Distribute paper plates, or ask students to use a sheet of paper and draw a plate on it. Have them draw the foods they eat the most during the week. Ask volunteers to come to the front and show the class what they eat. Then, have them draw a circle around the healthy foods. Display students' work.

Build Creativity!

Using Our Senses

Objective: A Different Point of View

Gather together a collection of fruits and vegetables. Look at them with the class, making sure students know the name of each item. Have students work in pairs. One student in each pair covers their eyes with a blindfold. Give the other student a fruit or a vegetable. Tell that student to allow their partner to smell the item and then to take a bite. Can the blindfolded student guess the food? Have partners switch roles.

7.4 Key Words 2 Use the flashcards and audio to pre-teach Key Words 2.

Pre-Reading

Read the title, and explain the meaning of the word *snacks* (small amounts of food you eat between meals). Have students look at the pictures in the text on pages 141 and 142, and ask them if they can identify these snacks. Also ask if they eat any of the snacks. Play Tracks 7.5 and 7.6, and invite students to follow the text.

7.5 **Page 141, section 1**

Play the part of Track 7.5 about Mexican popsicles. Pause and ask questions:

Where is Esteban from?
Teach the word *ingredients*. Then, ask:
What are the ingredients in a Mexican popsicle?
What can you use instead of water?
How do you keep popsicles cold?

Personalization

Ask: *Do you eat popsicles? What kind is your favorite?*

Digging Deeper

Ask: *Are popsicles healthy? Why or why not?*

7.5 **Page 141, section 2**

Play the rest of Track 7.5. Ask questions:

Where is Aom from?
Are insects healthy?
Where can people buy them?
How are they cooked?

Personalization

Ask: *Do you eat insects?*

7.4 Key Words 2

juice

water

oil

yogurt

tomato

rice

7.5 Snacks from Around the World!

Mexican Popsicles

Mexican popsicles are delicious. They're made from fruit, **juice**, and **water**. You put them in the freezer. You can also make them with **yogurt**.

I love popsicles!

Esteban from Mexico

Insects

Insects are a healthy snack. You can eat fried insects in Thailand. They are cooked in **oil**.

Mmm ... I like fried crickets!

Aom from Thailand

141

Objective: to understand the meaning of words in context and learn more about food people eat
Key Words 2: *juice, water, oil, yogurt, tomato, rice*
Materials: Audio CD 7.4, 7.5, Flashcards 7.7–7.12

7.6 Snacks from Around the World!

Plantains
Plantains are green bananas. They are cooked in oil. You can eat them in Cuba.

Lahmacun
Lahmacun is a Turkish snack. It has meat, **tomatoes**, and vegetables. It's delicious!

I like onigiri with seaweed!

seaweed

Onigiri (Rice Balls)
Onigiri is a Japanese food. They are balls of white **rice** with seaweed.

Hisao from Japan

I don't like cheese sandwiches. But I like peanut butter sandwiches!

Sandwiches
Sandwiches are a popular snack. They're made with bread. Are you hungry? You can make a sandwhich!

Think
Which foods in the pictures do you like? Which foods would you like to try?

Jake from Canada

142

7.6 Page 142, section 1

Play the part of Track 7.6 about plantains and lahmacun. Pause and ask questions:

What are plantains?
How do you cook them?
Where can you eat them?
Where is lahmacun from?
What is it like?
What ingredients does it have?

Personalization

Ask: *Do you eat lahmacun? If you do, do you like it? Do you know what other ingredients it can have?*

7.6 Page 142, section 2

Play the rest of Track 7.6. Ask questions:

Where is Hisao from?
Where is Jake from?
What are the ingredients in onigiri?
What type of sandwich does Jake like?

Personalization

Ask: *What types of sandwiches do you like?*

Think

Read the questions in the Think box aloud, and have volunteers answer them.

AB page 123

Differentiated Instruction

Below-level ★	On-level ★★	Above-level ★★★
Ask students to close their books. Start reading the nonfiction text aloud, and pause from time to time for students to say the next word. For example: *Mexican popsicles are so … (delicious). They're made from fruit … (juice).*	Ask students to close their books. Have them work in groups of three or four. Write sentences from the nonfiction text on the board with some words missing. Ask students to write the complete sentences in their notebooks.	Ask students to close their books. Have them work in groups of three or four. Write specific words from the nonfiction text on the board, and have students write complete sentences based on the text content and using the words. For example, you could provide the word *bananas*, and students could write *Plantains are green bananas.*

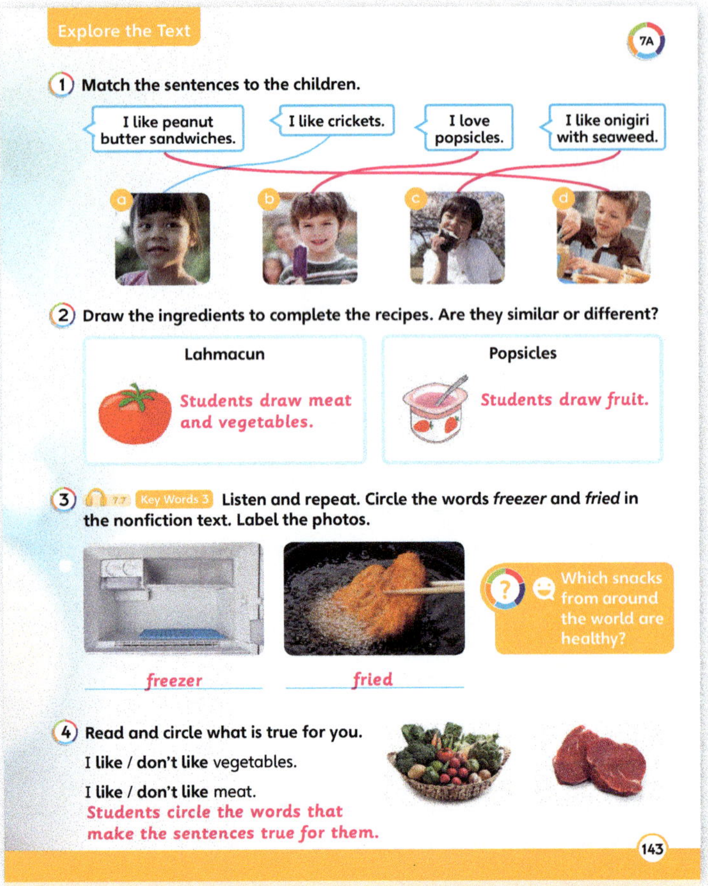

Explore the Text

7A

1 Match the sentences to the children.

I like peanut butter sandwiches.

I like crickets.

I love popsicles.

I like onigiri with seaweed.

a b c d

2 Draw the ingredients to complete the recipes. Are they similar or different?

Lahmacun	Popsicles
Students draw meat and vegetables.	Students draw fruit.

3 7.7 Key Words 3 Listen and repeat. Circle the words *freezer* and *fried* in the nonfiction text. Label the photos.

freezer

fried

Which snacks from around the world are healthy?

4 Read and circle what is true for you.

I like / don't like vegetables.

I like / don't like meat.

Students circle the words that make the sentences true for them.

143

Objective: to check reading comprehension and understand words in context

Key Words 3: ***freezer, fried***

Materials: Audio CD 7.7, paper

1 Match the sentences to the children.

Ask a volunteer to read one speech bubble, and ask the class which child said this. Do the rest of the activity as a class.

2 Draw the ingredients to complete the recipes. Are they similar or different?

Teach the word *recipe* by saying that a recipe has a list of ingredients. Then, as an example, guide students to tell you the ingredients of onigiri. Have students do Activity 2, and ask volunteers to show their work to the class. Then, tell the class to concentrate on the differences between lahmacun and popsicles. Encourage students to use *but* whenever possible. You may want to mention some similarities between lahmacun and popsicles, for example, that they are both fun to eat and are both snacks.

3 7.7 Key Words 3 Listen and repeat. Circle the words *freezer* and *fried* in the nonfiction text. Label the photos.

Ask students if they remember where the words *freezer* and *fried* were used in the nonfiction text. For example, *fried* referred to how the crickets were cooked. Then, do Activity 3.

Big Question Link

Read the question aloud. Have students share their opinions with you. Discuss what makes a snack healthy.

4 Read and circle what is true for you.

Ask students to do Activity 4, and ask volunteers to share their answers with the class.

Fun Corner!

Word Search

Form groups of three students. Students already know how to make a word search, but you may want to explain again how to make one and to specify the number of lines and columns. Ask groups to include five important words from the nonfiction text. Then, have groups exchange word searches to solve.

Build Creativity!

I Like It!

Objective: Try, Try, and Try Again

Tell students to visualize one food item they dislike. Ask them to imagine the food is on a plate in front of them. Have them pretend to smell the food and then take a small bite. Ask volunteers to name the food they imagined and to explain what they don't like about it. (They may need to use their home language for this.) Discuss as a class what students can do to learn to like these foods they dislike. Encourage students to commit to trying different techniques—eating the food in small pieces, telling themselves they like it, adding sauce to it, etc. Check in with students from time to time to see whether they are making progress in overcoming their dislike.

AB pages 124–25

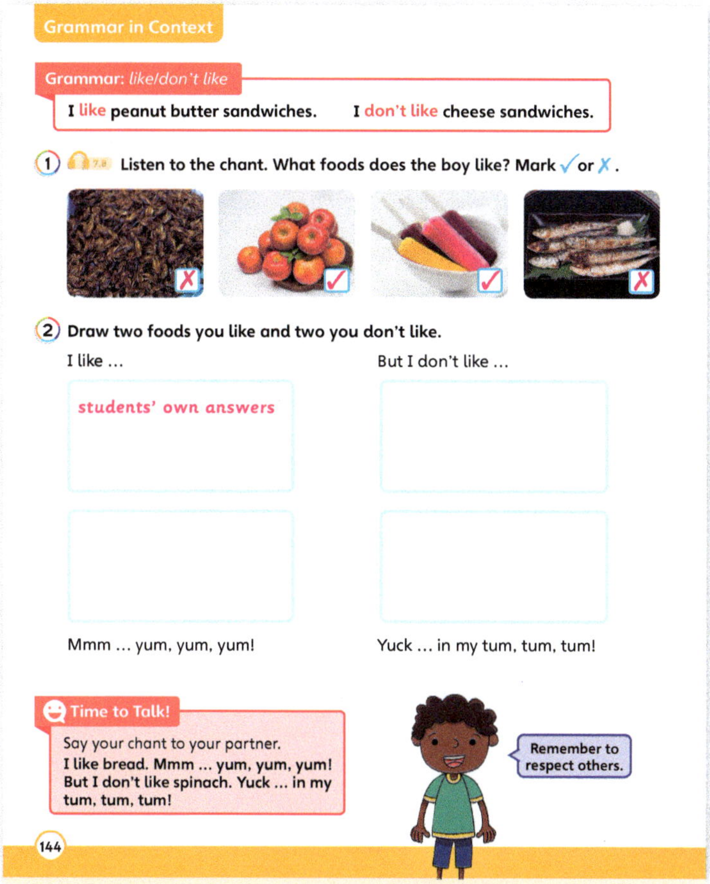
Grammar in Context

Grammar: *like/don't like*

I like peanut butter sandwiches. I don't like cheese sandwiches.

1 7.8 Listen to the chant. What foods does the boy like? Mark ✓ or ✗.

2 Draw two foods you like and two you don't like.

I like … But I don't like …

students' own answers

Mmm … yum, yum, yum! Yuck … in my tum, tum, tum!

Time to Talk!

Say your chant to your partner.
I like bread. Mmm … yum, yum, yum!
But I don't like spinach. Yuck … in my tum, tum, tum!

Remember to respect others.

144

Objective: to use *like* and *don't like*
Materials: Audio CD 7.8, a soft ball

Grammar Box

Draw a happy face and a sad face on the board. Point to the happy face, and read the first sentence in the Grammar box aloud. Then, point to the sad face, and read the second sentence aloud. Point out that *do not* becomes *don't*. You may want to provide more examples with other verbs, such as *eat*: *I eat (vegetables).*
I don't eat (meat).

1 7.8 Listen to the chant. What foods does the boy like? Mark ✓ or ✗.

Guide students to identify the food in the photos. Then, play Track 7.8 for students to do Activity 1.

Practice Time 1 Form two groups. Ask the groups to stand in lines facing each other. A student from one group throws a soft ball to a student in the other group and mentions a food like or dislike (e.g., *I like fish*). Have students continue in this manner and do the activity faster and faster.

2 Draw two foods you like and two you don't like.

Have students do Activity 2. You could also tell students that they can write the words instead of drawing, or do both.

Time to Talk!

Draw students' attention to Liam, the oracy character, and read the reminder aloud. Then, read the text in the Time to Talk! box, and ask students to work in pairs and share their chants.

Practice Time 2 Tell students that you will say a topic and they have to make sentences about that topic using *I like* and *I don't like*. For example, you could say *toys*, and students would mention toys they like or don't like. Animals are another possible topic.

Fun Corner!

Puppeteers

Pretend you are a puppeteer, and ask a volunteer to be the puppet. Draw a smiley face on the volunteer's back and an apple. The "puppet" has to produce a sentence: *I like apples.* Ask another volunteer to play the puppet, and draw a sad face and a fish on their back. The puppet says: *I don't like fish.* Then, form pairs and invite students to play, switching roles after each turn.

AB pages 126–27

Phonics

7A

1 7.9 Listen, point, and repeat.

box jam cub

fox arm tub

2 7.10 Listen and say the chant.

The fox is in the box. The fox is in the box. Where's the fox? It's in the box!	Where's the jam? Where's the jam? It's on my arm. It's on my arm.	The cub is in the tub. The cub is in the tub. Where's the cub? It's in the tub!

3 7.11 Listen and complete the words with *x*, *m*, or *b*.

a Look! It's a bear cu_b_!

b And over there is a fo_x_!

c I like ja_m_ on my bread.

d There is hot water in the tu_b_.

e Ouch! I hurt my ar_m_.

f Open the bo_x_.

145

Objective: to identify ending sounds *x, m, b*

Materials: Audio CD 7.9, 7.10, paper; Fun Corner: four copies of a word search, each including these words: *gym, him, gum, sum, cab, web, club, verb*; Build Creativity: construction paper

1 7.9 Listen, point, and repeat.

Play Track 7.9, and have students repeat the words. Pronounce each word in isolation. Exaggerate the pronunciation to help students get it right from the start. Emphasize *m* and *b*, and tell students that for both they have to press their lips together. Also, tell students that the letter *x* is pronounced with two sounds: */ks/.* Ask volunteers to pronounce the words in Activity 1. Monitor pronunciation.

2 7.10 Listen and say the chant.

Ask students to look at each drawing in Activity 2 and tell you what things from Activity 1 they see. Play Track 7.10 once for students to listen. Play it a second time for the class to say the chant.

3 7.11 Listen and complete the words with *x*, *m*, or *b*.

Play Track 7.11, pausing after each item for students to write the final sound. Check answers as a class.

Fun Corner!

Word Search

Form four groups, and distribute the word searches facedown. Tell students that there are eight words ending in *m* and *b* hidden in them. When you say *Go!*, groups turn their word searches over and search for the words. The first group to find all of the words wins.

Build Creativity!

Wall Charts

Objective: Focus

This activity was done in units 2 and 5 with the objective of having wall charts for the sounds taught throughout the year. Repeat the activity with the new sounds. Form six groups, and give each a sheet of construction paper. Assign one of the ending sounds to each group. Have groups write the sound at the top of the sheet and draw the items whose names end with that sound. Monitor students' work. Display students' work on the classroom walls.

AB page 128

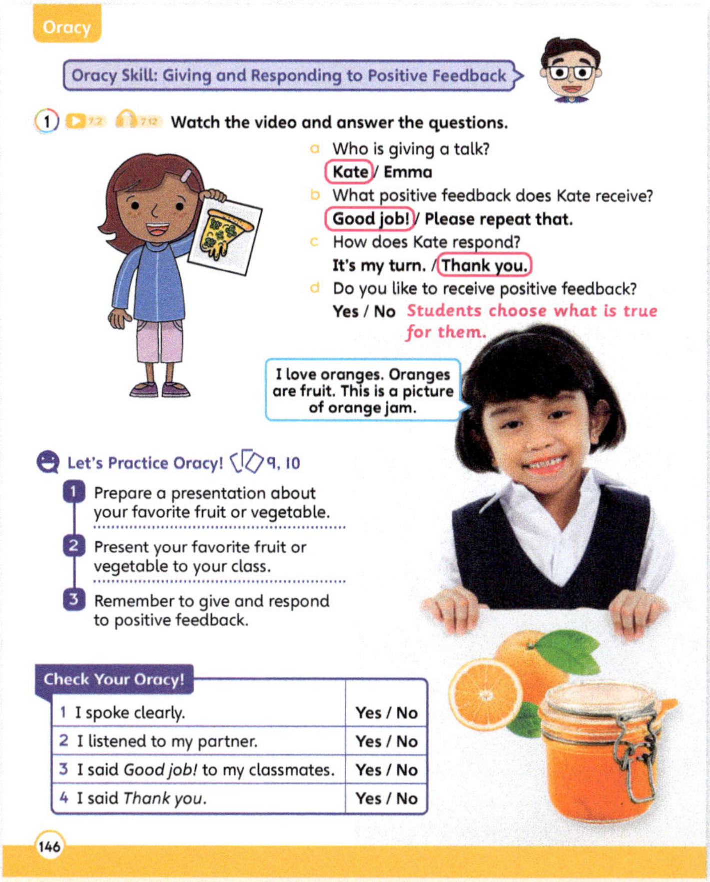

Oracy

Oracy Skill: Giving and Responding to Positive Feedback

1 7.2 7.12 Watch the video and answer the questions.

a Who is giving a talk?
Kate / Emma

b What positive feedback does Kate receive?
Good job! / Please repeat that.

c How does Kate respond?
It's my turn. / Thank you.

d Do you like to receive positive feedback?
Yes / No *Students choose what is true for them.*

Let's Practice Oracy! 9, 10

1 Prepare a presentation about your favorite fruit or vegetable.

2 Present your favorite fruit or vegetable to your class.

3 Remember to give and respond to positive feedback.

Check Your Oracy!

1 I spoke clearly.	Yes / No
2 I listened to my partner.	Yes / No
3 I said *Good job!* to my classmates.	Yes / No
4 I said *Thank you*.	Yes / No

146

Objective: **to learn to give and respond to positive feedback**

Cue Cards: **9.** ***Good job!*** **10.** ***Thank you.***

Materials: Video 7.2, Audio CD 7.12, Cue Cards 9–10

Oracy Skill

Ask students what people say to them in their language when they have done something well and what they say in response. Tell students that today they will learn how to say these things in English. Explain what *feedback* means. As an example, you could mention making a cake and people telling you how good it is. You may want to add that feedback is not always positive but that feedback that is not positive can still be helpful in showing ways to improve.

1 7.2 7.12 Watch the video and answer the questions.

Watch V7.2, and ask general comprehension questions: *What is Kate talking about? What is her favorite vegetable?* Watch the video again. Then, complete Activity 1 as a class.

Present and Practice Display Cue Cards 9 and 10 on the board. Ask a volunteer to come to the front and spell a simple word. Give them positive feedback by saying *Good job!* Encourage the volunteer to use *Thank you.* Ask other volunteers to do different things, and have the class give positive feedback to them. Encourage students to show the class things they can do well—sing, solve a difficult math problem, dance, etc.

Let's Practice Oracy! 9, 10

- Ask students to choose their favorite fruit or vegetable.
- **1** Read the example in the speech bubble of the girl giving a presentation on oranges. Tell students they should use that example to prepare a presentation about their favorite fruit or vegetable. You may also wish to provide an example of your own.
- You may want to give more example sentences, such as *Broccoli is green. Grapes are small.*
- **2–3** Have students give their presentations. Remind them to give and respond to positive feedback.
- Optional: Record or have students record one another's presentations to share their work.
- Have students complete Check Your Oracy!

Home-school Portfolio: Oracy

AB page 128

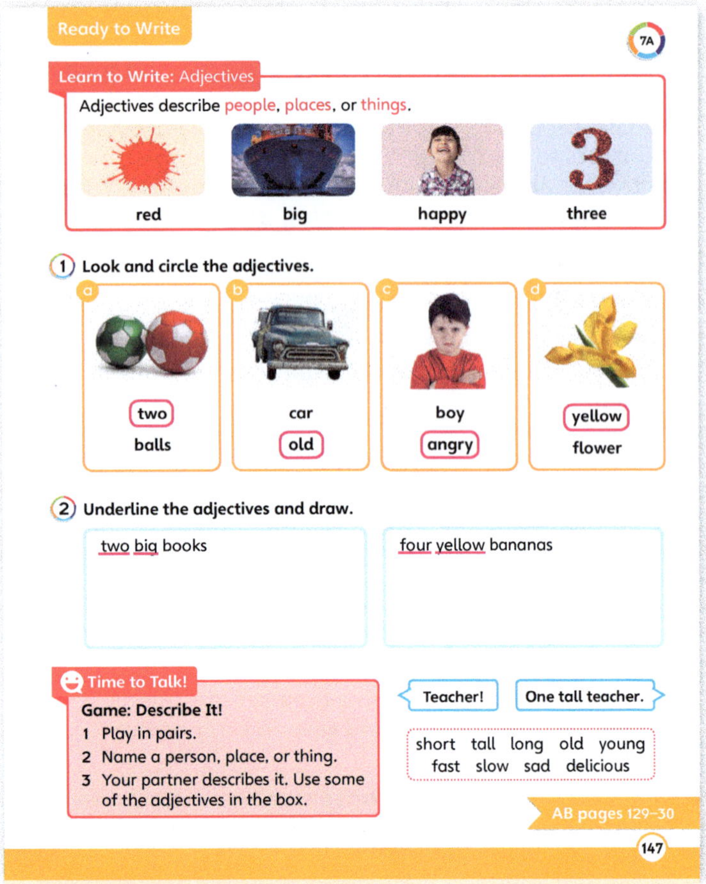

Ready to Write

7A

Learn to Write: Adjectives

Adjectives describe people, places, or things.

red big happy three

1 Look and circle the adjectives.

a two balls
b car old
c boy angry
d yellow flower

2 Underline the adjectives and draw.

two big books
four yellow bananas

Time to Talk!

Game: Describe It!

1 Play in pairs.
2 Name a person, place, or thing.
3 Your partner describes it. Use some of the adjectives in the box.

Teacher!

One tall teacher.

short tall long old young fast slow sad delicious

AB pages 129–30

147

Objective: to identify adjectives

Materials: Fun Corner: tape, 40 slips of paper with a word written on each (20 nouns: *box, teacher, girl, turtle, banana, ball, kitchen, boy, car, bicycle, family, bed, feather, pencil, schoolbag, robot, zebra, insect, bus, house;* 20 adjectives: *big, small, red, angry, happy, sad, old, young, short, tall, fast, slow, delicious, long, yellow, green, two, four, ten, cold*)

Learn to Write Box

Read the sentence in the Learn to Write box aloud. Point to the pictures and say the words. Say: *These are adjectives. We can use adjectives to describe things.* Provide an example to help students understand: Apple *is a noun. An apple can be green, red, big, or small.* Green, red, big, *and* small *are all adjectives.* Read the adjectives in the Learn to Write box aloud. Encourage students to provide more examples.

1 Look and circle the adjectives.

Ask a volunteer to read the two words in *a* in Activity 1. Ask: *Which word is an adjective:* two *or* balls? Continue with the rest of the pictures.

2 Underline the adjectives and draw.

Form pairs, and ask students to underline the adjectives. Check answers as a class. Then, ask students to draw individually. Have students check their partner's work.

Time to Talk!

Ask a volunteer to read the adjectives to the right of the Time to Talk! box. Review the adjectives, using gestures to remind students of their meaning. Form pairs, and explain to students how to play the game described in the Time to Talk! box. Then, have pairs play the game.

Fun Corner!

Adjective–Noun Match

Form two teams. Divide the board into two columns, one for each team. Place the slips of paper with adjectives in a pile, facedown. Do the same with the slips with nouns. Ask a student from Team 1 to take a noun, read it out loud, and tape it to the board in the column assigned to their team. Do the same with a student from Team 2. Continue in this way until all nouns have been taped to the board. Then, have teams choose adjectives. A student from Team 1 takes a slip, reads it out loud, and tapes it in front of an appropriate noun in their team's column. If the adjective does not go with any of the nouns, the student puts the slip down face up. This slip cannot be used by either of the two teams. The game continues until there are no more adjectives. The winning team is the one that correctly matched the most nouns with adjectives.

Build Creativity!

Think Fast!

Objective: A Different Point of View

Brainstorm names of different foods, and write them on the board. Do a rapid-fire prompt/response activity. Call out the name of a food, and ask volunteers to reply with the first adjective that comes to mind. Repeat with other food items. Then, call out adjectives and see which foods come to mind.

AB pages 129–30

Objective: **to make a memory game with adjectives**
Materials: 18 index cards per pair of students

Peer Writing

Working in pairs is extremely useful, especially at an early learning stage. Peer writing can help students feel more confident and become more creative. It also fosters peer correction, which is a good way to get better results at an early stage of writing.

1 IDENTIFY

Brainstorm with students the adjectives that they remember from the previous page, and write them on the board. Encourage students to provide additional adjectives.

2 WRITE

Hand out the index cards to pairs. Tell them they have to write adjectives on the cards. Allow students to use their books to check the spelling of words. One student writes an adjective on a card, and the other writes the same adjective on another card, making a pair of cards with the same adjective. Students continue writing until they have nine pairs. (See Differentiated Instruction.)

3 EDIT

Since pairs will be writing the same adjectives, peer correction will likely take place during the writing process. However, you may want to explicitly ask pairs to check spelling again by checking their partner's cards.

4 FOLLOW UP

Pairs place their cards facedown in random order on a desk. Then, they play a memory game. A student takes two cards, turns them face up. If the adjectives match, the student keeps the cards and takes another turn. If they don't match, the student returns the cards to their places, and it is the other student's turn. The winner is the student with the most matches.

Fun Corner!

Letter Drawings

Draw a smiley face using letters instead of lines. Encourage students to do the same with other simple drawings, such as a heart or a star. When they are finished, ask students to show their drawings to the class.

Build Creativity!

Relax to the Music

Objective: **Take a Break**

Ask students to put their heads down on their desks and close their eyes. Play soft music and give them time to relax. You can do this activity before a creative activity or after a difficult one.

Differentiated Instruction

Below-level ★	On-level ★★	Above-level ★★★
Instead of writing all the adjectives, students could make drawings representing adjectives. For example, a smiling face for *happy*, a face full of wrinkles for *old*, etc.	Students do the writing activity as described in the Write section.	Ask students to write adjectives that are not in the book.

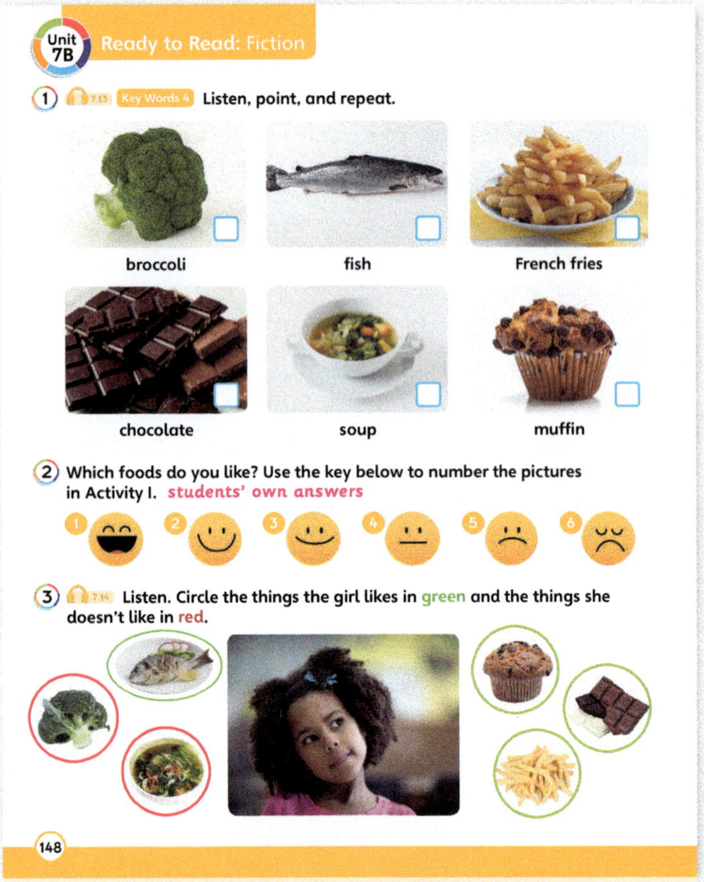

Unit 7B Ready to Read: Fiction

1 7.13 Key Words 4 Listen, point, and repeat.

broccoli fish French fries

chocolate soup muffin

2 Which foods do you like? Use the key below to number the pictures in Activity 1. students' own answers

1 2 3 4 5 6

3 7.14 Listen. Circle the things the girl likes in green and the things she doesn't like in red.

148

Objective: to learn vocabulary related to a fiction text

Key Words 4: ***broccoli, fish, French fries, chocolate, soup, muffin***

Materials: Audio CD 7.13, 7.14, green and red colored pencils; Build Creativity: tape, construction paper with two-column chart (pictures or drawings of food in the first column, nothing in the second)

1 7.13 Key Words 4 Listen, point, and repeat.

Play Track 7.13. Have students listen and point to the pictures. Play the track again for students to repeat the words. Ask: *What foods in the pictures are healthy?*

Practice Time 1 Ask a volunteer to come to the front. Spell one of the words in Activity 1 for the student to write on the board: *f - i - s - h*. Have the class check that the word has been spelled correctly. Ask another volunteer to come to the board, and assign another student to spell a different word from Activity 1. Repeat the activity as many times as you consider necessary.

2 Which foods do you like? Use the key below to number the pictures in Activity 1.

Have students look at the emoticons in Activity 2. Point to the first emoticon, and say: *Yum*. Then, point to the sixth emoticon, and say: *Yuck*. Have students use all the emoticons to show how much they like or do not like the foods in Activity 1.

3 7.14 Listen. Circle the things the girl likes in green and the things she doesn't like in red.

Ask students to take out a green and a red pencil. Say: *Green is for yum. Red is for yuck. What does the girl like? She likes fish. Yum.* Play Track 7.14, and ask students to circle as they listen to the dialogue.

Build Creativity!

Yum or Yuck?

Objective: A Different Point of View

Tape the chart to the board. Ask students to take out a green and a red pencil. Write a green checkmark next to the foods you like and a red *X* next to the foods you don't like. Then, have students do the same. Once all students have participated, add up the results with the help of the class to see what the most popular and least popular foods in the class are. As a follow-up, ask students to draw the most popular and least popular foods in their notebooks together with the words *yum* and *yuck*.

AB page 131

Reading Strategy: Main Idea

1 Look at the pictures from a story. Read the questions and trace the answers.

Stan Spinach | Bea Broccoli | Penny Peas | Zach Zucchini

a What are the pictures of? fruit vegetables

b What color are they? yellow green

c What is the story about? green vegetables yellow vegetables

2 Look at the pictures from a story. What is the main idea? Circle.

Alan | lunchbox | potato chips | candy | pizza

Alan's favorite snack | Alan's unhealthy lunch | Alan's healthy lunch

Draw what is inside your lunchbox. Is it healthy food?

149

Objective: to identify the main idea and prepare to read a fiction text

Materials: paper

1 Look at the pictures from a story. Read the questions and trace the answers.

Introduce each of the characters in Activity 1. Then, ask students each of the three questions about the characters, and have them trace the correct answers. Say: *The story is about green vegetables. This is the main idea, the most important idea.* Refer to fiction stories from previous units, and guide students to provide the main ideas.

2 Look at the pictures from a story. What is the main idea? Circle.

Introduce the boy in Activity 2. Then ask students: *What's this? (A lunchbox.)* Continue with the rest of the pictures. Then, ask: *Are potato chips, candy, and pizza healthy? (No.) What is the main idea of this story?* Read the three options, and have students choose the correct one.

Big Question Link

Read the instruction in the Big Question Link box. Give students time to draw, and then ask: *Is the food inside your lunchbox healthy?* Have various students share their drawings and answer your question.

Build Creativity!

Main Idea

Objective: Focus

Form groups of three students. Tell students you would like them to do something similar to what is shown in Activities 1 and 2—a set of drawings for other groups to guess the main idea. Draw a pencil, ruler, eraser, and glue on the board. Ask students what they think the main idea is. Students may come up with responses such as *my pencil case* or *school*. Accept all logical answers. Then, as groups begin working, go around the classroom and provide help if they are finding it hard to come up with ideas for their drawings. For example, you could tell them to draw insects, clothes, toys, emotions, water animals, fruit, etc. Once groups have finished their work, ask one group to share its drawing and another group say what the main idea is. Continue in this manner until all groups have participated.

Objective: to understand a fiction text
Materials: Audio CD 7.15, 7.16

Pre-Reading

Read the title aloud. Ask students to take a look at all the pages of the story. Then, ask general questions: *Who are the characters in the story? What foods can you see? What do you think the boy doesn't like?*

7.15 Page 150

Play Track 7.15 up to the end of the page. Pause and ask questions:

What is the boy's name?
What does Billy like?
What doesn't he like?
What's for lunch?

Personalization

Ask: *Do you like broccoli?*

7.15 Page 151

Play the rest of Track 7.15. Ask questions:

Who is on the phone?
What meal is Billy eating?
What time of day is it?

Think

Read the question in the Think box aloud. Accept all answers.

Fun Corner!

Performance 1

Encourage students to perform a short version of the first part of the story. Act as Billy's mom, and invite a volunteer to be Billy.

Billy: *Lunchtime. Yippee!*

Billy's mom pretends to be serving some food.

Billy: *Yuck! I don't like broccoli.*

Billy's mom: *Billy, eat your broccoli.*

No Broccoli, Please!

by Ángela Llanas

It's lunchtime. Yippee!
Billy likes fish.
Billy likes French fries.
Billy likes chocolate.
But Billy doesn't like broccoli! Yuck!
Billy pushes the broccoli away.

"Eat your broccoli," says Mom.
"I don't like broccoli," says Billy.

150

The telephone rings. It's Billy's grandma.
"We're eating lunch," Mom says. "Billy, eat your broccoli."
"I don't like broccoli," says Billy.

"What's that?" asks Grandma.
"Billy doesn't like broccoli!"

Think
How do you think Billy feels?

151

7.16 No Broccoli, Please!

On Sunday, Billy goes to his grandma's house to play with Fluffy, her dog.

"Lunchtime, Billy!" calls Grandma.
Grandma has a surprise. It's a little green dog.
"Hey, Fluffy," says Billy, "it looks just like you!"

152

78

Grandma's soup is green and creamy.
"Mmm! I like pea **soup**," says Billy.
"Good," says Grandma. "There are **chocolate** muffins, too."
"I love chocolate **muffins**!"

When Billy's mom comes, Billy shows her the little dog.
"I made it out of broccoli," Grandma says.
"We had pea soup for lunch."
"It was *broccoli* soup," says Grandma.
Billy's surprised. "There were chocolate muffins, too."
"Chocolate and *broccoli* muffins," says Grandma. "The recipe is on the Internet!"
Billy's mom laughs. "So, Billy, do you like broccoli now?" she asks.
"Yes, I do!" says Billy.

Think
Do broccoli soup and pea soup taste the same?

153

7.16 Page 152

Have students look at the scenes on page 152. Play Track 7.16 to the end of the page. Pause and ask questions:

Where does Billy go on Sunday?
Who is Fluffy?
What is Grandma's surprise?
Who is the green dog similar to?

Personalization

Ask: *Do you spend time with your grandparents? What do you do?*

Think

Read the question in the Think box aloud, and encourage students to guess what the green dog is made of.

7.16 Page 153, section 1

Play Track 7.16 to the end of the first paragraph. Pause and ask questions:

What color is the soup?
Does Billy like it?
What kind of soup does Billy like?
What does Billy love?

7.16 Page 153, section 2

Play the rest of Track 7.16. Ask questions:

Is the soup pea soup?
What are the muffins made of?
Where is the recipe from?
Does Billy like broccoli now?

Think

Read the question in the Think box aloud, and ask volunteers to answer the question.

Fun Corner!

Performance 2

Encourage students to perform a short version of the second part of the story. Act as Billy's mom, and guide two volunteers to be Billy and Billy's grandma.

Grandma: *Lunchtime, Billy!*

Billy: *Mmm! I like pea soup. I love chocolate muffins!*

Billy's mom arrives.

Billy: *We had pea soup for lunch. There were chocolate muffins, too.*

Grandma: *Chocolate and* broccoli *muffins.*

Billy's mom: *Do you like broccoli now?*

Billy: *Yes, I do!*

Explore the Text

1 What is the main idea of the story? Circle the answer.

a Billy doesn't like broccoli.

b Muffins can be made with broccoli.

2 Number the pictures 1–4. Then, tell the story to a partner.

3 Read the text again. Trace the answers.

Billy: I like soup / pea soup.

Billy: I don't like chocolate / broccoli.

Billy eats chocolate broccoli muffins / chocolate muffins.

The dog's name is Billy / Fluffy.

Time to Talk!

Do chocolate broccoli muffins sound yummy or yucky?

What interesting or unusual foods can you name?

Insects are yucky.

154

Objective: to deepen understanding of a fiction text

1 What is the main idea of the story? Circle the answer.

Ask a volunteer to read the two options in Activity 1, and have the class agree on what the main idea of the story is.

2 Number the pictures 1–4. Then, tell the story to a partner.

Have students number the pictures in Activity 2. Guide the class to provide information about each of the four scenes. Point to the scene numbered as *1*. Say: *Billy likes fish. Billy likes* ... Give students time to provide more information, and then say: *But Billy doesn't like* ...

Continue to guide the class to retell the story with you. Then, form pairs, and have them tell the story to each other. Have students take turns so that each one talks about two scenes.

3 Read the text again. Trace the answers.

Have students do Activity 3 on their own, then check answers as a class.

Time to Talk!

Draw students' attention to Liam, the oracy character, and read the reminder aloud. Students are already familiar with the words *yum* and *yuck*. Tell them they can also use *yummy* and *yucky* to show that they like or don't like something. Ask students the question in the Time to Talk! box. Then, encourage them to provide more examples of interesting or unusual foods they know about.

AB pages 132–33

Differentiated Instruction

Below-level ★	On-level ★★	Above-level ★★★
Ask students to close their books. Write the words *people* and *food* on the board. Have students tell you as many words as they can remember from the fiction story that fit in each category. Invite volunteers to write the words on the board.	Ask students to close their books. Write the words *people* and *food* on the board. Form small groups. In their notebooks, ask them to copy the words and write as many words as they can remember from the fiction story under each of the categories.	Do the activity as detailed in the On-level section. As a follow-up, ask groups to write five sentences about the fiction story using some of the words from their list.

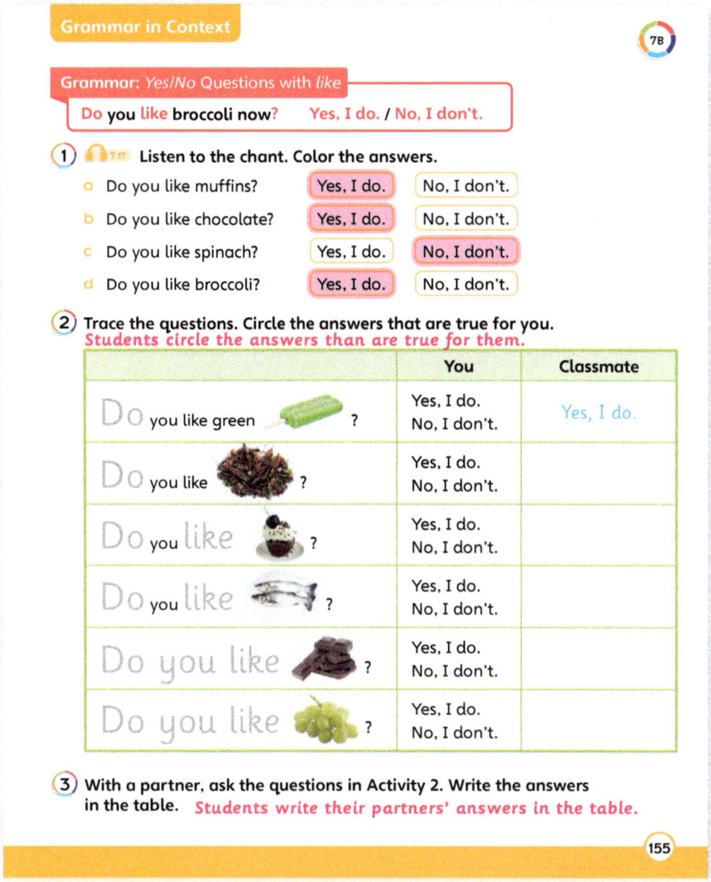

Grammar in Context

78

Grammar: *Yes/No* Questions with *like*

Do you like broccoli now? Yes, I do. / No, I don't.

1 7.17 Listen to the chant. Color the answers.

a Do you like muffins? Yes, I do. No, I don't.

b Do you like chocolate? Yes, I do. No, I don't.

c Do you like spinach? Yes, I do. No, I don't.

d Do you like broccoli? Yes, I do. No, I don't.

2 Trace the questions. Circle the answers that are true for you.

Students circle the answers than are true for them.

	You	Classmate
Do you like green ?	Yes, I do. No, I don't.	Yes, I do.
Do you like ?	Yes, I do. No, I don't.	
Do you like ?	Yes, I do. No, I don't.	
Do you like ?	Yes, I do. No, I don't.	
Do you like ?	Yes, I do. No, I don't.	
Do you like ?	Yes, I do. No, I don't.	

3 With a partner, ask the questions in Activity 2. Write the answers in the table. Students write their partners' answers in the table.

155

Objective: to use *yes/no* questions with *like*

Materials: Audio CD 7.17, slips of paper

Grammar Box

Read the question and answers in the Grammar box aloud. Write *Do you like … ?* on the board. Ask students to ask you questions with *Do you like … ?* Answer all questions. Remind students that *don't* is made up of *do* and *not*.

1 7.17 Listen to the chant. Color the answers.

Play Track 7.17. Then, play it again for students to chant. Do Activity 1 as a class.

Practice Time 1 Ask students to write four questions in their notebooks with *Do you like … ?* and a food they have learned in the unit. Have students work in pairs, and encourage peer correction.

2 Trace the questions. Circle the answers that are true for you.

Read the first part of the questions in the table in Activity 2, and let the class use the drawings to finish them. Then, have students do Activity 2 on their own.

3 With a partner, ask the questions in Activity 2. Write the answers in the table.

Ask students to write their names on a slip of paper. Go around the class, and gather the slips in a bag. Then, draw two slips from the bag, and read the names out loud. Ask those students to form a pair. Do the same with the rest of the class. (It is important to make sure students pair with different students over the course of the year.) Ask students to interview their partners by asking the questions in Activity 2. Have them write down the answers in their books.

Fun Corner!

Disgusting Food?

Ask students to think of two foods that together would make a food they would find disgusting. Give an example, such as fish muffin. Ask students to draw the two foods they have thought of and then the end result if they were combined; for example, a drawing of a fish, a drawing of a muffin, and then a muffin that has fins. Display students' drawings on the board. Ask students to vote for the most disgusting food, and count the votes.

Build Creativity!

Alphabet Food

Objective: Try, Try, and Try Again

Say the alphabet with the class as you write the letters on the board. Then, challenge students to think of a food starting with each letter. Work as a class. Encourage students to name foods in English, but, if necessary for some letters, accept names of local dishes.

AB pages 134–35

Listening

(1) Look at the pictures.
Which foods are unhealthy?

cookies broccoli French fries spinach
donuts zucchini pizza green beans

(2) 7.18 Listen to the song. Circle the main idea.
a yummy junk food (b) junk food vs. healthy food c healthy vegetables

(3) Circle the junk food in Activity 1 that is mentioned in the song.

(4) 7.18 Listen again and circle.

Healthy food makes you … Junk food makes you …

grow slow weak strong

Is it OK to eat some junk food?

Values AB page 136

156

Objectives: to talk about healthy and unhealthy food; to learn about healthy eating

Materials: Audio CD 7.18

(1) Look at the pictures. Which foods are unhealthy?

Ask students if they know what each picture in Activity 1 shows. Say each of the words, and have students repeat after you. Then, ask: *Which foods are unhealthy?* Explain that *unhealthy* means *not healthy.* Discuss as a class.

(2) 7.18 Listen to the song. Circle the main idea.

Teach the word *junk food,* and provide examples. Play Track 7.18, and read the three options in Activity 2 for students to choose from.

(3) Circle the junk food in Activity 1 that is mentioned in the song.

Play track 7.18 again. Then, have students circle the junk food in Activity 1.

(4) 7.18 Listen again and circle.

Teach the words *slow, weak, grow,* and *strong* with the help of the pictures in Activity 4. Play Track 7.18, and have students circle the correct answers.

ACTIVITY BOOK PAGE 136

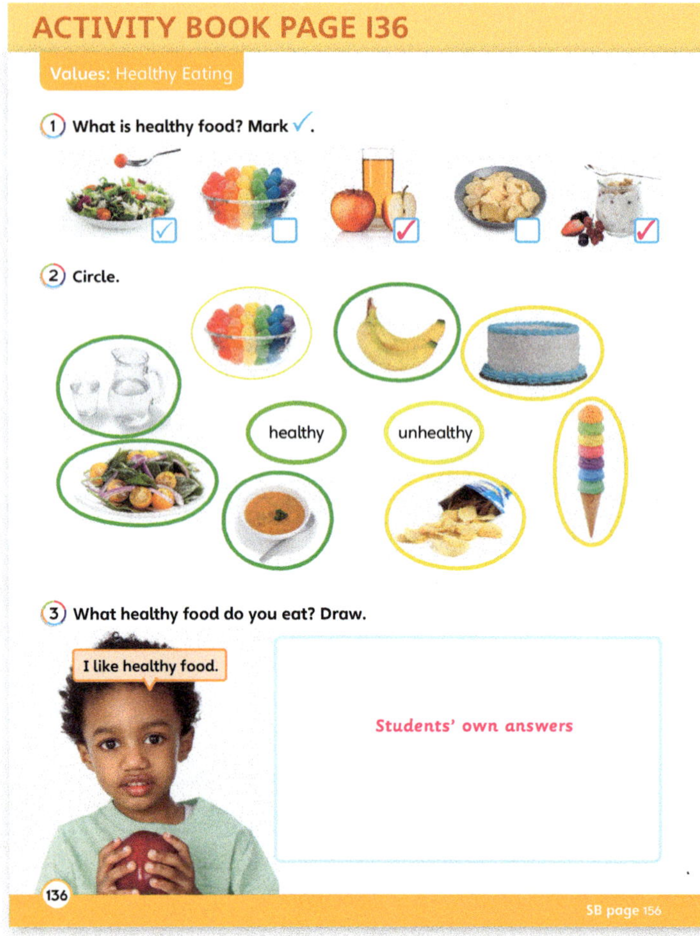

Values: Healthy Eating

(1) What is healthy food? Mark ✓.

(2) Circle.

healthy unhealthy

(3) What healthy food do you eat? Draw.

I like healthy food.

Students' own answers

136

SB page 156

(1) What is healthy food? Mark ✓.

Have students turn to page 136 of their Activity Books. Ask them to look at the pictures and mark the food that is healthy.

(2) Circle.

Have students look at the pictures. Focus on the example for students to understand the activity. Monitor, and provide support if necessary. Check answers as a class.

(3) What healthy food do you eat? Draw.

Ask students to think of a healthy food they eat often, and have them draw it.

AB page 136

Objective: to consolidate, extend, and personalize learning on the unit topic
Materials: paper

- Read the Big Challenge question and statement aloud.
- **1** Ask students to look at the recipe on page 157. Tell them they will make a similar recipe for a healthy dessert. Ask: *What are the healthy ingredients in Sam's Smoothies? (Banana, berries, yogurt, and water.)* Form pairs, and ask students to think of a healthy dessert.
- **2** Draw a cup, a spoon, and a glass on the board and teach the corresponding words. Have students write a list of the ingredients and the amount of each that they will need for their healthy dessert.
- **3** Ask students to follow the sample recipe to write theirs. First, they write the name of the dessert. Then, they include each ingredient: the amount needed, a picture of the ingredient, and the word for it.

Oracy Extension Activity

Before students give their presentations, draw their attention to Kate, the oracy character, and read the oracy reminder aloud. Then, display Cue Cards 9 and 10. Have students say which phrase they use to give positive feedback and which phrase they use to respond to positive feedback. Remind them to give and respond to positive feedback during their presentations. After their presentations, have students complete Check Your Oracy! on page 137 of the Activity Book.

- **4** Ask pairs to present their recipes to the class. Optional: Record or have students record one another's presentations to share their work.

Home-school | Portfolio: Big Challenge

Big Question Circle

Read the Big Question aloud. Have the class revisit the Big Question Links on pages 143, 149, and 156 and discuss what they have learned about healthy and unhealthy food.

- Use the following questions to help review the Big Question:

  What healthy foods can you name?
  What unhealthy foods can you name?
  What happens when you eat healthy food?
  What happens when you eat unhealthy food?
  What healthy foods do you like?
  What foods don't you like?
- Finally, have students turn to page 137 of their Activity Books to complete the Big Challenge self-assessment.

AB pages 137–39

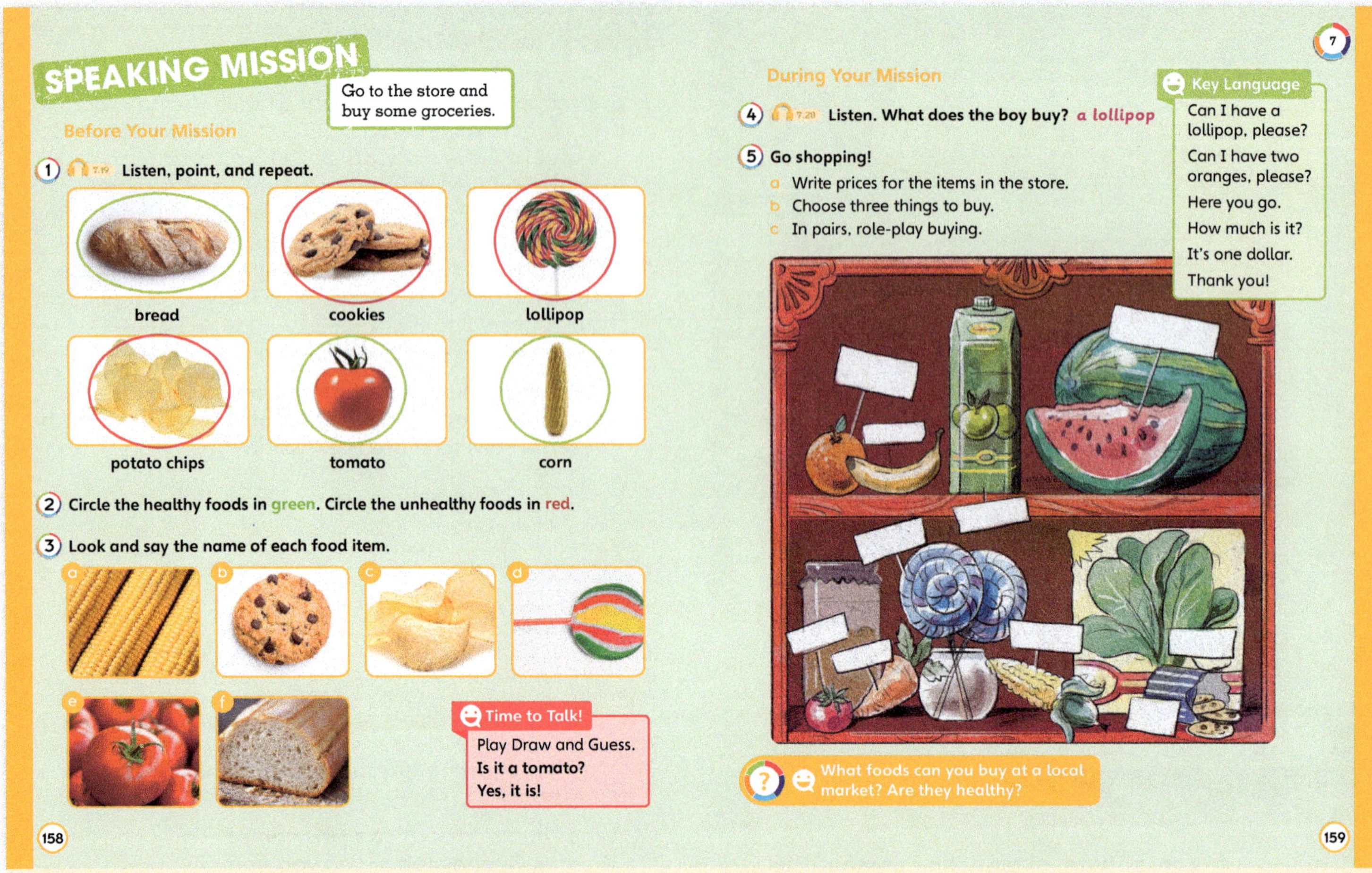

SPEAKING MISSION

Go to the store and buy some groceries.

Before Your Mission

1 7.19 Listen, point, and repeat.

bread cookies lollipop

potato chips tomato corn

2 Circle the healthy foods in green. Circle the unhealthy foods in red.

3 Look and say the name of each food item.

a b c d e f

Time to Talk!

Play Draw and Guess.

Is it a tomato?

Yes, it is!

158

During Your Mission

4 7.20 Listen. What does the boy buy? a lollipop

5 Go shopping!

a Write prices for the items in the store.

b Choose three things to buy.

c In pairs, role-play buying.

Key Language

Can I have a lollipop, please?

Can I have two oranges, please?

Here you go.

How much is it?

It's one dollar.

Thank you!

What foods can you buy at a local market? Are they healthy?

159

Objective: to buy some groceries at a store

Speaking Mission Words: ***bread, cookies, lollipop, potato chips, tomato, corn***

Materials: Audio CD 7.19, 7.20

1 7.19 Listen, point, and repeat.

Have students look at the pictures in Activity 1. Play Track 7.19, and ask students to point and repeat.

2 Circle the healthy foods in green. Circle the unhealthy foods in red.

Have students look at the pictures in Activity 1 again, and ask: *What is healthy? What is unhealthy?* Have students circle the food in green or red.

3 Look and say the name of each food item.

Point at a food item, asking a student to say what it is. Continue with other students, pointing at items in a random order. Then, work as a class. Say a letter, and have students say the food item.

Time to Talk!

Read the text in the Time to Talk! box aloud. Draw half an apple on the board, and have a volunteer guess using: *Is it … ?* Form two groups. Groups take turns drawing part of a food item on the board for the other group to guess.

4 7.20 Listen. What does the boy buy?

Play Track 7.20, and ask what the boy buys. Ask: *Where is he? (At the store.) How much is the lollipop? (One dollar.)*

5 Go shopping!

Have students tell you the food items they see in Activity 5. Teach words they are not familiar with. Have students write prices, either in dollars or in their own currency. Students choose three items to buy. They work with a student sitting next to them. Before role-playing, go through the key language and have students repeat after you. Play Track 7.20 if you think students need more practice. Optional: Record or have students record one another's role plays to share their work.

Home-school Portfolio: Speaking Mission

Big Question Link

Read the questions aloud. Have students share their opinions with the class.

AB pages 140–41

8 Are routines important?

Literacy

Read: a nonfiction text about a boy's healthy habits; a fiction text about an ant that doesn't follow routines

Reading Strategies: summarizing; making judgments

Ready to Write

Learn to Write: statements

Getting Ready to Write: write clues for a guessing game

Oracy

Skill: Speaking Up

Cue Card 4, II: 4. *Please repeat that.* II. *I don't understand.*

Speaking Mission: assign tasks to follow a class routine

Language

Key Words 1: *brush my teeth, eat breakfast, go to school, walk, ride my bike, take the bus*

Key Words 2: *sleep, do exercise, have fun, take a bath, change clothes, wash my hands*

Key Words 3: *before, after*

Key Words 4: *wake up, collect, march, find, carry, clean*

Speaking Mission Words: *take attendance, raise your hand, stand up / sit down, open your books, eat lunch, be quiet, take out / put away, draw, spell*

Grammar in Context

Present Simple: Affirmative: *I wash my hands. I sleep ten hours a day.*

Present Simple: Negative: *I don't sleep late on Saturdays! We don't work on Saturdays.*

Phonics

Ending Sounds: *-sk, -st, -nt*

Listening

Presentation: Describing Morning and Bedtime Routines

Values

Staying Healthy

The Big Challenge

How can we describe our routines?
Make a poster to show your routine

8

Are routines important?

Talk about daily routines.
Learn to speak up.
Identify statements.
Make a poster with your routines.
Assign tasks in the classroom.

What is a routine?

What are the children doing?

Do you have similar routines?

8.1 Key Words 1
brush my teeth
eat breakfast
go to school
walk
ride my bike
take the bus

1 8.1 Watch the video. Circle the routines you see.

2 8.1 Watch again. Complete the graphic organizer in the Activity Book.

AB page 142

160 161

Objective: to introduce the topic of routines
Key Words 1: ***brush my teeth, eat breakfast, go to school, walk, ride my bike, take the bus***
Materials: Video 8.1, Audio CD 8.1, Flashcards 8.1–8.6

ARE ROUTINES IMPORTANT?

- Ask students to open their books to page 160. Read the Big Question aloud. Encourage students to give their opinions on the topic and to give reasons for their answers. Read the first question, and help students answer the question by asking for examples and giving examples yourself: *Coming to school is a routine.* Ask the second question, and then, ask if each picture shows a routine. Finally, ask the last question.

8.1 Key Words 1 Use the flashcards and audio to present Key Words 1. Hold up the flashcards as you play Track 8.1. Have students repeat the words. Put the flashcards facedown on your desk. Hold them up one at a time, and have the class say the words. Then, call on individual students to do the same.

1 8.1 Watch the video. Circle the routines you see.

Watch the video, pausing after "Let's have a look!" Ask: *What is today's Big Question? (Are routines important?)* Continue the video. Pause after "But breakfast is different around the world." Ask comprehension questions, such as: *What routines are in the video?* Play the rest of the video. Then, ask what the children's names are and how they get to school. Have students do Activity 1. Check answers as a class.

2 8.1 Watch again. Complete the graphic organizer in the Activity Book.

Form pairs. Play the video again, and have students complete Activity 1 on AB page 142.

Fun Corner!

Charades

Play Charades with the class. Review the routines you have taught. Mime an action, and ask students to guess what you are doing. Then, ask volunteers to come to the front, and have them mime other routines for the class to guess.

AB page 142

Unit 8A Ready to Read: Nonfiction

Reading Strategy: Summarizing

1 Read the text. Then, point to the queen bee.

I am a honeybee.
My mother is the queen. She is very big!
I work with my sisters. I am busy all day.

I help the queen.

I collect food.

I make honey.

I clean my home.

2 Circle the best summary of the text.

a The text is about a honeybee and all the things she does.

b The text is about a bee's home.

Is the bee's routine important?

162

Objectives: to summarize and prepare to read a nonfiction text

Key Words 1: *brush my teeth, eat breakfast, go to school, walk, ride my bike, take the bus*

Materials: Audio CD 8.1; Build Creativity: colored pencils, paper

8.1 Key Words 1 Use the flashcards and audio to review Key Words 1.

1 Read the text. Then, point to the queen bee.

Point to the pictures as you read the text about the honeybee. Teach new vocabulary as you read. For example, when you teach *collect*, spread pencils out on your desk and then pick them up to show what the action involves. When you finish reading the text, ask students to point to the queen bee.

2 Circle the best summary of the text.

Tell students that a summary tells what happens in a text and that it has to be short and clear. Remind students of what they learned in unit 7 about the main idea of a text. Tell them that a summary must include the main idea. Read the two summaries in Activity 2, and have students choose the correct one.

Big Question Link

Point to the Big Question Link, and read the question aloud. Invite volunteers to answer the question. Encourage them to give reasons for their answers. Then, discuss the question as a class.

Build Creativity!

Workday Routines

Objective: Focus

Ask students to think of the jobs that their fathers, mothers, and other adults they know do. Have them choose one adult and their job. Ask students to draw four scenes to show what the adult they have chosen does each working day. Since students will find it hard to talk about routines at this stage, ask them only to show their work to a partner and say who the person is: *This is my (dad).* Then, have some volunteers come to the front, and ask them to show their drawings to the class. Ask: *Is your (dad's) routine important? Why?*

Fun Corner!

Zzz

Ask students if their parents are tired after their work routines. Perform a day in the life of a teacher. Exaggerate your performance, making it fun for the students. You could pretend that you are snoring when, suddenly, your alarm clock goes off and you realize it is late. Then, brush your teeth, drink a cup of coffee, and get dressed—all in fast motion. Continue in this way until you have shown your entire workday routine. End your day snoring again. Invite volunteers to pantomime their routines or a parent's or other adult's work routine for the class.

8.2 Key Words 2 Use Flashcards 8.7–8.12 and the audio to pre-teach Key Words 2. Hold up each flashcard as students listen to Track 8.2. Have students repeat each word.

Pre-Reading

Have students look at pages 163 and 164. Tell them that you will hold up flashcards in random order and that, for each, they should point to the picture in the nonfiction text that corresponds to the routine. For example, when you hold up the *do exercise* Flashcard, students point to the photo of Henry playing baseball. Point to the heading *4 Keep clean.* on page 164, and teach the word *clean*. Then, play Tracks 8.3 and 8.4 while students look through the text.

8.3 Page 163, section 1

Play Track 8.3 through "I sleep 10 hours every night." Pause and ask questions:

What's the boy's name?
How many hours does he sleep?

Personalization

Ask: *How many hours a night do you sleep?*

8.3 Page 163, section 2

Play the rest of Track 8.3. Ask questions:

What does Henry play?
Where does he play baseball?
What does he play with his friends?

Personalization

Ask: *What do you play with your friends?*

Fun Corner!

School Routines

Draw a chart with five columns on the board. Tell students that the chart represents a school week. Say: *Today is (Monday).* Write the day above the corresponding column. Teach the rest of the days of the week, and write each above its corresponding column. Divide the class into five groups, and distribute the materials. Assign one day to each group. Ask students to discuss what they study on the assigned day and to make drawings on separate pieces of paper representing what they study. They could draw a paintbrush to represent their art class, a ball for their gym class, etc. Have groups tape their drawings under the correct day in the chart.

Objective: to learn about a boy's healthy habits

Key Words 2: ***sleep, do exercise, have fun, take a bath, change clothes, wash my hands***

Materials: Audio CD 8.2, 8.3, Flashcards 8.1 and 8.2 (*brush my teeth, eat breakfast*), Flashcards 8.7–8.12; Fun Corner: colored pencils, paper

8.4 Page 164, section 1

Teach *morning* and *night* before playing Track 8.4. Then, play Track 8.4 through "after I play with animals." Pause and ask questions:

What does Henry do to keep clean?
When does he change his clothes?
When does he wash his hands?

Personalization

Ask: *When do you wash your hands?*

8.4 Page 164, section 2

Play the rest of Track 8.4. Ask questions:

What does Henry eat for breakfast?
Why?

Personalization

Ask: *What do you eat for breakfast?*

Big Question Link

Point to the Big Question Link, and read the question aloud. Discuss as a class.

Think

Read the question in the Think box aloud, and have students share their ideas.

AB page 143

Differentiated Instruction

Below-level ★	On-level ★★	Above-level ★★★
Do this activity as it is described in the On-level column, but give volunteers who come to the board more guidance when they say a sentence about their habits. For example, provide incomplete sentences. For the *sleep* Flashcard, say: *I sleep ... hours every night.* Students complete the sentence.	Display these flashcards in a column on the left-hand side of the board: *sleep, do exercise, eat breakfast, have fun, brush my teeth*. Write the number of hours you sleep per night next to the *sleep* Flashcard, and say: *I sleep (nine) hours every night.* Continue with the *do exercise* Flashcard. Draw a sport or exercise activity you do. If you do not do any exercise, draw a sad face. Say: *I (play basketball every day).* or *I don't do any exercise.* Draw healthy food you eat next to the *eat breakfast* Flashcard, and say: *I eat (fruit) for breakfast.* Then, draw an activity you do to have fun next to the *have fun* Flashcard. Say: *I (go to the park) with my friends.* Continue with the *brush my teeth* Flashcard. Draw a sun and a moon to show that you brush your teeth in the morning and at night. If you do not brush your teeth at night, for instance, cross out the moon. Say: *I brush my teeth in the morning. I (don't) brush my teeth at night.* Invite volunteers to provide information about themselves by drawing next to each flashcard and saying simple sentences about their habits. Then, invite all students to draw pictures about themselves in their notebooks under the title *My Habits*.	Do this activity as it is described in the On-level column, but, as a follow-up, ask students to follow a model to write sentences about themselves in their notebooks. Possible model: *I sleep (nine) hours.* *I play (tennis).* *I eat (fruit) for breakfast.* *I (play tag) with my friends.* *I brush my teeth (in the morning and at night).*

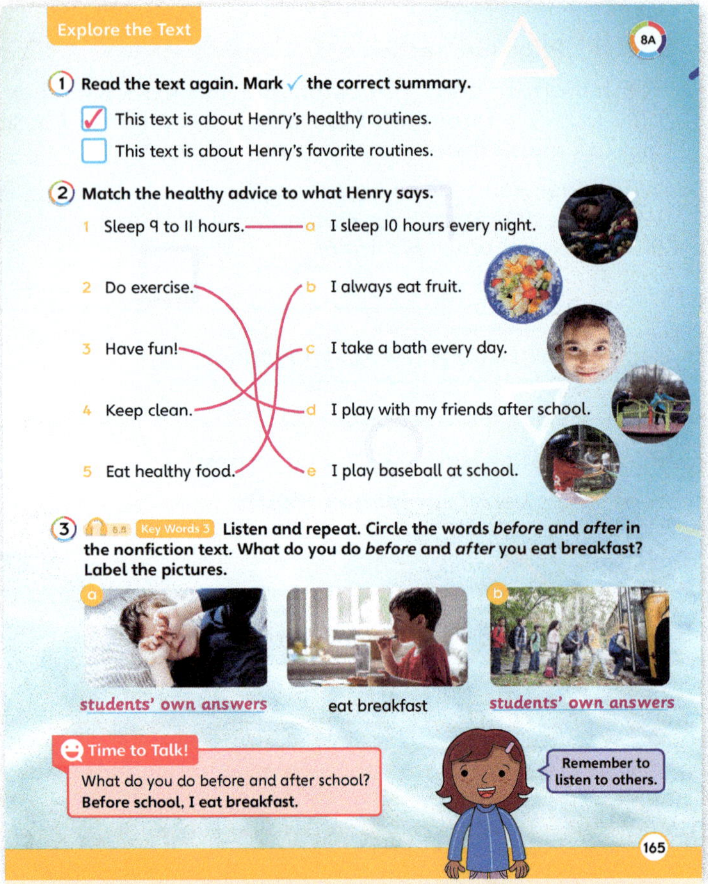
Explore the Text

8A

1 Read the text again. Mark ✓ the correct summary.

- [x] This text is about Henry's healthy routines.
- [ ] This text is about Henry's favorite routines.

2 Match the healthy advice to what Henry says.

1 Sleep 9 to 11 hours. — a I sleep 10 hours every night.
2 Do exercise. — b I always eat fruit.
3 Have fun! — c I take a bath every day.
4 Keep clean. — d I play with my friends after school.
5 Eat healthy food. — e I play baseball at school.

3 8.5 Key Words 3 Listen and repeat. Circle the words *before* and *after* in the nonfiction text. What do you do *before* and *after* you eat breakfast? Label the pictures.

a students' own answers | eat breakfast | b students' own answers

Time to Talk!
What do you do before and after school?
Before school, I eat breakfast.

Remember to listen to others.

165

Objective: to recall specific information from the text and identify words in context

Key Words 3: ***before, after***

Materials: Audio CD 8.5

1 Read the text again. Mark ✓ the correct summary.

Read the two options in Activity 1, and ask students to tell you which summary is the correct one. Correct as a class.

2 Match the healthy advice to what Henry says.

Do Activity 2 as a class. Read each sentence on the left, and have students point to the correct photo on the right. Ask volunteers to read the sentences next to the photos as you do the activity together.

3 8.5 Key Words 3 Listen and repeat. Circle the words *before* and *after* in the nonfiction text. What do you do *before* and *after* you eat breakfast? Label the pictures.

Play Track 8.5, and ask students to repeat. Then, have students do Activity 3 with you. Encourage peer correction to check performance. Explain to them that we can use these words when we are talking about routines. Ask students to follow the examples in the text to talk about themselves.

Time to Talk!

Draw students' attention to Kate, the oracy character, and read the reminder aloud. Then, read the question and the example answer in the Time to Talk! box aloud. Ask volunteers to answer the question about themselves.

Fun Corner!

Before or After?

In order to reinforce the meaning of *before* and *after*, write an incomplete row of numbers in order on the board, for example: *3 4 ___ 6 ___ 8 9 ___ 11 ___ 13*. Also write an incomplete row of the letters of the alphabet, for example: *e f g ___ i ___ k ___ m n ___ p*. Ask a volunteer: *What comes before 11? (10) What comes after g? (h)* Continue until the rows are complete. Then, form small groups, and ask them to write incomplete rows of numbers and letters for another group to complete. Have students ask questions using *before* and *after* while they play.

Build Creativity!

Backward Routines

Objective: A Different Point of View

Model a daily routine, and write the corresponding sentences on the board: *I wake up. I change my clothes. I eat breakfast. I brush my teeth. I go to school. I have fun. I eat dinner. I take a bath. I brush my teeth. I sleep.* Ask students to tell you their daily routine. Then, challenge them to see if they can tell you their routine backwards. Have them practice with a partner, and then encourage them to tell their backward routine to the class.

AB pages 144–45

Grammar in Context

Grammar: Present Simple: Affirmative

I wash my hands. I sleep ten hours a day.

1 8.6 Listen to the song. Number the pictures.

I brush my teeth. 2

I stretch and stretch. 1

I play with my friends. 4

I eat eggs and toast. 3

2 8.6 Sing the song. Act out the actions as you sing!

3 What things do you do every day? Tell a classmate.

Before I go to school, I ...

After school, I ...

What are your healthy habits? I brush my teeth in the morning.

166

Objective: **to use the present simple in the affirmative**
Materials: Audio CD 8.6, Flashcards 8.1–8.12, a bag with slips of paper with the names of each student in the class

Grammar Box

Read the sentences in the Grammar box aloud. Remind students that *wash* and *sleep* are verbs.

1 8.6 Listen to the song. Number the pictures.

Ask students to look at the pictures in Activity 1. Teach the words *stretch* and *toast*. Play Track 8.6, and ask students to number the pictures as they listen to the song.

2 8.6 Sing the song. Act out the actions as you sing!

Play Track 8.6 again, and act out the actions with the class. Then, split the class into girls and boys for them to perform their parts according to who is singing, the girl or the boy.

Practice Time 1 Write *After school ...* and *Before I go to bed ...* on the board. Then, display the *change clothes* Flashcard next to *After school ...* and the *take a bath* Flashcard next to *Before I go to bed ...* . Lead students in singing a new version of the song: *After school, I change my clothes, I change my clothes ... Every day. Before I go to bed, I take a bath, I take a bath ... Every day.* Leave the flashcards and text on the board.

3 What things do you do every day? Tell a classmate.

From the bag with the slips of paper, take out two slips. Read the names on them, and have the two students that you mention form a pair. Continue with the rest of the names. Keep the slips for future pair work. Then, ask pairs to do Activity 3. Have them follow the structure on the board (*Before ... After ...*) with any routines they can think of.

Big Question Link

Point to the Big Question Link, and read the question and example answer aloud. Discuss as a class.

Practice Time 2 Play a rapid-fire game to reinforce common collocations used when describing routines. For example, say: *eat*. Students respond with *I eat breakfast*, *lunch*, or *dinner.* Alternatively, say the second part of the collocation, and have students respond with the first part. For example, say: *dressed*. Students respond with *I get*. You may wish to repeat this activity as students are exposed to more collocations.

Fun Corner!

Charades

Make two teams. Put all twelve flashcards facedown on your desk. Ask a student from Team A to come to the front, take a flashcard, look at it, and then give it to you. The student has to mime the action for their team to guess. If the team does not guess, it is Team B's turn. Continue the game until all flashcards have been used. The team with the most correct guesses is the winner.

AB pages 146–47

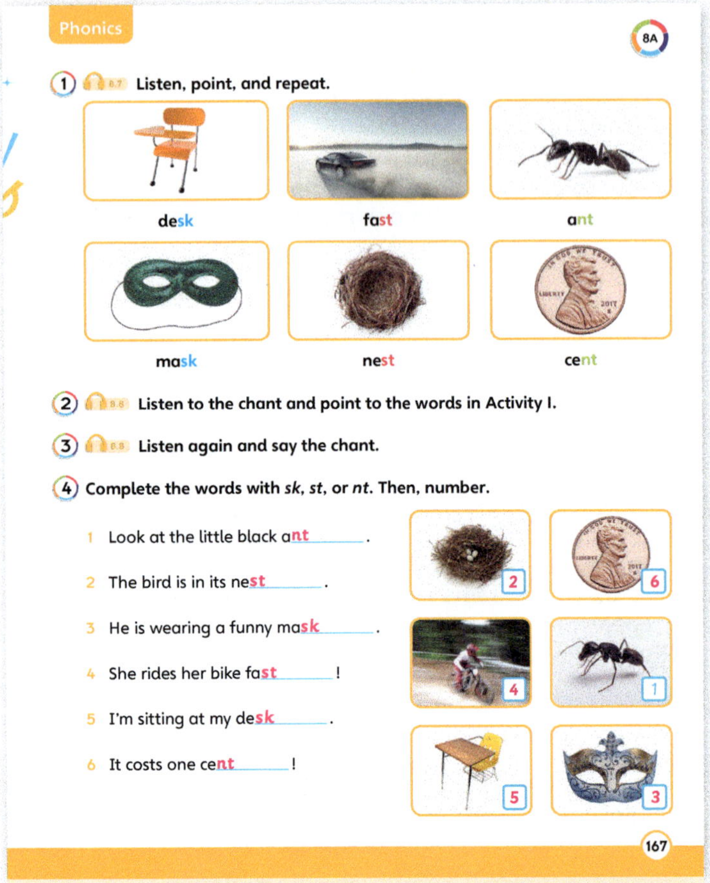

Phonics

8A

1 8.7 Listen, point, and repeat.

desk | fast | ant

mask | nest | cent

2 8.8 Listen to the chant and point to the words in Activity 1.

3 8.8 Listen again and say the chant.

4 Complete the words with *sk*, *st*, or *nt*. Then, number.

1 Look at the little black ant.

2 The bird is in its nest.

3 He is wearing a funny mask.

4 She rides her bike fast!

5 I'm sitting at my desk.

6 It costs one cent!

2 6 4 1 5 3

167

Objective: to identify the ending sounds *-sk*, *-st*, and *-nt*

Materials: Audio CD 8.7, 8.8

1 8.7 Listen, point, and repeat.

Ask students to look at the pictures in Activity 1. Play Track 8.7, and have them point and repeat. Then, point to the pictures in random order, and ask individual students to repeat after you.

2 8.8 Listen to the chant and point to the words in Activity 1.

Tell student they need to concentrate for this activity. Ask them to look at the pictures in Activity 1 and point to the corresponding pictures when they hear them in Track 8.8.

3 8.8 Listen again and say the chant.

Play Track 8.8 again, and encourage students to say the chant. Then, invite a group of students to say the chant faster. Call on another group, and ask them to say it faster than the previous group. You could also ask students to say the chant slower and slower.

4 Complete the words with *sk*, *st*, or *nt*. Then, number.

Form small groups, and have them do Activity 4 together. You may wish to use the slips of paper with students' names from the previous lesson to form the groups. When all groups have finished, check answers as a class. As a follow-up, write sentences on the board using the words in Activity 1. Have students draw what the sentences describe. For example, write: *Look at the big brown ant.* Ask a volunteer to read the sentence and then have everyone draw a big brown ant in their notebooks. You could also use the following: *I have a little old desk*, *There are four eggs in the nest*, etc. Ask volunteers to share their drawings with the class.

Fun Corner!

Which One Is It?

On the board, write the endings taught in this unit: *-sk*, *-st*, *-nt*. Point to each, and say it clearly. Then, form two teams. Call on a student from Team A, and say one word with any of the endings on the board. The student has to point to the correct ending on the board. Continue with the other team. The team that gets the most sounds correct is the winner. You may wish to use the following lists:

-sk: *dusk, ask, disk, tusk, task, mask, kiosk*

-st: *best, cast, dust, fist, must, lost, last, most, list*

-nt: *font, pant, want, tent, aunt, won't, mint, gent*

As a note, students do not need to know the words to practice identifying the ending sounds.

AB page 148

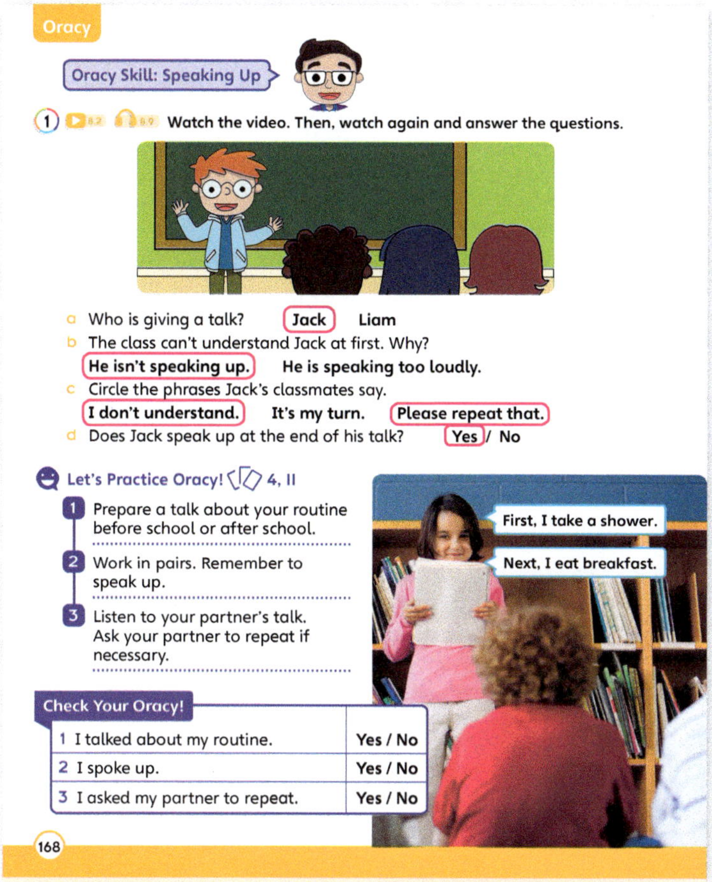

Oracy

Oracy Skill: Speaking Up

1 8.2 8.9 Watch the video. Then, watch again and answer the questions.

a Who is giving a talk? Jack Liam

b The class can't understand Jack at first. Why?

He isn't speaking up. He is speaking too loudly.

c Circle the phrases Jack's classmates say.

I don't understand. It's my turn. Please repeat that.

d Does Jack speak up at the end of his talk? Yes / No

Let's Practice Oracy! 4, 11

1 Prepare a talk about your routine before school or after school.

2 Work in pairs. Remember to speak up.

3 Listen to your partner's talk. Ask your partner to repeat if necessary.

First, I take a shower.

Next, I eat breakfast.

Check Your Oracy!

1 I talked about my routine.	Yes / No
2 I spoke up.	Yes / No
3 I asked my partner to repeat.	Yes / No

168

Objective: to learn how to speak up

Cue Cards: ***4. Please repeat that. 11. I don't understand.***

Materials: Video 8.2, Audio CD 8.9, Cue Cards 4, 11

Oracy Skill

Point out that the Oracy Skill is speaking up. Explain that we speak up when we talk loudly and clearly. This helps others to understand us.

1 8.2 8.9 Watch the video. Then, watch again and answer the questions.

Play V8.2, and ask a general comprehension question, such as: *What is the presentation about? (Routines.)* Have students watch again and, then, answer the questions in Activity 1 as a class.

Present and Practice Hold up Cue Cards 4 and 11. Read the sentences out loud, and ask students to repeat after you. Display the Cue Cards on the board. Ask two volunteers to come to the board. Assign one Cue Card to each of them. Pretend to be giving a talk about your routines, and deliver it in a low voice while looking at the floor. Students have to interrupt you by saying *I don't understand.* or *Please repeat that.* Ask groups of three students to come to the front and perform as you and the two volunteers did.

Let's Practice Oracy! 4, 11

- **1** Read the sample presentation in the book. Teach how to use *First*, *Next*, and *Finally*. Give students some time to think about three routines they do before or after school.
- **2** Form pairs. Ask students to give a presentation about their routines to their partner.
- **3** Encourage students to listen actively and to use the Cue Cards on the board if their partner is not speaking up.
- Optional: Record or have students record themselves as they practice oracy.
- Have students complete Check Your Oracy!

Home-school Portfolio: Oracy

Fun Corner!

In Crescendo

Tell students that speaking up does not mean shouting but, rather, speaking clearly and adapting to the noise level in a room. Have students get into a circle. Choose a student to start the activity. Tell students that you will say a word and the first student has to repeat it in a whisper. Moving clockwise, have students say the word louder and louder until you stop the activity. Repeat with other words.

AB page 148

Ready to Write

8A

Learn to Write: Statements

A statement is a sentence. A statement tells us something.

I play sports.

I wash my hands.

1 **Circle the statements. Match them with the pictures.**

I take the bus to school.

Is it a school bus?

I brush my teeth every day.

my teeth

a 

b 

2 **Read and draw.**

I eat a sandwich in the morning.	I play the piano every day.

Time to Talk!

In pairs, answer the question.

What do you do every day?

I read books and I play with my friends.

AB pages 149–50

169

Objective: to identify statements

Materials: paper; Differentiated Instruction: 2 bags, slips of paper with 10 questions, 10 statements, and 10 words (nouns, adjectives, verbs), 30 slips of paper (Above-level)

Learn to Write Box

Remind students that sentences begin with a capital letter. Explain that most sentences have more than one word. Write a simple question on the board. Remind students that some sentences are questions. Say: *Statements are not questions. Statements give information. They end in a period.*

1 Circle the statements. Match them with the pictures.

Ask students to do Activity 1 in pairs. Then, check answers as a class.

2 Read and draw.

Have students do Activity 2 individually. Remind students to use all of the information in the statement.

Time to Talk!

Ask students to work with the student sitting next to them. Read the question and example answer in the Time to Talk! box aloud for students to follow.

AB pages 149–50

Differentiated Instruction

Below-level ★	On-level ★★	Above-level ★★★
Put the slips of paper in a bag. Form three teams. Ask a student from Team A to go to the front and choose a slip of paper. Read the text on the slip, and then ask: *Is this a statement or a question?* Continue with the other teams. The team with the most correct answers is the winner.	Do this activity as described in the Below-level section, but have each student read the text on the slip that they have chosen.	Form two teams. Give each team 15 slips of paper and a bag to put the slips in. Ask each team to write five statements, five questions, and five words (nouns, adjectives, or verbs), each on a different slip of paper. Remind students of the correct punctuation for statements and questions, if needed. Then, have the teams swap bags. A student from one team chooses a slip and reads it. They say whether it is a statement or not. Then, a student from the other team does the same. The team with the most correct answers is the winner.

Objective: write clues for a guessing game
Materials: paper

Group Work

Discuss working in groups. Ask students if they prefer to work in groups or individually. Explain to students that working in groups can be helpful. Explain that, when you work with other people, you can share ideas. Explain that it is sometimes easier to solve a difficult problem with more people because we all know different things and have different abilities.

1 IDENTIFY

Write the word *crocodile* on the board. Ask students to give you information about crocodiles. Make a spider diagram with the information they provide. For example: *big teeth, water and land, long tail,* etc. Then, write statements: *I'm an animal. I live in water and on land. I have big teeth and a long tail.* Tell students that these statements are clues. Say: *Clues help someone guess what you are talking about.* Give clues about another animal.

2 WRITE

Form four groups: A, B, C, and D. Have them each think of one animal and write four clues about it in their notebooks. Tell students they must not write the name of the animal or say the name out loud yet because they will be playing a guessing game with the other groups. Go around the classroom to provide any needed assistance. (See Differentiated Instruction.)

3 EDIT

Remind students about using periods and capital letters and checking the spelling of words.

4 FOLLOW UP

Tell students they will play a guessing game with the clues they have written. Ask groups A and B to play the guessing game with each other, and groups C and D to do the same. For example, Group A reads the four clues to Group B. Group B tries to guess the animal. If Group B guesses on the first try, they get one point. If they guess on the second try, they get one point. If they need more guesses, they get no points. Continue with the game until each group has read its clues. The winner is the group that gets the most points.

Fun Corner!

Bingo

Draw a table made up of three columns and three rows to play Bingo. Have students copy the table into their notebooks. Then, have them choose nine key words from the unit and write them in the table. Call out key words until there is a winner. You may wish to give a prize to the winner or winners. Encourage the class to decide on the prize.

Build Creativity!

Mirror Drawing

Objective: Flow

Draw a vertical line on the board and draw half an object, animal, or person on the left-hand side. Ask a student to complete the other half. Ask students to do the same in their notebooks. Students exchange notebooks and complete their partner's drawing.

Differentiated Instruction

Below-level ★	On-level ★★	Above-level ★★★
Instead of asking students to write complete sentences, ask them to draw a spider diagram using words such as *big teeth*. They can then say complete sentences as they are playing the guessing game: *I have big teeth.*	Do Activity 2 as described above.	Do Activity 2 as described above, but tell students that their clues for the guessing game do not have to be about an animal but could instead be about a person, a place, or an object.

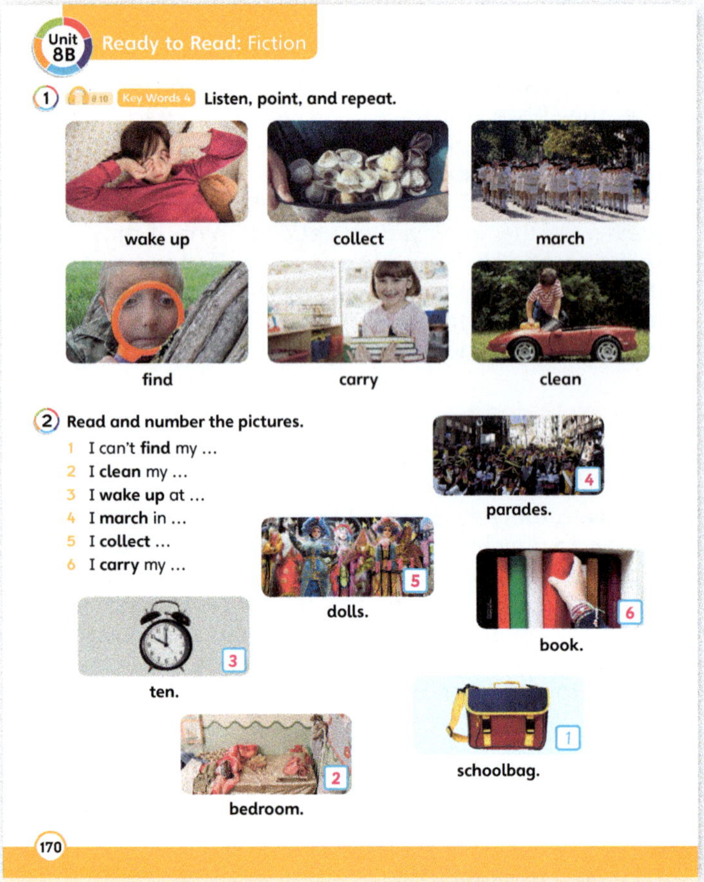

Unit 8B Ready to Read: Fiction

1 8.10 Key Words 4 Listen, point, and repeat.

wake up
collect
march
find
carry
clean

2 Read and number the pictures.

1 I can't **find** my ...
2 I **clean** my ...
3 I **wake up** at ...
4 I **march** in ...
5 I **collect** ...
6 I **carry** my ...

4 parades.
5 dolls.
6 book.
3 ten.
1 schoolbag.
2 bedroom.

170

Objective: to learn vocabulary related to a fiction text
Key Words 4: ***wake up, collect, march, find, carry, clean***
Materials: Audio CD 8.10

1 8.10 Key Words 4 Listen, point, and repeat.

Have students look at Activity 1, and ask them if they can name any of the actions they see. Then, play Track 8.10, and have students point and repeat. Correct pronunciation.

Practice Time 1 Ask students to write each of the six key words in Activity 1 in their notebooks with the letters scrambled (for example, *d i n f* for *find*). Then, have them swap notebooks with a classmate for them to unscramble the letters and write them in the correct order.

2 Read and number the pictures.

Give students time to look at the pictures in Activity 2. Encourage them to say what they see in the pictures. Then, complete the activity as a class.

Practice Time 2 Orally provide sentence starters, and invite volunteers to complete the sentences. For example, say: *Look at this picture.* Point to the picture of the collection of shells in Activity 1. Say: *I collect shells. What do you collect? I collect ...* Do the same with *I can't find my ... , I carry my ... to school,* and *I clean ... .*

Build Creativity!

Guess!

Objective: Focus

Ask students to make an activity similar to Activity 2. First, model how on the board. Write three of the sentences from Activity 2: *1. I can't find my ... , 2. I wake up at ... , 3. I collect ... .* Then, draw two options per sentence. For example, draw two clocks with different times next to *I wake up at ... .* Ask a volunteer to guess what time you wake up by matching *I wake up at ...* to one of the clocks. If the guess is correct, write a checkmark next to the choice. If not, write an X. Finally, have students write the three sentences in their notebooks and draw two options per sentence. Have pairs exchange notebooks to complete the activity. Check performance.

Fun Corner!

Mirrored Routines

Brainstorm routines with students, and write them on the board. Then, have students line up in two rows facing each other. Tell one row they are mirrors and they have to copy exactly what their partner does. The non-mirrors should act out a routine, for example, *brush your teeth.* The mirrors imitate their partners and say the phrase.

AB page 151

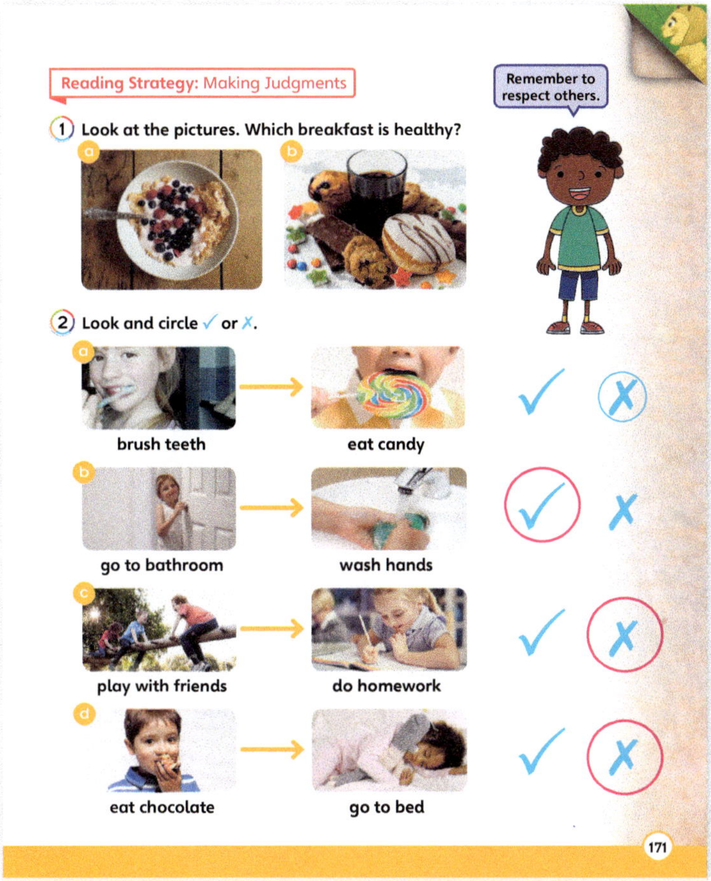
Reading Strategy: Making Judgments

Remember to respect others.

1 Look at the pictures. Which breakfast is healthy?

a b

2 Look and circle ✓ or ✗.

a brush teeth → eat candy ✓ ✗

b go to bathroom → wash hands ✓ ✗

c play with friends → do homework ✓ ✗

d eat chocolate → go to bed ✓ ✗

171

Objective: **to teach how to make judgments and prepare to read a fiction text**

Materials: Build Creativity: pictures with content about which judgments could be made (e.g., a person or people doing an action, food, sports)

1 Look at the pictures. Which breakfast is healthy?

Point to the first picture in Activity I. Ask students to tell you what they can see. *(Fruit, yogurt, cereal.)* Do the same for the second picture. *(Chocolate, cookies, a donut, soda, candy.)* Ask: *Which breakfast is healthy?* Once students have answered your question, tell them that they are making a judgment—they are saying if something is healthy or unhealthy.

2 Look and circle ✓ or ✗.

Draw students' attention to Liam, the oracy character, and read the reminder aloud. Then, complete the first item in Activity 2 as a class. Ask: *Do you eat candy after you brush your teeth? Is it good or bad? (Bad.) Is it good to brush your teeth after you eat candy?* Ask students to complete the rest of Activity 2 individually. Then, discuss their answers. Some students may not agree about item c. Tell students that we may disagree with others when we make judgments.

Fun Corner!

Hot or Cold

Discuss with students how routines can easily fall apart as a result of even small changes. For example, the routine of going to school or work can be disrupted by misplaced shoes. Ask students if the adults in their home ever lose their shoes. What do they do to find them? Play I Can't Find My … . Decide on an object. Have a couple of volunteers step outside while you hide the object. Invite the volunteers back into the classroom, and have students give them clues to help them find the object: *cold, very cold, hot,* or *very hot.*

Build Creativity!

Making Judgements

Objective: A Different Point of View

Tell students to pretend that they are aliens from outer space. Take out the pictures, and show them to the class, one by one. Encourage students to look at the pictures from the perspective of an alien and make judgments. For example, you could show a picture of people playing soccer. One student may say that the activity looks strange, while another may say the activity looks fun. The main objective of this activity is to show that people do not usually agree when they make judgments.

Objective: to understand a fiction text
Materials: Audio CD 8.11, 8.12, Flashcards 8.1–8.12

Pre-Reading

Read aloud the title of the story and the name of the author. Ask students to go through the story and identify the setting and the characters. Display the flashcards on the board, and also write these verbs: *stretch*, *help*, *clean*, *collect*, *play*, *wake up*, *carry*, and *march*. Ask students to look at all the pictures in the story. Then, ask volunteers to come to the board and put a checkmark next to the actions they can identify as being in the story.

8.11 **Page 172, section 1**

Play Track 8.11 through "… leaving Andy Ant sleeping tight." Pause and ask questions:

What day is it?
What do the ants do on Mondays?
Where is Andy Ant?

8.11 **Page 172, section 2**

Play Track 8.11 up to the end of page 172. Pause and ask questions:

What day is it?
What do the ants do on Tuesdays?
Where is Andy Ant?

Think

Ask the question in the box. Accept all possible answers.

8.11 **Page 173**

Play the rest of Track 8.11. Ask questions:

When do the ants look for seeds?
When do they carry leaves?
Where is Andy Ant?

Think

Ask the question in the box. If needed, remind students of the words *mad*, *happy*, *sad*, and *surprised*.

Personalization

Ask: *How do you feel about Andy Ant?*

Andy Ant

by Silvia Zapiain

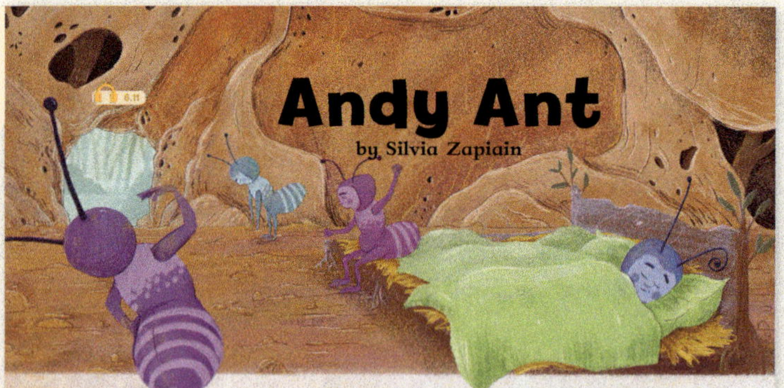

"Wake up, little ants!" says Mom.
"It's Monday morning! Let's collect bread crumbs."
"Coming, Mom!" say the little ants.
So, off they go, leaving Andy Ant sleeping tight.

The next day, Mom says, "Wake up, little ants!"
"It's Tuesday morning! Let's march!"
"Coming, Mom!" say the little ants.
So, off they go, leaving Andy Ant sleeping tight.

Think Why do you think Andy Ant is sleeping?

172

8B

The next day, Mom says, "Wake up, little ants!
It's Wednesday morning! Let's find seeds!"
"Coming, Mom!" say the little ants.
So, off they go, leaving Andy Ant sleeping tight.

The next day, Mom says, "Wake up, little ants!
It's Thursday morning! Let's carry leaves!"
"Coming, Mom!" say the little ants.
So, off they go, leaving Andy Ant sleeping tight.

Think How do you think Andy Ant's brothers and sisters feel?

173

Andy Ant

The next day, Mom says, "Wake up, little ants!
It's Friday morning! Let's clean the house!"
"Coming, Mom!" say the little ants.
So, off they go, leaving Andy Ant sleeping tight.

Think
Why do you think Andy Ant doesn't help?

174

8B

The next morning, Andy Ant is up early.
"I don't sleep late on Saturdays!" says Andy.
"I'm ready," he says. "I'm ready to help."
"I'm ready to collect bread crumbs."
"I'm ready to march."
"I'm ready to find seeds."
"I'm ready to carry leaves."
"I'm ready to clean the house!"
"But, Andy," says Mom. "It's Saturday!"
"We don't work on Saturdays!
Today we all go out and play!"

Think
Does Andy Ant help his mom on Saturday? Why?

175

8.12 Page 174

Play Track 8.12 up to the end of page 174. Pause and ask questions:

What day is it?
What do the ants do on Fridays?
Does Andy Ant help?

Think

Read the question in the Think box aloud. Ask students to give you reasons for Andy Ant's attitude.

8.12 Page 175

Play the rest of Track 8.12. Ask questions:

What day is it?
Is Andy Ant sleeping tight?
What do the ants do on Saturdays?

Think

Read the questions in the Think box aloud, and ask volunteers to answer them.

Personalization

Ask: *Do you help out at home? What do you do?*

Fun Corner!

Act It Out!

Form groups, and, in each group, assign the roles of Mom, Andy Ant, and other little ants. You could also ask a student to act as the narrator. Have students act out a short version of the story.

Narrator: *It's Monday morning.*

Mom: *Let's collect breadcrumbs.*

Some students pretend they are leaving.

Narrator: *Andy Ant is sleeping tight.*

Students continue in this manner for the rest of the story.

Explore the Text

1 Match what the ants do with the days of the week.

Monday Tuesday Wednesday Thursday Friday Saturday

2 Number the pictures in order. Retell the story in groups.

3 How do you think Mom feels about Andy Ant in each situation? Look and circle.

Do you think Andy Ant has a good attitude? Why or why not?

176

Objective: to deepen understanding of a fiction text
Materials: paper

1 Match what the ants do with the days of the week.

Ask students to look at the scenes in Activity 1 and tell you what the ants are doing in each one. Have students work in pairs and match the scenes with the days of the week. Then, encourage students to say: *On (Monday), the ants …* . Correct answers as a class.

2 Number the pictures in order. Retell the story in groups.

Form groups, and ask students to number the pictures in order. Have students retell the story by using only the four scenes in Activity 2. Monitor, and provide support as needed.

3 How do you think Mom feels about Andy Ant in each situation? Look and circle.

Discuss with students what they see in each scene in Activity 3. Then, ask students to look at scene *a*. Point to Mom's happy and sad faces and ask: *Andy Ant is sleeping. Is Mom happy or sad?* Ask students to circle the correct option. Do the same with scene *b*.

Big Question Link

Read the questions in the Big Question Link box aloud. Discuss the answers as a class.

Build Creativity!

I Can Help!

Objective: Focus

Ask students to think of two tasks they do at home to help out. Have them share the tasks with you. Make a spider diagram on the board. You will need to teach new vocabulary, such as *clean up*, *set the table*, and *sweep*. Have students make drawings in their notebooks of themselves doing the tasks. Then, ask them to write a complete sentence to accompany each drawing. Write some example sentences on the board as a model. (See Differentiated Instruction below.)

Daily Routines

Objective: Try, Try, and Try Again

Tell students that you will tell them part of your routine for each day of the week. Then, say: *On Mondays, I make pasta. On Tuesdays, I take a bath.* Continue with other examples, emphasizing the first letter of the day of the week and the first letter of the verb. Guide students to notice the connection. Then, as a class, come up with other examples for each day of the week.

AB pages 152–53

Differentiated Instruction

Below-level ★	On-level ★★	Above-level ★★★
Do the Build Creativity! activity as stated, but only ask students to draw.	Do the Build Creativity! activity as stated.	Do the Build Creativity! activity as stated but without the example sentences.

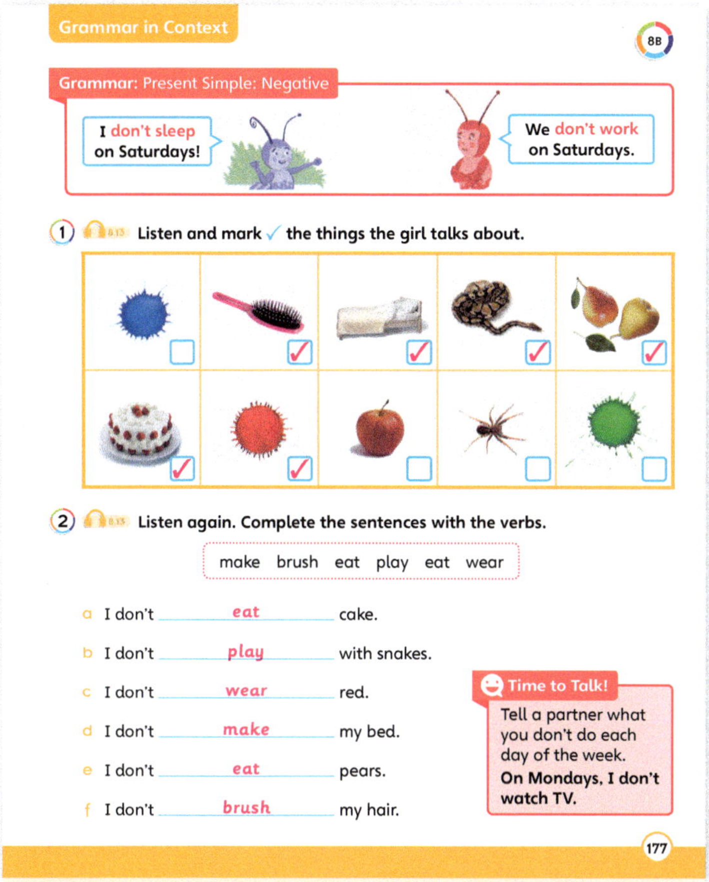

Grammar in Context 8B

Grammar: Present Simple: Negative

I don't sleep on Saturdays!

We don't work on Saturdays.

1 8.13 Listen and mark ✓ the things the girl talks about.

2 8.13 Listen again. Complete the sentences with the verbs.

make brush eat play eat wear

a I don't eat cake.

b I don't play with snakes.

c I don't wear red.

d I don't make my bed.

e I don't eat pears.

f I don't brush my hair.

Time to Talk!

Tell a partner what you don't do each day of the week.

On Mondays, I don't watch TV.

177

Objective: to use the present simple in the negative
Materials: Audio CD 8.13

Grammar Box

Ask students to look at the pictures in the Grammar box. Read the example sentences aloud. Write *don't* on the board. Point out that *don't* is a contraction of *do not*. Explain how the contraction is made.

1 8.13 Listen and mark ✓ the things the girl talks about.

Ask students to look at the pictures in Activity 1 and identify what they are. Teach students the words they do not know, such as *brush*. Then, Play Track 8.13 for students to complete the exercise. Check answers as a class.

2 8.13 Listen again. Complete the sentences with the verbs.

Do Activity 2 as a class. Then, ask students if they do or don't do the things mentioned in the activity.

Practice Time I Write *I don't eat …* on the board. Ask a student to complete the sentence orally: *I don't eat (yogurt)*. Then, have that student say *I don't eat …* and point to another student to complete the sentence. Continue with a few more students. Then, write another sentence for students to complete orally: *I don't wear … .* Continue this activity with as many sentences as you consider necessary for students to practice the negative form of the present simple.

Time to Talk!

Explain to students how to complete the Time to Talk! task. Review the days of the week before doing the activity, if necessary.

Fun Corner!

Chant Time!

Have students pretend that they are lazy children who do nothing at home. Form groups, and ask them to make a short chant using *I don't … .* Provide an example, such as: *I don't clean. I don't help. I don't wash my hands. Hooray, hooray, hooray.* Provide other expressions for students to use at the end of their chants, such as *yippee* or *oh yeah*. Invite groups to share their chants with the class.

AB pages 154–55

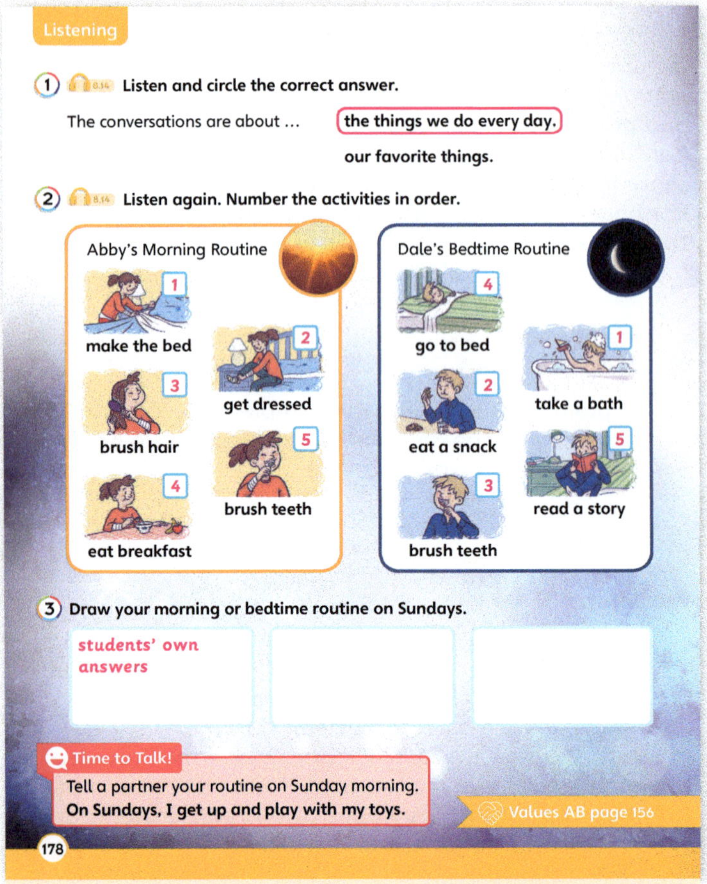

Listening

1 8.14 Listen and circle the correct answer.

The conversations are about … the things we do every day. / our favorite things.

2 8.14 Listen again. Number the activities in order.

Abby's Morning Routine: 1 make the bed; 2 get dressed; 3 brush hair; 5 brush teeth; 4 eat breakfast

Dale's Bedtime Routine: 4 go to bed; 1 take a bath; 2 eat a snack; 5 read a story; 3 brush teeth

3 Draw your morning or bedtime routine on Sundays.

students' own answers

Time to Talk!

Tell a partner your routine on Sunday morning.

On Sundays, I get up and play with my toys.

Values AB page 156

178

Objectives: to listen to children talking about their daily routines; to understand the value of staying healthy

Materials: Audio CD 8.14

1 8.14 Listen and circle the correct answer.

Play Track 8.14, and do Activity 1 as a class.

2 8.14 Listen again. Number the activities in order.

Go through the pictures in Activity 2. Ask students to pantomime the actions with you. Then, play Track 8.14 again, and have students number the activities. Check answers as a class.

3 Draw your morning or bedtime routine on Sundays.

Ask students to do Activity 3. Remind them that they should draw their routine on Sundays, not other days of the week.

Time to Talk!

Form pairs, and have students tell their partner about the routine they drew in Activity 3. If they drew their bedtime routine, have them talk about that. Ask them to follow the example: *On Sundays, … .*

ACTIVITY BOOK PAGE 156

Values: Staying Healthy

1 How can you stay healthy? Mark ✓.

2 What's healthy? Color.

3 What are your healthy habits? Draw.

Students' own answers

I do exercise.

156

SB page 178

1 How can you stay healthy? Mark ✓.

Have students look at the pictures in Activity 1 and mark the activities they can do to stay healthy.

2 What's healthy? Color.

Have students look at the drawings. Then, have them color the drawings of children doing healthy activites.

3 What are your healthy habits? Draw.

Have students draw one thing they do to stay healthy. Ask volunteers to share their drawings and talk about their healthy habits.

Fun Corner!

Repeated Steps

Talk about how routines are about doing the same things every day. Ask: *Do you think you walk on the same places every day?* Encourage students to guess how many steps they take to different parts of the classroom. For example, ask: *How many steps do you take to get your lunchbox?* Gather some guesses, then have students test their guesses. Encourage them to repeat the route several times to see if they get the same result each time.

AB page 156

Objective: **to consolidate, extend, and personalize learning on the unit topic**
Materials: Cue Cards 4, 11, paper, pictures, glue

- Read the Big Challenge question and statement aloud. Point to the girl showing a poster of her morning routine. Have students identify what each drawing represents—*brush teeth, change clothes*, etc.
- **1** Ask students to choose one day of the week and decide whether they want to focus on their morning, afternoon, or bedtime routine.
- **2** Have students think about their routine on the day and time they chose.
- **3** Tell students they should look for images from the Internet that represent the routines they want to show in their posters, or they can draw the routines. Ask students to prepare their posters at home. Remind them how to use arrows to show sequence. Also remind students of the meaning of *before* and *after*.

Oracy Extension Activity

Before students begin their discussions, draw their attention to Liam, the oracy character, and read the oracy reminder aloud. Then, display Cue Cards 4 and 11. Have students review why speaking up is important. After they have presented their posters, have students complete Check Your Oracy! on page 157 of the Activity Book.

- **4** Ask volunteers to come to the front and describe their routines. Encourage them to use *first, then*, and *finally*. (See Differentiated Instruction below.) Optional: Record or have students record one another's presentations to share their work.

Home-school Portfolio: Big Challenge

Big Question Circle

Read the Big Question aloud. Have the class revisit the Big Question Links on pages 162, 164, 166, and 176. Discuss what they have learned about routines.

- Use the following questions to help review the Big Question:

What is a routine?
Why are routines important?
Are routines always healthy?
Why is it important to be clean?
What do you do on Saturdays and Sundays that is different from other days of the week?

- Finally, have students turn to page 157 of their Activity Books to complete the Big Challenge self-assessment.

AB pages 157–59

Differentiated Instruction

Below-level ★	On-level ★★	Above-level ★★★
As a follow-up, ask students to use slips of paper to label their posters. For example, they place *brush my teeth* next to the corresponding picture. Go around the classroom to check students' work.	As a follow-up, ask students to go around the classroom with their posters to find a partner who follows a similar routine. Have pairs help each other to write complete sentences about the routines in their posters on separate sheets of paper. Go around the classroom to check students' work.	As a follow-up, ask students to individually write complete sentences about the routines in their posters. Go around the classroom to check students' work.

SPEAKING MISSION

Assign tasks to follow a class routine.

Before Your Mission

1 8.15 Listen, point, and repeat.

take attendance | raise your hand | stand up / sit down
open your books | eat lunch | be quiet
take out / put away | draw | spell

2 8.16 Listen and point to the actions in Activity 1.

3 8.16 Listen again and do the actions.

Time to Talk!
Play Simon Says.
Simon says, stand up!

180

During Your Mission

4 8.17 Listen. Mark ✓ the actions you hear.

a b c d e f g

Here!

5 Imagine you are the teacher. In your notebooks, make a list of six classroom activities for your class. students' own answers

6 In small groups, take turns role-playing the teacher.

Raise your hand.

Key Language
Hello, I'm (Ms./Mr. Brown).
(Sit down), please.
First, (open your book).
Let's (read).
Now, (stand up), please.
What do we do next?
Let's go to the playground.

Are school routines important? Why?

181

Speaking Mission Words: ***take attendance, raise your hand, stand up / sit down, open your books, eat lunch, be quiet, take out / put away, draw, spell***

Materials: Audio CD 8.15, 8.16, 8.17

1 8.15 Listen, point, and repeat.

Have students look at the pictures in Activity 1. Play Track 8.15 for students to point and repeat.

2 8.16 Listen and point to the actions in Activity 1.

Play Track 8.16, and ask students to point to the pictures in Activity 1 as they listen.

3 8.16 Listen again and do the actions.

Ask students to stand up and do the actions as you play Track 8.16 again.

Time to Talk!

Play Simon Says. Allow various students to give instructions.

4 8.17 Listen. Mark ✓ the actions you hear.

Play Track 8.17, and ask students to mark the actions that are mentioned.

5 Imagine you are the teacher. In your notebooks, make a list of six classroom activities for your class.

Ask students to choose six of the classroom activities in Activity 1 and write them in any order in their notebooks.

6 In small groups, take turns role-playing the teacher.

Before doing this activity, review the key language with students. If necessary, play Track 8.17 again for students to follow the example. Focus on the use of *Let's* … and … *please*. Form small groups, and have them do Activity 6. Optional: Record students' role plays.

Home-school | Portfolio: Speaking Mission

Big Question Link

Read the questions in the Big Question Link box aloud. Discuss answers as a class.

AB pages 160–61

9 Why do we wear different clothes?

Literacy

Read: a nonfiction text about traditional clothes from around the world; a fiction text about an emperor who is fooled by two thieves

Reading Strategies: identifying cause and effect; identifying beginning, middle, and end

Ready to Write

Learn to Write: questions

Getting Ready to Write: write a short story

Oracy

Skill: Standing Up Straight and Keeping Still

Cue Cards 1, 12: 1. *This is …* , 12. *These are …*

Oracy Performance Task 3: Presentation: give a final presentation

Language

Key Words 1: *clothes, cold, jacket, hot, T-shirt, shoes*

Key Words 2: *wear, hat, skirt, pants, gloves, dress*

Key Words 3: *wool, cool*

Key Words 4: *emperor, thief, palace, expensive, smart, fool*

Oracy Performance Task Expressions: *Please repeat that. I don't understand. Good job! Thank you!*

Grammar in Context

Present Continuous: Affirmative and Negative: *I'm wearing gloves and big boots. I'm not wearing a hat. She's wearing a long skirt. He's not wearing a jacket.*

Present Continuous: *Yes/No* Questions: *Are you wearing magic clothes? Yes, I am. Are you wearing your new clothes? No, I'm not.*

Phonics

Initial Sounds: *gr-, pl-*

Listening

Presentation: Describing What You Wear

Values

Taking Care of Your Clothes

The Big Challenge

How do we dress for special occasions? Make a jigsaw puzzle about clothes for special occasions

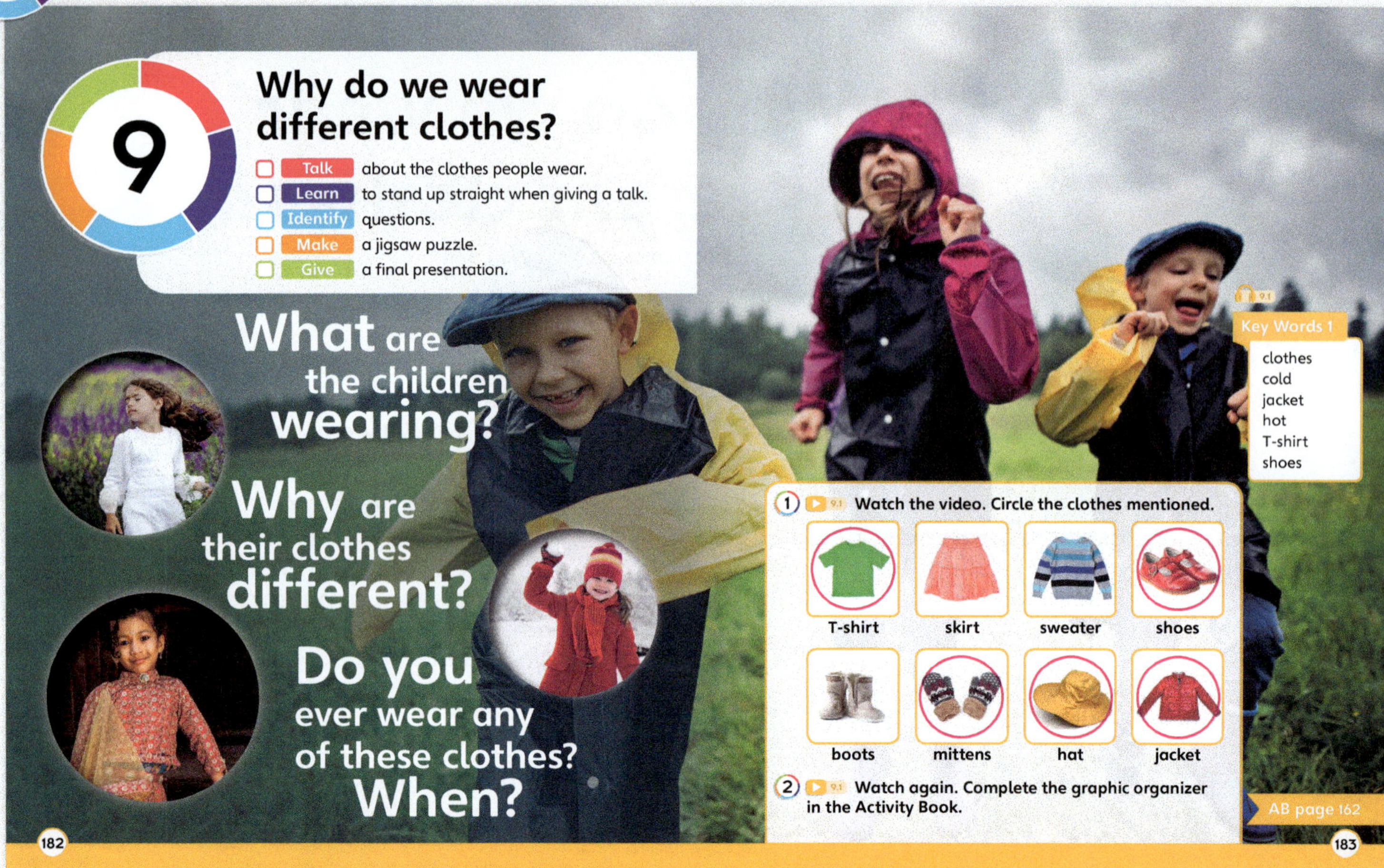

Objective: **to introduce the topic of clothes**
Key Words 1: ***clothes, cold, jacket, hot, T-shirt, shoes***
Materials: Video 9.1, Audio CD 9.1, Flashcards 9.1–9.6

WHY DO WE WEAR DIFFERENT CLOTHES?

- Ask students to open their books to page 182. Read the Big Question aloud. Encourage students to give their opinions on the topic and to give reasons for their answers. Lead students in talking about clothes from around the world as well. Read the questions, and guide students to answer them.

9.1 Key Words 1 Use the flashcards and audio to present Key Words 1. Hold up the flashcards as you play Track 9.1. Have students repeat the words. Put the flashcards facedown on your desk. Hold them up one at a time, and have the class say the words. Then, call on individual students to say the words.

1 9.1 Watch the video. Circle the clothes mentioned.

Watch the video, pausing after "Let's see what kind of clothes people wear!" Ask: *What is today's Big Question? (Why do we wear different clothes?)* Continue playing the video. Pause after "Look out!" Ask comprehension questions, such as: *Is it cold or hot? What are the children wearing?* Teach the word *warm*. Continue the video, and pause to ask questions about rainy days and then hot weather. Ask the last question in the video: *Is it hot or cold where you live?* Encourage students to talk about weather. Then, have students do Activity 1. Check answers as a class.

2 9.1 Watch again. Complete the graphic organizer in the Activity Book.

Form pairs. Play the video again, and have students complete Activity 1 on AB page 162.

Fun Corner!

Guess What I'm Drawing

Form two teams—Team A and Team B. Ask for a volunteer from each team to come to the front. Ask the volunteer from Team A to draw half of a piece of clothing on the board for their team to guess. If the team does not guess correctly on the first try, it is the other team's turn to draw. The winning team is the one with the most correct guesses.

AB page 162

Unit 9A Ready to Read: Nonfiction

Reading Strategy: Cause and Effect

Cause → Effect

1 Look at the pictures. Write *C* (cause) or *E* (effect).

a C E

b E C

2 Draw the effect.

Cause → Effect

Students should draw the boy tripping and falling or on the ground.

What do you wear when it's hot?

184

Objective: to identify cause and effect and prepare to read a nonfiction text

Key Words 1: ***clothes, cold, jacket, hot, T-shirt, shoes***

Materials: Audio CD 9.1, Flashcards 9.1–9.6; Fun Corner: yarn, cardboard

9.1 **Key Words 1** Use the flashcards and audio to review Key Words 1.

1 Look at the pictures. Write *C* (cause) or *E* (effect).

Ask students to look at the Reading Strategy box. Ask questions to guide students to identify cause and effect: *What's the weather like in the pictures? What is the boy wearing? Are they winter clothes? Why is he cold in the second picture?* Focus on the words *cause* and *effect*, and guide students to use *Why?* and *because*. You may want to ask students for more examples of situations like the one in the pictures. Then, complete Activity 1 as a class.

2 Draw the effect.

Ask students questions to help them describe the picture in Activity 2. If needed, point out the boy's shoelaces. Then, ask what they think the effect will be. Have students draw their ideas.

Big Question Link

Point to the Big Question Link, and read the question aloud. Invite volunteers to answer the question. Encourage them to give reasons for their answers.

Fun Corner!

What's the Effect?

Tell students that you will act out several situations and they have to act out the effect of each. For example, pretend you are eating a lot very quickly. Guide students to pretend they have a stomachache. Other situations you could act out are: you run fast in place (effect: you are tired; you are thirsty), you put on shoes that are too small for you (effect: your feet hurt). Also act out doing things that have a positive effect, for example, it is cold and you put a coat on (effect: you feel warm and comfortable).

Shoelace Tying

Ask: *Can you tie your shoelaces?* Invite a volunteer to demonstrate for the class. (Be sensitive to the fact that some students are probably still learning this skill.) Make the task a little harder by asking if they can tie another person's shoelaces. What about tying their shoelaces with their eyes closed? You may want to review with students how to tie their shoelaces. If possible, thread some yarn through a piece of cardboard to recreate shoelaces.

9.2 Key Words 2 Use Flashcards 9.8–9.12 and the audio to pre-teach Key Words 2. Hold up each flashcard as students listen to Track 9.2. Have students repeat each word.

Pre-Reading

Have students look at pages 185 and 186. Tell them you will hold up the flashcards in random order. For each flashcard, they should point to the corresponding piece of clothing in the nonfiction text. Then, play Tracks 9.3 and 9.4 while students look through the text.

9.3 **Page 185, section 1**

Play Track 9.3 through "They are part of who we are." Pause and ask questions:

When do people wear traditional clothes?
Why?

Personalization

Ask: *Do you wear traditional clothes?*

9.3 **Page 185, section 2**

Play the rest of Track 9.3. Ask questions:

Where is the first boy from?
What is he wearing?
Where is the second boy from?
What is he wearing?

Personalization

Ask: *What are you wearing now?*

Build Creativity!

What Are They Made Of?

Objective: Flow

Show a piece of fabric or a piece of clothing made from wool. Say: *This is wool. Touch it. Ponchos are made of wool.* Give students time to feel the wool. Then, show something made of faux fur. Say: *The Inuit boy is wearing boots made of fur.* Continue with silk to introduce the word to students before you work on the second part of the nonfiction story. Then, show more fabrics or pieces of clothing, such as cotton, leather, denim, etc. Let students touch them, and help students identify the materials. Ask students to bring a piece of clothing they wear from home into class. The following class, ask volunteers to show the clothing, identify its material, and tell you when they wear it.

Objective: to learn about clothes from around the world

Key Words 2: ***wear, hat, skirt, pants, gloves, dress***

Materials: Audio CD 9.2, 9.3, 9.4, Flashcards 9.8–9.12; Build Creativity: different fabrics or pieces of clothing made of different fabrics (including wool, silk, and faux fur)

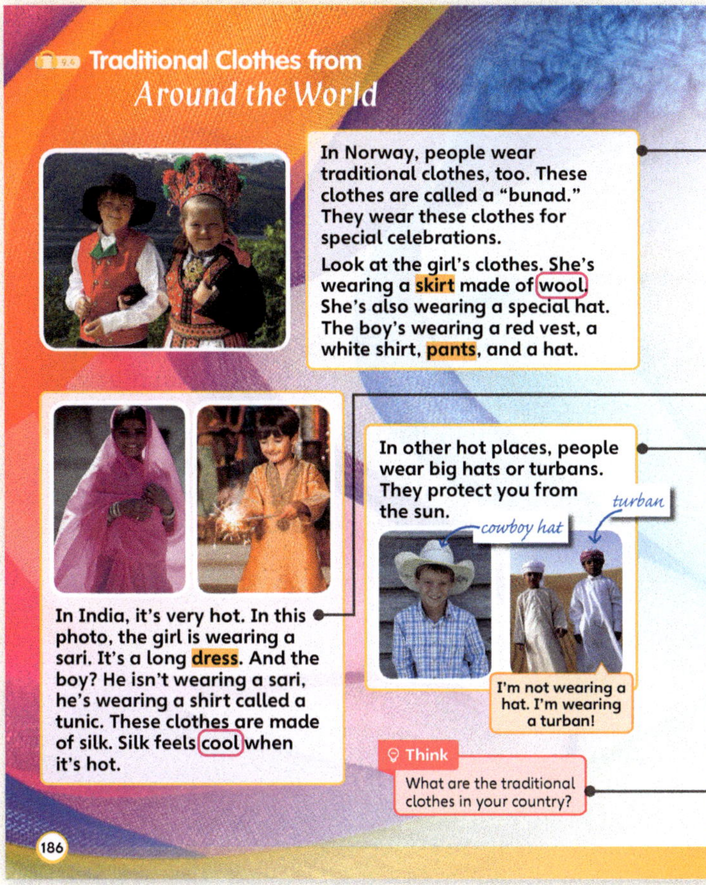

Traditional Clothes from *Around the World*

In Norway, people wear traditional clothes, too. These clothes are called a "bunad." They wear these clothes for special celebrations.

Look at the girl's clothes. She's wearing a **skirt** made of wool. She's also wearing a special hat. The boy's wearing a red vest, a white shirt, **pants**, and a hat.

In India, it's very hot. In this photo, the girl is wearing a sari. It's a long **dress**. And the boy? He isn't wearing a sari, he's wearing a shirt called a tunic. These clothes are made of silk. Silk feels cool when it's hot.

In other hot places, people wear big hats or turbans. They protect you from the sun.

Think: What are the traditional clothes in your country?

186

9.4 Page 186, section 1

Play Track 9.4 through "… and a hat." Pause and ask questions:

What traditional clothes do people wear in Norway?
What is the girl wearing?
What is the boy wearing?

Personalization

Ask: *What do you wear for special celebrations?*

9.4 Page 186, section 2

Play Track 9.4 through "Silk feels cool when it's hot." Pause and ask questions:

Where are the children from?
What is the girl wearing?
What is the boy wearing?

9.4 Page 186, section 3

Play the rest of Track 9.4. Ask questions:

What are the boys wearing on their heads?

Think

Read the question in the Think box aloud, and have students share their ideas.

AB page 163

Differentiated Instruction

Below-level ★	On-level ★★	Above-level ★★★
Do this activity as in the On-level section, but ask students to find words for only one category: clothes.	To help students internalize new lexical items from the nonfiction text, write these categories on the board: *Clothes, Materials, Weather.* Ask students to reread the nonfiction text and tell you what words go under each category. (Clothes: *hat, poncho, gloves, jacket, boots, bunad, skirt, vest, shirt, pants, sari, dress, tunic, cowboy hat, turban*; Materials: *wool, fur, silk*; Weather: *cold, hot*) Students already know the word *warm*. You may want to add this word under the *weather* category, together with the word *cool*.	Have students do this activity as in the On-level section but in small groups.

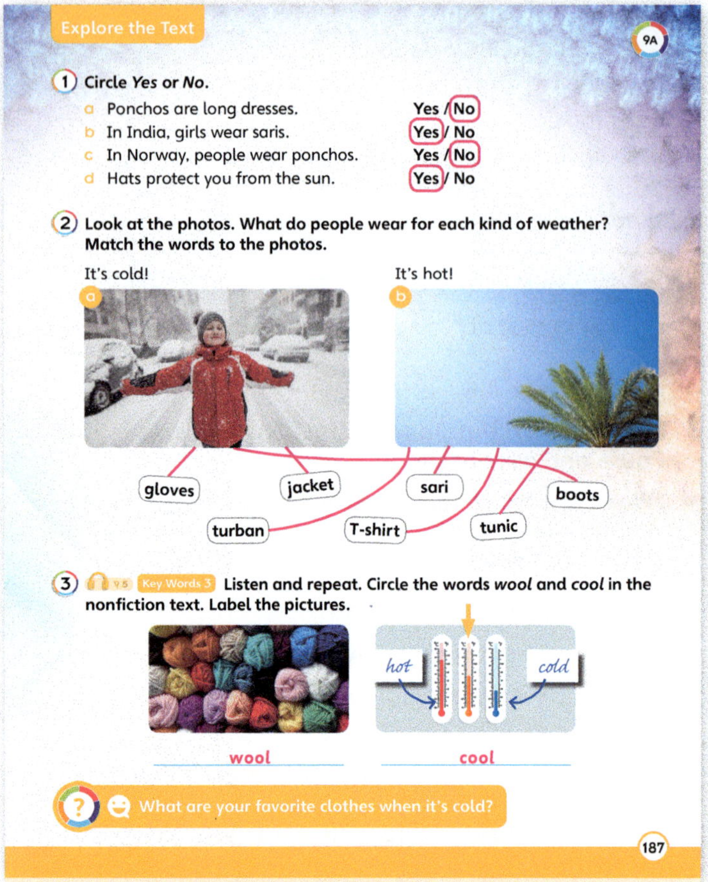

Explore the Text

9A

1 Circle *Yes* or *No*.

a Ponchos are long dresses. Yes / No
b In India, girls wear saris. Yes / No
c In Norway, people wear ponchos. Yes / No
d Hats protect you from the sun. Yes / No

2 Look at the photos. What do people wear for each kind of weather? Match the words to the photos.

It's cold! a
It's hot! b

gloves jacket sari boots turban T-shirt tunic

3 9.5 Key Words 3 Listen and repeat. Circle the words *wool* and *cool* in the nonfiction text. Label the pictures.

hot cold

wool cool

What are your favorite clothes when it's cold?

187

Objective: **to recall specific information from the text and identify words in context**
Key Words 3: ***wool, cool***
Materials: Audio CD 9.5

1 Circle *Yes* or *No*.

Have students work in pairs to do Activity 1. Then, check answers as a class. Encourage students to fix the sentences that are not true and to write the corrected versions in their notebooks.

2 Look at the photos. What do people wear for each kind of weather? Match the words to the photos.

Have students work in pairs but not with the same partner they worked with in Activity 1. Ask students to read the nonfiction text again and then do Activity 2. Check answers as a class. You may want to ask students to add more clothes words to each kind of weather.

3 9.5 Key Words 3 Listen and repeat. Circle the words *wool* and *cool* in the nonfiction text. Label the pictures.

Play Track 9.5, and ask students to repeat. Then, have students label the pictures in Activity 3.

Big Question Link

Point to the Big Question Link, and read the question aloud. Invite volunteers to answer the question. You could ask what their favorite winter clothes are made of.

Fun Corner!

Think Fast

Play a simple word association game. Say a word related to clothes, such as the word for an article of clothing, and encourage children to say (or write) the first word they think of. For example, if you say *glove*, they may respond with *hat* or with something completely different, such as *cold*. After a few rounds with the whole class, encourage students to play the game in pairs.

AB pages 164–65

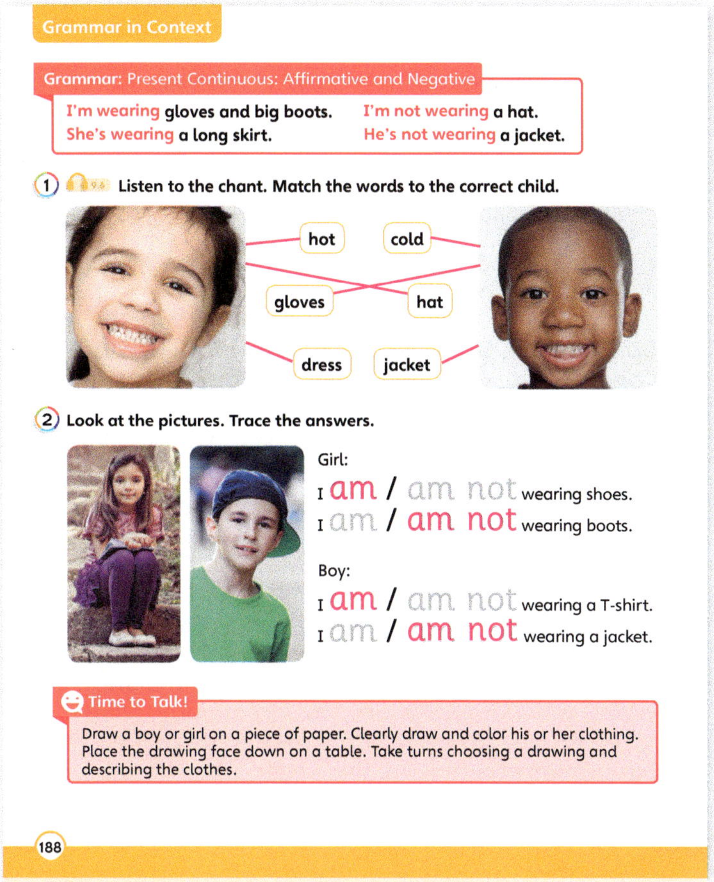
Grammar in Context

Grammar: Present Continuous: Affirmative and Negative

I'm wearing gloves and big boots. I'm not wearing a hat.
She's wearing a long skirt. He's not wearing a jacket.

1 9.6 Listen to the chant. Match the words to the correct child.

2 Look at the pictures. Trace the answers.

Girl:
I am / am not wearing shoes.
I am / am not wearing boots.

Boy:
I am / am not wearing a T-shirt.
I am / am not wearing a jacket.

Time to Talk!
Draw a boy or girl on a piece of paper. Clearly draw and color his or her clothing. Place the drawing face down on a table. Take turns choosing a drawing and describing the clothes.

188

Objective: to use the present continuous in affirmative and negative sentences
Materials: Audio CD 9.6, Flashcards 9.7–9.12; Build Creativity: pieces of clothing for dress-up and a fashion show (brought from home by students)

Grammar Box

Tell students what you are wearing: *Today, I'm wearing …* . Add a negative sentence about what you are not wearing. Then, describe what some students are or are not wearing. Show one flashcard at a time, and ask individual students: *What is (he) wearing? What isn't (she) wearing?* Ask a volunteer to read the examples in the Grammar box aloud.

1 9.6 Listen to the chant. Match the words to the correct child.

Ask a volunteer to read the words in Activity 1. Tell students they will be matching the words to the corresponding child. Play Track 9.6 for students to do the activity. Then, check answers as a class.

Practice Time 1 Write these sentences from the chant on the board:

Phew! It's hot, it's hot, it's hot today. But I'm wearing _______, so it's OK!

Brrr. It's cold, it's cold, it's cold today. But I'm wearing _______, so it's OK!

Ask students to write the sentences in their notebooks and to complete them with clothes that are different from the ones in the chant. Ask volunteers to sing their new version of the chant.

2 Look at the pictures. Trace the answers.

Have students do Activity 2 individually. Then, ask them to exchange books with a partner for peer correction.

Time to Talk!

Explain to students how to do the activity described in the Time to Talk! box. First, ask them to draw a boy or a girl wearing any kind of clothes. Make sure students draw and color the clothes clearly. Then, form small groups, and ask them to place their drawings in a pile, facedown on a table. Each member of the group takes a drawing, shows it to the group, and describes it. If a student gets their own drawing, they should choose another one. Go around the classroom, and check performance.

Build Creativity!

Fashion Show
Objective: Take a Break
If students have brought in clothing from home for the fashion show (see Materials), tell them where in the classroom or elsewhere in the school they can go to dress up. Do not force students to dress up if they do not want to. When everyone is ready, choose a part of the classroom to use as a catwalk. Have volunteers walk down the catwalk as other students take turns describing what they are wearing.

Design a T-Shirt
Objective: Focus
Discuss students' favorite colors. Ask if these colors are also the ones they like to wear. Have students design a pattern or draw a picture for a T-shirt. As they work, ask them about the colors they are using. Encourage students to take their time, and make suggestions about what they could add to make their pattern or picture more detailed.

AB pages 166–67

Phonics

9A

1 9.7 Listen, point, and repeat.

grow green grandma

plant play plum

2 9.8 Listen and follow along. Then sing the song.

Grandma's Plant Grows

Grandma's green plant
Grows and grows.
Come and see,
One, two, three.

Grandma's green plant
Grows into a tree, into a tree.
Come and see,
One, two, three.

Grandma's green plant
Grows into a plum tree, into a plum tree.
Come and see,
One, two, three.

Come climb and play with me
in Grandma's big plum tree!

3 Go through the book and find words starting with *gr* and *pl*.

189

Objective: to identify the initial sounds ***gr-*** and ***pl-***

Materials: Audio CD 9.7, 9.8

1 9.7 Listen, point, and repeat.

Ask students to look at the pictures in Activity 1. Play Track 9.7, and have students point and repeat. Then, point to the pictures in random order, and ask individual students to repeat after you.

2 9.8 Listen and follow along. Then sing the song.

Play Track 9.8, and have students follow along. Play the track once more for them to sing with you. Then, assign parts of the song to different groups. For example, one group could sing *Grandma's green plant grows and grows*, and another *Come and see, One, two, three.* You may wish to sing the second line of each verse until students get familiar with the song. Alternatively, you could assign boys and girls to different parts of the song, or use the classroom seating layout to assign parts of the song.

3 Go through the book and find words starting with *gr* and *pl*.

Form four groups. Ask students to find words starting with *gr* and *pl*. Have students write down the words as they find them. Some of the words they will come across are: *grapes, groceries, ground, group, graphic, great, play, please, plot, plan, plane.* Ask groups to share their findings with you, and ask volunteers to write the words on the board under two columns. (See Differentiated Instruction.)

AB page 168

Differentiated Instruction

Below-level ★	On-level ★★	Above-level ★★★
Instead of having students go through the book to find words with the initial sounds *gr* and *pl*, provide sentence frames to elicit particular words with these initial sounds; for example: *I _______ basketball very well. (play)* Ask volunteers to write the words on the board for the rest of the class to copy into their notebooks.	Do Activity 3 as stated above.	Do Activity 3 as stated above. As a follow-up, ask students to write sentences with some of the words they have found. For example, *Can you repeat that, please?*

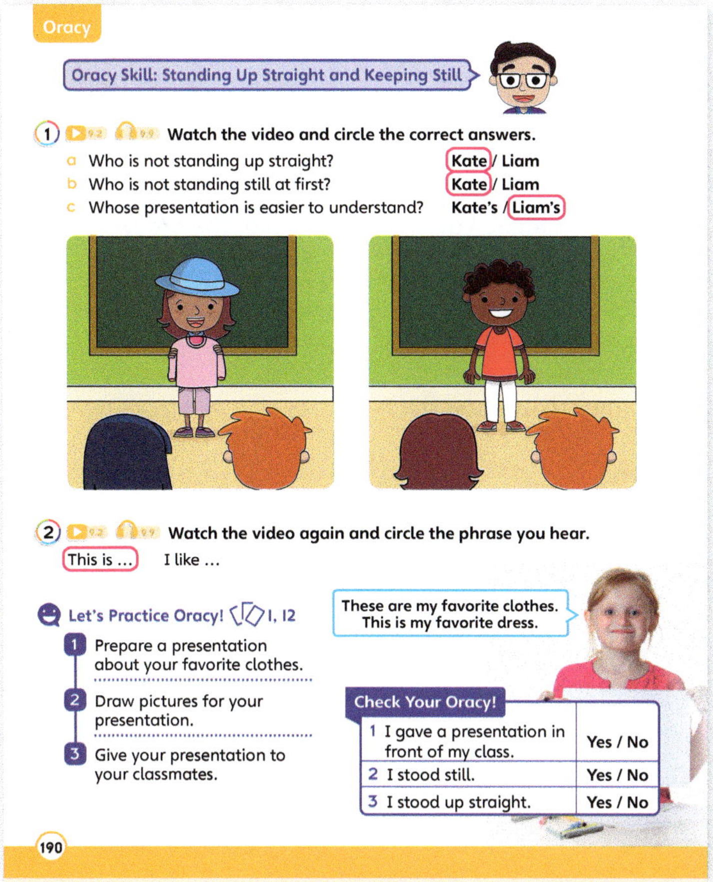

Oracy

Oracy Skill: Standing Up Straight and Keeping Still

1 9.2 9.9 Watch the video and circle the correct answers.

a Who is not standing up straight? Kate / Liam
b Who is not standing still at first? Kate / Liam
c Whose presentation is easier to understand? Kate's / Liam's

2 9.2 9.9 Watch the video again and circle the phrase you hear.

This is ... I like ...

Let's Practice Oracy! 1, 12

1 Prepare a presentation about your favorite clothes.
2 Draw pictures for your presentation.
3 Give your presentation to your classmates.

These are my favorite clothes. This is my favorite dress.

Check Your Oracy!	
1 I gave a presentation in front of my class.	Yes / No
2 I stood still.	Yes / No
3 I stood up straight.	Yes / No

190

Objective: **to learn how to stand up straight and keep still**

Cue Cards: **1. *This is ...* , 12. *These are ...***

Materials: Video 9.2, Audio CD 9.9, Cue Cards 1, 12, paper, colored pencils or crayons

Oracy Skill

Stand up straight, and then, slouch a bit. Ask students to tell you which posture they think is better to be in when giving a presentation. Then, demonstrate keeping still and moving around while giving a presentation. Ask students what they think is better. Ask students why it is important to stand up straight and keep still when they are giving a presentation. Explain that, if you do not keep still when giving a presentation, your audience may get distracted and not listen to you. Also, say that, if you do not stand up straight, you will not look confident.

1 9.2 9.9 Watch the video and circle the correct answers.

Play V9.2, and answer the questions in Activity 1 as a class. Note that the video must be shown to model this oracy skill.

2 9.2 9.9 Watch the video again and circle the phrase you hear.

Play V9.2 again. Have students circle the phrase they hear. Then, check the answer as a class.

Present and Practice Hold up Cue Cards 1 and 12. Read them out loud, and ask students to repeat after you. Display the Cue Cards on the board. Talk about your clothes using the two Cue Cards. For example: *This is my jacket. These are my shoes.* Ask volunteers to give more examples using the Cue Cards.

Let's Practice Oracy! 1, 12

- **1** Read the example presentation in the speech bubble. Ask students to think of two of their favorite clothes. If possible, encourage them to think of something plural (shoes, gloves, etc.) and something singular so that they use the two Cue Cards.
- **2** Have students draw and color their two favorite clothes on a sheet of paper.
- **3** Remind students of the presentation shown in V9.2. Encourage them to stand up straight and keep still while presenting.
- Optional: Record or have students record themselves as they practice oracy.
- Have students complete Check Your Oracy!

Home-school Portfolio: Oracy

Fun Corner!

Simon Says

Play Simon Says but with only four instructions: *Stand up straight. Don't stand up straight. Keep still. Don't keep still.*

AB page 168

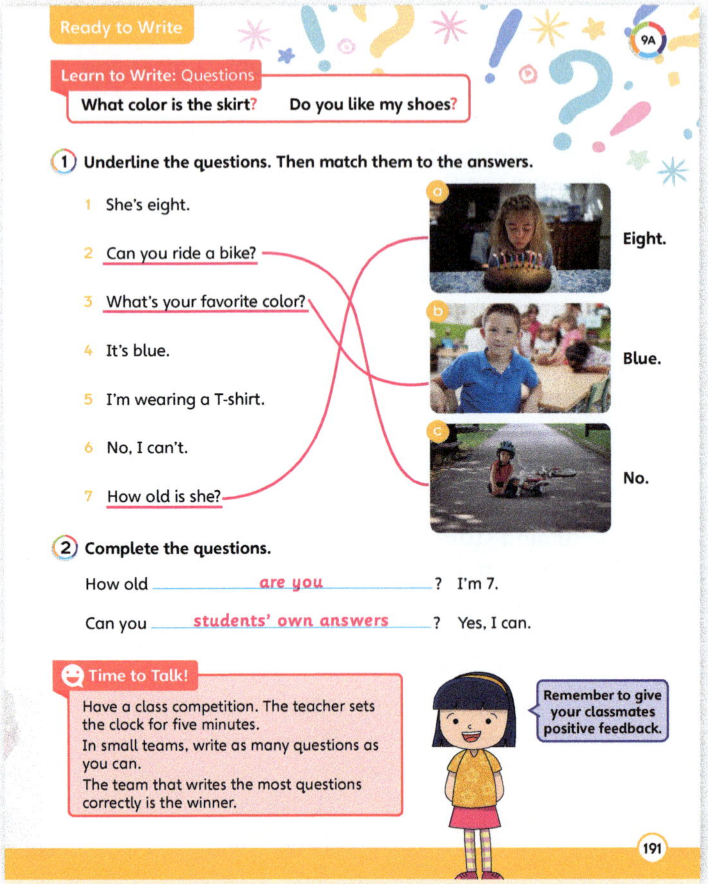
Ready to Write

9A

Learn to Write: Questions

What color is the skirt? Do you like my shoes?

1 Underline the questions. Then match them to the answers.

1 She's eight.

2 Can you ride a bike?

3 What's your favorite color?

4 It's blue.

5 I'm wearing a T-shirt.

6 No, I can't.

7 How old is she?

a Eight.

b Blue.

c No.

2 Complete the questions.

How old are you ? I'm 7.

Can you students' own answers ? Yes, I can.

Time to Talk!

Have a class competition. The teacher sets the clock for five minutes.

In small teams, write as many questions as you can.

The team that writes the most questions correctly is the winner.

Remember to give your classmates positive feedback.

191

Objective: to identify questions

Materials: paper; Build Creativity: scarves

Learn to Write Box

Read the two questions in the Learn to Write box. Encourage students to pay special attention to punctuation. Then, ask them to provide examples of questions.

1 Underline the questions. Then match them to the answers.

Have students look at Activity 1. Read the first item aloud. Ask: *Is this a statement or a question? (A statement.)* Remind students that statements give information and end in a period. Ask: *What do questions have? (Question marks.)* Read the second item aloud and ask if it is a question: *yes*. Have students underline the questions. Then, ask students to match the questions to the answers. Check answers as a class.

2 Complete the questions.

Have students do Activity 2 individually. Monitor, and provide support as needed.

Time to Talk!

Draw students' attention to Emma, the oracy character, and read the reminder aloud. Then, explain to students how to do the Time to Talk! activity. (See Differentiated Instruction.)

Build Creativity!

Fun with Scarves

Objective: Try, Try, and Try Again

Bring some scarves to class. Wrap a scarf around your neck, and tell students this is one way we wear a scarf. Form small groups, and, if you have brought in scarves, give one to each group. Ask them how many different ways they can think of to wear scarves. They may think of, for example, tying them around their heads or around their waists. Give students time to generate ideas. Then, have each group share its ideas with the class.

AB pages 169–70

Differentiated Instruction

Below-level ★	On-level ★★	Above-level ★★★
Provide help by writing sentence starters on the board before the competition takes place. Possible examples include: *Can you … ? Are you … ? Is she … ? Is it … ? What color … ? What are … ? Are they … ? Do you like … ?*	Do the Time to Talk! activity as explained in the Time to Talk! box.	As a follow-up to the Time to Talk! activity, ask students to have a short dialogue in pairs using five of the questions they have written down.

Objective: **write a short story**
Materials: paper

Literary Elements: Setting, Characters, and Plot

Throughout the book, students have been exposed to topics such as characters and characters' feelings, the order of story events, plot, setting, and main ideas. Put all the pieces together so that students see what a story is and understand what literary elements make up a good story. Write *Literary Elements in a Story* on the board, and make a mind map with the class. Say: *When we read a story, there are some basic elements in it, for example, the setting.* Elicit the meaning of *setting* from students, and start completing the mind map on the board by drawing an arrow from the main category (*Literary Elements in a Story*) to the word *setting*. Do the same with *character* and *plot*. Teach students that the events in the story can be divided into a beginning, a middle, and an end.

1 IDENTIFY

As a class, discuss a story students are familiar with, and guide them to identify the different literary elements in it. Then, tell students they will work in pairs to write a short story. First, have them think of a setting and share it with you. Then, have them focus on the characters. Give students time to think about the characters and invent names for them. Guide students to think about their characters' ages, physical appearance, etc. Finally, have students think of a simple plot that would involve drawing only three scenes.

2 WRITE

Have students draw the scenes first. Then, ask them to think of one or more short sentences they could write beneath each scene and/or in speech bubbles pointing to the characters' mouths. (See Differentiated Instruction.)

3 EDIT

Peer editing will be crucial after the stories are complete. Ask each pair to exchange its story with another pair. Write a list of things that editors should focus on, such as spelling and punctuation. Remind students that they should use only pencil to edit their classmates' work. When pairs receive their edited work, they can correct their errors. Check students' completed work.

4 FOLLOW UP

As a follow-up, make a storybook with the class's creations. Write a title on the cover, and have the authors write their names on it.

Fun Corner!

Favorite Character

Ask students to write the name of their favorite character from movies they have watched or stories they have read. Ask each student to say their character's name out loud and check who the most popular character is.

Build Creativity!

Itinerant Library
Objective: **A Different Point of View**
Give the storybook created with the class's short stories to different students to take home and read. Assign a specific quantity of days for students to keep it. Then, hold a class vote for students' favorite story.

Differentiated Instruction

Below-level ★	On-level ★★	Above-level ★★★
Instead of asking students to work in pairs, have them work in groups of four.	Do Activity 2 as stated above.	Instead of asking students to work in pairs, have them work individually.

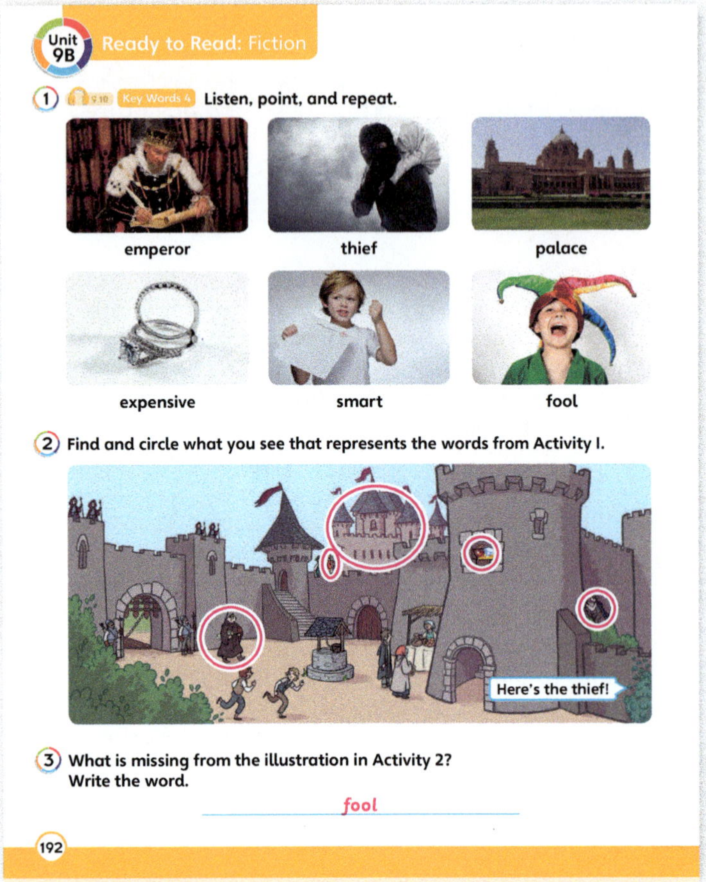
Unit 9B Ready to Read: Fiction

1 9.10 Key Words 4 Listen, point, and repeat.

emperor thief palace

expensive smart fool

2 Find and circle what you see that represents the words from Activity 1.

3 What is missing from the illustration in Activity 2? Write the word.

fool

192

Objective: to introduce vocabulary from the fiction text

Key Words 4: ***emperor, thief, palace, expensive, smart, fool***

Materials: Audio CD 9.10

1 9.10 Key Words 4 Listen, point, and repeat.

Have students look at Activity 1, and ask them if they can name any of the things they see. Then, play Track 9.10, and have students point and repeat. Correct pronunciation.

Practice Time 1 Ask a volunteer to go to the board. Spell one of the key words for them to write on the board. For example, spell *f - o - o - l*. Then, ask the student to spell a different key word for another volunteer to write on the board. Continue in this way until various students have participated.

2 Find and circle what you see that represents the words from Activity 1.

Give students time to look at the picture in Activity 2. Encourage them to say what they see in the picture. Then, complete the activity as a class.

Practice Time 2 Ask students to write in their notebooks each of the six key words but with the letters scrambled, for example: *fethi* for *thief*. Then, have them swap notebooks with a classmate for the classmate to unscramble the words, writing the letters in the correct order.

3 What is missing from the illustration in Activity 2? Write the word.

Ask students to look at the illustration in Activity 2 again and identify what is missing in the scene. Then, have students write what is missing on the line provided.

Fun Corner!

What Has the Thief Taken?

Ask five students to go out of the classroom. Assign another student to be a thief, and ask them to hide one thing in the classroom that has always been in the same place, such as a poster. Then, have the five students return to the classroom. Give them three minutes to guess what the stolen object is. Repeat with different students.

Do You Remember?

Tell students to close their eyes. Ask: *What am I wearing?* Can students describe your clothes? Ask volunteers to share what they remember. Next, ask students if they remember what a classmate sitting next to them is wearing. Then, ask who they saw this morning before they left the house. Do students remember what those people were wearing?

AB page 171

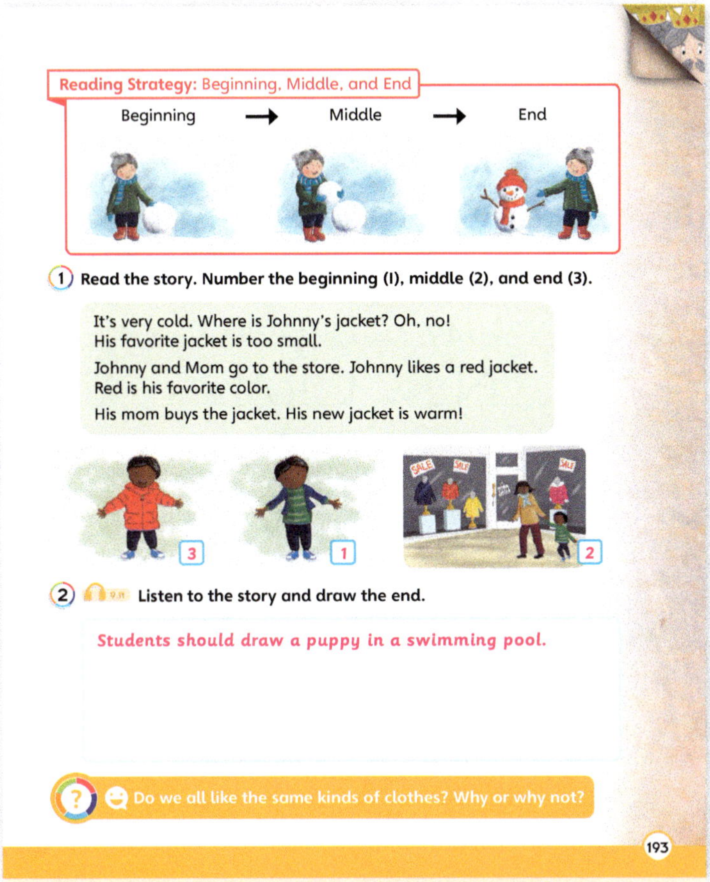

Reading Strategy: Beginning, Middle, and End

Beginning → Middle → End

1 Read the story. Number the beginning (1), middle (2), and end (3).

It's very cold. Where is Johnny's jacket? Oh, no!
His favorite jacket is too small.
Johnny and Mom go to the store. Johnny likes a red jacket.
Red is his favorite color.
His mom buys the jacket. His new jacket is warm!

3 1 2

2 9.11 Listen to the story and draw the end.

Students should draw a puppy in a swimming pool.

Do we all like the same kinds of clothes? Why or why not?

193

Objective: to identify the beginning, middle, and end of a story and prepare to read a fiction text

Materials: Audio CD 9.11; Build Creativity: paper

1 Read the story. Number the beginning (1), middle (2), and end (3).

Direct students' attention to the drawings in the Reading Strategy box. Give them time to analyze the pictures. Tell students that the pictures show the plot of a story, or what the story is about. Ask: *What is this story about?* Focus students' attention on the arrows that show the sequence of events. Explain that a story has a beginning, a middle, and an end. Ask students to write *1* next to the first picture, *2* next to the second, and *3* next to the third. Read the story in Activity 1 aloud. Ask simple comprehension questions: *What's the boy's name? What's the problem? Where do Johnny and his mom go? What's Johnny's favorite color? What do they buy?* Have students number the pictures so that they follow the sequence of the story—beginning, middle, and end. Then, check answers as a class.

2 9.11 Listen to the story and draw the end.

Play Track 9.11, and ask students simple comprehension questions. Have them tell you what the end of the story is. Then, ask them to draw the end in their books. Form pairs and have students show their drawings to their partners to see how similar or different their drawings are.

Big Question Link

Point to the Big Question Link, and read the questions aloud. Invite volunteers to answer the questions. Guide students so that they talk about their preferences by referring to aspects of clothes, including color, fabric, and size.

Build Creativity!

A Different Ending

Objective: A Different Point of View

Have students form small groups. Ask each group to choose one of the fiction stories in the book. Tell students that you would like them to draw a different ending to the story they have chosen. For example, if they choose *Snail Finds His Home*, they could draw Snail in his home with his friends. After students have drawn their alternative endings, ask them to write about the new ending. Allow students to use the text in the stories as a guide, altering it as needed. For example, for the new ending of *Snail Finds His Home*, students could write: *Snail goes inside his shell. It is his home! He invites his friends inside. They laugh and play until it stops raining.*

Objective: to learn that we cannot let pride interfere with the truth
Materials: Audio CD 9.12, 9.13

Pre-Reading

Read aloud the title of the story and the name of the author and adapter. Ask students if they know the original tale. Have students go through the story and identify the setting and the characters.

9.12 Page 194, section 1

Play Track 9.12 up to the end of the introductory paragraph. Pause and ask questions:

What does the Emperor like?
What color are the clothes he buys?

Personalization

Ask: *What color are the clothes you like?*

9.12 Page 194, section 2

Play Track 9.12 up to the end of the page. Pause and ask questions:

Who are the two men who go to the palace?
What do they have?
Why aren't the thieves wearing magic clothes?
Who can wear the magic clothes?

9.12 Page 195

Play the rest of Track 9.12. Ask questions:

What are the thieves showing to the Emperor?
What does the Emperor say about the clothes?
Does he like them?

Think

Read the question in the Think box aloud, and have students share their ideas.

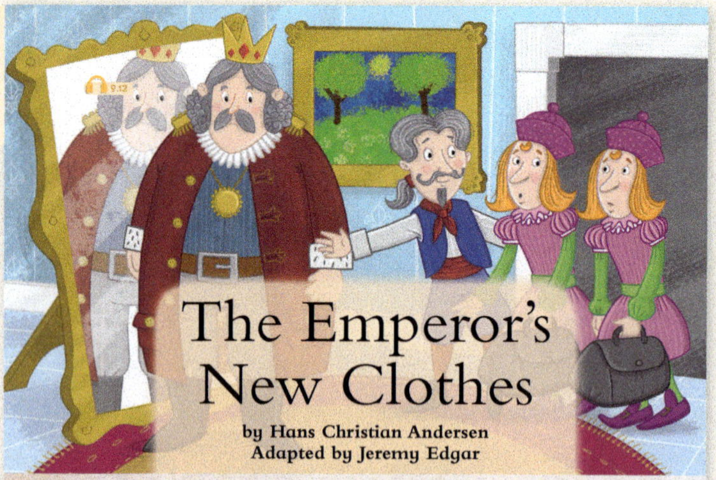

The Emperor's New Clothes

by Hans Christian Andersen
Adapted by Jeremy Edgar

This is the Emperor. He loves clothes. Every day, he buys new clothes—red clothes, blue clothes, purple clothes, green clothes, even gold clothes!

One day, two thieves go to the palace.
"We have magic clothes!" they tell the Emperor.
"Are you wearing magic clothes?" the Emperor asks one of the thieves.
"No, I'm not. They're too expensive."
"Really?" says the Emperor.
"Yes, because only very smart people can see them," the thieves say. "Fools can't."

194

9B

"Show me the magic clothes!" the Emperor says.
The thieves hold up the clothes. But there is nothing there.
The Emperor is worried. "Am I a fool?" he asks himself.
"Oh, those clothes look magnificent!" the Emperor says.
"I want to buy them."

Think
Can the Emperor see the clothes?

195

The Emperor's New Clothes

The Emperor calls his minister.
The minister is surprised. "Are you wearing your new clothes?" he asks.
"Yes, I am," the Emperor says.
He tells the minister about the magic.
The minister doesn't see anything.
"Those clothes look wonderful!" he says.
"Show them to the people. Have a parade!"

Think
Can the minister see the clothes?

196

Everyone is at the parade.
One boy shouts, "What is the Emperor wearing?"
"I'm wearing my magic clothes," the Emperor says.
"But I can only see underwear!" the boy laughs.
"It's true!" the people shout. They all laugh.
The Emperor is embarrassed. He will never wear his "magic" clothes again.

Think
Is the boy smart or a fool? Why?

197

9.13 Page 196

Play Track 9.13 up to the end of page. Pause and ask questions:

Who does the Emperor call?
What does the Emperor tell his minister?
What does the minister say about the new clothes?

Think

Read the question in the Think box for students to answer. Ask them if they think the minister is a fool or if he is smart.

9.13 Page 197

Play the rest of Track 9.13. Ask questions:

What does the boy ask?
What is the Emperor wearing?
How does the Emperor feel?

Think

Read the questions in the Think box aloud and discuss them with the class.

Fun Corner!

Act It Out!

Ask students how many characters there are in the story. Assign roles to a group of students to act out a short version of the story. You could also ask a student to act as the narrator. For example:

Narrator: *This is the Emperor. He loves clothes! One day, two thieves go to the palace.*

Thieves: *We have magic clothes!*

Emperor: *Are you wearing magic clothes?*

Thieves: *No, we aren't. They are too expensive. Only smart people can see them.*

Narrator: *The Emperor can't see the magic clothes.*

Emperor: *Am I a fool?*

Narrator: *The Emperor calls his minister. He tells the minister about the magic clothes.*

Minister: *Those clothes look wonderful! Have a parade!*

Narrator: *Everyone is at the parade.*

Boy: *What is the Emperor wearing?*

Emperor: *I'm wearing my magic clothes.*

Boy: *You are only wearing underwear!*

Explore the Text

1 Circle *Yes* or *No*.

a Are the magic clothes expensive? Yes / No (Yes circled)
b The emperor can see the magic clothes. Yes / No (No circled)
c The minister can see the magic clothes. Yes / No (No circled)
d The boy is a fool. Yes / No (No circled)

2 Number the beginning (1), middle (2), and end (3) of the story.

2 The emperor is worried. "Am I a fool?" he asks himself.
1 "We have magic clothes!" they tell the Emperor.
3 "But I can only see underwear!" the boy says.

3 Number the pictures in order. Retell the story in pairs.

What are you wearing?
What color are your clothes?

Remember to speak up so that others can hear you.

198

Objective: to deepen understanding of a fiction text

Materials: Fun Corner: bag, ten slips of paper, each with one sentence from the fiction story (*We have magic clothes! They're too expensive. Fools can't. Am I a fool? I want to buy them. Those clothes look wonderful! Have a parade! What is the Emperor wearing? I'm wearing my magic clothes. But I can only see underwear!*)

1 Circle *Yes* or *No*.

Ask students to get into pairs. Give them time to go through the fiction story and do Activity 1. Correct answers as a class, and ask volunteers to provide the true versions of the sentences that are false. For example: *The boy isn't a fool. He is smart.*

2 Number the beginning (1), middle (2), and end (3) of the story.

Ask students to do Activity 2 on their own. Then, ask a volunteer to read the beginning and another two students to read the middle and the end.

3 Number the pictures in order. Retell the story in pairs.

Number the scenes as a class. Then, write key words for each scene on the board; for example:

Scene 1: *thieves, magic clothes, smart, fools*

Scene 2: *show, worried, fool, buy*

Scene 3: *minister, magic, parade*

Scene 4: *wearing, boy, underwear*

Retell the story with the class using as many of the words on the board as possible. Then, form pairs, and ask students to retell the story to each other again. Each student should retell two scenes. Go around the classroom, and check performance. (See Differentiated Instruction.)

Big Question Link

Draw students' attention to Liam, the oracy character, and read the reminder aloud. Then, read the questions in the Big Question Link box aloud. Ask volunteers to answer them.

Fun Corner!

Who Says What?

Write the characters in the story on the board: Emperor, thieves, minister, boy. Put the slips of paper in the bag. Form two teams. Tell students that you will ask one team at a time to take a slip from the bag. The student who takes the slip should read the sentence on it and say who in the story said the sentence. Make sure everyone participates. The winning team is the one with the most correct answers.

AB pages 172–73

Differentiated Instruction

Below-level ★	On-level ★★	Above-level ★★★
Do Activity 3 as specified above but with four groups instead of pairs. Make sure that you include enough words on the board for each scene. The students in each of the four groups work together to figure out and rehearse a retelling of one scene of the story. Then, have each group retell its scene, providing them with as much support as needed.	Do Activity 3 as specified above.	Do Activity 3 without the step of retelling the story as a class. (However, give students support by writing as many words on the board as you feel are appropriate.) Then, as a follow-up, ask various pairs to retell their scenes to the class.

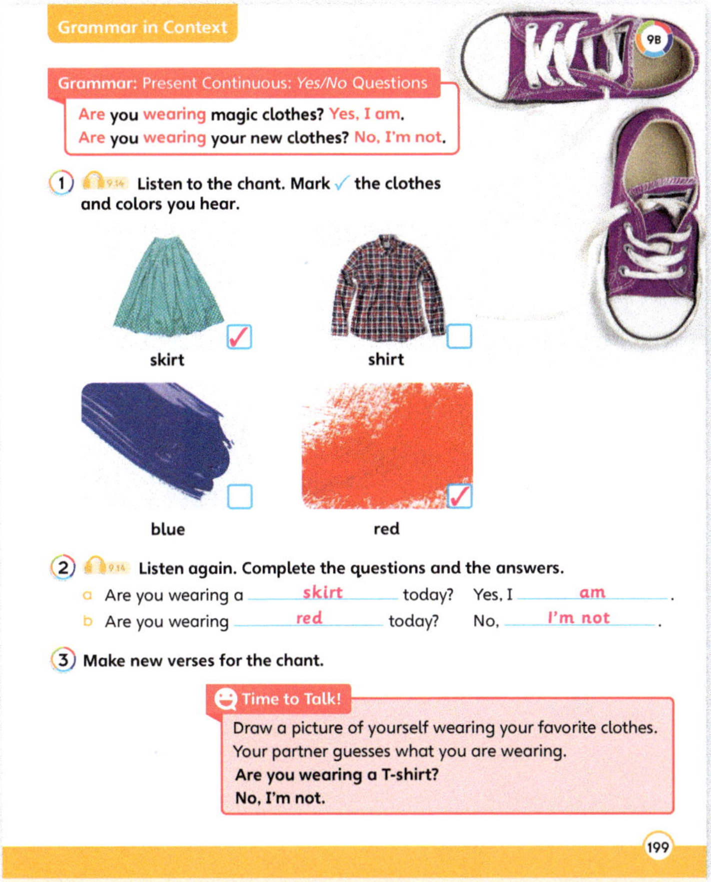

Grammar in Context

9B

Grammar: Present Continuous: *Yes/No* Questions

Are you wearing magic clothes? Yes, I am.
Are you wearing your new clothes? No, I'm not.

1 9.14 Listen to the chant. Mark ✓ the clothes and colors you hear.

skirt ✓ shirt
blue red ✓

2 9.14 Listen again. Complete the questions and the answers.

a Are you wearing a skirt today? Yes, I am.
b Are you wearing red today? No, I'm not.

3 Make new verses for the chant.

Time to Talk!

Draw a picture of yourself wearing your favorite clothes. Your partner guesses what you are wearing.
Are you wearing a T-shirt?
No, I'm not.

199

Objective: to ask and answer *yes/no* questions in the present continuous

Materials: Audio CD 9.14, articles of clothing that can be put on top of other clothes, such as jackets, shirts, T-shirts, skirts, dresses (brought by volunteers from home)

Grammar Box

Write an affirmative sentence on the board: *You are wearing magic clothes.* Show how you make a question by changing the word order in the sentence: *Are you wearing magic clothes?* Point out the questions in the Grammar box and read the second question aloud. Point out and read the affirmative and negative answers.

1 9.14 Listen to the chant. Mark ✓ the clothes and colors you hear.

Ask students to look at the pictures in Activity 1 and identify what they show. Then, play Track 9.14 for students to complete the activity. Check answers as a class.

2 9.14 Listen again. Complete the questions and the answers.

Play Track 9.14 again, and then ask students to complete Activity 2 in pairs. Check answers as a class.

Practice Time 1 Ask students who have brought articles of clothing from home to show them to the class. Have the class say what each article of clothing is and what color it is. Choose five articles of clothing and put them on your desk. Ask two volunteers to come to the front. Student A faces a wall while Student B puts on any of the articles of clothing. Student A has to guess what Student B is wearing and its color by asking *Are you wearing (the blue T-shirt)?* Allow students three guesses. Repeat with different students and different articles of clothing.

3 Make new verses for the chant.

Ask students to get into pairs and think of a new version of the chant. Then, invite pairs to share their chants with the class.

Time to Talk!

Ask students to draw a picture of themselves wearing their favorite clothes. Make sure that partners for this activity are sitting far away from each other to ensure that they have not seen each other's pictures before the guessing game begins. Students have to guess two pieces of clothing. When you say *Go!*, the guessing game starts. Go around the classroom and check performance. Once one partner has guessed the two pieces of clothing, it is the other partner's turn to guess.

AB pages 174–75

Listening

1 9.15 Listen. Who likes their school uniform?

Holly Wayne

2 9.15 Listen again and mark ✓ the clothes Holly and Wayne mention.

	Holly	Wayne
tie	✓	
skirt	✓	
shorts		✓
hat	✓	✓
shirt	✓	✓
coat	✓	
socks		✓

Stand Up Straight and Keep Still

1. Draw what you usually wear to school. Then, draw what you usually wear after school.
2. In groups, take turns describing the clothes you wear. **At school, I wear a blue skirt and a white shirt.**
3. Remember to stand up straight and keep still while you are talking.
4. Complete **Check Your Oracy!** on Activity Book page 177.

Values AB page 176

200

ACTIVITY BOOK PAGE 176

Values: Taking Care of Your Clothes

1 How can you take care of your clothes? Mark ✓.

2 Match.

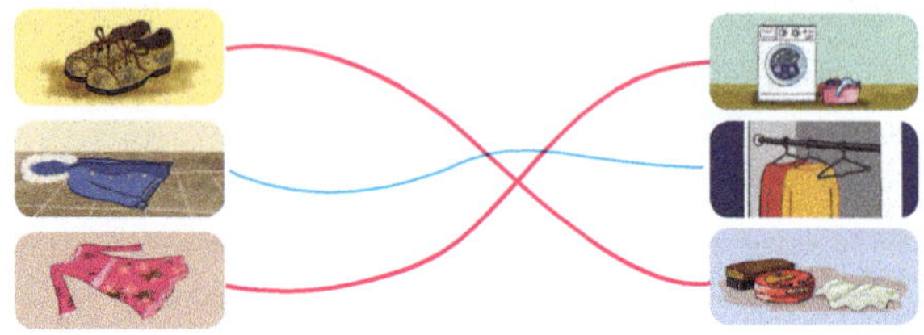

3 How do you take care of your clothes? Draw.

Students' own answers

176

SB page 200

Objectives: **to listen to children talking about their school uniforms; to understand the value of taking care of your clothes**

Materials: Audio CD 9.15

1 9.15 Listen. Who likes their school uniform?

Ask students to look at the children in the photos in Activity 1. Ask: *What are they wearing?* Play Track 9.15. Then, ask: *Who likes their school uniform?*

2 9.15 Listen again and mark ✓ the clothes Holly and Wayne mention.

Go over each of the pictures in Activity 2 with students. Play Track 9.15 again for students to do the activity. Check answers as a class.

Oracy Extension Activity

Read the steps in the Oracy Extension activity aloud. Form groups for students to do the activity. Ask students to complete Check Your Oracy! on page 177 of their Activity Books.

1 How can you take care of your clothes? Mark ✓.

Have students look at the pictures in Activity 1 and mark those that represent things they can do to take care of their clothes.

2 Match.

Have students look at the pictures closely and then match them. Correct as a class.

3 How do you take care of your clothes? Draw.

Read the question in the instructions aloud. Point to the picture of the boy and read what he says. Then, have students draw one thing that they do to take care of their clothes. Ask volunteers to share their drawings with the class and talk about what they do.

AB page 176

Objective: **to consolidate, extend, and personalize learning on the unit topic**
Materials: students' photos or drawings of a person wearing special clothes; evelopes, paper, glue

- Read the Big Challenge question and statement aloud. Point to the girl showing a puzzle, and tell students they will be making a similar jigsaw puzzle for clothes for special occasions.
- **1** Encourage students to mention special occasions and to tell you what they usually wear on those occasions.
- **2** Have students choose their favorite special occasion.
- **3** As homework, ask students to look for a photograph or draw a person wearing special clothes for the occasion they have chosen.
- **4** Tell students they should cut the photo or drawing into pieces for a puzzle. Explain that the pieces should be neither too small nor too big. Students should bring the pieces to class in an envelope.
- **5** Ask students to get into pairs and exchange envelopes with their partner. Students put their partner's pieces together and glue them onto a piece of paper. Then, the puzzles are returned to their owners.
- **6** Partners show each other the jigsaw puzzles and describe what the people are wearing. Optional: Record or have students record one another as they describe their puzzle to share their work.

Home-school   Portfolio: Big Challenge

Big Question Circle

Read the Big Question aloud. Have the class revisit the Big Question Links on pages 184, 187, 193, and 198. Discuss what they have learned about clothes.

- Use the following questions to help review the Big Question:

  What do you wear when it's hot?
  What do you wear when it's cold?
  What are you favorite clothes?
  What special clothes do people around the world wear?

- Finally, have students turn to page 177 of their Activity Books to complete the Big Challenge self-assessment.

AB pages 177–79

Differentiated Instruction

Below-level ★	On-level ★★	Above-level ★★★
As a follow-up, ask students to label the pieces of clothing in their jigsaw puzzles. Have students include colors as well. For example, *red T-shirt*.	As a follow-up, ask students to write sentences based on their jigsaw puzzles using *wearing*.	As a follow-up, do as stated in the On-level section, but encourage students to add more adjectives to their sentences (*favorite*, *silk*, *expensive*, etc.). If you think students need guidance, brainstorm adjectives with them before they write the sentences.

Oracy Performance Task 3: Presentation

7–9

① Read and number the pictures.

1 Giving and Receiving Positive Feedback · 2 Speaking Up · 3 Standing up Straight and Keeping Still

② Read and match the speech bubbles to the two options.

Please repeat that. — Speaking Up
I don't understand. — Speaking Up
Good job! — Giving and Receiving Positive Feedback
Thank you! — Giving and Receiving Positive Feedback

YOUR TASK

a Prepare to give a final presentation.
b Draw pictures for each category on page 203. You can look back through your book.
c Choose a category and plan your presentation. Draw pictures on a separate piece of paper.
d Give your 1- to 2-minute presentation to your class.

202

All About Me	My Favorite Toy
My Bedroom	My Favorite Wild Animal
My Favorite Foods	My Routine
My Clothes	My Friends

Check Your Oracy!

	☺	☺☺	☺☺☺
1 I planned my presentation.			
2 I stood up straight and kept still.			
3 I spoke up.			
4 I gave positive feedback to my classmates.			

203

Objective: **to apply oracy skills in presentations**
Oracy Performance Task Expressions: *Please repeat that. I don't understand. Good job! Thank you!*
Materials: Cue Cards 1–12

① Read and number the pictures.

Remind students of the oracy skills that they have learned. Show the Cue Cards, one by one, and display them on the board. Then, read each of the categories in Activity 1, and have students do the activity. After checking answers as a class, guide students to associate the Cue Cards with the categories. Explain that some of the Cue Cards may not belong to any of the three categories.

② Read and match the speech bubbles to the two options.

Do Activity 2 as a class.

YOUR TASK

- **a** Tell students that they will give a final presentation.
- **b** Invite students to draw pictures for each category. Take this opportunity to review vocabulary.
- **c** Have students choose a category and draw pictures. Give a presentation for students to follow as a model. Then, ask students to plan their presentations. Tell them that their presentations should be one to two minutes long.
- **d** Invite volunteers to give their presentations to the class. Remind them to put into practice the oracy skills they have learned. Optional: Record or have students record their presentations to share their work.
- Have individual students self-assess by filling in the Check Your Oracy! chart.

Home-school · Portfolio: Oracy Performance

Build Creativity!

End-of-the-Year Poster

Objective: **Start Again**

As a follow-up to their presentations, have students write a draft of a short text that corresponds to their presentation. Check students' work. Form small groups, and ask students to exchange their drafts with the other students in the group to edit their work. For homework, have students make a poster with their drawings and their edited text below them.

AB pages 180–81

Audio Script

Track 0.1

1
Boy 1: Hello. What's your name?
Boy 2: I'm Cemil.

2
Teacher: Hello. What's your name?
Girl: I'm Karen.
Teacher: Nice to meet you, Karen.

3
Bus driver: Hello. What's your name?
Boy: I'm Pablo.
Bus driver: Nice to meet you, Pablo.

Track 0.2

Orange, green, yellow,
purple, red, and blue.

Orange, green, yellow,
purple, red, and blue.

What color is it?
I ask you.

Orange, green, yellow,
purple, red, and blue.

Track 0.3

one, two, three, four, five, six, seven, eight, nine, ten

Track 0.4

Show me your hands,
Show me your hands.
Now, let's count,
Now, let's count,

From 1 to 10,
From 1 to 10.

1, 2, 3,
1, 2, 3.

4, 5, 6,
4, 5, 6.

7, 8,
7, 8.

9, and 10,
9, and 10.

We can count,
We can count,

From 1 to 10,
From 1 to 10.

Track 0.5

Sunburn

Legs and head,
Legs and head.
I'm so red!
Ouch!

Arms and hands,
Arms and hands.
I can't stand!
Ouch!

Eyes and ears,
Eyes and ears.
Oh, my dear!
Ouch!

Feet, mouth, nose.
Feet, mouth, nose.
Even my toes!
Ouch!

Track 1.1

favorite, color, hair, girl, brown, boy

Track 1.2

eyes, hair, brown, orange

Track 1.3

1 Hello. I'm Larissa.
2 I'm six years old.
3 I'm from the United States.
4 I have blue eyes.
5 I have brown hair.
6 My favorite color is orange. I have an orange cat! Here's a picture of him.

Track 1.4

short, long, tall, curly, straight, blond

Track 1.5

Nonfiction text p. 9

Track 1.6

Nonfiction text p. 10

Track 1.7

1 class
2 different

Track 1.8

1 I am five years old.
2 She is seven.
3 He is eight.

Track 1.9

I'm tall. He's short.
I'm eight. He's six.
Blond hair. Black hair.
I have straight hair.

Track 1.10

The Alphabet Song

A, B, C, D,
E, F, G,
H, I, J, K,
L, M, N, O, P,
Q, R, S, T, U, V,
W, X, Y, Z.
Now I know my ABCs.
Next time won't you sing with me?

Track 1.11

These are the ground rules for our classroom.
1 Listen to others.
2 Take turns.
3 Respect others.
4 Share your ideas.
5 Raise your hand to speak.

Track 1.12

old, slow, fast, tired, young, happy

Track 1.13

1 The girl is young.
2 The girl is tired.
3 The woman is old.
4 The boy is fast.
5 The turtle is slow.
6 The girl is happy.

Track 1.14

Fiction text pp. 18–19

Track 1.15

Fiction text pp. 20–21

Track 1.16

Grandma Turtle is old.
Young Turtle is young.
Young Turtle is slow.
Grandma Turtle is tired.
Grandma Turtle and Young Turtle are happy.

Track 1.17

I am special.
This is true.
I am six.
How about you?

They are special.
This is true.
They are fast.
How about you?

Track 1.18

1 bicycle
2 tablet
3 colored pencils
4 puzzle
5 coloring book
6 ball

Track 1.19

Girl: Wow! You have a lot of fun things.
Boy: Yeah. Look at this. It's my tablet.
Girl: A tablet! It's cool! And what's this? Is it a coloring book?
Boy: No, it's a puzzle. It's fun.
Girl: Wow! I like it! You have a lot of things! What's your favorite thing?
Boy: My bicycle.
Girl: It's great!

Track 1.20

1 My bicycle is fast.
2 My puzzle is big.
3 My tablet is small.
4 My ball is old.

Track 1.21

yes, no, name, phone, numbers, lost

Track 1.22

Police officer: Hello. Are you OK?
Boy: No! I'm lost!
Police officer: What's your first name?
Boy: Demir.
Police officer: Demir?
Boy: Yes.

Police officer: What's your last name?
Boy: Tosun.
Police officer: Can you spell it, please?
Boy: T - O - S - U - N.
Police officer: OK. Demir Tosun. And how old are you?
Boy: I'm six.
Police officer: Six! What's your phone number, Demir?
Boy: 3743-1235.
Police officer: 3743-1235?
Boy: Yes.
Police officer: Thank you.

Track 1.23

Police officer: What's your first name?
Boy: Sam.
Police officer: What's your last name?
Boy: Black.
Police officer: How old are you?
Boy: I'm six.
Police officer: What's your phone number?
Boy: 4268-9120.

Track 2.1

desk, teacher, classroom, gym, bathroom, playground

Track 2.2

In my classroom,
I can see
A board and a teacher.
Point with me.

In my classroom,
I can see
Classmates and a window.
Point with me.

In my classroom,
I can see
A desk and a chair.
Point with me.

Track 2.3

library, schoolbag, pencil case, notebook, colored pencil, eraser

Track 2.4

Nonfiction text p. 31

Track 2.5

Nonfiction text p. 32

Track 2.6

1 classmates
2 apple

Track 2.7

1 a pencil
2 a desk
3 a pen
4 an eraser
5 an orange
6 an apple

Track 2.8

Dad! My schoolbag!
An apple, a pencil.
My book? Oh, look!
An eraser.
And my paper?

Track 2.9

C, c, c … car. Car.
P, p, p … pen. Pen.
T, t, t … ten. Ten.
N, n, n … net. Net.
B, b, b … boy. Boy.
H, h, h … hi. Hi.

Track 2.10

1 C, c, c.
cat, book
2 P, p, p.
hand, pet
3 T, t, t.
toy, boy
4 N, n, n.
nine, pup
5 B, b, b.
big, pot
6 H, h, h.
ball, hat

Track 2.11

Liam: I'm Liam.
Emma: I'm Emma.
Kate: I'm Kate.
Jack: I'm Jack.

Liam: School is fun! Do you agree?
Emma: Yes!

Kate: Puzzles are fun! Do you agree?
Jack: No!

Track 2.12

a b c d e f g h i j k l m n
o p q r s t u v w x y z

Track 2.13

story, sad, mad, hungry, lunchbox, surprised

Track 2.14

I'm hungry! My lunchbox is in my schoolbag.

Track 2.15

happy, sad, surprised, mad

Track 2.16

Fiction text pp. 40–41

Track 2.17

Fiction text pp. 42–43

Track: 2.18

1 This is my schoolbag.
2 This is her book.
3 This is your chair.
4 This is his schoolbag.

Track 2.19

read books, play games, play sports, study

Track 2.20

This Is My School

This is my school.
This is my school.
It's so cool.
It's so cool.
This is the classroom.
Here, I love to study
At my school,
At my school.

This is my school.
This is my school.
It's so cool.
It's so cool.
This is the big gym.
Here, I love to play sports
At my school,
At my school.

This is my school.
This is my school.
It's so cool.
It's so cool.
This is the library.
Here, I love to read books
At my school,
At my school.

This is my school.
This is my school.
It's so cool.
It's so cool.
This is the playground.
Here, I love to play games
At my school,
At my school.

Track 2.21

1 Crayon. Crayon.
2 Glue. Glue.
3 Scissors. Scissors.
4 Pencil sharpener. Pencil sharpener.
5 Marker. Marker.
6 Ruler. Ruler.

Track 2.22

1
Boy 1: Oh, no! I don't have my red pencil. Can I borrow your red pencil?
Boy 2: Sorry! I don't have one.
Boy 1: No problem.

2
Boy 1: Oh, no! I don't have my storybook. Can I borrow your storybook?
Boy 2: Sure! Here you are.
Boy 1: Thank you!

Track 3.1

toy, box, house, paper, airplane, tablet

Track 3.2

This is Tim.
He has a car.
The car is blue.

Track 3.3

robot, fun, dollhouse, tent, train, jump rope

Track 3.4

Nonfiction text p. 53

Track 3.5

Nonfiction text p. 54

Track 3.6

children, jump

Track 3.7

1 Listen!
2 March!
3 Sit!
4 Stop!
5 Jump!
6 Stand!

Track 3.8

Listen!
Stand!
March!
Stop!
Sit!
Stand!
Jump!
Sit!

Track 3.9

bat, cat, hat, pen, hen, ten

Track 3.10

cat, cat
hen, hen
hat, hat

Track 3.11

Liam: I'm Liam.
Emma: I'm Emma.
Kate: I'm Kate.
Jack: I'm Jack.

Narrator: Class 1
Teacher: It's story time!
Children: Yay!
Teacher: Are you ready?
Children: Yes!
Teacher: Look at this picture. What's this?
Children: A cat!
Teacher: Correct! Now let's read. Once upon a time, there was a very fat cat. The fat cat had a friend who was a hen. Yes, Liam.
Liam: Ms. Green, please repeat that.
Teacher: Sure, Liam. The fat cat had a friend who was a hen.

Narrator: Class 2
Teacher: It's story time!
Teacher: Are you ready? Look at this picture. What's this?
Teacher: It's a cat! Now let's read. Once upon a time, there was a very fat cat. The fat cat had a friend who was a hen. Emma, Liam, Jack, Kate, please pay attention!

Track 3.12

The Action Song

This is the action song.
Come and move with me!
Come and move with me!
Let's start at the count of three:
One, two, three!

Everybody run in place.
Everybody run in place.
Everybody run in place.
Look at me!

Everybody jump up high.
Everybody jump up high.
Everybody jump up high.
Look at me!

Everybody dance like this.
Everybody dance like this.
Everybody dance like this.
Look at me!

This is the action song.
Come and move with me!
Come and move with me!
Let's start at the count of three:
One, two, three!

Track 3.13

monkey bars, bike, car, action figure, dinosaur, spaceship

Track 3.14

1 The monkey bars are red.
2 The bike is green.
3 The car is yellow.
4 The action figures are purple.
5 There are three dinosaurs.
6 The spaceship is gray.

Track 3.15

1
Dennis: Hello, lion!
Ada: Grr, I'm hungry. Grr.
Dennis: This is fun.

2
Dennis: Oh, no! My toy! I'm sad.

3
Dennis: Mom, help! Look at my toy!
Mom: Mmm ... Don't worry.
Dennis: Thank you, mom.

4
Dennis: I'm so happy!
Ada: I'm happy, too!

Track 3.16

Fiction text pp. 62–63

Track 3.17

Fiction text pp. 64–65

Track 3.18

1 Don't touch my dinosaur!
2 Don't sit on the chair!
3 Don't talk in the library!
4 Don't play on the swings!

Track 3.19

Girl: Let's play I Spy!
Boy: Yes! Good idea!
Girl: OK. I spy ... with my little eye ... something blue and green.
Boy: It's the dinosaur!
Girl: No.
Boy: The monkey bars!
Girl: Yes! Your turn.

Boy: I spy ... with my little eye ... something yellow, red, and blue.
Girl: It's the train!
Boy: No.
Girl: It's the robot!
Boy: No.
Girl: It's the ball!
Boy: Yes!

Track 3.20

Boy: Let's buy a ball. Do you agree?
Girl: Yes.
Boy: A ball, please.
Girl: Here you go.
Boy: Thank you.

Track 4.1

home, family, dining room, living room, bedroom, kitchen

Track 4.2

bedroom , bathroom, playroom, kitchen, living room, dining room

Track 4.3

Narrator: What's your favorite place in your house, Ahmet?
Ahmet: I like my bedroom. It's green. Green is my favorite color. My bedroom is big. And I have a car collection!

Narrator: And you, Sabita? What's your favorite place in your house?
Sabita: My favorite place is my bedroom. It's pink. I love pink! My bedroom is not big. It's small. I have lots of books.

Track 4.4

apartment, room, water, garden, stove, bed

Track 4.5

Nonfiction text p. 75

Track 4.6

Nonfiction text p. 76

Track 4.7

1 roof
2 stairs

Track 4.8

a
1 The book is on the table.
2 The book is under the table.
3 The book is in the schoolbag.

b
1 The ball is under the chair.
2 The ball is on the chair.
3 The ball is in the basket.

Track 4.9

nut, nut
cut, cut
hut, hut

big, big
wig, wig
dig, dig

Track 4.10

a hut
b wig
c nut
d big

Track 4.11

(Song 1)
Look at this chick.
His name is Stig.
He has a wig,
A big, big wig!
He likes to dig,
With his big wig.
His name is Stig.

Look at this chick.
His name is Stig.
He has a wig,
A big, big wig!
He likes to dig,
With his big wig.
His name is Stig.

(Song 2)
Nuts, nuts,
I love nuts.
A nut in a hut.
Big nuts,
Peanuts,
Any kind of nut.
I love nuts!

Nuts, nuts,
I love nuts.
A nut in a hut.
Big nuts,
Peanuts,
Any kind of nut.
I love nuts!

Track 4.12

Liam: I'm Liam.
Jack: I'm Jack.

Liam: Let's play tic-tac-toe. I'll start.
Jack: It's my turn. Now it's your turn.
Liam: It's your turn.
Jack: It's your turn.
Liam: I win!
Jack: Good job!

Track 4.13

snail, ladybug, forest, spider, butterfly, mouse

Track 4.14

Fiction text pp. 84–85

Track 4.15

Fiction text pp. 86–87

Track 4.16

Teacher: Oh, no! Where is the red marker?
Boy: Is it on the desk, Miss White?
Teacher: No, it isn't. Hmm.
Boy: Is it in your bag?
Teacher: No, it isn't. Hmm ... Where is it?
Boy: Is it in your pocket?
Teacher: Yes, it is. Thank you, Tom!

Track 4.17

My Home!

In my home,
I sleep,
I eat,
I play,
I am myself all day.

In my home,
I paint,
I draw,
I read,
I get the love I need.

Track 4.18

Socks. Socks.
T-shirt. T-shirt.
Hat. Hat.
Jacket. Jacket.
Skirt. Skirt.
Glasses. Glasses.

Track 4.19

Point to ... the ... jacket.
Point to ... the ... socks.
Point to ... the ... hat.

Point to the ... skirt.
Point to the ... glasses.
Point to the ... T-shirt.

Point to the hat.
Point to the glasses.
Point to the T-shirt.

Point to the skirt.
Point to the jacket.
Point to the socks.

Point to the glasses.
Point to the hat.
Point to the T-shirt.

Track 4.20

Girl: Mom! Where is my jacket? I can't find it! Where is it? Where is it?
Mom: Your jacket? Is it on the chair?
Girl: No, it isn't. Where is it?
Mom: Is it in the closet?
Girl: No, it isn't. Where is it?
Mom: Is it under the bed?
Girl: Hmm ... let me see. Yes, here it is! It's under the bed! Thanks, Mom!

Track 5.1

zebra, land, elephant, octopus, ocean, dolphin

Track 5.2

crocodile, parrot, penguin, blue whale, brown bear, panda

Track 5.3

1 (brown bear)
2 (blue whale)
3 (parrot)

Track 5.4

It lives on land. It's black and white. It has four legs. It looks like a horse.

Track 5.5

It lives in the ocean. It has eight legs.

Track 5.6

teeth, tail, beak, jungle, claw, fur

Track 5.7

Nonfiction text p. 97

Track 5.8

Nonfiction text p. 98

Track 5.9

a feathers
b insects

Track 5.10

What Are They?

They have tails.
They have beaks.
They're smart.
They can speak.
They're red, yellow, orange,
Green, white, and blue.
Where are they?
They're in the zoo.

Track 5.11

queen, queen
sun, sun
fish, fish
jar, jar
goat, goat
ring, ring

Track 5.12

Look! A queen, a queen, a queen,
Sitting in the sun, the sun, the sun.
She is having fun!

Look! A fish, a fish, a fish,
Swimming in a jar, a jar, a jar.
It can't swim very far!

Look! A goat, a goat, a goat,
With a golden ring, a ring, a ring.
See how it can sing!

Track 5.13

a I have a big white rabbit.
b Please, close the gate.
c Let's sing a song.
d The fish moves its fins.
e Sharks have big jaws.
f This is a difficult quiz.

Track 5.14

Emma: I'm Emma.
Kate: I'm Kate.

Emma: Hi, Kate. Let's play a game!
Kate: OK, Emma!
Emma: Let's play with our dolls!
Kate: No, that's boring! Let's draw pictures!
Emma: No, that's boring! Let's play charades!
Kate: Animal charades?
Emma: Yes!
Kate: OK!

Track 5.15

a Is it a parrot?
b Hello!
c Let's play!
d What color are they?

Track 5.16

a Are you six?
b Thank you!
c Don't touch!
d Is it on the table?

Track 5.17

rabbit, moon, snake, tongue, sun, stars

Track 5.18

1 It's big and white.
2 It has fur.
3 It's big and yellow.
4 You can see lots of these in the sky at night.
5 It's in your mouth.
6 It has a long body.

Track 5.19

Fiction text pp. 106–107

Track 5.20

Fiction text pp. 108–109

Track 5.21

a Are zebras black and white?
b Are pandas brown?
c Are Ketzi and the little rabbit friends?
d Are blue whales small?

Track 5.22

nose, eyes, legs, ears, wings, feet

Track 5.23

1 It has wings and six legs.
2 It is very big. It has four legs and two big ears. It has a trunk.
3 It is black and white. It has four legs. It's similar to a horse.
4 It has fur and claws. It's very big.
5 It has a long tongue. It lives on land and in water.
6 It is black and white. It has two webbed feet.

Track 5.24

a board game
b dice
c game piece
d square
e lose
f win

Track 5.25

Girl 1: Let's play the Animal Game.
Girl 2: You start. Throw the dice.
Girl 1: I got a two! One, two … It's a tiger!
Girl 2: My turn … I got a six. It's a panda! Your turn …
Girl 1: I got a five. One, two, three, four, five. It's an elephant!
Girl 2: I got a six. I win!

Track 6.1

ability, paint, run, skate, play basketball, talk

Track 6.2

see, ride, climb, say, spell, swim

Track 6.3

Nonfiction text p. 119

Track 6.4

Nonfiction text p. 120

Track 6.5

a blind
b backwards

Track 6.6

I can run, and I can walk.
I can speak, and I can talk.
I can read, and I can sing,
But …
I can't do everything!

I can't swim, and I can't write.
I can't see well at night,
But …
I can do lots of things!

Track 6.7

hop, hop
top, top
pop, pop
mad, mad
bad, bad
dad, dad

Track 6.8

Do the hop dance!
Hop, hop,
Hop, hop, hop!
Get off your seat!
Dance to the beat!

Do the top dance!
Top, top,
Top, top, top!
Get off your seat!
Dance to the beat!

Do the pop dance!
Pop, pop,
Pop, pop, pop!
Get off your seat!
Dance to the beat!

Track 6.9

Give me an M. M!
Give me an A. A!
Give me a D. D!
What does that spell? Mad.
Say it three times.
Mad! Mad! Mad!

Give me a B. B!
Give me an A. A!
Give me a D. D!
What does that spell? Bad.
Say it three times.
Bad! Bad! Bad!

Give me a D. D!
Give me an A. A!
Give me a D. D!
What does that spell? Dad.
Say it three times.
Dad! Dad! Dad!

Track 6.10

Kate: I'm Kate.
Jack: I'm Jack.

Kate: Hey, Jack. I think fish is delicious! Do you agree?
Jack: No! I don't like fish. But what about hamburgers? I think hamburgers are delicious. Do you agree, Kate?
Kate: Yes!

Track 6.11

music, love, dancer, practice, read, puppy

Track 6.12

Fiction text pp. 128–129

Track 6.13

Fiction text pp. 130–131

Track 6.14

Susie can't dance,
But she can run.
So we have lots of fun.

Tom can't walk,
But he can play.
So he plays with me all day.

Track 6.15

1 tie
2 open
3 draw
4 find
5 say
6 spell

Track 6.16

Teacher: Good morning, class.
Class: Good morning, Ms. White.

Girl: Can you help me, please? I can't say this word in English.
Teacher: Yes, let me see.

Track 6.17

1
Girl: Ms. White, I can't tie my shoe. Can you help me, please?
Teacher: Yes, of course.

2
Boy: Teacher, I can't find my book. Can you help me, please?
Teacher: Sure.

3
Girl: Teacher, I can't write this word. Can you help me, please?
Teacher: Of course.

4
Boy: Ms. White, I can't open my lunchbox. Can you help me, please?
Teacher: Yes, one moment, please.

5
Girl: Ms. White, I can't spell this word in English. Can you help me please?
Teacher: Sure. H - O - R - S - E. Horse.
Girl: Thank you.

Track 6.18

Boy 1: What do you want to do?
Boy 2: Let's play marbles.
Boy 1: OK. Do you agree, Millie?
Girl: No, marbles are boring. Let's play hopscotch.
Boy 2: OK. Do you agree, Sam?
Boy 1: No, I'm not good at hopscotch. How about tag?
Girl: Yes! I love tag!
Boy 2: Me, too. Let's play tag.
Boy 1: Great!

Track 7.1

fruit, banana, grapes, vegetable, spinach, sugar

Track 7.2

sandwich, water, banana, grapes, nuts, apple, cookies

Track 7.3

Anna: Hi, I'm Anna. This is my school lunchbox. I have an apple, a sandwich, grapes, and some water. Oh, and a banana!

Noah: Hello, my name is Noah. This is my school lunchbox. I have an apple, a sandwich, nuts, and some cookies.

Track 7.4

juice, water, oil, yogurt, tomato, rice

Track 7.5

Nonfiction text p. 141

Track 7.6

Nonfiction text p. 142

Track 7.7

freezer, fried

Track 7.8

I like popsicles.
Mmm … yum, yum, yum!
But I don't like crickets.
Yuck … in my tum, tum, tum!
I love apples.
Mmm … yum, yum, yum!
But I don't like fish.
Yuck … in my tum, tum, tum!
What do you like?

Track 7.9

box, box
jam, jam
cub, cub
fox, fox
arm, arm
tub, tub

Track 7.10

The fox is in the box.
The fox is in the box.
Where's the fox?
It's in the box!

Where's the jam?
Where's the jam?
It's on my arm.
It's on my arm.

The cub is in the tub.
The cub is in the tub.
Where's the cub?
It's in the tub!

Track 7.11

a Look! It's a bear cub! Look! It's a bear cub!
b And over there is a fox! And over there is a fox!
c I like jam on my bread. I like jam on my bread.
d There is hot water in the tub. There is hot water in the tub.
e Ouch! I hurt my arm. Ouch! I hurt my arm.
f Open the box. Open the box.

Track 7.12

Kate: I'm Kate.
Emma: I'm Emma.

Kate: I'm Kate. I'm going to talk about my favorite vegetable.
I love broccoli. Broccoli is green.
And it's delicious.
Broccoli makes you strong.
It makes you grow!
Sometimes I eat broccoli pizza. Yum!
Emma: Good job, Kate!
Kate: Thank you.

Track 7.13

broccoli, fish, French fries, chocolate, soup, muffin

Track 7.14

Mom: Lunch is ready!
Girl: Oh, Mom! I don't like soup, and it's broccoli soup. I don't like broccoli, either!
Mom: Well, there's also fish and French fries.
Girl: Mmm … I love fish and French fries.
Mom: And there's a chocolate muffin for dessert.
Girl: Thanks, Mom! I like chocolate, and I like muffins. And I love chocolate muffins!

Track 7.15

Fiction text pp. 150–151

Track 7.16

Fiction text pp. 152–153

Track 7.17

Girl: Do you like muffins?
Boy: Yes, I do! Yes, I do!
Girl: Do you like chocolate?
Boy: Yes, I do! Yes, I do!
Girl: Do you like spinach?
Boy: No, I don't! No, I don't!
Girl: Do you like broccoli?
Boy: Yes, I do! Yes, I do! Yum!

Track 7.18

Please Eat Your Greens

Spinach, broccoli, zucchini, and beans.
Healthy! Healthy!
Please eat your greens.
Pizza, donuts, cookies, and fries.
Junk food! Junk food! Say goodbye!
'Cause junk food makes you weak and slow.
Healthy food makes you strong and helps you grow!
So, junk food, junk food, say goodbye!
And healthy food, come on! Let's try!

Track 7.19

bread, cookies, lollipop, potato chips, tomato, corn

Track 7.20

Boy 1: I'm hungry. Let's go to the store.
Boy 2: OK.

Narrator: At the store …

Boy 1: Can I have a lollipop, please?
Shop assistant: Here you go.
Boy 1: How much is it?
Shop assistant: It's one dollar.
Boy 1: Thank you!

Track 8.1

brush my teeth, eat breakfast, go to school, walk, ride my bike, take the bus

Track 8.2

sleep, do exercise, have fun, take a bath, change clothes, wash my hands

Track 8.3

Nonfiction text p. 163

Track 8.4

Nonfiction text p. 164

Track 8.5

before, after

Track 8.6

When I wake up,
I stretch and stretch,
I stretch and stretch,
I stretch and stretch.
When I wake up,
I stretch and stretch,
Every day.

After I eat,
I brush my teeth,
I brush my teeth,
I brush my teeth.
After I eat,
I brush my teeth,
Every day.

Before I go to school,
I eat eggs and toast,
I eat eggs and toast,
I eat eggs and toast.
Before I go to school,
I eat eggs and toast,
Every day.

After school,
I play with my friends,
I play with my friends,
I play with my friends.
After school,
I play with my friends,
Every day.

Track 8.7

desk, desk
fast, fast
ant, ant
mask, mask
nest, nest
cent, cent

Track 8.8

Tell me, tell me.
What do you prefer?
Desk or mask?
Desk or mask?
Tell me, tell me.
What word do you prefer?
Desk or mask?

Tell me, tell me.
What do you prefer?
Fast or nest?
Fast or nest?
Tell me, tell me.
What word do you prefer?
Fast or nest?

Tell me, tell me.
What do you prefer?
Ant or cent?
Ant or cent?
Tell me, tell me.
What word do you prefer?
Ant or cent?

Track 8.9

Jack: I'm Jack.
Emma: I'm Emma.
Liam: I'm Liam.

Jack: My name is Jack. My topic today is my morning routine.
Emma: What? Please repeat that.
Jack: My topic today is my morning routine. First, I eat breakfast. I eat eggs and toast.
Liam: Sorry, I don't understand.
Jack: I eat eggs and toast. Next, I get dressed. Then, I brush my teeth. Finally, I go to school! I take the school bus.

Track 8.10

wake up, collect, march, find, carry, clean

Track 8.11

Fiction text pp. 172–173

Track 8.12

Fiction text pp. 174–175

Track 8.13

Girl: I don't eat cake.
I don't play with snakes.
I don't wear red.
I don't make my bed.
I don't eat pears.
I don't brush my hair.
Mom: Tell me! Tell me!
What else don't you do?

Track 8.14

Teacher: OK, Abby. It's your turn! Tell the class about your morning routine.
Abby: I get up at 7 o'clock in the morning. First, I make the bed. Then, I get dressed and brush my hair. After that, I eat breakfast with my family. Finally, I brush my teeth.
Teacher: Thank you, Abby. Good job! OK, Dale. Can you tell us about your bedtime routine, please?
Dale: Yes. First, I take a bath. Then, I eat a bedtime snack. Next, I brush my teeth. Finally, I go to bed and read a story in bed. I am in bed at 8 p.m. every night.
Teacher: Very nice. Thank you, Dale.

Track 8.15

take attendance
raise your hand
stand up / sit down
open your books
eat lunch
be quiet
take out / put away
draw
spell

Track 8.16

Teacher: Let's play Simon says!
Class: Yay!
Teacher: Simon says, raise your hand.
Teacher: Simon says, take out your books.
Teacher: Simon says, sit down.
Teacher: Stand up. But I didn't say Simon says! The students that stood up are out!

Track 8.17

Girl 1: Hello, everybody. I'm Ms. Brown. Let's take attendance. Burak.
Boy 1: Here.
Girl 1: Canan.
Boy 2: Here.
Girl 1: Sofia.
Girl 2: Here.

Girl 1: Now, let's stand up! Everyone stand up, please! ... Let's wash our hands. Everyone, let's go to bathroom and wash our hands. ... It's lunchtime. Let's eat lunch!
Boy 1 and 2: Hurray!

Track 9.1

clothes
cold
jacket
hot
T-shirt
shoes

Track 9.2

wear, hat, skirt, pants, gloves, dress

Track 9.3

Nonfiction text p. 185

Track 9.4

Nonfiction text p. 186

Track 9.5

wool, cool

Track 9.6

Phew! It's hot, it's hot, it's hot today.
But I'm wearing a hat, so it's OK!

Phew! It's hot, it's hot, it's hot today.
But I'm wearing a dress, so it's OK!

Brrr. It's cold, it's cold, it's cold today.
But I'm wearing gloves, so it's OK!

Brrr. It's cold, it's cold, it's cold today.
But I'm wearing a jacket, so it's OK!

Track 9.7

grow, grow
green, green

grandma, grandma
plant, plant
play, play
plum, plum

Track 9.8

Grandma's Plant Grows

Grandma's green plant
Grows and grows.
Come and see,
One, two, three.

Grandma's green plant
Grows into a tree, into a tree.
Come and see,
One, two, three.

Grandma's green plant
Grows into a plum tree, into a plum tree.
Come and see,
One, two, three.

Come climb and play with me
in Grandma's big plum tree!

Track 9.9

Kate: I'm Kate.
Liam: I'm Liam.

Kate: My topic today is my favorite clothes. This is my pink sweater. It's very warm. It's my favorite! This is my blue hat. I love this blue hat. I wear it when it's a sunny day. My pink sweater and blue hat are my favorite clothes.

Liam: My topic today is my favorite clothes. Today I'm wearing my favorite clothes! This is my red T-shirt. Red is my favorite color. These are my white pants. I think these pants are super cool!
My T-shirt and pants are my favorite clothes. I love wearing them.

Track 9.10

emperor, thief, palace, expensive, smart, fool

Track 9.11

Where is Anna's puppy? Is he in her bedroom? No. Is he under her bed? No. Anna is sad. Where is her puppy?
It's very hot. Look! Anna's puppy is in the swimming pool!

Track 9.12

Fiction text pp. 194–195

Track 9.13

Fiction text pp. 196–197

Track 9.14

Are you wearing a skirt today,
Skirt today, skirt today?
Are you wearing a skirt today?
If you are, shout, "Yes, I am!"

Are you wearing red today,
Red today, red today?
Are you wearing red today?
If you're not, shout, "No, I'm not!"

Track 9.15

Hi, I'm Holly. In this photo, I'm wearing my school uniform. I'm wearing a dark blue coat and skirt. I'm also wearing a white shirt and tie. My tie is blue and yellow. My hat has a black ribbon. I like my uniform.

Hello, I'm Wayne. In this photo, I'm wearing my school uniform. I'm wearing dark blue shorts, a blue shirt, and a big sun hat. I'm also wearing blue and white socks with black shoes. I don't like my uniform.

Activity Book Answer Key

Unit 1

p. 2 Video

1 Max: Canada, red (favorite color), blue eyes, blond hair;
Ela: Turkey, 5 years old, brown eyes, brown hair
2 Students circle:
a picture 1
b picture 2
c picture 2
d picture 1

p. 3 Ready to Read: Nonfiction

1 Students trace: o, l, t, g, d
2 curly–straight, blond–brown, long–short

p. 4 Reading; Nonfiction

1 Students circle:
a pictures 1 and 2
b pictures 1 and 3
c pictures 2 and 3
2 Similar: Ula is a girl, Maya is a girl.
Different: Ula is tall, Paul is short; Maya is a girl, Ban is a boy.

p. 5 Explore the Text

3 Ben, curly hair; Paul, straight hair; Maya, blond hair; Ula, red hair
4 Students trace the words.
5 Students color:
1 red 2 yellow 3 brown 4 brown

p. 6 Grammar in Context

1 a I'm not tall.
b She is six years old.
c I am five years old.
d He's not short.
2 a am b is c
3 1c 2b 3a

p. 7

4 a He is 6 years old.
b I am 5 years old.
c She is tall.
d I am short.
My Life students' own answers

p. 8 Phonics

1 Students trace: F, L, O, S, X
2 Students color: A (green), I (blue), P (gray), T (yellow), X (brown), M (purple)

Oracy

1 a Share.
b Listen.
c Ask.

p. 9 Ready to Write

1 Students check (✓): ABC.
2 RED–red, COLOR–color, FAVORITE–favorite, BROWN–brown, BOY–boy, GIRL–girl
3 My name is Dana. D-A-N-A.
This is Julio. He is from Mexico.

p. 10

1 Students trace: K, S, L
2 Students color: F (yellow), I (green), V (blue), E (brown); S (red), X (purple)

p. 11 Ready to Read: Fiction

1 a old
b fast
c slow
d tired
2 1a 2d 3e 4c 5b

p. 12 Reading: Fiction

1 a real
b fantasy
c real
d fantasy
2 students read with the teacher

p. 13 Explore the Text

3 3, 4, 1, 2
4 a picture 1
b picture 2
c picture 1
d picture 1
e picture 1

p. 14 Grammar in Context

1 You aren't I am She is They are
2 1c 2a 3b
3 a are b am c are d aren't e is

p. 15

4 1a 2c 3b
5 a I am not old.
b You are young.
c He isn't tired.
d They are happy.
My Life students' own answers

p. 16 Values: Respecting Differences

1 Students check (✓): c and d
2 1b 2c 3a 4d
3 students' own answers

p. 17 How Did I Do?

students' own answers

p. 18 Unit 1 Review

1 a boy
b hair
c girl
d brown
e eye
f young
2 a She has short hair.
b I have curly hair.
c He is tired.
d You have brown hair.
3 Students trace: l, s, i, e, t
4 a am
b is, am
c am, is
d is, am
5 a I am happy.
b You are my friend.
c He is short.
d She is tall.
6 students trace

p. 20 Speaking Mission

1 name: left
phone: right
number: right
yes: left
no: right
lost: left
2 a What's your name? Abu Naser.
b How old are you? I'm 6.
c What's your phone number? 5566-7823.
3 3, 1, 2

p. 21 Wrap-up

1 long
2 I am tired.
3 students circle 1st crayon
4 fast–slow, long–short, old–young
5 B–b
6 students trace
Big Question students' own answers

Unit 2

p. 22 Video

1 teacher: picture 2
classroom: picture 1
playground: picture 2
2 teacher, bathroom, playground, desk, gym, classroom

p. 23 Ready to Read: Nonfiction

1 library: left
schoolbag: right
pencil case: right
notebook: left
colored pencil: left
eraser: right
2 eraser, notebook, pencil case, schoolbag

p. 24 Reading: Nonfiction

1 Students circle: desk, classroom, playground, gym
2 students read with the teacher

p. 25 Explore the Text

3 pencil 😊 apple 😊 chair ☹
4 schoolbag, notebook, pencil case
5 Students circle and color:
blue chair: picture 2
red apple: picture 3
green pencil: picture 1

p. 26 Grammar in Context

1 a It's a chair.
b It's an eraser.
c It's a pencil case.
d It's an apple.

2 Students check (✓):
  a picture 1
  b picture 2
  c picture 1
  d picture 1
  e picture 1

p. 27

3 students trace and draw
4 a an b a c an d a e an f a
My Life students' own answers

p. 28 Phonics

1 c, p, h, t, n, b
2 a ten–toy
  b car–cat
  c boy–big
  d hat–hello
  e nine–net

Oracy

1 students' own answers

p. 29 Ready to Write

1 students color
2 a ant, apple
  b car, cat
  c eight, eraser
  d hat, hen

p. 30

1 1a desk 2b eight 3c fish 4d girl
2 pencil, red, nine, schoolbag, orange, ten

p. 31 Ready to Read: Fiction

a story b hungry c lunchbox d mad
e surprised f sad
b a story, lunchbox, surprised, hungry

p. 32 Reading: Fiction

1 happy, sad, happy, sad
2 students read with the teacher

p. 33 Explore the Text

3 This is Ada.
  This is Hira.
  Ada is 6.
  Ada has a red pencil.
  Hira has a blue pencil.
4 hungry, surprised, sad
5 Students trace: p, p, d, u, r

p. 34 Grammar in Context

1 His pencil is blue.
  My pencil is green. Your pencil is green.
  Her pencil is red.
2 a my b your c his d her

p. 35

3 a picture 2 (red)
  b picture 1 (green)
  c picture 3 (yellow)
4 students trace
My Life students' own answers

p. 36 Values: Taking Care of Your School Objects

1 a 🙂 b 🙁 c 🙂 d 🙁 e 🙂 f 🙂
2 Students check (✓) (top to bottom, left to right): pictures 3, 4 and 5
3 students' own answers

p. 37 How Did I Do?

students' own answers

p. 38 Unit 2 Review

1 a classroom
  b bathroom
  c library
  d playground
2 pencil case (green), eraser (yellow), notebook (brown), desk (blue), colored pencil (orange), lunchbox (red)
3 Students trace:
  a s b p c d y e h f m

p. 39

4 a, an, a, an, an, a
5 a my b his c her d your
6 1 apple
  2 bathroom
  3 eraser
  4 library
  5 playground

p. 40 Speaking Mission

1 (top to bottom, left to right) marker, ruler, scissors, glue, pencil sharpener, crayons
2 a marker
  b ruler
  c crayon
  d pencil sharpener
3 Conversation 1:
  1 Can I borrow your ruler?
  2 Sorry! I don't have a ruler.
  3 No problem!
  Conversation 2:
  1 Can I borrow your crayon?
  2 Sure. Here you are!
  3 Thank you.

p. 41 Wrap-up

1 gym
2 a desk, an orange
3 hat–hello, library–long, car–cat
4 students trace
5 his, mad
6 students circle the ruler (final object)
Big Question students circle pictures 2 and 4

Unit 3

p. 42 Video

1 (clockwise) pictures 1, 3 and 5
2 toy, airplane, house, tablet, box, paper

p. 43 Ready to Read

1 tent, dollhouse, robot, fun, train, jump rope
2 1, 3, 2, 5, 4

p. 44 Reading: Nonfiction

1 Students circle in blue (toys):
  jump rope, train;
  Students circle in green (names):
  Lucas, Emma;
  Students circle in blue (colors):
  white, black
2 Rob has a red and brown house.
  Ayaz has a red car.
  Lisa has a blue and white airplane.
  Ian has a blue, green, and black train.
  Irina has a green jump rope.

p. 45 Explore the Text

3 (clockwise) a, e, c, d, b
4 names: Ayaz, Rob, Lisa;
  toys: train, airplane, jump rope;
  colors: blue, brown, green
5 School Objects: schoolbag, eraser, pencil;
  Toys: bat, robot, dollhouse

p. 46 Grammar in Context

1 (clockwise) d, a, e, c, b
2 a Jump!
  b Stop!
  c Stand!
  d Run!

p. 47

3 students trace
4 Students color:
  Stand! Sit! Stop!
My Life students' own answers

p. 48 Phonics

1 (top to bottom, left to right) bat (blue), hen (yellow), hat (blue), ten (yellow), cat (blue), pen (yellow)
2 a bat b hat c ten d hat e cat

Oracy

1 Students check (✓): pictures 2 and 3

p. 49 Ready to Write

1 Students trace:
  a R, . b S, . c T, . I, .
2 a I have an airplane.
  b brown eyes
  c the yellow train
  d an orange car
  e I have a toy box.
  f two blue pencils
  g Aiko has black hair.

p. 50

1 a This house is red.
  b The girl has a jump rope.
  c The boys have a tent.
  d That train is brown.
2 She has a tablet.
  It's an airplane.
  This is a box.

p. 51 Ready to Read: Fiction

1 a monkey bars
 b bike
 c spaceship
 d action figure
 e dinosaur
 f car
2 students color the picture

p. 52 Reading: Fiction

1 3, 1, 2
2 Students circle:
 Look! Look! Look! Run! Jump!

p. 53 Explore the Text

3 2, 3, 1
4 Look! Jump! Run!
5 students' own answers

p. 54 Grammar in Context

1 a, d, f
2 (left to right, top to bottom) c, d, a, b
3 Don't sit! Stop! Don't touch!

p. 55

4 Students check (✓):
 a left b right c left d right
5 students trace
My Life students' own answers

p. 56 Values: Sharing

1 Students check (✓): a, b, d, f
2 Students circle (left to right, top to bottom): toy, pencils, ruler
3 students' own answers

p. 57 How Did I Do?

students' own answers

p. 58 Unit 3 Review

1 Students color:
 a picture 2
 b picture 2
 c picture 2
 d picture 1
2 (left to right in picture) spaceship, house, car, airplane, train
3 students trace

p. 59

4 (clockwise)
 Jump! Look! Stop! Run! Listen!
5 students trace
6 Students color: a, c, d

p. 60 Oracy Performance Task 1: Discussion

1 (clockwise)
 board game, soccer ball, play dough, boat, dinosaur
2 a jigsaw puzzle
 b doll
3 1 A jump rope, please!
 2 Here you go!
 3 Thank you!

p. 61 Wrap-up

1 spaceship, bike, monkey bars
2 boat
3 Students circle in blue: cat, hat, bat;
 Students circle in green: hen, pen, ten
4 Ela
5 Don't jump! Run!
6 The toy is yellow.
Big Question students color the dinosaur

Unit 4

p. 62 Video

1 students draw
dining room: eat
living room: watch TV
bedroom: read stories
kitchen: cook

p. 63 Ready to Read: Nonfiction

1 (clockwise) garden, bed, stove, water
2 Students trace: o, o, o, e, e
3 (clockwise) water (blue), bed (yellow), stove (red)

p. 64 Reading: Nonfiction

1 Students circle the differences:
 The position of the birds is different in picture 1 and picture 2;
 In picture 1 there are apples in the tree, but not in picture 2;
 There is water coming from the hose in picture 1, but not in picture 2;
 There are flowers missing in picture 1 that appear in picture 2;
 The flowers in picture 1 are yellow, but purple in picture 2.
 6 similar: both are houses, the bed and the table are small;
 different: the dollhouse has three rooms, but the treehouse has only one

p. 65 Explore the Text

3 dollhouse: pictures 2, 3 and 4; tree house: picture 1
4 (left to right, top to bottom) right, left, left, right
5 students' own answers

p. 66 Grammar in Context

1 on, under, in
2 under, on, in
3 students draw and color

p. 67

4 (left to right) The robot is on the table.
 The cars are under the bed.
 The dinosaurs are in the box.
 The ball is under the chair.
5 students trace
My Life students' own answers

p. 68 Phonics

1 students say and color
2 a nut, hut
 b wig, Stig
 c big, dig
 d but, nut
3 Students color blue: nut, but; nut hut
 Students color green: big, dig; wig, big

Oracy

1 (clockwise)
 It's my turn. It's your turn. Let's play.

p. 69 Ready to Write

1 fish–animal, apartment–place, chair–object, boy–person
2 place: gym; person: girl; animal: turtle; object: toy
3 boy, home, water, teacher

p. 70

1 Students check (✓): box, stove, roof, stairs, book
2 Students trace: garden, tree, house, roof, stairs

p. 71 Ready to Read: Fiction

1 snail, ladybug, spider, butterfly, mouse
2 students color

p. 72 Reading: Fiction

1 picture 1, picture 2, picture 1
2 students read with the teacher

p. 73 Explore the text

1 (left to right, top to bottom) 4, 3, 1, 2
2 picture 2

p. 74 Grammar in Context

1 (left to right, top to bottom) Yes, it is.
 No, it isn't. No, it isn't. Yes, it is.
2 (left to right, top to bottom)
 No, it isn't.
 Yes, it is.
 Yes, it is.
 No, it isn't.
3 Yes, it is.
 Yes, it is.
 No, it isn't.

p. 75

4 Yes, he is.
 No, she isn't.
 Yes, they are.
5 Students trace:
 Yes, it is.
 No, it isn't.
My Life students' own answers

p. 76 Values: Helping Others

1 a, c
2 (left to right, top to bottom)
 Omar helps in the kitchen.
 Mairi helps in the garden.
 Jack helps in the living room.
 Asya helps in her bedroom.
3 students' own answers

p. 77 How Did I Do?

students' own answers

p. 78 Unit 4 Review

1 (left to right, top to bottom) bedroom, bathroom, living room, dining room, kitchen, garden
2 r o o m, s t o v e, b e d, w a t e r
3 Students trace: o, f, a, i

p. 79

4 students draw
5 Yes, it is.
No, it isn't.
Yes, it is.
No, it isn't.
6 boy–place, toy–object, mouse–animal, apartment–place

p. 80 Speaking Mission

1 (left to right, top to bottom) right, right, left, right, left, right
2 What color is the T-shirt? It's purple.
Is the T-shirt on the chair? Yes, it is.
What color is the hat? It's green.
Is the hat on the chair? No, it isn't.
3 1 I can't find my glasses.
2 Are your glasses on the table?
3 Yes, they are.

p. 81 Wrap-up

1 living room
2 butterfly, ladybug
3 cut, but, hut; wig, big, dig
4 teacher, kitchen, boy, rabbit
5 It's on the chair.
6 No, it isn't.
Big Question students circle picture 1

Unit 5

p. 82 Video

1 Students draw:
Land: a zebra and an elephant;
Ocean: an octopus and a dolphin
2 (top to bottom) ocean, octopus, land, elephant, dolphin, zebra

p. 83 Ready to Read: Nonfiction

1 students color
2 Students trace: t, t, h, a, i, e, a, c, w
3 students color

p. 84 Reading: Nonfiction

1 students own answers (may include crocodile, bear, lion, tiger; zebra, panda)
2 students read with the teacher

p. 85 Explore the Text

3 (left to right) teeth, tail, beak, feathers
4 Ocean: whale, octopus; Land: elephant, bear
5 students match and color

p. 86 Grammar in Context

1 What are they? They're bears.
What color are they? They're brown.
Where are they? They're in the tree.
What is it? It's a fish.
What color is it? It's blue and green.
Where is it? It's in the ocean.
2 It's in the forest.
They're elephants.
It's black and white.
3 students trace

p. 87

4 (left to right, top to bottom)
What color is it?
What's your name?
How old are you?
What are they?
5 What, How, Where
My Life students' own answers

p. 88 Phonics

1 q, f, g, r, s
2 a fin
b jaws
c jar
d fish
e song
3 fin–fish, jar–jaws, goat–gate, ring–rabbit

Oracy

1 picture 2

p. 89 Ready to Write

2 Look!
What is it?
Is it a mouse?
No, it's a rabbit!
Where's the rabbit?
Look!
Are they dolphins?
Yes!
Where are they?
They are in the ocean.
Dolphins are my favorite animal!
5 Question ?: Is it a bird? Is it an insect?
Exclamation !: Look! Yes! No!

p. 90

1 students trace
2 ! ? ! ? ! ? !

p. 91 Ready to Read: Fiction

1 (top to bottom) moon, rabbit, sun, snake, star, tongue
2 (left to right, top to bottom) right, right, right, left

p. 92 Reading: Fiction

1 a picture 1
b picture 2
2 students read with the teacher

p. 93 Explore the Text

1 a No b Yes c No
2 Snake, Rabbit
3 picture 2, picture 1, picture 2

p. 94 Grammar in Context

1 Are the dolphins in the water? Yes, they are.
Are the lions in the jungle? Yes, they are.
Are the giraffes in the tree? No, they aren't.
2 (left to right, top to bottom)
No, they aren't.
Yes, they are.
Yes, they are.
No, they aren't.
3 students draw blue whales in the water

p. 95

4 Students color the mice brown, the crocodiles green (or any color but yellow), and the fish orange.
5 Students trace: No, they aren't; Yes, they are.
My Life students' own answers

p. 96 Values: Taking Care of Animals

1 Students check (✓): a, c, d
2 picture 1–picture 2, picture 2–picture 4, picture 3–picture 1, picture 4–picture 3
3 students' own answers

p. 97 How Did I Do?

students' own answers

p. 98 Unit 5 Review

1 (left to right, top to bottom) octopus, zebra, elephant, snake, dolphin, rabbit
2 (left to right, top to bottom) teeth, claws, beak, tongue
3 Students trace: a, h, s, n, e, c

p. 99

4 What, Where, What
5 students trace
6 ?: Is it a zebra?
What is it?
Is it an elephant?
!: Look!
No, it's not!
Yes!

p. 100 Speaking Mission

1 (left to right, top to bottom) left, left, right, right, left, left
2 Are you a tiger? Yes, I am.
Are you a rabbit? No, I'm not.
Are you a zebra? Yes, I am.
3 1 What's this?
2 It's a board game.
3 Throw the dice!
4 I win!

p. 101 Wrap-up

1 left to right)
It's an elephant.
It's a dolphin.
It's an octopus.
2 It's on land.
3 What are they?
Is it a bird?
4 song–sun, fins–fish, rabbit–ring

5 tongue
6 moon
Big Question students' own answers

Unit 6

p. 102 Video

1 Students draw (in any order): somebody running, painting, talking, roller-skating, dancing, playing basketball
2 (left to right, top to bottom) talk, run, play basketball, paint, ability, skate

p. 103 Ready to Read: Nonfiction

1 (left to right, top to bottom) see, spell, climb, ride, say, swim
2 (left to right, top to bottom) ride, see, spell, say, climb, swim

p. 104 Reading: Nonfiction

1 (left to right, top to bottom)
Run!
My Skates
Basketball
2 students read with the teacher

p. 105 Explore the Text

3 (left to right, top to bottom)
I can't swim.
I can climb.
I can see.
I can read.
4 Spell!–top row, I Can Paint!–top row, Let's Swim!–bottom row

p. 106 Grammar in Context

1 (left to right) ✓ ✗ ✓ ✓ ✗
2 (left to right, top to bottom)
I can play.
I can spell.
I can't run.
I can draw.
3 students trace

p. 107

4 (left to right, top to bottom)
can, can't, can't, can
5 can, can, can't
My Life students' own answers

p. 108 Phonics

1 Students trace: d (brown), p (green), m (yellow), b (purple), t (red)
2 2a bad
b top
c mad
d hop
e mad
f box

Oracy

1 students' own answers

p. 109 Ready to Write

1 paint, swim, skate, paint
2 happy, tired, book
3 Students trace: see, swim

p. 110 Ready to Write

4 a noun: pencil; verb: draw
b noun: teacher; verb: play
5 skate, run, jump, climb

p. 111 Ready to Read: Fiction

1 (left to right, top to bottom)
right, left, right, left, right, right
2

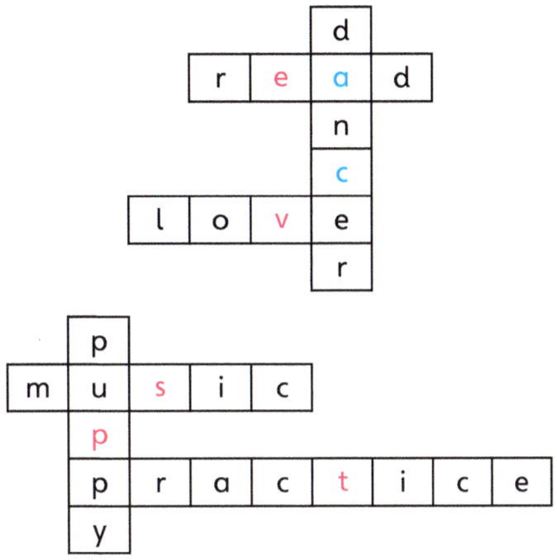

p. 112 Reading: Fiction

1 Students draw: a fully-grown tree or plant; a pizza on the floor
Students read with the teacher

p. 113 Explore the Text

1 a 2, 1, 3
b 3, 1, 2
2 a top right
b top left
c bottom left
d bottom right
3 a picture 2
b picture 1

p. 114 Grammar in Context

1 (left to right, top to bottom)
No, she can't.
Yes, he can.
Yes, she can.
No, he can't.
2 Can it dance? No, it can't.
Can she roller-skate? Yes, she can.
Can he ride? Yes, he can.
Can it climb? Yes, it can.
3 students trace

p. 115

1 Yes, he can.
No, she can't.
Yes, she can.
No, he can't.
2 Students trace:
Yes, they can.
No, he can't.
My Life students' own answers

p. 116 Values: Perseverance

1 (left to right, top to bottom)
To skate well.
To read well.
To paint well.
To play basketball well.
To dance well.
2 students trace
3 students' own answers

p. 117 How Did I Do?

students' own answers

p. 118 Unit 6 Review

1 (top to bottom)
ride, paint, swim, climb, run
2 music, puppy, dancer, read
3 students trace

p. 119

4 can't, can, can, can
5 Lola can dance.
Lola can't skate.
Gib can climb.
Gib can't ride.
6 Students color: spell, read, write, talk

p. 120 Oracy Performance Task 2: Discussion

1 (left to right)
hide-and-seek, hopscotch, marbles, tag, board games, telephone
2 students' own answers
3 1 Let's play tag!
2 No! Tag is boring!
3 Let's play hopscotch!
4 Yes! Hopscotch is fun!

p. 121 Wrap-up

1 can
2 (left to right) climb, skate, play basketball
3 can't
4 Yes, I can.
5 run, swim, spell, talk
6 Students trace: h, b, m, t, d, p
7 hip-hop
8 hopscotch
Big Question students circle picture 2

Unit 7

p. 122 Video

1 Students draw (2 of each of the following options):
fruit: banana, grapes;
vegetable: spinach;
sugar: candy, ice cream, cake
2 (left to right, top to bottom)
left, left, right, right, right, left

p. 123 Ready to Read: Nonfiction

1

e	w	a	t	e	r	b
m	k	l	p	o	i	l
r	i	s	b	a	c	a
w	j	u	i	c	e	p
y	o	g	u	r	t	g
r	a	p	u	b	a	n
t	o	m	a	t	o	j

3 students trace
4 students draw and color

p. 124 Reading: Nonfiction

1 Different: b, c;
Same: a, d
2 students read with the teacher

p. 125 Explore the Text

3 I love popsicles!
I don't like meat.
I love fried rice!
4 I love vegetables with fried rice!–big picture 1–pictures of oil and rice;
Tomato sandwiches are my favorite snack–big picture 3–pictures of bread and tomatoes;
Popsicles are delicious!–big picture 2–pictures of yogurt and bananas

p. 126 Grammar in Context

1 ✓ ✗ ✓ ✗
2 Students circle: pictures of corn, carrots, and broccoli
3 students trace

p. 127

4 I like vegetables.
I don't like rice.
I like fruit.
I don't like juice.
5 like, don't like
My Life students' own answers

p. 128 Phonics

1 b: tub, cub; tub; Bob
m: arm; arm, jam; jam, arm
x: box, fox; fox
2 (left to right, top to bottom)
cub, fox, jam, box
3 (left to right, top to bottom) x, b, m, b

Oracy

1 students trace

p. 129 Ready to Write

1 (left to right) old, slow, short, red, green
2 (left to right, top to bottom) toy, girl, apples, hair, eat
3 Students trace: old, tall, happy

p. 130

4 noun: bed, grape, banana, parrot;
verb: jump, eat, ride, climb;
adjective: blue, big, yellow, sad
5 students draw and color

p. 131 Ready to Read: Fiction

1 broccoli, fish, French fried, chocolate, soup, muffin
2 bliccoro–broccoli, suop–soup, cohocalte–chocolate, fhis–fish, Fenrhc riesf–French fries, mufifn–muffin

p. 132 Reading: Fiction

1 Kim's healthy lunch.
2 students read with the teacher

p. 133 Explore the Text

3 4, 2, 1, 3
4 Mark's favorite snack
5 picture 1: sandwiches, chocolate;
picture 2: French fries, broccoli, fish, soup

p. 134 Grammar in Context

1 top left–top right, top right–bottom right, bottom left–top left, bottom right–bottom left
2 Do you like muffins? Yes, I do.
Do you like chocolate? No, I don't.
Do you like yogurt? Yes, I do.
Do you like juice? No, I don't.
3 students' own answers

p. 135

4 Students trace: Yes, I do. Yes, I do.
5 Yes, I do. No, I don't.
My Life students' own answers

p. 136 Values: Healthy Eating

1 Students check (✓): pictures 3 and 5
2 healthy: bananas, soup, vegetables, water; unhealthy: candy, cake, ice cream, potato chips
3 students' own answers

p. 137 How Did I do?

students' own answers

p. 138 Unit 7 Review

1 (left to right) tomato, spinach, grapes, broccoli, apple, banana
2 (clockwise from top left) fish, juice, soup, vegetables, yogurt, French fries
3 fruit, sugar, muffin

p. 139

4 I don't like chocolate.
I like soup.
I don't like French fries.
I like rice.
5 Do you like grapes? Yes, I do.
Do you like yogurt? No, I don't.
Do you like muffins? No, I don't.
Do you like broccoli? Yes, I do.
6 Students color: two, small, green

p. 140 Speaking Mission

1 (left to right, top to bottom) tomato, bread, corn, lollipop, cookie, potato chips
2 It's one dollar.
It's two dollars.
Here you go!
3 1 Can I have a lollipop, please?
2 Here you go!
3 How much is it?
4 It's one dollar.

p. 141 Wrap-up

1 I like water.
2 I don't like bananas.
3 spinach, broccoli, grapes
4 long, delicious, small
5 box–fox, jam–arm, cub–tub

6 students trace
7 cookies
8 picture 2
Big Question No, but encourage children to discuss which foods are unhealthy, why, and that a little unhealthy food is OK.

Unit 8

p. 142 Video

1 Students draw:
Morning Routine: someone eating breakfast, someone brushing their teeth;
Going to School: someone walking, someone taking the bus
2 (top to bottom, left to right) go to school, walk, ride my bike, eat breakfast, brush my teeth, take the bus

p. 143 Ready to Read: Nonfiction

1 Students color: my clothes, my hands, exercise, fun
2 4, 1, 2, 3

p. 144 Reading: Nonfiction

1 Susan's morning routine.
2 students read with the teacher

p. 145 Explore the Text

3 (top to bottom) 2, 5, 7, 1, 4, 6, 3
4 Cara's after-school routine.
5 After–picture 2, Before–picture 1

p. 146 Grammar in Context

1 I do exercise.
I sleep ten hours.
I ride my bike.
I wash my hands.
I take the bus.
2 I wash my hands.
I do exercise.
I have fun.
I walk home.
I take the bus.
3 students trace

p. 147

4 Students color: right, left, left, left
5 a I walk to school.
b I take the bus.
c I brush my teeth.
d I do exercise.
My Life students' own answers

p. 148 Phonics

1 st: nest, fast; sk: desk, mask; nt: ant, cent
2 ant, nest, cent, mask
3 students trace and draw

Oracy

1 Can you repeat that?

p. 149 Ready to Write

1 I eat breakfast.
I do exercise.
I brush my teeth.

2 my teeth, school, good exercise, I like, after school
3 students trace

p. 150

4 students trace and draw
5 (pictures top to bottom)
I go to school.
I ride my bike.
I eat breakfast.
I have fun.

p. 151 Ready to Read: Fiction

1 students trace
2 students' own answers

p. 152 Reading: Fiction

1 It's bad. It's good.
2 students read with the teacher

p. 153 Explore the Text

3 (pictures top to bottom)
I love fruit!
Let's find food.
Can you carry that?
I don't like vegetables!
Yes, I can.
4 Robbie:
I don't like vegetables.
I love fruit!
Yes, I'm hungry!
Mama Rabbit:
Carrots are delicious!
Let's eat breakfast!
5 students trace

p. 154 Grammar in Context

1 (left to right, top to bottom) ✗ ✓ ✗ ✓ ✗
2 Students color: don't wake up, brush, play
3 I don't eat snacks.
I don't clean the table.
I don't play in the park.

p. 155

4 take, collect, eat
5 Students trace: march, don't do, make
My Life students' own answers

p. 156 Values: Staying Healthy

1 Students mark (✓) (left to right, top to bottom): pictures 2, 4, and 5
2 Students color (left to right): pictures 1, 2, and 4
3 students' own answers

p. 157 How Did I do?

students' own answers

p. 158 Unit 8 Review

1 take a bath
brush my teeth
eat breakfast
take the bus
go to school
2 (left to right, top to bottom) my bike, my clothes, my hands, fun
3 students trace

p. 159

4 I take the bus.
I don't ride my bike.
I don't take the bus.
I ride my bike.
5 students' own answers
6 I change my clothes.
I go to the park.
I wash my hands.
I sleep ten hours.

p. 160 Speaking Mission

1 (left to right, top to bottom)
Be quiet.
Take out your pencil.
Take attendance.
Open your books.
Put away your book.
Raise your hand.
2 Open your books.
Raise your hand.
3 Let's read.
Sit down, please.
Hello!
Open your books, please.

p. 161 Wrap-up

1 eat
2 I wash my hands.
I have fun.
I brush my teeth.
3 I play in the park.
4 I change my clothes.
5 desk–mask, ant–cent, fast–nest
6 sleeps
7 students trace
8 sleep
Big Question Yes, but encourage children to say why and to understand routines can vary and change.

Unit 9

p. 162 Video

1 Students draw (2 of each of the following options)
Hot Weather: a T-shirt, shorts, sandals
Cold Weather: a winter jacket, gloves, a hat, boots
2 (left to right, top to bottom) left, right, left, left, right, right

p. 163 Ready to Read: Nonfiction

1 hat, gloves, dress, pants, skirt, wear
2 1 hat
2 skirt
3 pants
4 gloves
5 dress
3 students trace

p. 164 Reading: Nonfiction

1 hot weather–picture 2; cold weather–picture 1
2 students read with the teacher

p. 165 Explore the Text

3 (top to bottom)
This is her favorite Sari.
It's cold. He wears gloves.
He wears boots.
His jacket is warm.
It's hot. She wears sandals.
4 picture 1: India, sandals, 40 °C, hot
Picture 2: Russia, boots, -40 °C, cold

p. 166 Grammar in Context

1 (clockwise from top left) a, c, d, b
2 She's not wearing a skirt.
He's wearing a hat.
3 students trace

p. 167

4 Students color: He's not, He's, I'm
5 (left to right, top to bottom) She's, She isn't, He's, He isn't
My Life students' own answers

p. 168 Phonics

1 We play in Grandma's garden.
We see two green plants in Grandma's garden.
We eat the plums from the plants in Grandma's garden.
2 (left to right, top to bottom) 4, 2, 3, 1
3 plant, grow, grandma, plum

Oracy

1 students trace

p. 169 Ready to Write

1 What's your favorite jacket?
Do you like these red gloves?
What color is your hat?
How old are you?
2 How old are you?
What's your favorite color?
Do you like it?
What color is it?
3 Is it cold? No, it's not. It's hot.
What are you wearing? I'm wearing a T-shirt.
Do you like it? Yes! I love it!
What color is it? It's orange.
Can you play? Yes, I can. Let's go!

p. 170 Ready to Write

4 students trace
5 Students write a question mark for each of the sentences on the left and a period for each of the sentences on the right.

p. 171 Ready to Read: Fiction

1 (left to right, top to bottom) emperor, expensive, palace, smart
2 (left to right, top to bottom) expensive, emperor, thief, palace

p. 172 Reading: Fiction

1 3, 1, 2
2 students read with the teacher

p. 173 Explore the text

3 2, 4, 1, 3
4 1 Oh, no! The shoes aren't real!
2 The emperor is smart.
3 The thief is a fool!
4 Here are the real shoes!
5 picture 1: real shoes, emperor, smart
Picture 2: not real shoes, thief, fool

p. 174 Grammar in Context

1 Yes, I am. No, I'm not. Yes, I am.
No, I'm not.
2 Are you wearing pants?
Are you wearing shoes?
Are you wearing a jacket?
Are you wearing a hat?
3 students trace

p. 175

4 Are you, I am; Are you, I'm not;
Are you, I am
5 1 Are you wearing a dress?
2 Are you wearing a hat?
My Life students' own answers

p. 176 Values: Taking Care of Your Clothes

1 Students check (✓) (left to right, top to bottom): pictures 1, 2, 4, and 6
2 top left–bottom right, middle left–middle right, bottom left–top right
3 students' own answers

p. 177 How Did I Do?

students' own answers

p. 178 Unit 9 Review

1

f	g	h	c	s	w	c	o
d	o	g	l	o	v	e	s
r	g	r	o	t	g	t	k
p	a	n	t	s	a	h	i
e	l	s	h	a	t	e	r
s	k	t	e	h	c	r	t
d	r	e	s	s	l	m	v

2 students color
3 students trace

p. 179

4 He's wearing a hat.
I'm wearing a dress.
She's not wearing a skirt.
I'm wearing a jacket.
I'm not wearing gloves.
5 students' own answers
6 you wearing a jacket?
What is your favorite color?
Do you like this hat?

p. 180 Oracy Performance Task 3: Presentation

1 Students circle in appropriate colors (left to right, top to bottom):
school (orange): pictures 4 and 14
toys (blue): pictures 10 and 11
home (green): pictures 6 and 9
animals (red): pictures 7 and 12
routines (pink): pictures 1 and 5
clothes (gray): pictures 2 and 13
food (brown): pictures 3 and 8
2 Please repeat that.
I don't understand.
Good job!
Thank you!
3 picture 1: This is my drawing. Thank you!
picture 2: Please repeat that. Good job!

p. 181 Wrap-up

1 I'm not wearing a dress.
2 He's wearing a hat.
She's wearing a hat.
3 No, I'm not.
4 shoe
5 How old are you?
6 Students trace: gr, pl
7 Two
8 hot
Big Question students circle *It's cold*, *It's my birthday party*, and *It's hot*.